T0385114

The Last Charge of the
AUSTRALIAN LIGHT HORSE

PETER FITZSIMONS

The Last Charge of the
AUSTRALIAN LIGHT HORSE

hachette
AUSTRALIA

Published in Australia and New Zealand in 2023
by Hachette Australia
(an imprint of Hachette Australia Pty Limited)
Gadigal Country, Level 17, 207 Kent Street, Sydney, NSW 2000
www.hachette.com.au

Hachette Australia acknowledges and pays our respects to the past, present and
future Traditional Owners and Custodians of Country throughout Australia
and recognises the continuation of cultural, spiritual and educational practices
of Aboriginal and Torres Strait Islander peoples. Our head office is located on
the lands of the Gadigal people of the Eora Nation.

A catalogue record for this
book is available from the
National Library of Australia

ISBN: 978 0 7336 4667 6 (hardback)

Cover design by Luke Causby/Blue Cork
Cover and endpapers images courtesy of Australian War Memorial and Trove. Front cover, top: Light Horse-
man with horse (Trove: State Library of South Australia RSL Collection/SRG 435/1/235); bottom: 1st ALH
Brigade advancing over sand dunes at Esdud (AWM B01510); back cover: Light Horsemen on parade (Trove:
239706285); endpapers: George Lambert, *The charge of the Australian Light Horse at Beersheba, 1917*,
1920, painting, oil on canvas (AWM ART02811).
Maps by Jane Macaulay
Author photo courtesy of Peter Morris/Sydney Heads
Typeset in 11.2/15.1 pt Sabon LT Pro by Bookhouse, Sydney
Printed and bound in Australia by McPherson's Printing Group

To Trooper Ion Idriess, Lieutenant Guy Haydon, Lieutenant Alaric Pinder Boor, Major Banjo Paterson, General Sir Harry Chauvel, and all those who served with the Australian Light Horse throughout this extraordinary saga. I can only hope to have done justice to your extraordinary story.

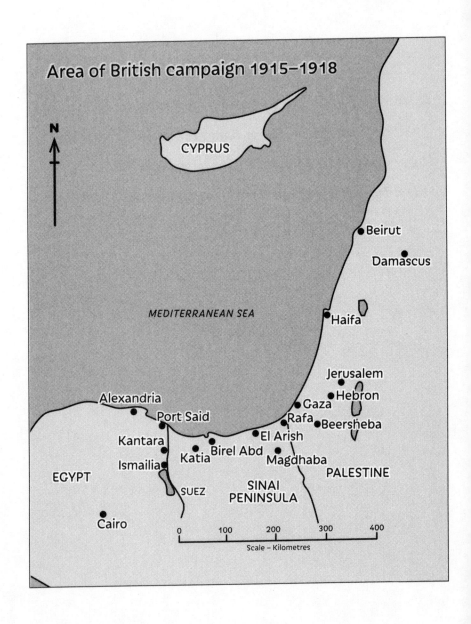

Area of British campaign 1915–1918

N

CYPRUS

MEDITERRANEAN SEA

Beirut

Damascus

Haifa

Jerusalem

Hebron

Alexandria

Port Said

Gaza

Rafa

Beersheba

Kantara

El Arish

Katia

Birel Abd

Magdhaba

Ismailia

EGYPT

PALESTINE

SUEZ

SINAI
PENINSULA

Cairo

0   100   200   300   400

Scale – Kilometres

'Then someone shouted, pointing through the sunset. There, at the steady trot, was regiment after regiment, squadron after squadron coming, coming, coming! It was just half-light, they were distinct yet indistinct. The Turkish guns blazed at those hazy horsemen but they came steadily on.'[1]

Ion Idriess

CONTENTS

LIST OF MAPS

DRAMATIS PERSONAE

General Sir Archibald James Murray. Veteran of the Anglo–Zulu War of 1879 and the Boer War (1899–1902), he was Chief of the Imperial General Staff in the early months of the Great War before moving on to become the Commander-in-Chief of the Egyptian Expeditionary Force.

General Sir Edmund Allenby. A graduate of Haileybury College and Sandhurst, veteran of the Boer War, where he was mentioned in dispatches, and the 5th Irish Royal Lancers, Allenby's background was as a cavalry officer, holding senior positions in the British Expeditionary Force on the Western Front before taking command of the Egyptian Expeditionary Force from June 1917 to the end of the Great War.

General Harry Chauvel. Born in Tabulam, New South Wales, he attended Sydney Grammar School before joining the Upper Clarence Light Horse. He first saw action in the Boer War, where he commanded the Queensland Mounted Infantry, being mentioned in dispatches and rising to the rank of Lieutenant Colonel. At the outbreak of the Great War he was on a ship en route to London to serve as Australia's sole representative on the Imperial General Staff, travelling to Egypt to take command of the 1st Australian Light Horse Brigade. By the end of the war he was commanding 30,000 men of the Desert Mounted Corps.

General John 'Galloping Jack' Royston, also known as 'Hellfire Jack'. Described by Banjo Paterson as an officer who was 'by instinct a bandit chief and by temperament a hero'[1] Royston was, though South African, ideally suited to command Australians as he cared little for protocol, and everything for the fight. Born in 1860, the fact he lived beyond 20 was a miracle, given his attitude to risk. He was already a legendary figure in the Boer War, mentioned in dispatches at Ladysmith, and led the Western Australian contingents he commanded as though they were the commandos. In the Zulu rebellions, he raised 'Royston's Horse', consisting largely of Australian ex-pats who loved his daring and his extraordinary luck. Royston was the special aide-de-camp to Lord Kitchener at the Coronation of Edward VII.

General Philip Chetwode. A British aristocrat and old Etonian (if that is not a tautology?) his long military career included the Chin-Lushai Expedition of 1889 in Burma and he was twice mentioned in dispatches during the Boer War. In 1914, he gained fame through the Curragh incident, where a near mutiny of British officers in Ireland was averted by his leadership. He was given command of the 5th Cavalry Brigade in August 1914 when the Great War began.

Brigadier General William Grant. A Boer War veteran and career officer, he became the Commanding Officer of the 11th Australian Light Horse Regiment in the Australian Imperial Force in 1915. In the words of the Official Historian Henry Gullett, referring to what happened at Beersheba: 'Somewhat more excitable and impulsive than most of the Light Horse leaders, Grant possessed the temperament for the exploit . . . which was to give lasting distinction to his name.'[2]

Brigadier General Granville Ryrie. Born into a family of graziers in Michelago, New South Wales. As a competent bushman and skilled horseman, Ryrie first served overseas in the Boer War, achieving the rank of Honorary Major. He entered Federal Parliament in 1911 as Member for North Sydney. Duty called in 1914 when war was declared, and Ryrie was given command of the 2nd Light Horse Brigade.

Lieutenant Colonel George Macarthur-Onslow. Commissioned in the New South Wales Mounted Rifles early in his military career, steady advancement followed. In October 1915, he was promoted to Lieutenant Colonel commanding the 7th Light Horse Regiment.

Major Banjo Paterson. Australia's most famous poet began the Great War with disappointed hopes of becoming a war correspondent, as he had been in the Boer War, before working as a volunteer ambulance driver in France. Finally, he officially joined the Army to be a squadron commander in the 2nd Australian Remount Depot.

Lieutenant Guy Haydon. Born in 1890 at the old homestead at *Bloomfield* in the Hunter Valley, New South Wales, Guy could practically ride before he could walk. In February 1915, with his brother Barney, he joined the Australian Imperial Force and served with the 12th Light Horse Regiment, B Squadron, taking with him his famous horse, Midnight.

Lieutenant Alaric Pinder Boor. The son of a draper in Carnarvon, Alaric attended Christian Brothers' College in Western Australia, where he became Dux, School Captain and Captain of the cricket and football teams. He was awarded a Rhodes Scholarship in 1913, but gave up his studies in England to enlist first in the 7th Battalion Oxfordshire and Buckinghamshire Light Infantry, before achieving his dream to become a pilot. He became attached to the No. 113 Squadron Royal Flying Corps, serving in the desert campaigns.

Major Richard Meinertzhagen. Born in 1878 to a merchant banking family second only to the Rothschilds, he attended Harrow with Winston Churchill, before joining the Hampshire Yeomanry in 1897. A brilliant eccentric, he served in Burma, Kenya and South Africa with a success only matched by his savagery, once ending the Nandi Resistance in Kenya by shooting its leader while shaking hands with him. He joined British Intelligence when World War I broke out and was awarded the Distinguished Service Order in 1916. In 1917 he was transferred from East Africa to the Sinai and Palestine campaign.

Trooper Ion Idriess. An itinerant Jack-of-all-trades, he joined the AIF early in the war, abandoning his previous life, which to that point had included crewing on a paddle-steamer, boundary riding, droving and prospecting.

Trooper Tibby Cotter. A great Australian Test fast bowler, who joined the Light Horse in April 1915, despite his notable lack of ability in riding a horse.

Colonel T. E. Lawrence, Lawrence of Arabia. A British archaeologist and Intelligence officer who became famous for his role in supporting the Arab Revolt against the Ottoman Empire during World War I.

Colonel Ismet. A Turkish army officer. A brilliant student, he graduated from the Ankara Military Academy as first rank staff captain in 1906. After a brief flirtation with revolutionary politics, he discovered his real skill; suppressing the rebellions that plagued the dying days of the Ottoman Empire. In October 1917, he commanded the III Corps at Beersheba, which ultimately bore the brunt of the British attack that opened the Palestine front in the Third Battle of Gaza.

Ahmed Djemal Pasha. Born into a military family in Lesbos in 1872, Ahmed followed tradition into the Military Academy and Staff College in Istanbul. One of the young Turks who profited from the Young Turk revolution in 1907, he became one of the 'Three Pashas' who came to effectively rule Turkey in an awkward triumvirate after their audacious coup of 1913, following the Balkan Wars that foreshadowed World War I. He commanded the Ottoman Fourth Army from November 1914 to September 1917.

Mersinli Djemal Pasha. Born in Mersin in 1873, he graduated from the War Academy in 1898. He served as Chief of Staff in the Balkan Wars of 1912–13 and was also made commander of the 10th and 42nd Divisions. On the outbreak of World War I, he became a General. He commanded the Ottoman Eighth Army from April 1914 until February 1918 when he succeeded to the command of the Fourth Army.

Colonel Friedrich Kress von Kressenstein. A German officer from Nuremberg. During World War I he served chiefly with the Ottoman Army. He was responsible for Turkish operations for the First Suez Offensive in 1915, and later commanded the Ottoman Desert Force.

INTRODUCTION AND ACKNOWLEDGEMENTS

The fabled 'Last Charge at Beersheba'?

I had heard of it, just as I knew a little of the 'Australian Light Horse', in part because my grandfather, Trooper Frederick Harper Booth had served with the 4th Victorian Light Horse in the Boer War. Having written many books on other iconic Australian battles, campaigns and war heroes – the Boer War, Gallipoli, Fromelles & Poziéres, Villers-Bretonneux, Kokoda, Tobruk, Long Tan, Nancy Wake and Sir John Monash among them – I had Beersheba in mind for some time as a story I would get to.

It was only while so engaged over this last year or so, however, that I truly realised the wonder of the story and how what the Australian Light Horse achieved in the whole campaign was so significant and enthralling. Thus, in a similar manner to my books that were initially just on Sir Charles Kingsford Smith and Sir Douglas Mawson before being expanded to take in much of the history of early aviation and Antarctic exploration respectively – because the stories were so wondrous – I ended up expanding the scope of this book well beyond just the fabled 'Last Charge at Beersheba', which was my original intention.

(And yes, on that subject, as I went along I came to appreciate the point made by the academic, Dr Jean Bou, that there were plenty of charges both before and after Beersheba. But it was *not* just another charge of many. This was the largest force of mounted infantry charging entrenched positions to achieve a major victory, at a pivotal point of a vital campaign. And, in the contemporary words of the British supremo, General Sir Edmund Allenby himself, this was every bit 'the most marvellous charge in modern warfare!'[1] In their recorded remarks, the Generals Chauvel and Chaytor felt the same, as did so many of the Troopers. But we'll get to that!)

It was, frankly, a delight to research and write as I kept discovering detail that put wondrous flesh on the bones of the story and showed it in all its glory.

What men!

What times!

What a charge!

My principal researcher for this book was the indefatigable Barb Kelly, who digitally trawled as mightily as ever to bring to the surface long-lost treasures of previously unrevealed detail. Happily, she became as obsessed with the story as me, and was able to provide the exact material to help bring to life previously obscure and unknown episodes. As with some of my previous books it was wonderful that her son Lachlan was able to lend valuable assistance, finding obituaries, death notices, and contemporary accounts that had previously escaped the rest of us.

My long-time researcher and beloved cousin, Angus FitzSimons, was as insightful as ever, constantly turning up new angles to pursue, even while finding the info on previous angles. This book is in his great debt. Dr Libby Effeney was very helpful on the Turkish side of things and was generous with her scholarship in the whole field of Ottoman history.

My warm thanks also to Dr Peter Williams, the Canberra military historian who has worked with me on eight books now. As ever, I relied on the depth and width of his military knowledge and lore to inform my writing – not to mention his extensive library of wartime literature and contacts, including the excellent Lieutenant Colonel Renfrey Pearson (retired) of the British Army, who was able to dig out much valuable documentation in London from the National Army Museum, National Archives and the Liddell Hart Centre for Military Archives.

Thanks, too, to Peter Finlay for expertise on matters of military aviation; to Gregory Blake for his expert advice on all things to do with the weapons of the time; while in terms of specific Light Horse expertise, I am indebted to Mick Batchelor, a re-enactor with the

7th Light Horse, and John Baines and Adrian Younger of the 8th Indi Light Horse Heritage Troop, another re-enactor group. I also thank Delia Parker and Brother Brian Clery of Aquinas College (formerly Christian Brothers' Perth) in Western Australia for their kind help with information on Alaric Pinder Boor. Emeritus Professor Bill Gammage gave me valuable help on key detail of the Gallipoli saga. Max Bonnell gave me great counsel on Tibby Cotter, and I warmly thank him.

And a particular thanks to Peter and Ali Haydon of *Bloomfield*, in the Upper Hunter Valley, who hosted me and my wife at their wonderful property in early 2023 and allowed me to trawl through Guy Haydon's letters and diaries, while Peter was a great source of advice and information thereafter. Thanks, too, to Bradley Olden, the grandson of Colonel Arthur Olden, for his help in bringing to life my favourite only-in-Australia episode of the whole saga.

As ever, and as I always recount at the beginning of my historical writing, I have tried to bring the *story* part of this history alive, by putting it in the present tense, and constructing it in the manner of a novel, albeit with close to a thousand footnotes as the pinpoint pillars on which the story rests. It was also a great pleasure to revisit previous Australian sagas I have worked on, like my book on Gallipoli, which gave me handy familiarity for some of the building-blocks of the Light Horse experience leading up to Beersheba.

For the sake of the storytelling, I have occasionally created a direct quote from reported speech in a journal, diary or letter, and changed pronouns and tenses to put that reported speech in the present tense. When the story required generic language – as in the words used when commanding movements in battle, I have taken the liberty of using that dialogue, to help bring the story to life, just as very occasionally I have tweaked the chronological order of scenes to help with flow.

Always, my goal has been to determine what were the words used, based on the primary documentary evidence presented, and what the feel of the situation was. All books used are listed in the Bibliography, but I relied particularly on the incomparable first-hand reportage of Richard Preston, Henry Gullett, Cyril Falls, Charles Bean, Lawrence of Arabia and Banjo Paterson.

My greatest debt though is to the incomparable Trooper Ion Idriess of the 5th Australian Light Horse Regiment, who was present for much of the action of this book, and wrote the seminal work describing the times, *The Desert Column*. No author who wants to capture the Light Horse experience in World War I can go past Idriess and I returned to his bountiful well repeatedly and with great pleasure. Meanwhile, Oliver Hogue's book, *Trooper Bluegum*, was particularly strong for the Light Horse experience at Gallipoli, while Major Banjo Paterson's book *Happy Dispatches* was also enormously valuable in providing the wonderful colour and feel of the times – and I was blessed to be able to use select verses of his poetry to also illustrate the era.

In terms of more contemporary work, I loved *A Thousand Miles of Battles*, the book of my old friend, the late Ian Jones, who first encouraged me to write on the wider Light Horse story, when he was helping me on my Ned Kelly book. It was a delight to go back to his town of Beechworth to talk to Ian's old friend, John Baines, who is also an expert and was kind enough to hand me an entire treasure trove of material.

I also consulted my friend Paul Daley, who wrote his own fascinating book, *Beersheba*, and inhaled his enthusiasm and advice. This book owes a particular debt to the work – and spoken words in the café and over the blower – of the generous Phillip Bradley, who wrote *Australian Light Horse: The Campaign in the Middle East 1916–1918*. Bradley's book was a constant and valuable guide to me, and I am in his debt.

My long-time sub-editor, Harriet Veitch, took the fine-tooth comb to the whole thing, untangling hopelessly twisted sentences, eliminating many grammatical errors and giving my work a sheen which does not properly belong to it. She has strengthened my stuff for three decades now, and I warmly thank her.

In all my books, I give a draft of the near finished product to the eldest of my six siblings, David, who has the best red pen in the business. When his interest flags, it is a fair bet so too will that of the reader, and I generally slash what doesn't grab him, so long as it is not key to the story. In this book, he was as astute as ever, and I record my gratitude.

My thanks also to my highly skilled editor, Deonie Fiford, who, as ever, has honoured my request that she preserve most of the oft esoteric – I'm told – way I write, while only occasionally insisting that something come out because it just doesn't work.

I am also grateful to my friend and publisher, Matthew Kelly of Hachette, with whom I have worked many times over the last three decades, and who was enthusiastic and supportive throughout, always giving great guidance.

I have loved doing this book, and hope you enjoy it.

Peter FitzSimons
Neutral Bay, Sydney
May 2023

THE CHARGE OF THE LIGHT BRIGADE

25 October 1854, Balaclava, the valley of death

Half a league, half a league,
Half a league onward,
All in the valley of Death
Rode the six hundred.

If they should die, think only this of them. While they advance with the ghosts of their forebears who, in the service of the British Empire have died due to everything from bullets to bombs, dysentery to drowning, spears to splinters . . . they risk shuffling off this mortal coil because of a sleeve.

'Forward, the Light Brigade!
Charge for the guns!' he said.

Certainly, but which guns exactly? For the Commanding Officer of the Cavalry Division, the Earl of Lucan, the answer is not obvious as he gazes at a bloody battlefield on the floor of this valley, which now has Russian artillery blazing on three sides. For the written order, which has just arrived in the hands of Captain Louis Nolan, is confusing:

> Lord Raglan wishes the cavalry to advance rapidly to the front,
> follow the enemy, and try to prevent the enemy carrying away
> the guns. Troop horse artillery may accompany. French cavalry
> is on your left. Immediate.[1]

What? Does the Army commander, Lord Raglan, refer to our own cannon on the causeway, which the Russians have captured and may try to take away, or does he mean the mass of the Russian guns, pointed at them directly, a mile away, at the far end of the valley?

Captain Nolan?

'Attack immediately!' he says, recalling this as the verbal instruction he was meant to pass on.

Certainly, but *which* guns?

Nolan simply throws his arm out pointing roughly to the left, the sleeve billowing out as his sweeping gesture is absorbed by Lucan. So, the far guns, at the end of the valley, glinting in the sunshine. Very well.

Lord Lucan passes the order on to Lord Cardigan, who is stunned. A charge straight at guns a mile away, firing straight at them, even while guns on their flanks tear into them from both sides! Lord Cardigan cannot help but question the order vigorously and is rebuked by Lord Lucan for his trouble. (The conversation is not helped by the fact that they are brothers-in-law, with Lucan married to Cardigan's sister. They are two men who despise each other with a passion in the way only forced families can.)

Orders are orders, and I will ask you to follow them.

So be it. As you command. In short order, 607 men of Her Majesty's Light Cavalry ride, their sabres and lances glittering in the sun as they set off.

> Into the valley of Death
>   Rode the six hundred.

> 'Forward, the Light Brigade!'
> Was there a man dismayed?
> Not though the soldier knew
>   Someone had blundered.

In fact, one man observing is more than dismayed. It is Lord Raglan himself who, watching aghast through field-glasses from the Sapoune Heights, cannot believe that Lord Cardigan is leading a charge towards the wrong guns! In horror, he watches as the Light Brigade thunder forward in a cloud of dust and the fog of war, their sabres forward, their fate sealed.

There is no time to stop them. And no sense in sending reinforcements. For you do not reinforce a suicide.

> *Theirs not to make reply,*
> *Theirs not to reason why,*
> *Theirs but to do and die.*
> *Into the valley of Death*
> *Rode the six hundred.*

Lord Cardigan rages at the insanity of it all, at the hide of his damn brother-in-law in insisting such orders be followed, and even at Captain Nolan, who now has the cheek to ride ahead of him. Cardigan has just decided to place Nolan on report should they make it back, when a Russian cannonball turns Nolan into bloody mush, instantly left behind.

> *Cannon to right of them,*
> *Cannon to left of them,*
> *Cannon in front of them*
> *Volleyed and thundered;*
> *Stormed at with shot and shell,*
> *Boldly they rode and well,*
> *Into the jaws of Death,*
> *Into the mouth of Hell*
> *Rode the six hundred*

Nolan is not the only one. In no more than two minutes, 107 worthies of the Light Brigade are blown apart by pieces of lead small and large, while their brethren charge on, their blades high, the primal roar of their lungs soon competing with the guns themselves.

> *Flash'd all their sabres bare,*
> *Flash'd as they turned in air,*
> *Sabring the gunners there,*
> *Charging an army, while*
> *All the world wonder'd*

Lord Cardigan is among the first to reach the Russian guns, wielding his sword with savage skill, only to recognise a friend from their days together in London high society, before the war. Why, it is Prince Leon Radziwill!

Despite Radziwill being more than a little occupied at the moment commanding the assembled Russian forces, he acknowledges Lord Cardigan and gives the order – *noblesse oblige* – that Cardigan is to be captured rather than killed if possible.

> *Plunged in the battery-smoke*
> *Right thro' the line they broke;*
> *Cossack and Russian*
> *Reel'd from the sabre-stroke*
> *Shatter'd and sunder'd.*

Lord Cardigan is not captured, or killed, and, regarding his bloody brother-in-law's order fulfilled, turns and trots back up the valley. He refuses to speak to Lucan as the remnants of his men return in bloody disarray, choosing to leave the field in disgust and ride to Balaclava Harbour, where his yacht and his champagne await.

> *They that had fought so well*
> *Came thro' the jaws of Death,*
> *Back from the mouth of Hell,*
> *All that was left of them,*
> *Left of six hundred.*

'The Charge of the Light Brigade', penned by the Poet Laureate Alfred Tennyson just two weeks later, will be recited ever after, a timeless classic that demonstrates that while warfare might have entered an industrial age, signalling the end of grand cavalry charges, honour, bravery, duty and self-sacrifice endure.

> *When can their glory fade?*
> *O the wild charge they made!*
> *All the world wonder'd.*
> *Honour the charge they made!*
> *Honour the Light Brigade,*
> *Noble six hundred!*

CHAPTER ONE

THE GUNS OF AUGUST

The Australians shook their heads when they saw men of the first contingent about the city streets. 'They'll never make soldiers of that lot,' they would say. 'The Light Horse may be all right, but they've got the ragtag and bobtail of Australia in this infantry'.[1]

Charles Bean, *Official History of Australia in the War of 1914–1918*

Late June 1914, Australia, a shot in the distance

The crack of distant gunfire is *so* distant it only just registers. It comes with no warning, but gives no alarm. It barely breaks breakfast, let alone news, and comes with no sense of what it presages. Yes, apparently in Sarajevo, wherever that is, an Archduke and his missus from Austria, or somewhere, have been shot and killed by a pistol-wielding Serbian called Gavrilo Princip but, so what?

The account in the *Sydney Morning Herald* comes with no clash of cymbals, and simply reminds readers that the Archduke, Franz Ferdinand, was the curious cove who came on a state visit to Australia a couple of decades back and while on a hunting trip in the Blue Mountains had no sooner brought down some kangaroos than his own retinue of royal taxidermists had moved in to gut, stuff and mount them! Strange bloke.

And even when things had started to turn ugly shortly after the assassination, with Austria-Hungary declaring war on Serbia, the whole thing remains barely a smudge on an otherwise sunny horizon.

Up in northern New South Wales, a country lad by the name of Maurie Evans will later recall just how dull the beginning of the whole thing was.

'At the breakfast table at Kyogle one morning in late July [1914] I was but languidly interested to hear that another war had started in the Balkans. I had never interested myself in international politics and so took another helping of eggs & bacon without a thought to the monstrous possibilities.'[2]

Alas, it proves not to be just another war in the Balkans, and that single shot fired in Serbia can later be pinpointed as the moment that the entire world started spinning out of control and on a different axis . . .

For at this time Europe is less a continent than a mesh of secret treaties which sees encircled empires move onto a war footing with extraordinary speed, and each declaration of war immediately triggering another.

Russia backs Serbia; Germany not only backs Austria-Hungary but attacks Luxembourg, who are backed by France, which means France is at war with Germany, which sees Germany attacking Belgium, who has a treaty with Britain, that sees the Brits declare war on Germany, which . . . brings in Australia. From Melbourne, Prime Minister Joseph Cook promptly promises the Home country, that it would

```
despatch an expeditionary force 20,000 men of any suggested
composition to any destination desired by the Home
Government. 3
```

Most of them will be foot soldiers, but 2000 are to be mounted Troopers.

For there are already 23 regiments of the Australian Light Horse in operation around the country – some 9000 mounted citizen soldiers, riding their own steeds and training in their spare time under professional commanding officers. The Australian Light Horse had its origins in cavalry, mounted infantry and mounted rifles regiments raised to defend the colonies before acquitting themselves so well in the Boer War that they had entered the realms of legend. The existing Light Horse Regiments are to be swept up into Brigades which will form part of the 'Australian Imperial Force', to soon be sent o'er the waves to the service of the Motherland.

Already, the government, while calling 'upon horse owners to repeat the generosity shown during the Boer War and donate any horses suitable for military purposes',[4] has started buying some of the 2300-odd horses thought necessary. Nearly all of them are 'Walers', a quintessentially Australian breed of mixed pedigree. That is, just as other animals in this tough and rugged land of Australia had evolved to be just as tough and rugged, or perish . . . so too, the Walers. No, these magnificent horses – predominantly from New South Wales, hence the name – do not have the classic lines of the fine English thorough-bred with heads as delicate as porcelain and bodies as slim and trim as they are shining with sheen, but that is just as well.

For the Walers are already deeply admired for their ability to travel long distances in hot weather and even go for as long as 60 hours without water, all while carrying a total load of over 20 stone!

Across Australia thus, there is a sudden flurry of hurry. Change is not just afoot, it is galloping. Battalions are forming up, recruitment depots are flooded and plans made for the massive movement of men, munitions, horses and ships.

It is the tenor of the times, with many nations around the world and whole empires either reacting swiftly to the cataclysmic news from Europe, or at the very least trying to work out how not to be engulfed by the cannon's roar.

Early evening, 10 August 1914, Constantinople, a son has been born to us

The capital of the Ottoman Empire – the empire of the Turks – is abuzz.

War!

They have not yet declared themselves to be on one side or the other, but in this war of empires it is inevitable that the Ottomans will have to choose.

The Turkish leadership are already engaged in heated debate over whether to join with the Triple Entente alliance – Great Britain, France and Russia – or side with the Central Powers of Germany and Austria-Hungary. The fact that only two days before Britain had entered the war the First Lord of the Admiralty, Winston Churchill, had given orders for the confiscation by armed troops of two dreadnoughts which had just been built in Britain's Elswick shipyard at Newcastle-on-Tyne for

Turkey, and that were about to be launched by a Turkish crew taking possession, had not helped the Turks warm to the British side of the war.

It is an *outrage*, and the people of Turkey had risen in righteous anger.

Furthermore, if the Triple Entente prevails, the risk is that the Dardanelles – that enormously significant narrow stretch of water that leads from the Mediterranean to the Sea of Marmara, where the Bosphorus at Constantinople joins it to the Black Sea – would be given to the Russians. So perhaps the Ottoman Empire should side with Germany?

Perhaps. On this evening, the most powerful man in Turkey, the Ottoman Minister of War, Enver Pasha – one of the three Young Turks effectively running the country, together with Djemal Pasha and Talaat Pasha – is meeting with the redoubtable Colonel Hans Kannengiesser of the German Military Mission discussing the possibilities and . . .

Ne oluyor şimdi? And what now?

Suddenly, there is something of a commotion outside.

It proves to be the very pushy German nobleman officer, Lieutenant Colonel Friedrich Kress von Kressenstein, who has news that cannot wait, and which – he bristles with righteous authority and glares through his monocle – needs an urgent decision.

'Fort Canakkale,' Kress von Kressenstein says portentously, naming the principal fort guarding the entrance to the Dardanelles, 'states that the German warships *Goeben* and *Breslau* are lying at the entrance to the Dardanelles and request permission to enter. The fortress asks for immediate instructions . . .'[5]

An ascetic German aristocrat whose ambition is nearly equalled by his ability, Kress von Kressenstein had taken his country's martial traditions with his mother's milk and his father's every utterance. There is an intensity about him which is unsettling.

Enver Pasha prevaricates, which is unlike him.

The *Goeben* and *Breslau* have had the Royal Navy in hot pursuit of them across the Mediterranean since the day war had broken out between Germany and Britain. If they are allowed in under these circumstances, Turkey's current claim of neutrality will be neutered, but on the other hand the Ottoman army is simply not ready for a major confrontation.

'I can't decide that now,' the Turkish Minister for War says in rapid staccato.

'But,' Kress von Kressenstein insists, 'we need to wire *immediately*.'[6]

Enver pauses. He deliberates. Is this the moment?

Perhaps.

Britain has already confiscated the Turkish ships, while Germany has been framing itself as a Turkish ally for years, and has been particularly solicitous since the war broke out. Could they really allow German ships to be sunk at the door of the Dardanelles?

Thus . . .

'They are to allow them to enter,' Enver Pasha intones, deeply aware of the significance of what he is doing.

Lieutenant Colonel Kress Von Kressenstein is relieved, but still not satisfied.

'If the English warships follow the Germans,' he asks, 'are they to be fired on if they also attempt an entrance?'

Again, Enver Pasha would rather not rule on it.

'The matter,' he says gravely, 'must be left to the decision of the Council of Ministers. The question can remain open for the time being.'

But Kress von Kressenstein will not take neither *Nein*, nor *Nocht nicht*, *not yet*, for an answer.

'Excellency,' Kress von Kressenstein persists, 'we cannot leave our subordinates in such a position without issuing immediately clearly defined instructions. Are the English to be fired on or not?'[7]

'. . .

'. . .

'*Evet*. Yes . . .'[8]

The German cruisers may enter.

The British ships will be stopped with artillery and mines.

The die is cast.

•

Maurie Evans finds more than his breakfast interrupted now; his life is stopped, his home farewelled, he is just one of many men across Australia who are rushing to join up, to be a part of it, to defend the British Empire! He can get back to his agricultural studies later, and for now heads to the recruitment centre for the Australian Light Horse at Sydney's Victoria Barracks.

Everywhere it seems, adventurous young men – once apprised of the chance to engage in that ultimate adventure that is war – pack up their old kitbag, and head to the nearest towns where they can join up.

From Maryborough comes a wild stockman who, since his birth in the saddle, has never met a brawl he didn't want to join, seen a drink he hasn't drunk, or met trouble he hasn't made a serious effort to deepen, just on principle. It will take a few months, and a few brawls along the way, but Thomas O'Leary is heading to the hastily erected enlistment tent at Winton in Queensland.

In Sydney, the most famous fast bowler of his day, the Test tearaway Tibby Cotter, will soon give up his job at the Riverstone Meat Company as a bookkeeper. He has worn the baggy green cap for Australia in 21 Tests, now it is time to test out the slouch hat. No, he can't ride a horse, particularly, but he'll ride his luck and see how it goes.

On the family farm just outside the tiny town of Walpeup in north-western Victoria, it matters little that Harry Bell is just 13 years old, and only knee-high to a grasshopper.

He *wants* to join up. He dreams of joining up. He curses wicked fate that has him as too young to join up. But he is determined to be in uniform at the first possible opportunity; legal or otherwise. All he can do meantime is keep working on the family farm with his father Thomas and brother Sam, and hope that there is enough war left over for him. His father is confident the war will be over by the time Harry is 18, while Sam is confident that Harry won't wait that long.

To others, the news has come a little more slowly.

Up in far north Queensland, a smile creeps across Ion Idriess's face as he sees the white sail crest the horizon. The face of this slender fellow is filled with character. The eyes have it – ever and always, filled with amused mischief – and a moustache that looks like it should be finished in a week or so, but never quite gets there. His fine aquiline nose looks as if it might have been nicked from one of the colonial statues in Brisbane, but the rest of him is Australian to a fault – a little rough around the edges, but proudly so. He sees being Australian as a virtue beyond all others. The sail? Well, that smudge of white coming ever closer here on the east coast of Cape York means news, don't you see?

Idriess clambers towards it; there is nothing he loves so much as diversion.

Just gone 25 years old, Idriess has known tough times before, through everything from working as a rabbit poisoner, drover, boundary rider, shearer, opal miner, itinerant rough-rider to dingo shooter and a dozen jobs in between. He knows how to live off the land and was taught by the best – living for a time with an Aboriginal clan on Cape York. But his current caper, prospecting for tin up around Cape Melville, is tougher than dried kangaroo meat carried in your gunny sack for a month, so no sooner has the approaching lugger dropped anchor than Ion rows out towards it and soon finds himself in a quite animated conversation with the captain.

A what?

A *war*!

Fine, can you take me back to Cooktown, so I can join up?

Nuh. He is heading up north.

No matter, there's always Shanks's pony. Idriess quickly packs his kit and starts to walk south, down the coast. Yes, it is 200 miles, and to get there he will have to get across wild, unsettled country with snakes, and a river featuring crocodiles *and* sharks, but he will cross that river or find another way entirely when he comes to it. The important thing is to join up, to not miss out on the adventure of a lifetime!

One way or another, hundreds, and soon *thousands*, of young men are riding their horses along the highways and byways of the bush and beyond, all heading in the same direction – to war; towards the nearest already inundated recruitment depot. Fresh-faced farmhands, pauper prospectors, rich members of the squattocracy, bronzed jackaroos and even a few townies are all part of the mix.

First, they must pass a basic riding test, which most do with ease, but not all.

At the Claremont Showgrounds in Western Australia, an aspirant for the 10th Australian Light Horse Regiment first climbs up on the wrong side of the horse – the correct side is on the left, a tradition which began from knights having their swords on their left-hand side, allowing them to easily draw it out with their right-hand – and then is thrown for his trouble. The young man has never ridden a horse in his life. What's impressive is his desperation to join the Light Horse, and the recruiting sergeant tells him, 'Practise for a week, and come back.'[9]

He does exactly that, and is accepted.

At the Broadmeadows recruiting station in Melbourne, another man initially has his application denied, because he has false teeth.

'I want to shoot the damned Germans,' he replies, 'not bite them to death!'[10]

Which is a fair point.

The key is to be so keen to join, you'll overcome any obstacle.

After all, being a member of the Light Horse is as close as an Australian can get to being a Knight of Camelot. Stories of the Light Horsemen's feats in the Boer War are legion, they were masters at fighting the commandos in the relentless heat of South Africa, and there is no more prestigious branch of the armed forces to join.

The new recruits are soon getting to know the senior officers of each regiment, experienced campaigners who have effectively been preparing for this very eventuality – *war* – since the days of the Boer War, a decade and a half earlier.

One such senior officer is Lieutenant Colonel William Grant, who commands the 3rd Light Horse on the Darling Downs. At 43 years old, some think that Grant should have handed over to a younger man some time ago, but Grant would never consider it. For one thing, he is as fit as he ever was, and still highly regarded by his superiors.

'He was a typical light horse subaltern,' his own commander, General Sir Harry Chauvel, would later say of his days training Grant in Queensland, 'tall, lithe and wiry, and full of dash and energy, and I early had my eye on him as a possible leader.'[11]

Colonel George Macarthur-Onslow, who is with the 7th Light Horse Regiment, based in Sydney's Rosebery Park, is also excited. Descended from major landowner John Macarthur, who had famously been the key driver of Sydney's Rum Rebellion of 1808, the young Colonel Macarthur-Onslow had served in the Boer War with the Australian Light Horse and steadily risen in the officer ranks from there.

In Melbourne, Lieutenant Colonel Alexander White happens to take command of the newly formed 8th Australian Light Horse Regiment on the day his beloved wife of less than a year, Myrtle, gives birth to a beautiful baby boy. White will pause at home long enough to organise a photo of his wife and infant son to be put in a locket that he hangs around his neck, but must quickly get back to the business at hand. White is an officer and a gentleman, a kind soul of enormous energy who now devotes himself to laying the foundation stones for their nascent regiment.[12]

In the Australian Parliament in Melbourne, the member for North Sydney, Granville Ryrie, is not long in deciding his political career is to be halted for a bit of practical non-diplomacy. Raised on the land down Monaro way, a crack marksman, brilliant horseman and a boxer with thunder in one fist and lightning in the other, the 50-year-old conservative MP is also a veteran of the Boer War, where he had gained a reputation for being a first-rate officer, ending the conflict as an honorary Major.

Can he resist getting back in uniform and answering the call? He cannot. The Light Horse is in his blood, and though he will remain a Member of Parliament even while serving in the AIF, his destiny is to take charge of the 2nd Light Horse Brigade, with the rank of Brigadier General.

(Those brigades are structured so that they are made up of regiments coming from different states. We must move on from our colonial mentality, and think nationally!)

By way of farewell to Ryrie, his loyal constituents of North Sydney present him with a magnificent stallion, christened 'Plain Bill'. Bill has been especially selected for strength, as weighing in at enough stones to build a dam, Ryrie is the biggest man in Parliament, and will be one of the largest men in this man's army.

There is just time for a farewell dinner at Parliament House in his honour – hosted by the newly installed Prime Minister, Andrew Fisher, and the Minister for Defence, Sir George Pearce. It is attended by members of both Houses, and after the Prime Minister – whose most famous utterance on the war to date is the promise that 'Australians will stand beside the mother country to help and defend her to our last man and our last shilling'[13] – makes a toast, Ryrie makes warm reply.

'I feel that, perhaps, the Australian Light Horse will be in at the triumphal entry into Berlin,' he finishes. 'If I can ride my charger down the streets of Berlin with the Belgian flag in front, I will be a happy man.'[14]

Cheers.

One Australian, Alaric Pinder Boor, is already in paradise when war breaks out.

There has always just been something about Western Australia's outstanding young son, Alaric, and it is not the sheer effortlessness with which he dominated on the cricket and Aussie Rules football fields, both as player and captain. It is not that he is also a force to be reckoned with in the boxing ring, the swimming pool and on the athletics track, while being a near Nijinsky at gymnastics grace, all while being the most outstanding academic scholar in the school. For these things are to do with his extraordinary physical and intellectual attributes. No, the most stand-out thing about Alaric is his character – his decency, his modesty despite his dominance, his sense of fair play that trumps even his fierce will to win.

Raised in Carnarvon in Western Australia, the only son of John Arthur Boor and his wife Emily, he had been sent to school at Christian Brothers' College in Perth, where he had risen to be both School Captain and Dux in the final year, before winning a three-year scholarship to Ormond College at the University of Melbourne, worth £125 per annum. There, his dominance of all things academic and sporting had been so outstanding – which included captaining Ormond's First XVIII side for two successive years, shining in cricket, rowing, running, hurdling, boxing, swimming, gymnastics, shooting *and* topping the college's Academic Honours list – he then won a Rhodes Scholarship to study Medicine at Oxford from October 1913.

Here now, in Oxford, it is a comfortable, wonderful life at Brasenose College, filled with everything he loves – scholarship, wonderful friendship and endless sporting opportunities. But can he truly stay doing that, while others go off to do their duty to King and country by fighting the Germans? He cannot.

Less than a month after the outbreak of hostilities, Boor sends his father in Carnarvon, Western Australia, a cable with just three words:

CAN I ENLIST?[15]

No sooner has the answer come back in the affirmative than – pausing only to cable thanks to his parents and write a long letter to the love of his life, sweet Ida Rawlings, back in Perth – Alaric joins up, heading off to training at Epsom before joining Oxfordshire and Buckinghamshire Light Infantry in actions around the Western Front.

For her part, Ida is naturally worried, and all the more so because her brother Frank Rawlings has also joined up, with Western Australia's only mounted unit, the 10th Australian Light Horse.

Among the officers at the 10th Light Horse is 2nd Lieutenant Arthur Olden – a dental surgeon by trade – who, finding the officer ranks of the 10th already filled the year before, had joined as a Trooper and was soon peeling potatoes for his trouble. His horse skills? Well, they mainly come from playing polo. His spud-peeling skills? Not so great, but it didn't matter as he had soon been promoted to the officer ranks anyway.

A softly spoken man, Olden knows not what awaits abroad, only that it is his duty to find out.

•

Watching proceedings with a weather eye from downtown Sydney Town way is the Poet Laureate of Australia, that Sydney Grammar boy who somehow managed to capture the spirit of the Australian bush better than any born in it, Banjo Paterson. He considers his position. It is one thing to be a living legend, and quite another to be able to live off it. He is not quite yesterday's man, but certainly at the point that if he is to die suddenly there will be more than a few reading his obituary who will be surprised to know he was still alive in the first place. What to do in the face of this war? Banjo is 50, and feeling it, and far too old for a front-line position holding a rifle. But he feels he can still hold a pen, and his own against other war correspondents – just as he had demonstrated so well in his famous dispatches from the Boer War and the Boxer Rebellion. Banjo announces to the press that he is to depart at first opportunity as War Correspondent; but for who exactly? Well, he will work that out when he gets there. Right now he will go a'waltzin' to war with lead in his pencil and a spring in his step. On a sunlit plain extended, he hopes for a vision splendid to revive his fortunes once more.

•

The first thing for you Australian Light Horse recruits is to be issued with your kit, so you look the part. First, here is your famous Australian slouch hat, made so by the Victorian Mounted Rifles since 1885 and always worn at a rakish tilt. For Queenslanders it comes complete with an emu plume, a prized tradition of the Light Horse, established, if you can call it that, by bored members of the Queensland Mounted Infantry in 1891. Assigned 'special duty' to patrol Capella during the Great Shearers' Strike, the men had grown weary of endless uneventful patrols and decided to see if they could not only chase emus in the scrub, but be skilled enough to reach down at full gallop, swerving left and right, and pluck a tail feather.

Those who can do so proudly have . . . a feather in their cap. The lark has become uniform, but the feathers still signal that sly streak of mischief that is also standard issue with these men.

Now, as with all icons, there are different legends as to how they started; and the famous feather is no different. Another story has it that the actual originator was a young officer by the name of Captain Harry Chauvel and his mate, serving in the West Moreton Mounted infantry. After a pet emu had died and the stockmen had nailed its hide to the saddle shed at a property called *Franklyn Vale*, Chauvel and his mate had playfully plucked the feathers to put them in their hats. Advised that they looked smart, they kept them!

Either way, the feather has even been immortalised by Australia's greatest versifier, Banjo himself, in the last war before this:

> There's a very well-built fellow, with a swinging sort of stride,
> About as handy sort as I have seen.
> A rough and tumble fellow that is born to fight and ride
> And he's over here a-fighting for the Queen.

He's Queensland Mounted Infantry – compounded 'orse and foot.
He'll climb a cliff or gallop down a flat.
He's cavalry to travel but he's infantry to shoot.
And you'll know him by the feathers in his hat.[16]

Completing their kit and caboodle are such things as a khaki jacket, breeches, leggings and spurs, waist belt with ammunition pouches, a bandolier, water bottle, haversack and – most importantly, a .303 rifle and hooked Quillion bayonet.

Now, for those of you who have brought horses with you, if your horse meets our standards, we will pay £30 for it, but – unless we decide it is only fit for hauling carriage or artillery – you may keep carriage of it. If accepted into the Army it will be branded with the government broad arrow, and have its army number carved on one hoof.

Each horse has its saddle and equipment placed directly in front of it; ready to be placed on the animal after the daily watering, grooming and feeding is completed. The men will eat after the horses do. At night they sleep eight men per bell tent – essentially the Australian Army's answer to teepees – with each man's feet pointing to the central pole. Being adept with a rifle and a mount is assumed, but the most important thing now is to learn how to drill, use Light Horse tactics, both mounted and dismounted, and function as a section.

A what?

A section! It is the most basic building block of our force, as Trooper Ion Idriess declares: 'We are all concentrated in sections. A section is four men. A section lives together, eats together, sleeps together, fights together, and when a shell lands on it, dies together. A full troop of men has eight sections. There are four troops to a squadron, three squadrons to a regiment. I'm not going further than the regiment. Our big world is the regiment and even then most of us don't know intimately the men out of our own squadron. Our life is just concentrated in the "section". We growl together, we swear together, we take one another's blasted horses to water, we conspire against the damned troop-sergeant together, we growl against the war and we damn the officers up hill and down dale together; we do everything together – in fact, this whole blasted war is being fought in sections.'[17]

Now, time for drill, and across the country the likes of Fred Rawlings, Maurie Evans, Ion Idriess and all the rest learn how to fire from the saddle; how to dismount in the shortest amount of time; find good cover and keep firing; how to scout, patrol and skirmish. In such skirmishes, only three men of the section will join in after they dismount their horse; the fourth man will hold and lead the horses, waiting for the signal to advance or withdraw.

Meantime, remember! When firing at moving targets approaching, you must constantly adjust the sights on your rifles, otherwise as they get closer you will end up firing well over their heads. Each man and horse rides in concert with the others, each racing to position, charging together in drills that forge the four into one.

Obviously, there is a sad lack of experience among the new recruits. But, at least at Sydney's Liverpool Army Camp, even the more experienced riders can stand to have a bit of swagger knocked out of them by ... 'Bill the Bastard'. Now, that might seem like an impolite name for a horse, but few who've been put upon him will argue, as he swiftly brings even the most accomplished riders back to earth.

Literally and eventually! Bill likes to kick them up first before gravity takes and does the second bit. Look, now!

For there goes another one, sent careering skywards before landing with a shattering thump on the muddy ground of Liverpool's horse corral, as the men roar. It is almost a rite of passage.

While the average Waler is around 14 hands tall, Bill the Bastard stands an extraordinary 17.2 hands – 5 foot 9 inches in the old money – a giant of a chestnut gelding of highly uncertain breeding, but well named. For he really *is* a bastard, in fact a bastard's bastard, and besides that, no bastard can ride the bastard! Unscrupulous outback stations have sold wild horses to the Army which they claim have been broken, but some of the horses are not only no such thing, they *refuse* to be broken.

Recruit after recruit to the Light Horse does his best on this buckjumper to beat them all, but to the growing delight of all who are in on the phenomenon *even the best and boldest riders* – those who have broken in horses from the Overflow down to the Back'o'Bourke and out to the Black Stump – can hold for no longer than ten seconds at best. This horse is like none they have ever seen before.

What to do with him?

Send him anyway.

Whatever else, the horse's phenomenal strength will surely come in useful for carrying supplies and munitions, not to mention the phenomenal horsepower required to haul guns forward with their limbers. Fortunately, Bill doesn't seem to mind that kind of work. It's just people he can't stand. So, get him ready with the thousands of other horses we are preparing to send to England with the troops.

But truly?

There is not time for much more, and much of whatever else specialist training the recruits need can be done on the spot.

Quick now!

The Germans have already invaded Belgium. The brutes are advancing at the rate of three miles a day, which might not sound like much, but at that rate Belgium is only about a month long. It is a matter of urgency to get these Australian infantry and Light Horsemen onto ships – where many onboard lectures can sharpen their knowledge if not their skills – and then get them to England, where they can complete their training on the Salisbury Plain. And then they can be sent to Europe to take on the Hun!

The weeks of training rush by.

•

Here in the English town of Epsom, everything is so exciting!

Yes, for Alaric Boor it had really been a wrench to leave the wonderful warmth and familiarity at Brasenose College and Oxford to join up with the Public School Corps and to begin training in France. But of course it had been his duty to King and country, and in the second place he is filled with exhilaration at being part of something so *extraordinary*, as trains and buses continue to disgorge thousands of similarly high-spirited young men of the Empire, all come to begin their training in the fields outside Epsom, just 13 miles south of London.

'Everywhere, it appears,' young Alaric writes home to his fond parents, 'the spirit of optimism prevails, and despite the German advance at the time of writing, [we] confidently believed that the Allies' turn for the offensive would shortly arrive . . .'[18]

The *Sunday Times* agrees and paints the novel picture for its readers of this small town turned training ground overnight.

'Epsom was invaded on Saturday, but not by Germans. Through its streets there was the march of many men, but they were all sons of the British Empire, and though none of the three thousand, two hundred and fifty – the first detachment of the Old Public Schools and University Corps – carried a rifle, all of the men hope and expect to cross the water and get face to face with the Germans in unusually quick time. The brigade consists of five thousand men; men who are the flower of the young manhood of England, men who bear with them the stamp of a vigorous healthy athletic life spent in the playing fields, or on the rivers of England. Epsom had its first sight of these about 4 o'clock one Friday afternoon, and from then until sleep drew the curtain down, the inhabitants had plenty to see and talk about. We arrived at Epsom Downs Station and marched into Epsom town square. When the many detachments of the invading army had assembled in the centre of the place; the old High Street presented a new and wonderful spectacle.'[19]

So say it, Alaric, for you know you must and give us at least a few words worth.

> Bliss was it in that dawn to be alive,
> But to be young was very heaven.

•

It has all happened so fast.

For now Victoria's 8th Light Horse Regiment is on its way. Under the earnest command of Lieutenant Colonel Alexander White, the men have trained hard, worked well, gelled as a fighting unit and received their embarkation orders just days before.

Inevitably, as the troopship *Star of Victoria* steams out of Port Phillip Bay, the men gaze earnestly at Melbourne Town for a last look – how long before they see it again, if ever. Few gaze with more emotion than White himself, wearing the locket with the picture of his beloved wife, Myrtle, and baby son Alexander around his neck, so that they are always with him. But unlike his men, on this day White genuinely has some chance of actually *seeing* his family, as the ship passes by the shoreside suburb of Elsternwick, right where his family home lies.

And there it is, Cole Street! Adjusting the focus of his field-glasses, he can clearly see his elderly neighbour, Armstrong, and his even more aged dog! A tiny swivel to the right and he can see it clearly. It is the lovely house he and Myrtle had purchased just before their marriage, the one he had laughingly carried her over the threshold into, after the wedding and there . . . there . . . there . . .

Alas, *alas*, he cannot see Myrtle and baby Alex, try as he might. They must be inside. If only he could have been more precise as to what time the ship was leaving, he could have arranged for them to be outside. Still hopeful, White keeps the binoculars trained until their blessed home disappears from view and Elsternwick itself fades into the hazy horizon. Sadly, he brings his glasses down. No matter that he is in command of 500 Troopers, it is only the locket he keeps brushing his fingers against that keeps him from feeling completely alone.

•

Australia takes her pen in hand
To write a line to you,
To let you fellows understand
How proud we are of you.

From shearing shed and cattle run,
From Broome to Hobson's Bay,
Each native-born Australian son
Stands straighter up today.

The man who used to 'hump his drum',
On far-out Queensland runs
Is fighting side by side with some
Tasmanian farmer's sons . . .

The old state jealousies of yore
Are dead as Pharaoh's sow,

We're not State children any more —
We're all Australians now!

'We're All Australians Now' by Banjo Paterson

November 1914, leaving shore, pyramid scheme

For the 30,000 Australian and Kiwi soldiers now steaming towards Europe aboard 48 transport ships, there is no question. These men of what is known as the 'First Contingent', are the southern sons of the Empire and they won't have it forgotten. Armed service is more than a duty, it is an honour and a privilege. Banjo Paterson certainly thinks so, and spends his time aboard the *Euripides* writing for the *Sydney Morning Herald*:

'It is strange to look out over the grey sea, not a ripple on the water, the horizon shrouded in haze, and to think of England calling up men from the ends of the earth – to think of these great flotillas ... of which one is, perhaps, even now behind that haze, all steaming steadily and purposefully towards the goal. Has anything like it ever been seen in the world before? The ends of the earth are called in for troops, the sea is furrowed with keels, and the very air is called into service to carry messages. If anything would cure a man of being a "little Australian", it would be such an expedition as this.'[20]

For now the news breaks, as reported by the Foreign Office in a bulletin that comes over the ship's radio, 'Owing to hostile acts committed by Turkish forces under German officers, a state of war exists between Great Britain and Turkey as from today.'[21]

It is *wonderful* news. Their greatest fear had been that the war would be over before they got there, but now those fears can settle.

And in other news, Kingsburgh, ridden by the four foot tall wonder George Meddick, has won the Melbourne Cup! Good God Almighty, what would that be *like* – to round the final turn at Flemington, and thunder to the finish atop your charging steed!

In the meantime, however, what is that bloody *smell*?

It is the horses. Their horses. It is always the horses. Eleven thousand of them are secured in hastily constructed stalls on and below decks, across all the ships. It is unbelievable just what stench their daily ablutions can emit and a large part of the Troopers' ship-life is engaging in the Herculean task of trying to keep those stalls clean, as well as get the horses exercised on deck. Even now it looks like it's going to be a close-run thing to get them to England in shape to perform, as so many are simply collapsing. Horses are supposed to sleep standing up, but not lately, not on Banjo's ship, where they are dropping like flies and they don't bloody get up unless you lift them.

Banjo being Banjo, he writes a poem about it, entitled, 'There's Another Blessed Horse Fell Down'.

When you're lying in your hammock, sleeping soft and
  sleeping sound,
Without a care or trouble on your mind,
And there's nothing to disturb you but the engines going round,
And you're dreaming of the girl you left behind;
In the middle of your joys you'll be wakened by a noise
And a clatter on the deck above your crown,
And you'll hear the corporal shout as he turns the picket out,
'There's another blessed horse fell down.'

The most troublesome of them all, albeit on another ship, is of course Bill the Bastard. Even when boarding he had very nearly been left behind because of his demeanour.

Yes, he'll be an incredible packhorse for his formidable strength alone. But it is that very strength which is such a handful in the confined space of a ship. It takes four Troopers pulling hard on his ropes to get him to go anywhere.

In truth, Bill the Bastard is so wild that there is a growing view that the best thing would be to shoot him, throw him over the side and feed him to the sharks. But Bill had retained some support, almost in the spirit of Banjo's most famous poem.

I think we ought to let him come, he said.
I warrant he'll be with us, when he's wanted at the end.

For it's his strength, don't you see?

He is the strongest horse anyone has ever seen. Yes, it'll be a long haul to England to get Bill the Bastard there in one piece, but it can be done.

•

Colonel Harry Chauvel, Australia's just arrived representative to the War Office in London, is concerned. Several trips out to the camps into which the Australians are due to go – at various spots around the Salisbury Plain – have confirmed his worst fears. The promised barracks have not been built, the whole thing is a shambles and, possibly, simply unworkable. (The nearest stable structure would appear to be Stonehenge.) After all, even the Canadians – who as a people take ice cubes with their mothers' milk – complain that it is freezing, while the miles of mud make movement as impossible as it is filthy. What's worse, and particularly makes Colonel Chauvel worry about what is coming – his countrymen, *en masse* – is that those same Canadian soldiers have been raising hell in the nearby cathedral city of Salisbury, causing shocking headlines. If that is what the relatively genteel Canadians do, just what kind of hell will a further 20,000 *Australians* raise when it is even more crowded, muddier and colder?

In his quiet but no-nonsense manner, Chauvel is not long in putting his views to Australia's High Commissioner, Sir George Reid. We *must* do something, Sir George. Plans must change. The first ships of our soldiers are no more than a week away from reaching the Suez Canal on their way here. Instead of putting our troops on Salisbury Plain in the freezing cold, it makes much more sense to have them train in Egypt. After all, with Turkey now in the war, they may well be required to fight in those parts and, if not, it is still far better to have them train there in the warmth. They can always be brought on to England and sent to France, if necessary.

Sir George takes his point, as he has learnt is always the best way with the sage Chauvel.

This late in the piece, there is only one man in Britain who could intervene to have those ships stopped in Egypt. Happily, Sir George knows Lord Kitchener, the Secretary of State for War, very well and quickly goes in search of him. Leave it with me, Colonel Chauvel.

•

The sound of cheering and animated conversation breaks out all over every ship in the convoy as the glad tidings wash from stern to starboard to port to bow and back again. They say the word has come from the Admiralty, that we're *not* going to be landing in the Old Dart after all. Nup, apparently we're going to land in Egypt, and do our training there!

If proof is not in the pudding that night, it comes with official confirmation during lunch the next day: after steaming 100 miles up the Suez Canal we'll be heading west to make a landing in Alexandria, where trains will await to take us to Cairo.

Mid-November 1914, Constantinople, the rule of three

It had all been so easy when they started out, branded as the Young Turks.

For they had been every bit of that, and more.

Enver Pasha, Djemal Pasha and Talaat Pasha are united not just by a title but by a passion to save their empire. They are the revolutionary leaders of the Committee of Union and Progress who, on 13 January 1913, had seized control of the Sublime Porte – the seat of Ottoman power in Constantinople for the last 400 years. The Young Turks had stormed the palace, gunning down the War Minister and his Adjutant Major, and forcing the 90-year-old Grand Vizier Kamil to resign.

Ya Namus Ya Ölüm! Honour or death! The three men will soon be known across the land as 'the Three Pashas'. Enver Pasha has become the powerful Minister of War and Chief of the General Staff – making him the political *and* military leader of the armed forces – while his key ally, Djemal Pasha, is Minister of the Navy and Enver's right-hand man, Talaat Pasha, is the Minister of the Interior.

And now here they are, at war with an implacable foe, which makes Enver Pasha the most powerful man in the land. On this day he has invited Djemal to his glorious home above the Bosphorus to unveil his next glorious idea.

'Djemal Pasha,' he says, with that touch of unnecessary formality that is his trademark, intoning his words as if he were a textbook working up the nerve to be an encyclopedia: 'I want to start an offensive against the Suez Canal to keep the English tied up in Egypt, and thus not only compel them to leave there a large number of Indian divisions, which they are now sending to the Western Front, but prevent them from concentrating a force to land at the Dardanelles.'

Djemal realises he is not hearing a thought, but a typically detailed Enver plan, already being enacted even before being revealed! And sure enough, as Enver Pasha continues his stately speaking, that truth is unveiled.

'With that end in view,' Enver continues, 'I've been making preparations in Syria for a month or two. I've earmarked the 8th Army Corps, under the command of Mersinli Djemal, for this business. As the Germans attach the greatest importance to the execution of this operation, I've appointed Lieutenant Colonel Kress von Kressenstein Bey as Chief of Staff and sent him to Damascus as attaché of the German Military Mission.'[22]

Djemal is immediately uneasy. The Germans are gifted at many things – alas, taking and following orders from people who are not also German is not among them. But do go on, Enver Pasha.

'The news from Syria points to general disturbance in the country and great activity on the part of the revolutionary Arabs. In these circumstances I have wondered whether Your Excellency would not give a further proof of your patriotism by taking over the command of the Fourth Army. In doing so you would have to prepare (and carry through) the attack on the Canal, and also maintain peace and internal order in Syria. I don't know if I may venture to make this proposal to you?'

Djemal Pasha accepts, as both knew he would: 'I consider it my sacred duty to go.'

And within two days, Djemal Pasha is on his way, farewelled at Constantinople's principal station by many officials, one of whom says to him with heartfelt passion, 'The nation expects from you great exploits and speedy news of victory.'[23]

Does it indeed?

'I am fully conscious of both the greatness and the immense difficulties of the task before me,' Djemal Pasha replies, meeting the eyes of his well-wishers with his intense, dark glare. '*If* our enterprise fails, and my corpse and those of the brave men going with me are left at the Canal, the friends of our country will then have to take up our work, must sweep over us and rescue Egypt, the rightful property of Islam, from the hands of the English usurpers.'[24]

That will be your task, gentlemen. With that, he doffs his black fez to the crowd and boards the train, on his way to that shining jewel in the crown of the Ottoman Empire that is Damascus, from where he will gather his forces before moving on the Suez Canal.

•

For the Australians heading out aboard the *Euripides*, the big wide world they'd been looking forward to seeing is suddenly closing in. Just a couple of hours ago their ship had been a small speck on a vast and shimmering ocean, a tiny crawling mite on an endless blue canvas. But now the Australians are suddenly aboard a gigantic vessel in this mostly man-made canal, the Suez waterway only just big enough to fit their ship going north while also accommodating all the ships heading south.

On this bright moonlit night of 1 December 1914, not even four months since the war had begun, the Australian soldiers and Troopers crowding the decks can look to both port and starboard to see vast tracts of trackless desert. Those with a sense of geography quickly get their bearings. To their right must be Egypt's vast Sinai Desert and beyond it the Biblical realms of the Holy Land with towns like Bethlehem and Jerusalem. Well over the horizon on the left is the Nile, which weaves its way to Cairo.

On the western bank, in the wan luminescence, they can see ghostly regiments of the netherworld – actually Indian soldiers, complete with turbans and swords, standing guard behind what look to be entire forts of sandbags and rolls of barbed wire.

Dawn reveals a slowly moving picture show of endlessly exotic things, starting with an eternity of tiny mud huts beside pocket-handkerchief vegetable patches tended by heavily veiled women carrying huge water jars amazingly balanced on their heads.

'I have just witnessed,' one Australian soldier records, 'a tribe of natives paying their tribute to their God . . . kneeling and bobbing up and down like a Jack in a box, then they would mutter something to themselves, with their hands up in the air, then nearly knock their brains out with bowing to the sun.'[25]

Somewhere in the distance comes a weird wailing of origin unknown.

For those aboard the *Euripides* though, the most extraordinary thing is still to come. On the hazy horizon to their north, they suddenly see a major town with spires and towers, just sort of floating above the shimmer only for it to slowly . . . . fade . . . . from view as they approach! Yes, a mysterious mirage, but so real!

'This ghostly desert town,' Banjo Paterson records, 'made more impression on the men than anything that they saw; it seemed uncanny.'[26]

Onwards.

Instead of passing the port to the left, as has long been the tradition in the maritime world, the *Euripides* soon berths at that most ancient of port cities, Alexandria – founded and named by Alexander the Great himself, that masterful military commander of the ancient world who had conquered these very parts.

Within three hours the soldiers are on the train, steaming south through the Delta country on the 120-mile trip to Cairo.

'I fairly drank it all in,' one soldier will recall, 'for we were now in the land of mystery and wonderful things.'[27] Another notes, 'The native villages are most peculiarly laid out and the method of tilling the land somewhat strange to us Australians. It is quite common to see an ox and a camel, or a camel and a donkey pulling an old wooden plough.'[28]

After arriving at Cairo's Central Station the Australians begin the march to their training camp at a place called Mena, 10 miles away, and shortly after traversing a bridge that takes them over the mighty moonlit ribbon of the Nile, they see them.

Pyramids!

The Mena Camp – where they will shortly put up tents and build latrines – proves to lie within the moon-shadow of the towering 482-foot Great Pyramid of King Cheops, with the surrounding desert to be their principal training ground. Ever more members of the Light Horse will arrive in succeeding days, weeks and months. Hopping around the camp at the Pyramids are at least a half-dozen of the smarter kangaroos and wallabies the troops brought from Australia – the ones who had not jumped overboard on the way over. (The kangaroos, babies when they left port, are supposed to be mascots, now they are a source of fascination to locals and irritation to officers trying to work out what to do with them. The Cairo Zoo will soon have some new recruits.)

•

Few are more pleased at news of the Australians' safe arrival and successful establishment than Colonel Chauvel. He is particularly interested to get reports on how the 1st Light Horse Brigade is faring, and for good reason. Even before Chauvel had made the suggestion for the Australian troops to be trained in Egypt, a cable had arrived from Australia informing him that instead of being Australia's representative in London to the War Office he was to journey to Egypt himself and assume command of the 1st Light Horse Brigade when it arrives. Officers of his calibre, with his level of experience with the Light Horse, are simply too valuable to waste on the War Office. Someone else can do it. Chauvel is soon on the high seas, on the ocean liner SS *Mooltan*, heading for Egypt and his men. It had been shockingly difficult to leave his wife and three children in their comfortable digs in London where he had so recently installed them, but there is nothing for it.

This is war, this is duty; all else must wait and be missed. Onwards.

•

For most of the Australian soldiers now settled into the endless line of sandy tents in the desert that is the Mena Camp, the strangeness of the environment is soon matched by the sense of time. Is it really only six weeks ago that they left Australia, and all that was familiar to them? It seems so long ago, another world, another life. They dream of home when they can, which is not long, for every day starts with reveille at 5 am SHARP, the sound of the bugle whipping across the desert sands and through their thin canvas tents before drilling right into their ears.

Up! Up! Up!

Now clean the horse lines, feed your mounts, water them, groom them, and *then* you can eat. Look after them like silkworms and they will look after you in battle. And make no mistake – they are more important than you. Together you are a complete fighting unit!

After a breakfast of eggs and bread and jam washed down by tea stewed in the curious British standard issue 'Tommy Cooker' – small stoves – now we are back at it, falling in for the first of many inspections and roll-calls for the day.

And then back to the endless pill of drill, drill, drill. Yours not to reason why, yours to drill until you die, apparently. (The instructors are aware we are in Egypt, yes? It's so hot it makes Darwin look like Hobart. *Sigh*.)

It is at Mena, just a couple of weeks after the first arrivals, that Charles Bean, often spied with his pad in hand jotting notes all the while in his mad dash of a scrawl, reports back to his readers: 'All day long, in every valley of the Sahara for miles around the Pyramids, were groups or lines of men advancing, retiring, drilling, or squatted near their piled arms listening to their officer . . . At first, in order to harden the troops, they wore as a rule full kit with heavy packs. Their backs became drenched with perspiration, the bitter desert wind blew on them . . .'[29]

Meanwhile, the Troopers of the Light Horse regiments are equally busy getting both themselves and their horses in shape. By now the best of the Troopers and their horses have a bond close enough to be like family members, each understanding, trusting and depending on the other. Look after your horses, and they will look after you. Look after your Troopers, and they will look after you.

On 18 December, a fortnight after their arrival, an intrepid reporter from the *Egyptian Gazette* records the scene.

'The many lines of beautiful and much loved horses strike the onlooker immediately; they have practically constant attention night and day. Being packed on the boats as they were the whole time from Australia, standing for seven or eight weeks has for the time weakened and stiffened their legs and joints and at present not one of them is being ridden. They are exercised daily, at first gently, increasing to 10 mile exercises and training they are now undergoing.'[30]

In coming weeks, the men will be taking their horses on long treks through the desert to toughen both before making rapid attacks on a designated sandhill three miles away, dismounting and firing a dozen times, fixing bayonets and charging, and so on and so forth as the sun blazes down and they can return at the end of the day to the Sphinx that awaits at the base of the Pyramids, just as the cat used to greet them at home after a hard day's work.

For all the hard yakka of this training, the Australian Troopers can still find the funny side of things, no matter how exhausted they are. On one occasion a company from the 7th Battalion is on the march near Cairo, when they pass by a group of hawkers and their donkeys.

Left ... left ... left, right, left ...

At that very moment a male donkey becomes so excited by a nearby female donkey that the soldiers roar with ribald laughter. Annoyed, the nearest hawker gives the donkey's ear a vicious twist, at which point the donkey's excitement instantly dissipates.

Just a few minutes later, two beautiful Englishwomen in a fine carriage heave into view, whereupon the Captain outdoes himself to first halt the Company and now engage the women in lightly flirtatious greetings, whereupon a laconic drawl comes from deep within the ranks: 'Twist his ear, sergeant.'[31]

They march on through the Egyptian streets, by the vendors, the beggars, the street-kids in this riot of a city. Though they have only been here for a few weeks, the Australians have already come to understand and even use some of the local language.

Baksheesh is not just the cry from the Cairo beggars asking for alms for the poor, but is also the small bribe seemingly required from anyone to do anything in a hurry. For in these parts hurry itself is in exceedingly short supply.

When will something be ready, or be completed?

The answer is invariably *inshallah*, meaning 'tomorrow, Allah willing', while you must understand that tomorrow does not mean something between dawn on the morrow and dusk. It means sometime in the future if Allah wills it, but if he doesn't so be it, do not fret. Allah is in charge of everything that happens, so there is no point in fretting when it hasn't happened yet, or when it hasn't happened in the way you want it to have happened. Everything happens, *inshallah*, when Allah wills it, in the way he wills it to happen.

Meantime, a *wadi* describes the usual watercourses that criss-cross the desert. And any geographic feature that has a *Tel* in it means it most likely comes complete with ruins, as *Tel* is an Arabic word denoting ancient mounds, often composed of the remains of centuries of different structures.

There are also words which the Troopers use as short-hand for their own, purely military world. Anti-aircraft guns are known as 'Archie', the officer class is known as 'Brass'. And those pooncey Poms prancing about on their thoroughbreds who, with swords actually part of their kit, call themselves the British cavalry? They are 'donkey wallopers'.

What can the Australian Troopers do on those rare occasions when they are allowed time off from training? The obvious: drinking and chasing women in 'the Wazza', Cairo's extraordinarily exotic, erotic, red-light district, where the air is filled with an intoxicating mix of perfume, hashish smoke, strange languages and edgy excitement. It is a place of labyrinthian alleys, dimly lit rooms and shouting hawkers where – and this is extraordinary – for only a few shillings you can get an actual nail that Jesus was nailed to the cross with!

As to the women, they are *everywhere* and hail from the same: coming from as far afield as Italy, Greece, Armenia, Persia and Sudan; and are present in all shapely shapes, sizes and states of undress. They titter, teeter and totter on the balconies beckoning the Australian soldiers to come hither.

If you do, all the soldiers know – they hand out more roots than a mangrove swamp for as little as six 'disasters' (piastres) a pop, the equivalent of just a single shilling! All while we are getting paid six shillings a day!

What better place to run riot, drink like a mad dog, and maybe pick fights with Pommies, knowing your mates will back you up. After all, the only real authority hereabouts is the fat Nubian, Ibrahim al-Gharbi, known as the 'King of the Wazza', an odd sod who dresses in sheila's clothing and wears a white veil. No, seriously.

Of course their senior officers don't like the Australians heading into the Wazza in such numbers, and drinking so heavily, but so what?

We can sort that out when we get back.

Our reputation, when we do turn up at camp precedes us, and it is reflected in a running joke about the nightly exchange that goes on between the camp sentries and new arrivals.

Sentry: 'Halt! Who goes there?'
Voice: 'Ceylon Planters' Rifles.'
Sentry: 'Pass, friend.'
A little later.
Sentry: 'Halt! Who goes there?'
Voice: 'Auckland Mounted Rifles.'
Sentry: 'Pass, friend.'
A little later again.
Sentry: 'Halt! Who goes there?'
Voice: 'What the fuck has it got to do with you?'
Sentry: 'Pass, Australian.'[32]

CHAPTER TWO

DEATH IN THE SUN

The joy-spots of this old Bible desert are the oases. They seem to be about twenty-five to thirty miles apart, except when there are groups within a few miles of one another as in the huge Katia oasis area. Each little group of date-palms among the sandy hills shelters that most precious thing to man – water. It is in tiny wells which have been used since countless centuries before Moses.[1]

Ion Idriess, *The Desert Column*

Tibby Cotter is the match-winner, stump-breaker, and sensation-provider of Australia. He started this season by getting six wickets for 12, the last five for three, and smashed a stump.[2]

From a 1908 *Sydney Mail* profile of the leading Test cricketers of the day. Cotter was the third one profiled after Victor Trumper and M. A. Noble.

15 January 1915, Jerusalem, singing in the Suez

Hark!

It is men singing.

Many men singing.

It is practically a Turkish anthem: 'The red flag flies over Cairo.'

In the middle of the throng is the Commander of the Fourth Army, the man with jet-black eyes, which match his black fez and thick black beard, Djemal Pasha, surrounded by his usual squadron of gaily attired guards on camels. He is feeling strong as they march through the ancient streets, on their way south to Beersheba, where a force of 15,000 men from the Ottoman 8th Corps will join the advance, and they will go all the way to the Suez Canal, which they intend to cross and get all the way to Cairo! They are supported by 1500 Arabs

30

and eight batteries of field artillery, and drag 10 enormous pontoons which, strung together, should allow them to cross and establish a beach-head on the far shore of the Canal to enable a place for them to cross *en masse*.

Now, Djemal Pasha has been described as a 'bon vivant with a weakness for pomp and circumstance', and for 'beautiful Jewesses', who plays poker, races horses and smokes cigars. But on matters military he is nothing if not capable, and in this parade he has already boasted to his troops: 'We'll meet on the other side of the Canal or in Heaven!'[3]

For now, they must settle down as the long haul gets underway in the growing moonlight. The first major stop will be Beersheba, where they can replenish their water supplies. They will continue to move at night, and camp in the desert during the day, the men on small canvas sheets, while Djemal Pasha will take his rest amid 'magnificent tents, hat stands, commodes'.[4]

'Everyone was absolutely convinced that the Canal would certainly be crossed,' Pasha will recall, 'that we should dig ourselves in securely on the further bank, and that the Egyptian patriots would then rise and attack the English in the rear.'

Djemal himself is not quite so confident, having been informed of the bristling British defences that await, but no matter.

'I used to talk to the troops every night about the victory in store, and what a glorious victory it would be . . .'[5]

For their parts, both Mersinli Djemal and Colonel Kress von Kressenstein – who, as Commander of the Fourth Army's 8th Corps and his Chief of Staff, will have operational control of the actual attack – are more sanguine.

They plan to order their men to fight to the death, maintaining the attack until the objective is reached.

February 1915, Liverpool, cometh the horsemen

And so they keep coming, from all over the country, to join the Australian Light Horse.

Among them on this day is a notably good-looking fellow with an educated, well-bred air about him, projecting a sense of both 'can-do' and 'has-done'. His name is Guy Haydon, he is 25 years old, hails from the Upper Hunter Valley famous Haydon horse stud, *Bloomfield*, established in 1838, and comes complete with the stud's prize pedigree mare. She is in fact one of the most legendary steeds in New South Wales, Midnight – born at exactly that time – out of Tester by Moonlight.

Haydon, a strapping six-footer and graduate of the Shore School in Sydney, had raised Midnight from a foal and been riding her for most of the last decade. Just as Guy had been practically able to ride before he could walk, Midnight had known Guy's steady hand long before she could trot. The bond between them is so strong it is spiritual. When Guy is on her back, they are not two, they are *one*.

And yes, few horses of her pedigree would be sent to the war, but the Haydons come to the conclusion that, given Guy's bond and mastery of Midnight's majesty, it will improve the chances of him coming home safe. A mighty mare, she is distinctive not only for her coal-black coat, but also for the fact that on her forehead is a 'small white star with three little peaks like the petals of a tiara pointing upwards. There was a distinctive white triangular peak on the front of her near hind coronet, standing all alone, matching the upward peaks on her star.'[6]

While his older brother Fred has stayed back to help his parents on the stud, Guy joins the Australian Light Horse in the company of his younger brother, Barney, on the firm promise made by Guy to his parents that he will keep a close eye on Barney.

They will be following their much-admired cousin Stuart Haydon, who had joined up in the early days of the war. Guy Haydon is one of those men who spent more time on the saddle than in the high chair when he was a toddler. He'd excelled at rowing, rugby and cricket throughout his time at school in Sydney, but never lost his passion for putting a foot in a stirrup.

When they arrive at Liverpool enlistment camp it is to the wry amusement of all the Hunter Valley men that they are required by the Light Horse instructors to put themselves and their mounts through a series of manoeuvres to prove they are actual horsemen – to ride, gallop, jump and steer with a flick of the reins as though these were tests instead of reflexes for them – it's like asking a bloke from west

of Dubbo if he can knock back a beer before you let him join up –
handling a horse is something that all of them just do.

Haydon dominates the day, just as he and Midnight have dominated
all the bushman carnivals and camp drafting competitions up Hunter
Valley way for most of the last decade. Together, the two are the pride
of the squadron, which is being formed practically from the moment
of their arrival in camp.

4.20 am, 3 February 1915, Suez Canal, West Bank check

Movement in the moonlight!

It is the soldiers of the 62nd Punjabis, of the 22nd Indian Infantry
Brigade, who spy them first – men on rafts and pontoons trying to
cross the Suez Canal from east to west! Extraordinarily, a large mass
of Turks has indeed succeeded in crossing the Sinai, and the first of
them – the vanguard of Djemal Pasha's 'Suez Expeditionary Force',
15,000 soldiers strong, with nine batteries of field artillery – are trying
to get across the Canal itself to fight up close with those defending
on the west bank.

But not tonight, Ahmed.

Indian machine-gunners from the 62nd quickly cut a swathe through
the would-be invaders on the water, together with those massed on
the other shore, and are soon joined by their fellow Indians from the
128th Pioneers, as well as an Egyptian artillery battery. They, in turn,
come under heavy fire from the Turks on the other side – including
artillery, which they have somehow dragged across the Sinai! At the
first light of dawn, the Turks redouble their efforts, both here and
further north at the key Suez Canal port of Kantara.

Courtesy of pontoons, two companies of Turkish and Arab soldiers
actually succeed in crossing under the cover of heavy machine-gun fire
from the eastern shore, but come under the brave and concentrated fire
of the defending soldiers, together with the British gunships arriving
from their base at Port Said. Seven of the pontoons are destroyed by
artillery.

From a hill two miles back, Djemal Pasha is watching closely through
his glasses, his worst fears near confirmed. They have done mightily

well to come this far, but, yes, the British defences look to be simply too strong. By noon he is convinced that getting more troops across the Canal and seizing the city of Ismailia on the other side must surely be out of the question. He sends for Mersinli Djemal, the Commander of the 8th Corps. Mersinli Djemal is not ready to give up, insisting that if he can get full artillery support by nightfall, they could perhaps get more men across at dawn the next day, a proposition that his Chief of Staff, Colonel Kress von Kressenstein, agrees with.

But Djemal Pasha's ink-black eyes flash in stern disagreement.

'The attempt to cross the Canal a second time is dependent upon the resources at our disposal, and according to the reports you have sent in we have not more than three pontoons left. The proposal to swim across the Canal is perfectly hopeless. How, then, do you propose to carry out your scheme?'[7]

There is no firm reply, but what Djemal Pasha can see is that Kress von Kressenstein – who has been working on this expedition for nearly three months – 'regarded this campaign as his life's purpose, was in utter despair at the apparent failure, and considered death the only remedy'.[8]

Glistening 'neath his monocle, the German now bursts out.

'Your Excellency! In my view it is now the duty of the Expeditionary Force to die to a man on the Canal!'

Djemal Pasha answers him quietly, his voice as dark as his glare.

'I didn't call you here to hold a council of war and share the responsibility for my decisions with you . . .'

The point is taken in cold silence and Kress von Kressenstein listens as his commander goes on.

'I gather from what you say that there is nothing more to be done. If we stay another day by the Canal, the Expeditionary Force will be entirely destroyed. This force represents all that is available to the Ottoman Empire in an emergency for the defence of Syria and Palestine. I have no higher duty than to preserve this force from danger, and put it to the best uses until the end of the war. I think it is preferable to hold our positions until evening, keeping up the artillery duel with the enemy, and then utilise the darkness to withdraw the troops to the lines they left yesterday evening. From there we can march back slowly to Beersheba . . .'[9]

And so it is done. By nightfall, all the Turks laying siege to the Suez Canal have pulled back, and by dawn they are out of sight, disappeared into the Sinai whence they came. They have suffered 1300 casualties.

For the exhausted but victorious British forces they leave behind, there is exultation. They have taken on the Turks and beaten the bastards back!

The worry is that they will clearly be trying again.

But there is also incredulity at just how close the Turks had come, how many men they had massed for the attack. For it is nothing less than extraordinary!

The reason they had been able to arrive essentially undetected had been because they had eschewed the route taken by all invaders since the time of the Pharaohs through to Napoleon – pushing along the caravan road by the sea, where there is more water, cover and food. Instead, close questioning of the Turkish prisoners reveals that, mostly by marching through the night and resting by day in the *wadis*, they had succeeded in crossing the trackless Sinai Desert, coming via the Palestinian town of Beersheba right out in the middle of those desert wastelands. It is an amazing achievement, previously thought impossible.

The Suez will have to be reinforced; the Turks, Germans and Arabs stopped; and – if all goes well – the forces of the British Empire can begin to push Johnny Turk back across the Sinai.

After all, as General Kitchener himself will observe when first having a close look at the set-up, 'Are you defending the Canal, or is the Canal defending you?'[10]

This whole thing may indeed need a rethink.

But whatever they do, they will definitely need plenty more troops to do it – and they will have to come from the British Empire. Recruitment drives must be picked up, and perhaps even conscription introduced into those countries that can manage it.

Send us your finest!

1 March 1915, Sydney, ride to the bridle register

The orders are in, their time has come at last. The 12th Australian Light Horse Regiment is issued with authority for active service abroad and proceed in formation out of Liverpool Camp to nearby Holsworthy Camp.

The only interruption for the newly arrived men from the Hunter Valley is when they are granted one weekend's leave so that all can be present when Guy Haydon marries the love of his life, the beautiful Bonnie Hindmarsh. A dear friend of his sister Madge, she hails from Lismore, is the daughter of a well-known New South Wales parliamentarian, and neither bride nor groom could be happier. It had come as a shock to both of them to have had the thrill and wonder of a joyous engagement, only to realise that Guy would be going away to war, but what can they do?

Like everyone else, only the best they can.

On the Saturday night at Strathfield, the wine and beer flow, the speeches are made, the bridal waltz is followed by dancing that goes well past midnight and, after one blessed night with his bride, Guy Haydon and his fellow new recruits of the 12th Light Horse must again get into their uniforms and head back to Holsworthy for more training.

Good Friday, 2 April 1915, Cairo, a pox on both your houses

Bloody *locusts*. There is a plague of locusts in Egypt. True, frogs are not falling from the sky and water isn't turning into blood, but it still feels a little too like the Biblical Armageddon for comfort. Swirling, whirling little bastards, the insects flock and block out the sun, sprawling and crawling over every bloody thing, their wings like 'whirring wheels'.[11]

Never mind. The word is it's *on*, from tomorrow, as we embark for parts unknown. Which means we have just one night left to enjoy ourselves in Cairo in parts well known.

We will drink until we are drunk and then keep going until all the booze is gone. We who are about to depart are going to make a bloody good start at painting this town redder than the Red Sea.

Where can one obtain fine grog and girls?

Well, where else but the Wazza!

So it is that by 3 o'clock on this hot afternoon, it seems like entire brigades of Australian and New Zealand soldiers are joyfully stumbling around the Wazza, as tight as two Lords, and in the mood for love, in a back room if possible. Now, in this drunken haze a blazing row with some pimps begins, and when we say blazing, we mean it. For look up there, no falling frogs, but blazing mattresses falling from the sky, wending their way quickly to the flaming streets of the Wazza. *What the hell is going on?*

A blue, in the upper floors of the whorehouse at Number 8, Darb al-Muballat. After the mattresses come furniture, clothes, chairs and shutters, all raining down to the bleary cheers of the soldiers beneath. What to do with all this debris? How about a bonfire? The mattresses are still alight and they are soon not alone, a proper Guy Fawkes blaze now breaches the peace in the Egyptian streets. From above, yelling continues; from below the Egyptian police arrive, and if there is a sober witness to tell them what is going on, they are surely not speaking English. *Well, what did happen?*

Not enough! 'Finish the bastards off!'[12] the soldiers yell as the police are now attacked! There is no arguing with a mob, especially a mob of drunken Aussies and sloshed En Zedders. Thirty British Military Police arrive to restore order and order that fire out. But the 'Red Caps' find that the Australians have 'reinstoushments' at the ready, three bloody thousand of them! Now the Red Caps, too, are being attacked, by their own bloody men! (Well, colonial men, but still.) And nobody knows what started all this! *Well?*

The reinstoushed are very well and prove it by hurling bottles, stones and – HOLY CHRIST – A PIANO! A bloody piano is attacking them from the sky and smacking down on the street. Right, this is getting serious. The Captain of the Red Caps orders pistols to be drawn.

And WATCH OUT!

'If you don't disperse,' he yells to the rioters, 'I will order them to fire!'[13]

Really? Well, let's see you do it . . . His bluff called, the Captain yells 'FIRE!' and they do, over the heads of the mob. The Australians have seen far more impressive fires this night and have started at least three bigger than that pop-gun chorus. Got anything else, mate?

Yes, a whole battalion of Lancashire Territorials arrive with *rifles* and bayonets fixed and by 10 o'clock order is restored and swaying Australians promise to return to barracks, or at least go to a quieter brothel.

Well, it's been a night out, as one happy Trooper notes in his diary: 'It was the greatest bit of fun since we've been in Egypt . . . not a pane of glass remained intact.'[14]

Australian officers like Colonel Alexander White of the 8th Australian Light Horse Regiment are appalled at the behaviour. He is an officer and a gentleman – kind, resolute, strongly conservative and opposed to all vices like drinking, swearing and gambling – and his view is that this kind of behaviour disgraces the AIF. The motto he has chosen for the 8th Regiment is *More majorum* – after the manner of our ancestors. And even being *around* this kind of behaviour is not on. Given that a lot of the British already think of the Australian soldiers and Troopers as jumped-up convicts in khakis, this outrage makes you wonder if they're not right! Paint the town red, but then go to bed, boys – your own. The sooner these men are out on the battlefield the better.

There will be few repercussions, for as soon as the following day the news breaks: we are on the move!

But what about us poor bastards of the Australian Light Horse in Maadi Camp? They say the landing place is unmanageable for horses, so we must stay behind. It is outrageous! I mean, good luck to the blokes who are going, but it is a fair bastard not being able to go with them.

Colonel John Monash would record that when the time came for his own 4th Brigade to leave, 'Thousands of Territorials, and Australians and New Zealand Light Horsemen, many weeping with regret at not being allowed to come, gathered around to give us a royal send-off . . .'[15]

•

Alas, alas!

Even before the end of April, over half of the AIF's once proud 1st Australian Division – those men who had marched out – is either dead or wounded on the Gallipoli Peninsula. The Turks had been waiting for our blokes when they landed on 25 April and the carnage was catastrophic.

(Among them, Guy and Barney Haydon soon learn to their deep distress, had been their cousin Stuart, shot shortly after he had hit the beaches.)

To replace the men who have been lost, and keep their solid foothold on Gallipoli Peninsula, the Brass do not have to look far . . .

Granville Ryrie, Commander of the 2nd Australian Light Horse Brigade, gets word to the Englishman commanding the Australians in the Middle East, General Birdwood, that, 'my brigade are mostly bushmen, and they never expected to go gravel-crushing, but if necessary the whole brigade will start tomorrow on foot, even if we have to tramp the whole way from Constantinople to Berlin'.[16]

Colonel Henry George Chauvel makes a similar offer for his men of the 1st Light Horse Brigade. No, it is stronger than that; he *insists* they join the fray at once.

Late afternoon, 9 May 1915, Maadi Camp, to arms by sea for thee

At Maadi Camp in Egypt, where the 2nd Australian Light Horse Brigade are training, they call it 'The Stadium' – a glorified name for what is little more than a rough ring of sand, surrounded by some ropes, where boxing matches are put on to entertain the men. On this evening, as they all cheer themselves hoarse, an Irish soldier, with the most amazing *luck*, has managed to beat an Australian, winning on points over the regulation ten rounds.

But now, through all the shouting and carry-on, the 2nd Light Horse's 'Old Brig', the famed parliamentarian and now Brigadier General, Granville Ryrie, raises his hand, as he wishes to be heard. They immediately fall silent. For perhaps he is going to say what they have all been praying for, and confirm the rumours that have been swirling for the last few days?

Ryrie – so enormous he could hold his own on a seesaw with a rhinoceros, and has a hide to match; who sleeps beneath a dingo skin and keeps a boomerang under his bunk – pauses before he speaks.

'Lads,' he starts out, in his stentorian tones, 'this is the first chance I've had of addressing you since our mates fixed bayonets in earnest over yonder, and I want you to join me in three cheers for our gallant comrades in the Infantry, the men who made the world ring with their deeds on the 25th of April, and who are now hanging on and in dire need of help.'

Hip-hip! HOORAY!

The next cheer is louder, and the third louder still.

That landing is already a legend among the Australians in Cairo, just as it is at home. Widely reported and cherished is the comment of a Royal Navy sailor who had stood awestruck on the deck of his ship watching as the first Diggers on the shore had hared up the slope without waiting for their officers, only to start tearing into the Turks on high.

'The Australians will do me,'[17] he had said within earshot of a journalist, and the comment is already well on its way to entering the Australian vernacular. And now they may be able to join those at Gallipoli? The prospect is thrilling.

Hip-hip! HOORAY!

'Now then,' Brigadier General Ryrie resumes, when at last the tumult dies down. 'I know that you're all anxious to give them all the help you can, and I can tell you tonight on the best authority that it won't be many days before we are alongside of them.'[18]

This time the noise near raises the canvas roof.

Yes, it will be a wrench for these Troopers to leave their horses behind – as there is no space on that confined beach-head for a mounted force to do what they are designed for – but the steeds will be looked after by those who remain. And the main thing is the men will be able to see some action themselves, and aid their brother soldiers of the Australian Imperial Force.

The men of the 1st Australian Light Horse Brigade feel exactly the same.

'I have offered to go dismounted,'[19] Colonel Chauvel initially writes to his wife when the possibility had first come up, before confirming, on 11 May: 'The men although very disappointed would rather come dismounted than not at all.'[20]

True, General Sir William Birdwood had asked for 1000 Light Horse volunteers to be inserted into infantry battalions to replace casualties on Gallipoli, but General Chauvel had strongly resisted. Such a move would inevitably see another call for volunteers, followed by ever more until his 1st Light Horse Brigade would be completely dispersed among infantry battalions on Gallipoli – a couple of dozen here, 50 more there and so on. No, Chauvel had insisted that all Australian brigades should remain intact, albeit as a dismounted formation, retaining its structure, its commanders, and its *esprit de corps*.

•

Just days later, some of the horsemen of the 2nd Light Horse Brigade, of course sans horses, climb to the top of their ships and peer into the distance. Is that? It is! Anzac Cove!

Through the murky dark it looks like a great furnace, spewing and billowing from a dozen places at once.

Trooper Ion Idriess gazes, completely mesmerised and awaiting the sun to reveal more of just what they are facing.

Sure enough, cometh the dawn, cometh the vision horrid.

'Opposite is a tiny beach,' he will write, 'which rises abruptly into cliffs merging into steep peaks on a gloomy range of big, dark, scrub-covered hills. Mists curl rather drearily over the larger hills but at the beach the sun glints on stacks of ammunition cases, and dugouts and numerous queer things littered about. Cloud-puffs are continually forming over the beach – shrapnel!

'On either side of us are silhouetted the masts of battleships: the deep echoes of guns roll sullenly over the water.'

All are twitching and itching to get on shore, but just as Brigadier General Ryrie has always reserved the right to have the last word, here he wants the first word, as he gathers the men on deck to highlight just what they will be facing on shore.

'Two divisions of Turks, numbering fifteen thousand each, reinforced the Turkish position yesterday and last night attacked the trenches with the intention of driving the Australians into the sea.'[21]

So we must be careful. Bravery is wonderful, bravado alone can be dangerous.

'My only fear,' he says, 'is that you will be too impetuous. Your comrades who have gone before have made history. Their courage and dash and their invincible charge on a well-nigh impregnable position will be a theme for historians throughout the ages. Their only fault was – they were too brave. They were ordered to take one strongly fortified line of trenches and they actually took three.'[22]

Concluding, the Colonel says: 'If I get back to Australia and some of you fellows don't, I know I shall be able to tell your people that you fought and died like heroes. If you get back and I don't, I hope you will be able to tell my countrymen that Colonel Ryrie played the game.'[23]

In short order, small steamers have deposited the Troopers on shore and they are trudging forward right by a Digger, who is being held down by an orderly while having what is left of his arm cut off by a doctor.

Welcome, new chums, this is Gallipoli.

High up on the slopes, right by the Turkish trenches, the Troopers of Harry Chauvel's 1st Light Horse Brigade are already facing an even more torrid baptism of fire as they have taken over a sector that includes the already notoriously difficult Quinn's Post, Courtney's Post and Steele's Post, and busy themselves defending against the endless attacks coming from the Turks on high.

'Men passing the fork in Monash Valley, and seeing and hearing the bombs bursting up at Quinn's,' Charles Bean will chronicle, 'used to glance at the place as a man looks at a haunted house.'[24]

And for good reason.

Within hours many of the Troopers are making their way towards that haunted house, passing Australian Diggers coming the other way – the very ones they had farewelled from Cairo just a few weeks ago with cheers – now looking completely different.

'To us these soldiers of only two weeks' battle experience,' Trooper Humphrey Kemp will comment, 'looked strangely drawn with grey faces of fatigue and shock and grey uniforms dusty from close contact with clays of shallow scrapes and dugouts. I remember being struck with their unsmiling unshaven gravity, sure of themselves, but to our sharpened sense carrying a look in their faces touched with strokes of the old religious representations of Christ.'[25]

For Christ's sake, just what are they getting into?

This. They find parapets sometimes built from dead Diggers and mud – actual *dead Diggers in the wall*, do you hear? – where Turkish bombs are constantly hurled into their trenches and the trick is to hurl them back before they explode. Turkish snipers only have to see the top of your head extend an inch above the parapet and they will blow your head off, where blokes you've come to regard as your best mates on earth in recent months are regularly slaughtered before your very eyes.

After one bomb goes off leaving Trooper Kemp the last man left standing, he records: 'Tinned bully beef lying on the floor of the trench, together with uniform and web equipment, had been blown . . . into the clay walls of the trench. They were speckled with meat and khaki. The body of a Turk built into the trench wall showing only a pair of huge soles had sprung a leak of indescribable matter. Here, the air was thick with bullets, so much so that some sandbags on the parapets held more ammunition than soil.'[26]

Chauvel himself is a much-needed presence. Yes, his hair is grey now, and in partial retreat, but the outline of the dashing young officer he once was is still there, complete with an elegant moustache. His jockey-like physique belies an easy calm that in any other might be mistaken for complacency.

Despite the horror of their conditions, and the odds they face, to his subordinates Chauvel seems notable for both his calm, and his care for their lives.

'The Brigade Commander [Chauvel],' Major Sydney Rowell, adjutant of the 3rd Light Horse Regiment under Chauvel's command, will note, 'was never fussed and appeared the model of what a commander should be.'[27]

•

As it happens, the men of the 2nd Light Horse Brigade have arrived at a time of deep sadness, even by Gallipoli standards. For they are mourning not just the death of a Digger, as that is something that happens every day by the dozen, all around them. No, this is a *particular* Digger, they hear, a bloke by the name of Simpson who had become famous and beloved for heading forward right into the middle of murderous maelstroms and taking the wounded out – get this – on his *donkey*!

'Simpson and his donkey' had quickly become legendary. Alas, alas, on the very day that the 2nd Light Horse had landed, Simpson had been killed and his donkey injured, and the body of Simpson had been hauled back for burial on the back of another legendary figure,

Bill the Bastard, the strongest horse in this whole place, even if he is completely unrideable by those still living. With the dead, however, like Simpson, he is formidable – gentle, and almost caring – and he has been seen winding down the tracks with as many as five or six dead Diggers at a time, taking them for burial.

Despite their fearful casualty rate, the 2nd Light Horse Brigade under Granville Ryrie also perform exceedingly well. So well, in fact, that Ryrie writes to a friend, in late May: 'The boys are still in the best of nick, and anxious to get out of the trenches at the Turks. Rashness would be criminal with so many machine guns, batteries, and barbed wire entanglements about. We cannot afford to throw away valuable lives. Our boys have already proved themselves the best fighting troops in the world. When roused they are tigers and nothing frightens them.'[28]

But yes, the casualty rate is indeed so fearful, that it is clear that fresh troops from Australia are not only needed, but will be rushed here as soon as they arrive in Cairo.

Late May 1915, Sydney, reign on their parade

Coming up Sydney's George Street on this fine wintry morning, band after band are leading a grand procession of our best and our brightest, our finest and most fearless, our marvellous soldiers on their way to the war.

With their slouch hats, bayonets, tunics and breeches, don't they look just . . . well, there's no shortage of young women who've come out to bid them farewell.

The pageant proceeds, the crowd cheers – an estimated 200,000 have turned out for the occasion – and the many Union Jacks wave gaily in the morning breeze.

There is a delirious aspect to it, a real sense of it being a timeless moment, one that will live long in the memory of all who are there. Our boys have been doing it tough in Gallipoli, and no doubt about it, but help is on the way!

Stiff of back, clear of eye, resplendent in their brightly coloured uniforms, the soldiers of the 5th Infantry Brigade keep marching, closely followed by the most impressive of the lot, the men of the 12th and 7th Australian Light Horse Regiments!

Just a short time later they are on their way, heading out the Heads of Sydney Harbour, aboard the steamship *Suevic*, as the people on the wharves cheer, the ferries toot and the seagulls themselves sing their cawing praises.

At the back of the *Suevic*, Guy Haydon leans over the back railing, straining to keep his new bride in sight for as long as possible as she waves from the Finger Wharf jutting out into the harbour. They had managed to have a couple of precious nights together just before departure, but it was never going to be enough for the newlyweds, who had barely slept on their last night together.

They had both said the right things, that they'll surely be back together again soon, that worrying is pointless, that Midnight will help keep him safe – but there is no getting around the truth – the time before they are back together again will, at best, still be an eternity. Bon keeps waving – as the cry keeps going up from the wharf, in the words of the popular song, 'Australia will be there!' – finally the ship steams out of view, turning for the Heads.

Yes, Australia will be there. And Guy Haydon with his Australian comrades.

Bon, like all of those left on the wharf, simply can't help wondering how many of them will be coming back. Tonight, Guy won't be there, except in Bon's thoughts and ever in her heart. There is one thing that neither Bon nor Guy will know for several weeks, Bon is pregnant with their child.

•

More than one Digger muses on the possibilities. If only they could bring their horses over here from Cairo, land them in the dark, perhaps a mounted charge on some of the lower Turkish trenches could break the deadlock? Yes, that's it!

With enough horses going straight at Jacko, some of them would have to get through, and once on the other side they could sow havoc! And from there, who knows? With our horses, back to our best at last, we could race right up the peninsula and be halfway to Constantinople before the Turks knew what hit them!

Sigh. In the meantime, pass me a can of bully beef – our endless rations for breakfast, lunch and dinner, more relentless than Jacko himself.

As summer settles on the Dardanelles, the heat rises to intolerable levels, only to be outdone by the stench of rotting corpses, then topped in turn by the number of pestilent flies that abound all around. A general malaise envelops Gallipoli. Both sides now realise that they are here for the long haul, that breakthroughs are unlikely and the only thing in their future that is certain is more deaths, with the only question being whether their own will be among them. A perpetual target of the British artillery from both land and sea is the towering 'Achi Baba', the literal height of the formidable Turkish defences. Four attempts to fell it by blizzards of shells fail. Achi Baba might as well be Ali Baba in terms of its imperviousness to attack, and the fact that it continues to loom and gloom above them no matter what they do is a permanent reminder of their impotence.

In his bunker just down from a spot called the Nek, Colonel Alexander White is shattered with exhaustion but takes the time to write to his wife Myrtle, and child, Alexander Jnr.

'Dear little wife and kiddie,

I do not want to speak about the war, it's horrible. If I let myself think about it too much my nerves would go. Have seen things and done things I want to forget . . .'[29]

What he wants to remember is their look, their feel, their smell, the wonder of the last day when they were all together, holding each other tight before he had to come away to this war. Every day he does a tour of the 8th's front-line trenches, ensuring that all is as it should be, that the sandbags are in place, that their heads are down, that the Turks just 50 yards away are constantly under surveillance from the Australian 'periscopes'.

On this hot afternoon, White is just making his way back to those front-line trenches when he hears a sudden whistle, and before he can take cover a Turkish shrapnel shell explodes just 100 yards or so from him. One of the balls inside the shell roars forth and hits White in the head, dropping him like a sack of spuds.

Lieutenant Colonel Alexander White, husband of Myrtle, father of Alexander Jnr in faraway Melbourne, is . . . all right. Yes, the ball – about a third of an inch in diameter – has lightly penetrated the skull, but not so badly that it can't be fairly quickly dug out. White is carried away to an aid post and evacuated from there to a field hospital, but will be back within the week.

His relief is overwhelming. Not just that his own life has been saved, but that his wife will not go through the agony of losing him, and his son grow up without a father. Onwards!

•

The official record tells the tale, and Colonel Percy Abbott of the 12th Australian Light Horse Regiment writes it down.

In the shooting competition held on the back deck of the SS *Suevic* as they make their way to Alexandria, on a wooden target being towed 150 yards behind on the bobbing swell of the Indian Ocean, the newly promoted Sergeant Guy Haydon and Trooper F. Bell tie for first place, both scoring an extraordinary 49/50! In four further shoot-offs they are still tied, and so are declared joint winners.

Oh how the men cheer.

It has been good for morale and also helps mark down those two Troopers as first class. It is not that firing from a rocking ship at a bobbing target is the equivalent of firing at a moving enemy from a galloping horse, but it certainly bespeaks an extraordinary skill. Haydon is already well known to the Colonel for his skill with his amazing steed, Midnight, but this performance really makes him top drawer. How will he go in the real thing? They are about to find out; and none can sleep at the thought of it.

7 August 1915, Gallipoli, the Nek, *pro patria mori*

While it the nature of catastrophe that it usually flows raggedly from chaos, the most shocking thing about what happens on this morning is that it is built on such organised order.

Orders are read – and followed to the letter.

British naval ships off Anzac Cove are to bombard the Turkish lines at the Nek for 30 minutes from 4 am, on the reckoning that at 4.30 am precisely four waves of 150 Australian Troopers of 8th and 10th Light Horse Regiments will charge the 50 yards across no-man's-land to get stuck into the Turks. Bullets will not be required, the Diggers will by order use only bayonets and bombs, as there will be no time to stop and fire in any case. Speed and pluck will serve. Two minutes will elapse between each wave. When the Turks are reached and breached, place your mark flags along the advance to guide the next wave.

At 4 am, shellfire starts to land on the Turkish trenches at the Nek. The Light Horsemen can see the Nek before them, its trenches just up a small slope, and behind that the hill of Baby 700, on which Turkish trenches are situated, all of them with guns aimed *right* at them.

Charles Bean will later say that sending men charging along this narrow ridge, to trenches situated above them, 'was like attacking an inverted frying pan from its handle'.[30]

The first Troopers due to go after the top are those of the 8th Light Horse Regiment.

Colonel Alexander White is expected to stay back, to control his regiment as the fight develops. But honour will not allow it, decency will not allow it. Death is beckoning and he feels an urge to answer.

'Damn it!' White declares to his Brigade Major, John Antill. 'I'll lead my regiment.'[31]

After removing his coat, White offers his hand.

'Goodbye, Antill.'[32]

Antill begs him to reconsider, to no avail. White moves among his brother officers, with his watch in his hand.

'Men,' he tells them, 'you have ten minutes to live.'[33]

The comrades shake hands, their next greeting will be in the next world. Time to go over the top. But now, strangely, the bombardment stops.

White takes his eyes off his open locket, where he has been gazing at the photo of his wife and child, to look at his watch. It is only 4.23 am.

The bombardment should continue until 4.30 am, but, unaccount-ably, it has stopped. They will be climbing those parapets to Turks at the ready, not Turks in defence!

Somewhere, a terrible mistake has been made. But it is too late to alter course now.

'Three minutes to go,'[34] Colonel White tells his men.

The Turks make ready in earnest now, not believing their fortune, they are lined two deep between the machine-gunners – aiming their Maxims right at the top of the Australian parapet and unleashing a quick chattering burst, just to make sure everything is in working order. The first wave of the 8th Light Horse Regiment is jostling forward, ready if not steady.

'Two minutes.'

Now the Turkish firing becomes intense, both from their machine guns and from their 3-inch field guns near Hill 60. The shells are landing thickly around the Australians, the salty and acrid fumes so thick many begin to cough.

'One minute.'

The officer next to White brings the whistle up to his lips an instant after taking a long, deep breath.

White roars 'GO!', the whistle goes, they go and are gone . . .

The first wave of men of the 8th Light Horse, 150 horseless horsemen, charge forward, 'GIVE IT TO THEM, BOYS.'[35] That last cry silenced by the instantaneous roars of 500 rifles, and five machine guns, firing not only from the Nek, but also from Baby 700 behind and above it.

'It was one continuous roaring tempest,' Charles Bean would recount. 'One could not help an involuntary shiver – God help anyone that was out in that tornado. But one knew very well that men were out in it – the time put the meaning of it beyond all doubt.'[36]

Colonel White is running with the best of them, leading his men, when the fusillade hits only 'ten paces'[37] from their beginning. White falls dead, as do his men, not one by one but all at once. It is, one eye-witness will record, as if 'the men's limbs had become string'.[38] The bodies and heads of the fallen horsemen are so riddled with bullets that they continue to shake as bullets and now grenades and now shrapnel from exploding Turkish shells hit them. No Trooper makes it to the enemy trenches. Not one. As the second wave gets ready to go over the top into Dante's hell of blood, spilt intestines, severed legs and mates with missing arms, they listen for the whistle above the screams.

The whistles blow, and over they go . . .

This time the roar is even greater, the fire and bombs even more concentrated, the devastation even more catastrophic. In little more than three minutes, the 8th Light Horse Regiment has been wiped out, half killed outright and the rest grievously wounded. Again, no Trooper makes it to the Turkish trenches. The marker flags of progress are not required, none has been made. Chaos surrounds them, the earth is soaked with blood.

Is this not enough?

Colonel Noel Brazier, Commander of the 10th Light Horse, rushes to HQ to try to get the orders changed, but his request is declined. The 10th Light Horse will be next.

Brazier trudges back to the front line to give his men the news.

'I am sorry, boys, but the order is to go.'[39]

Trooper Harold Rush – a softly spoken farmer from Western Australia, just 23 years old – turns to his mate beside him, offers his hand and says, 'Goodbye, cobber, God bless you.'[40]

His cobber takes his hand, and then the two turn, put their feet on the firing step, and start to pray together. Just along from them is Trooper Frank Rawlings.

Theirs not to reason why. Theirs but to do and die.

'For bravery,' Brazier would record, 'each line was braver than that which went before. Death stared them in the face and not a man wavered.'[41]

But now, from the Turkish lines, comes a strange . . . *pleading* . . . call. '*Dur!*' '*Dur!*' '*Dur!*'[42]

Stop! When even your enemy begs you to cease, well, you know you are beyond hell. It is too late to stop.

The whistle blows, and with a cheer for the ages . . . for all eternity . . . the vast wave of Australian humanity rolls out, even as the five Turkish Maxim machine guns start chattering at the oncoming wave, and some 500 Turkish soldiers all around keep loading again and again the five bullet magazines into their Mausers and firing into the throng.

'The air,' one officer of the 10th will note, 'was hazy with lead.'[43]

'As they rose to charge,' another will recount, 'the Turkish machine guns just poured out lead and our fellows went down like corn before a scythe.'[44]

One more time, the Australian soldiers are cut to pieces, including Trooper Harold Rush and his cobber, shot dead within yards of their trench. Their prayers unheard or unheeded, no interventionist God could allow this morning to occur. Charles Bean states it plain and true:

'With that regiment went the flower of the youth of Western Australia, sons of the old pioneering families, youngsters – in some cases two and three from the same home ... Men known and popular, the best loved leaders in sport and work in the West ... rushed straight to their death.'[45]

Trooper Fred Rawlings is shot through the head and instantly killed.

The fourth wave? Of course they move forward too, to their equal slaughter before finally, dreadfully, this 'assault' is called off.

'During the long hours of that day,' Charles Bean would record, 'the summit of the Nek could be seen crowded with their bodies. At first here and there a man raised his arm to the sky, or tried to drink from his water-bottle. But as the sun of that burning day climbed higher, such movement ceased. Over the whole summit the figures lay still in the quivering heat.'[46]

At the first roll-call for those 500 Troopers who have gone over the top, just 47 shattered men are capable of answering 'Present'.

Two hundred and thirty-four members of the Australian Light Horse have been killed, 138 wounded.[47]

And death on the Nek doesn't stop. Just the following morning, in an attempt to bring in the wounded, Trooper Maurie Evans – serving with the 1st Field Ambulance – charges out onto the field beside two mates, both of whom are cut to pieces while he, miraculously, remains untouched. The two dead? 'Threlfall and Jimmy.' Jimmy is Jimmy McGovern, the son of a former Premier of New South Wales. Threlfall? He is Sergeant Reggie Threlfall, of the Field Ambulance, who was running out to tend to the wounded when a burst of shrapnel killed him in an instant. 'We buried him at night where he fell in a soldier's grave, even then under fire, with a wooden cross at his head to mark the place. His career in this corps was an unblemished one, and he gave every promise of becoming a man in a thousand, whose word was his bond and whose every action was honourable.'[48] A man in a thousand, his name joining the thousands of dead. Remembered by his family in Turramurra, New South Wales, by his comrades who survive and by a small wooden cross, that, God willing, will be replaced and the grave graced by a fitting tombstone.

Survivors of the whole affair are devastated, and few more than the Ballarat dental surgeon Lieutenant Arthur Olden, who now lies in a hospital ship having suffered his second severe Gallipoli wound – this one from a bomb – just days before, which had seen him evacuated. Over 100 of the men and officers he had left behind have been killed? Olden can barely believe it, but knows he must, quietly weeping as the ship makes its way back to Alexandria, where he will be transferred to a Cairo hospital. He inevitably makes his way past the reinforcements coming from Cairo, heading to Gallipoli to replace those killed.

Among them are the men and officers of Guy Haydon's 12th Australian Light Horse. They think they are ready. Before leaving their camp, Colonel Reginald Spencer-Browne gathers his men in and proudly tells them: 'You are fit to meet the enemy after only four weeks training in Egypt. No other regiment has left this country with less than three months training. I am proud to have commanded such officers, non-commissioned officers and men. I believe Australia has never sent out a finer brigade.'[49]

And they are off, first by train to Alexandria, then by ship, which – despite actually taking a few bullets from the distant hills as it approaches the shore – is able to get them close enough that they land at Anzac Cove at midnight on 29 August.

An entirely new life begins, of trenches, snipers, wild charges and burying your mates. Haydon performs well and will soon be promoted to the rank of 2nd Lieutenant in charge of B Squadron, 7th Australian Light Horse Regiment now defending the line at Shell Green, at the far right of the Anzac line.

Late August 1915, Gallipoli, spot of bother

It has been a *brutal* few months at Gallipoli. And rarely more brutal than now, as the Battle for Hill 60 – a crucial summit with devastatingly clear views across Allied lines if held by the enemy – enters its seventh day.

In one last heroic charge across no-man's-land, just before midnight, the commander of the 9th Light Horse, Lieutenant Colonel Carew Reynell, with 140 of his horseless troop actually make it to, and *take*, the Turkish trenches just beneath the summit of Hill 60 – only to suffer a massive counter-attack by an overwhelming force of the enemy. Reynell is hit and killed by a spray of machine-gun fire, one of half the regiment who fall this day, as they must beat a bloody retreat. Who, *in extremis*, can replace him? They need an officer with a bold personality, with an approach of never holding back. Lieutenant Colonel William Grant – formerly of the 3rd Light Horse Regiment and commanding the 11th Light Horse Regiment since March – who has only landed at Gallipoli the day before, is picked to take command and finish the job.

He is an old boy of Bright Grammar and Ormond College, an exceptional engineer and proud pastoralist, and the weight of leadership rests easily on Grant's shoulders. Yes, their situation is desperate, but it will be all the more desperate if he doesn't give his men firm direction, and that is exactly what he provides now.

Their direction is forward, calmly, precisely. Their job is to kill the enemy and avoid being killed while doing so. That and to not go mad amidst the daily slaughter that will surround them.

It is a gruelling, appalling existence, occasionally leavened by bright spots. Like this, on the early morning of 20 August . . .

Suddenly, from the Turkish trenches a man comes running, waving a white flag. Don't shoot! Don't shoot!

The Australians don't and it proves to be an Arabic officer by the name of Muhammad Sharif al-Faruqi, who proves to not only speak French but also comes with a lot to say! According to the 28-year-old, he is one of many Arabs fighting with the Turks who has had enough, who want to revolt! Oh yes, we are 10,000 strong, and no less than

90 per cent of the Arab officers of the Ottoman Army belong to our secret Arab nationalist society, Al-Ahd.

So convincing is he that he is soon brought before the highest-ranking officer at Gallipoli, Commander-in-Chief of the Mediterranean Expeditionary Force, General Sir Ian Hamilton – at his headquarters on the island of Imbros – where he tells his story again, and adds detail.

We of Al-Ahd, General Hamilton, want what you want – the end of the Ottoman Empire. We Arab nationalists want to reclaim our own lands. And we want to work with you British to defeat them – us from the inside, you from the outside.

'Nationalism is the principal drive for most Arabs,'[50] he tells Hamilton.

The way forward, he insists, is for the British to connect with and support the Arabs who would revolt. It is in the interests of both the Arabs and British to bring down the Ottoman Empire which has, after all, occupied Arab lands for the last 400 years, so why not quietly unite? Hamilton is wary, but interested. The Arab is put in the hands of British officers and extensively interrogated – whereupon he does divulge a lot of fascinating intelligence, which will likely prove very useful. He knows all about what the Turks are doing in Gallipoli, where their reserve forces are and how strong – and is also the full bottle on Turkish manoeuvres against Russia and in Mesopotamia.

Look, it is true that the Arabs are not remotely one nation, so much as many tribes oft warring with each other, but the idea of organising the Arabs to revolt against the Turks is intriguing.

However, after Hamilton receives the go-ahead from the War Office to explore this matter further, al-Faruqi finds himself in Cairo being closely questioned by the Director of the Arab Bureau, General Sir Gilbert Clayton, who is running British Intelligence in this part of the world. To help with the questioning of al-Faruqi, Clayton asks an able, if slightly eccentric, young lieutenant by the name of Tom Lawrence to assist.

It is an astute choice. Lawrence, a former archaeology student – who quietly lets drop to anyone who might believe him that he is descended from Richard the Lionheart of Crusaders' fame – had arrived at the newly established Arab Bureau intelligence unit in Cairo late in 1914, sent there as 'a youngster . . . who has wandered about in the Sinai Peninsula',[51] and prospered from the first. The effete young man's knowledge of Arab customs and language, not to mention the Crusades, which is his academic specialty, and his ability to blend in with the locals, has proved priceless in providing intelligence of just what the Arabs are up to.

And now Sir Gilbert wants him to put aside his recent work, focused on updating ancient maps, to talk to a high-ranking Arab who wants to help? Lawrence can't get enough of it, and day after day, and late into the night, he listens intently to the Arab, asking questions, taking notes, forming up ideas for action and testing them against his knowledge. Lawrence has a powerful idea of how to really hurt the Turks by organising, energising and then unleashing the Arabs against them . . . *inshallah*.

•

Near a destroyed French village on this day, right by the hideous carnage of the Western Front, the newly promoted Lieutenant Alaric Boor of the 7th Battalion Oxfordshire and Buckinghamshire Light Infantry is walking along when his head momentarily passes a spot where the sandbags have not been properly put in place, meaning his head is exposed for a split second.

There is a curious *zzzzip* as a bullet hits the sandbag on the other side, and his neck is showered with French dirt.

'Missed me,'[52] Boor murmurs lightly, before proceeding with his head down a little more.

In short order, until the trench walls can be reconstructed, a signboard is put up on the spot, reminding soldiers:

> Your King and country wanted you;
> they have got you, and want to keep you,
> so keep your head down.[53]

Your country needs you . . . to *duck*.

In the meantime, look way over there, Alaric, to the French town of Albert, shimmering in the distance!

It is a 35-foot statue of the Virgin Mary leaning precariously out from the top of the red-brick church tower of Notre-Dame de Brebières. She's been hit by a German artillery shell and it is anyone's guess when she will fall. To many of the soldiers marching through – both Germans heading west and then Allies heading east – it looks as if she was consumed with grief at the sheer and bloody tragedy of what God's children are doing to each other in this war. But the Diggers had taken a different slant. To them she looks like the great Fanny Durack, the famed Sydney lass who had won a gold medal swimming for Australia in the 100-yard sprint at the 1912 Stockholm Olympics, because if you look at 'Our Fanny', as they call her, just right, it dinkum looks as if Mother Mary is about to dive in and win gold for the Holy Land.

One way or another, different myths have grown up around her.

The Allied soldiers assure each other that when the Virgin falls into the street, the war will be over, while the Germans have come to embrace 'a superstition that the nation which shot down the Virgin would be vanquished'.[54]

Alaric is merely content because the French matron of the house near Albert where he has been billeted has told him that merely having *seen* this Madonna means that, '*Vous aurez de la chance!*' You will have good luck![55]

Hopefully.

Alaric's war goes on and he continues to impress his superiors with his dedication to duty and his quick grasp of every task.

He has no thoughts about leaving before fulfilling his duty to King and country, but . . .

But the number of aeroplanes constantly flying overhead – these chevaliers of the skies, who usually cavort their way through the endless puffs of anti-aircraft fire – certainly does make him start to think about other ways he might contribute . . .

Could he perhaps become a pilot himself? It is true there are many risks. As a matter of fact, on this day he had been fascinated and then horrified as a British biplane, a Bristol, had taken on a German Taube in a dog-fight, only for the biplane to tumble from the skies and hit the ground with a fiery explosion, resulting, as he mournfully writes to his parents, 'in two more fellows experiencing the "great adventure"'.[56]

Yes, a terrible risk. But really no more of a risk than life in the trenches, both here on the Western Front and at Gallipoli, where by all reports things are grim and getting grimmer.

•

Gentlemen, place your bets.

This Pommy officer, Captain Anthony Bickworth, who his mob reckons is one of the best cavalrymen in Britain, says he is going to ride Bill the Bastard the four miles from Suvla Bay over to British Campaign Headquarters to get an important dispatch through.

Bill the Bastard!

No *bastard can ride him!*

Well, they reckon Captain Bickworth could ride a lightning bolt in a tropical storm, and bets are placed accordingly, most of the money going down on Bill arriving riderless.

Easy. Eassssy. Eassssssssy.

They're off! With a snort and a lunge, Bill the Bastard tears off down the track, the dispatch, as usual, encased in a leather satchel secured to the saddle. To Bickworth's credit, he stays in the saddle for an extraordinary mile before he is thrown to land in a crumpled heap. Bill the Bastard gets through, the dispatch is delivered, and the money changes hands accordingly.

But Bill is not unscathed, the brave bastard has taken a bullet in the flanks.

Whether or not he'll recover is anyone's guess. But one who does not want to guess is Major Michael Shanahan – a builder from Roma before the war – who now does everything he can to help nurse Bill back to health. This includes daily leading him into the waters at Anzac Cove so the salt water can clean his wounds, while offering Bill his own special treat: liquorice allsorts, sent to Shanahan all the way from Australia! And now he talks to Bill softly, grooms the bastard with a brush, pats and straps and shows him nothing but kindness and patience. And still more liquorice!

While Bill is nursed, the private betting still mixes with daily duty and delivery. In fact, there is now a daily race along the shores of Gallipoli as the men of the Light Horse volunteer to have the only chance they will get in this infernal place to go at full gallop, delivering dispatches, while others wager on whether or not they will make it.

'The rider was fired at the moment he left the shelter of Lala Baba,' Chauvel will write to his wife, 'until he reached the wide communication trench near Anzac, yet all the brave young Light Horsemen were tumbling over each other to get the job, such was their desire to do what they had enlisted to do: to ride horses.'[57]

Yes, that and the purse . . . still, what the commander doesn't know won't hurt him.

•

Beyond Gallipoli, the Ottoman Empire is also looking forward to advancing on other fronts. Yes, the thwarted attack on the Suez Canal had hurt, but Djemal Pasha has new plans. Impressed by the skill of Colonel Kress von Kressenstein, he has decided to offer him command of a specifically designed *Çöl Komutanlığı, Wüstenkraft*, 'Desert Force', whose job it will be to operate in the Sinai and, above all, defend Palestine.

'Von Kressenstein,' Djemal Pasha will note, 'who regarded the Canal Expedition as the object of his life, and the tussle with the difficulties with the desert as compensation, accepted my proposal without hesitation . . .'[58]

Mersinli Djemal, meantime, and his 8th Corps, can be pulled back to Damascus, to defend Syria in case of a landing there. Djemal Pasha also looks to the necessary future; where a particular battle in the east must be won: 'One of the first questions I took up was the construction of a road connecting Beersheba and all the bases in the direction of Ismailia, and thus permitting the transport of all kinds of wagons and cars . . . It was also necessary to sink wells . . . and erect all kinds of buildings, such as hospitals, depots, and so forth . . .'[59]

Always, however, there is a rider for the riders.

'If we left these working posts unguarded, they would unquestionably be harassed the whole time by the bold and highly mobile cavalry of the English. Thus it was necessary to effectively fortify the desert.'[60]

November 1915, Gallipoli, now is the winter of our discontent

As winter approaches, the low, slow malaise continues over the Anzacs, above and beyond the physical sickness they have all been struggling with for so long. Making matters worse is the creeping cold that sometimes climbs from the depths of the Dardanelles to lay siege to your soul, and more often comes as a howling, biting wind that turns your flesh to ice, and gets into the very *marrow* of your bones – so cold that you less shiver than shudder. Yes, like everything, they treat their misfortune with humour and joke that when they grab some kip in the night, instead of blowing the candle out in their trench, they have to knock the flame off with the butt of their .303, but even that humour doesn't make it any less cold. And those shots that ring out in the night? They'll tell the Sergeant they thought they saw some Turks, but the truth is some of the Diggers fire 'five rounds rapid' just for the sake of 'hugging the rifle barrel'[61] for warmth!

As the weeks pass, and the brass monkeys scamper hither and thither, the only thing they know for sure is that it is getting worse, as winter starts to grab the 'Dards' by the throat.

'In the Trenches-Gallipoli,' Guy Haydon writes home to his pregnant wife, Bon, 'the trenches are 7 feet deep . . . it is impossible to get hit by a bullet if you keep your head down. I can assure you we do . . . we dig little rests in the side of the trenches to sleep in and as long as it doesn't rain we will be fairly comfortable . . . dysentery is playing the devil with the man . . . the smell is pretty awful as there are scores of bodies unburied lying out beyond the trenches . . . we can see bodies of dead Australian and Turks lying together . . . they had been there for about a month . . . it is getting cold here now and if we are here for winter we'll have a pretty rough time of it as it rains heavily at that time.'[62]

Haydon, of course, is not the only one to recognise just how appalling things will be if the Australians remain in Gallipoli over the winter.

Even as he writes, steps are underway to evacuate the Australians without the enemy being aware. In the meantime, however, the fight against the Turks goes on, and the Diggers are manufacturing their own 'jam-tin bombs', jammed with explosives and every bit of scrap metal they can find, starting with old cartridge cases.

The favourite method of delivering them?

Well, in these latter months the Diggers are blessed to suddenly have among them one of the greatest hurlers of a cricket ball the world has ever seen – none other than Australia's most famous Test fast bowler . . . Trooper Tibby Cotter.

Not so long ago, our Tibby was the most feared man in England, at least when dressed in white and coming at you from 22 yards away.

And yes, in the very occasional quiet times in the trenches, he can tell them stories of his fellow Test stars.

Victor Trumper, you say?

One of the finest men I've ever met. One time when I took his wicket, and broke his stump in half, Vic picked up both halves of the stump and held it up to the crowd so they could see how fast the ball was. When Vic died just before I embarked, I was given leave from the Army to be one of the pall-bearers at his funeral.

'Cotter was extremely popular in the Regiment,' one Trooper will recount, 'being esteemed for his cheerful, unassuming good nature. He always spoke in glowing terms of the hospitality enjoyed in England by the Test teams. Whenever he chose to relate his numerous interesting and amusing experiences while on tour, he was always assured of a good hearing from the assembled Diggers.'[63]

And so here he is, working as a stretcher-bearer as his eyesight has not been strong enough to be a front-line soldier, but in between gathering in the wounded, he is hurling jam-tin bombs for Australia. Look, Tibby can send 'em at *least* 30 yards further than any other bastard here.

Speaking of cricket, it will have a strange role in the final weeks of the Australian occupation of Gallipoli, but that is to come . . . shortly.

Brigadier Granville Ryrie is one of the many officers who secretly has the rumours confirmed in late November. We are getting out, abandoning the peninsula. In the wake of this disaster – 10,000 men already killed, for no advance, and winter setting in – we are going to evacuate, starting on 15 December.

You, Ryrie, will be among the last to leave and the job of you and your men will be most particular. For, as we take out 10,000 a night from the 15th, those who remain must become ever busier with every succeeding tranche that goes, to disguise the evacuation. Your 2nd Brigade will be last off, giving you the greatest responsibility of all, and putting you in the greatest danger.

Ryrie is worried from the first, 'sure that their spies would get hold of the information and that of course the Turks would attack and half of the troops had gone'.[64]

But no matter. It simply has to be done. They have to get as many Diggers out alive as possible, so that the graveyards won't fill up even more.

It will take an extraordinary amount of ingenuity to make the Turks think they are still there, but at least Australians are good at that.

'We used every device imaginable to make them think we were preparing to attack them,' Ryrie will recount, 'instead of going away.'[65]

The first method?

Shhhhh. Lieutenant Guy Haydon carefully notes it down. It is a 'silence stunt', an ingenious double bluff.

Hear that?

Exactly. It is the sound of Australian guns *not* being fired. After months of chattering machine guns, sniper shots and exploding grenades, the Diggers down tools, or at least all of the above. No sound at all comes from their trenches, and no digging work is done, with no clods of earth flying over the parapet as was the usual way. It is three days for the Turks before they can bear it no longer and, convinced they must have gone, venture forth, only to find – *surprise!* – they are there in force!

'The result,' Guy Haydon records, 'they were badly cut up.'[66]

The point is that the next time the Australians go quiet – during the evacuation – the Turks will have hopefully learnt to hold back longer before venturing forth, by which point the Australians will have gone.

Meantime, Lieutenant Colonel George Macarthur-Onslow approaches Ryrie with an idea.

Why not put on a cricket match?

Ryrie likes the idea! It will lift morale for those who remain, display activity and . . . confuse the Turks. The match is set down for the afternoon of 17 December at the spot known as Shell Green, and will be between the Troopers of the 7th Australian Light Horse and anyone else who wants to play, including many from the New South Wales 4th Battalion.

Macarthur-Onslow captains his side, wins the toss and walks out to take strike on a remarkably 'sticky wicket' – a scratch in the soil already littered with shrapnel. Now just what the Turks in the trenches above make of all the running, hitting, throwing and cheering that takes places is unclear – grenade-throwing practice perhaps? – but at least in the first instance they seem to be entranced? At the very least they hold their fire and simply watch, until as the shadows start to lengthen they send down some mortar fire to clear the Australians out.

As recorded by Ryrie, 'the game continued anyway, just to let them see we were quite unconcerned . . . and when the shells whistled by we pretended to field them. The men were wonderfully cheerful and seemed to take the whole thing as a huge joke.'[67]

The Turks, however, decide they are less than impressed by the invaders' insistence on continuing this strange practice, and so now unleash doubly heavy salvos of mortar fire. Given that it had been on this very spot that, a couple of months earlier, the Old Brig had stopped a piece of shrapnel with the right side of his neck, crying out cheerily, 'Holy Moses, they've got me where the chicken got the axe',[68] he knows better than most it might be time to call it a day, and the game is reluctantly called off. The job has, in any case, been done.

That happiness over, tension returns. Tomorrow, everyone now knows, the final stage of the evacuation begins, with all of the remaining soldiers – some 20,000 at Anzac Cove, with the same number at Suvla – due to be taken off in just two nights.

More tricks are put into play, many of them overseen by Lieutenant Colonel William Grant, who is now commanding the 9th Regiment.

The best method, invented by Lance Corporal Bill Scurry, involves filling a kerosene can with water, and then puncturing the can so that it has a slow drip into a second can.[69] At a certain point, when the second can – attached to a string connected to the trigger of a rifle – has sufficient weight, it will topple and the rifle will fire. Another way is to have two pieces of string attached to a weight, with the short string wrapped around a candle. When the candle burns down, it burns the string too, meaning the weight – with the longer piece of string attached to the trigger – drops, thus firing the rifle.

Other systems are put into play to activate the self-firing rifles, all while the Diggers continue destroying the supplies that they won't be able to take with them.

'Into our latrine pit,' one officer records, 'we threw 70,000 rounds . . . 1500 grenades and bombs. The enemy are welcome to this if they like to clean it.'[70]

Many of them also put final touches to their endlessly diverse farewell messages to the Turks on whatever pieces of cardboard or paper they can find:

Au revoir, Abdul. See you later on.[71]

Good-bye, Mahomet. Better luck next time.[72]

Abdul, you're a good clean fighter and we bear you no ill-will.[73]

Merry Christmas, Abdul; you're a good sport anyhow, but the Hun is a fair cow.[74]

And yes, of course, there is the odd aggressive message as well, in one case mixed with an unspeakably crude drawing of Kaiser Bill and the Sultan above the scrawled words: 'Abdul: you silly c— !'[75]

But it works. By late on the night of 19 December, the last of the Australians – including 6000 men of the Australian Light Horse – are on their way.

For the final act, the Old Brig divides his remaining men into A, B and C parties, and as each tranche files down to the waiting boats, the others move along the trenches firing rifles from different places, setting timers on other guns, and setting booby-traps. Finally Ryrie and George Macarthur-Onslow are left on Gallipoli, with just 110 men to keep them company.

At 3 am, Ryrie gives the order and, with cloth wrapped around their boots to muffle their sound, they . . . scarper in the night . . . filing down the trenches and tracks to the last of the boats that await, and are soon heading back to their Egyptian bases.

'We hadn't a man killed and I think everyone was brought off,' Granville Ryrie writes proudly to his wife, Mary, from the ship that has evacuated him and his men.

Lieutenant Guy Haydon, also among the last to leave, looks back at the receding peninsula with real emotion.

Like all of them, he reflects on the comrades they are leaving behind to lie there for all eternity. Their loss is such a tragedy. And the pity of it is that, despite their sacrifice, Australia has not only not won the day, but they are leaving in the dead of night.

It hasn't really been a fair fight. They are Light Horsemen, and had been obliged to fight without their horses, in trench warfare, with the enemy coming at them from the heights.

He, like all of them, hungers to be reunited with his horse and take on the Turks in open spaces. *Then* we will see how this goes, Abdul!

CHAPTER THREE

THE SINS OF THE SINAI

A bugle blowing lot of bastards.[1]
Thomas O'Leary to his guards while being arrested at Tel el Kebir, prior
to being court-martialled for striking a local inhabitant, bashing his guard,
and using insubordinate language to a superior officer

*They are a fine race of men these Turks. They can beat any of
us as regards chest measurement and are about the cleanest race
I've seen.*[2]
Trooper Stanley Broome of the 12th Australian Light Horse Regiment, on
working in a POW camp in Maadi, on the edge of Cairo

*Calm, debonair, crop on thigh. Moving quietly, almost impass-
ively. Quiet decisive words. Moving like a note of calm confidence.
Easy natural leader. In contrast to wild galloping Royston.*[3]
War correspondent Henry Gullett on the style of General Harry Chauvel

Early 1916, Mena Camp, Egypt, midnight at the oasis

For so many of those returned safely to Egypt from Gallipoli – ready
for 'rest, reinforcement and retraining' – it's the nagging sense of guilt
that gets them.

Why me?

Why have so many of my mates died, and somehow I am still here?
And at the going down of the sun, and every morning, you really do
remember them. They haunt you.

As Ion Idriess notes in his diary, 'It was real lonely wandering down
the familiar line, looking for familiar faces, and saddening to find only
an odd one here and there. I think the boys of my regiment were the
nicest lads in the world. The regiment is filled up with reinforcements.

We landed on the Peninsula nearly five hundred strong. Our casualties were eleven hundred and forty-five. As fast as the reinforcements dribbled across, they were knocked. Only two original officers survived right through the Peninsula without being casualtied away. In my own troop, there are only four old hands left, and two of them are first reinforcements who came over with us.'[4]

And yet the shadows that stalk the night are not just their nightmares. One of them is real and it is Guy Haydon, who cannot rest until Midnight comes – not the hour, but the horse, *his* horse. Guy last saw Midnight on the dock at Adelaide, from then travelling on separate ships to Egypt but only Guy is present and accounted for on the distant shore. A minor snafu, he is assured, Midnight will be found shortly. But she is not, and Guy suspects that somebody could not resist a horse of such quality and has 'requisitioned' and renamed her. But part of him is always lost – at least until he can find her. So the search resumes; the horses are tied together at the end of a day, and each stretch of rope is visited by Guy looking through the night for his Midnight.

But now, just like that, one of the blokes of the 12th sidles up to him and says, 'I found your mare.'

Oddly, the thing that identified her was not her appearance, but the distinctive Haydon Stud brand on her right shoulder – an H with a small mark high up the left upright – well known and revered by horsemen across Australia; the most famous in the country.

Guy races to the designated corral and Midnight whinnies happily at his very sight, while Guy throws his arm around her neck, immediately a little alarmed at how much condition she has lost. Where her coat had once been smooth it is now mottled, where her muscles had once been bulging, they now retreat within the sagging skin. But it's her! Midnight found again! And never to be lost again if he has anything to do with it.

Similar reunions are taking place across the camps of the Australian Light Horse in Egypt, though not always with horses that had been left behind. In at least one case there is a reunion between a Gallipoli man and a horse that had been in Gallipoli.

It doesn't take long for Lieutenant Michael Shanahan to locate Bill the Bastard. He only has to ask around the camps for the most unruly, unrideable horse you've ever seen and . . . there he is. Standing in a pen on the edge of the Mena Camp, Bill the Bastard glares at Shanahan the way he glares at everyone, daring them to try and ride him. Yes, with no more dead or wounded to carry at Gallipoli, Bill has reverted to his behaviour from long ago back at Liverpool, a source of amusement for those in the know who encourage newcomers to try their luck at riding him.

And no-one knows more than Major Banjo Paterson, one and the same, who, after a stint as war correspondent, had turned his hand to driving an ambulance for Lady Dudley's Army Hospital in Boulogne in France, before finding his way here, in charge of a squadron of the Australian 2nd Remount Depot.

'The work,' as Banjo describes it, 'is to take over the rough uncivilized horses that are bought all over the world by the Army buyers; to quieten them and condition them and get them accustomed to being heel-roped; and finally to issue them in such a state of efficiency that a heavily-accoutred trooper can get on and off them under fire if need be.'[5]

The horses arrive in lots of 2000 at a time, and the 100 or so rouseabouts under Paterson's command must feed and water them three times a day, groom them, exercise them and . . . ride them, bring them to heel, turn them into malleable war-horses!

By now, many thousands of horses have come through Banjo's Remount Depot, known affectionately by the Troopers as 'Methusaliers', the 'Horsehold Cavalry' and the 'Horse-dung Hussars'.[6] But he's never seen one like Bill the Bastard.

Knowing how it lifted the morale of all, Banjo has enjoyed taking bets on who could ride him, and he's never lost yet.

Major Shanahan, care to have a go?

As a matter of fact he does.

Very well then, give it a go, and let's see how long you last!

Shanahan does precisely that, quietly reaching for the liquorice he has in his pocket and slipping Bill a piece. The wildly whinnying Bill, bucking his head about in reluctance to be mastered for even a moment, pauses a little.

Liquorice?

Before he knows it, Shanahan has got not just a saddle on him, but has leapt on top himself and dug his heels in, *commanding* Bill the Bastard to charge.

The men of the Remount Depot cheer, but, to their amazement, Shanahan is not sent skywards to land in a shattered pile, and Shanahan and the rogue horse are soon charging off into the desert in a cloud of dust!

Thirty minutes later they are back. Placid. Shanahan has, if not broken him, at least got the heat to beat his temper down from a tempest to a sweating sulk, and 'Bill the Bastard' is a lot closer to just 'Bill' from this point on, even if he will never lose the moniker. But he is Shanahan's horse all right, and Major Banjo Paterson honours the bet and reluctantly bids the beast good day.

Less exalted common Troopers must make the best of whatever they are given. One such is Trooper Chook Fowler, who, returning from Gallipoli, finds himself allocated a notably difficult horse, without obvious redeeming features on first acquaintance.

Not to worry, he is given a lecture by an English staff major, who finishes by saying, in all seriousness, 'Take care of your horses, men, they cost money. Men are of no value, we can get plenty of men.'[7]

In any case, for the likes of Chook and Guy Haydon and their comrades of the 12th Regiment, their days are necessarily filled now with more training.

Yes, they had acquitted themselves well in Gallipoli, but now, having been either reunited with their horses or allocated fresh ones, it is time to become a cohesive unit of the Australian Light Horse once more.

The sense of renewal is compounded by the fact that the 12th Light Horse Regiment has just been assigned a new Commanding Officer, Colonel Jack Royston – variously known as 'Hellfire Jack' or 'Galloping Jack', for very good reason. For, legendarily, his style of leadership is not one of signing orders, consulting maps and giving dry dissertations on military tactics. It is hands-on, in everything.

Royston is a huge South African and had so covered himself in glory during the Boer War by commanding 'Royston's Horse' – a fast-moving unit of veteran irregulars, composed mostly of Australians, which had been notable for turning up where least expected before striking savagely and getting out again – that Lord Kitchener *himself* has given orders that Royston is to travel to Egypt and be given 'the first available Australian command'.[8]

They say that, in battle, he insists on being *involved*, with the men, not just at the front, but at the forefront of the front. As it happens, that is also his approach to training, which he supervises, charging back and forth and riding horse after horse to a complete standstill, roaring orders all the time.

Every day now – within sight of the Pyramids, which have seen such things for centuries – Royston roars at his Troopers as he puts them and their steeds through their paces. First as sections, then as troops, then as squadrons, and finally the whole regiment goes through endless drills to ensure once more that, in battle, their horses will swiftly deliver them to exactly where they need to be to attack the enemy.

Among other things, they practise moving in different formations, depending on the terrain or the objective. If passing through a gap in rough ground, they form long single columns with a horse length between you and the horse ahead. (You can tell a horse length by looking through the ears of your horse and if you can just see a hock of the horse in front then the distance is about right.)

Of course they never practise a straight charge over distance at enemy trenches, because it would be a waste of time. That is certainly a romantic notion some retain about the role of the Light Horse at its best – if you can believe it, the English still have actual cavalry regiments, and specifically train to charge like in days of yore, even being issued swords for the purpose – but that era is gone and everyone knows it. The men of the Light Horse are *not* cavalry, they are mounted Troopers, and there is a huge difference.

For most of the training now is advancing into action, moving forward until the enemy fire becomes too hot at 1000 yards or more, whereupon they – 'Sections, dismount!' – get off their horses and operate as infantry, the men continuing on foot while the horses have their reins gathered in and are collectively pulled back to safety.

And now do it so it forms part of a cohesive action with the batteries of Royal Horse Artillery that each Brigade now has attached to it. This level of fire-power makes them far more dangerous, but it can be lethal to the soldiers charging forth unless their timing is precise and they are aware at all times where their own shells are landing.

But whatever is happening around you, remember, the challenge is to keep the formation, no matter the speed of advance. While horses can of course walk, trot, canter or gallop, the Light Horse have only three rates of movement, with orders and signals given from a standstill for 'Walk-march', followed by 'Trot' and finally 'Gallop'. As detailed in the 1908 Australian Light Horse manual that all officers are issued with, a walk is at 4 miles per hour, a trot is 8 miles per hour and a gallop is 15 miles per hour.

But remember, you are *not* cavalry. There is no chance that you will ever be charging into battle with your swords drawn, to the fore as in days of yore. You won't even be issued with swords. And yes, it's true that as recently as 1909, the *British Cavalry Journal* had opined that, 'The charge will always remain the thing in which it will be the cavalryman's pride to die, sword in hand'[9], but they don't get it. We are Australians. We do. This is *modern* warfare. You are first and foremost soldiers, and your horses are simply the means of getting you to the battle at the greatest speed, and then you swiftly manoeuvre, ideally using skill and speed, to get in behind the enemy, whereupon you must dismount and fight as infantry.

Again and again and again they keep practising their manoeuvres. The Sphinx does not blink. Seen it all before.

February 1916, Cairo, in the pipeline

It wasn't all that long ago that a bloke around these parts had turned water into wine. The challenge right now, however, is just to have enough water in the first place.

For moving a large army through the most remote parts of the desert might need a miracle on par with anything in the Bible. And yet the newly arrived General Archibald Murray, the highest-ranking British officer in the Middle East, after days gazing at maps and trawling through maps, is convinced it not only can be done but *must* be done.

And he has just the men to do it, right before he sends them where *they* want to go.

'I think we should aim at sending one or more Australian Corps to France in due course,' he reports to London shortly after arriving. 'The Australians expect and hope for this and it is a great incentive to make them efficient. They are the finest body of men I have ever seen, bigger men than the Canadians. Their discipline is not good and they are troublesome in all the Egyptian towns. Their battle discipline is no doubt good and the best place for them is the trenches.'[10]

The English officer commanding Australians in the Middle East, General Birdwood, quite understands, noting in his reply to Murray: 'On the [Gallipoli] Peninsula we had two great advantages: One, drink was unobtainable; two, there were no women.'[11]

And speaking of drink, the challenge of the logistics of moving this particular large mass of men is not the usual one. For, in this unrelenting desert, an army marches less on its stomach than on its canteen bottle.

If you do not have a sure supply of water where those canteens can be refreshed, you simply cannot win. Having thousands of camels bearing water is one thing, and living off oases you have captured is another. Under this blistering sun a man generally needs over a gallon of water a day just to stay alive and two gallons to stay healthy, while six gallons a day is the bare minimum for a horse and ten gallons for health – meaning a mounted division of 8000 men and 11,000 horses requires at least 120,000 gallons of water daily.

Similarly, one man needs 2 pounds of rations – usually bully beef, onions, biscuits, tea and sugar, carried in a haversack – while a horse needs 20 pounds of chaff, carried in bags hanging from the saddle.

The sheer logistics of moving thousands of men and horses forward becomes overwhelming.

Truly, the only certain way to give his army the water and *materiel* they need is to build a pipeline and railway line across the terrain, and so, in the late February of 1916, the work begins. Starting from the Sweet Water Canal near the Suez and intending to head out into the Sinai via the oases of Romani and Katia, the pipeline runs alongside a four foot eight and a half inch gauge railway, in order that the dual defeat of the Sinai and the Turks can begin this summer, building up reservoirs along the way – in particular, the one at Romani will hold more than two million gallons.

3 March 1916, Cairo, bloomin' good news

Wonderful news! Glorious news! Come and behold it . . .

The cable is handed to Lieutenant Guy Haydon just after breakfast. *Unto thee a child is born, unto thee a daughter is given.* Well, look, the cable doesn't say exactly that, but that's certainly the way it feels when he reads the telegram in this ancient land. *I'm a father!* Guy's hand is shaken, his back slapped, his good fortune toasted and the name of a lady is, for once, spoken in the mess. Her name? Pat! Patricia Haydon! *May we all live to see her grown!*

Guy's joy is tempered however, by just that crippling thought. Will he even be able to make it home safely to see Bon and their bonny baby? Or will his fate be that of so many others, to take a Turkish bullet, and be quickly buried in a shallow grave before the rest of the army moves on? He will not know his child through telegrams and photographs.

He *must* survive.

March 1916, Suez Canal, ships in the night

God, what a place! Ion Idriess is not fond of the Suez Canal. As canals go, this one is in his bottom five, at number five actually. Yes, it's an engineering marvel, but it's what surrounds the great passage that maddens him and all the men. How to describe it? Well, it is the land version of *water, water, everywhere, and not a drop to drink.*

'Sand, sand, sand, flying sand, blooming sand everywhere.'[12]

Yes, they are sentry men, guarding the desert, treading sand while watching water. And it is not just the sand beneath their feet.

For the worst thing of all comes with what the Arabs call a '*khamsin*' but the Australians call a 'bloody awful sandstorm'. Friends, this is not 'sand', the way Cottesloe Beach and Bondi Beach have 'sand'. This is sand so fine that gravity barely grips it; sand that can swirl and whirl all around you for hours on end. When the *khamsin* is blowing a bastard, it is like being in front of an open blast furnace belching fiery dust that burns all it touches before insinuating itself through all parts of your clothes and body. Troopers become phantom figures moving about in this twilight world of the dead, until the only thing is to do as the Arabs and the camels do, curling yourself into almost a foetal position, with your greatcoat over you.

If it is necessary and you must keep working, you can do another Arab trick, and cover all of your face with a wrap-around cloth, leaving only the eyes exposed, ideally never straight into the wind – though a few of the lucky ones manage to secure goggles, and with handkerchiefs over their mouths and nostrils like bank robbers they can manage.

Look, it's so bad that anything is preferable, even fighting for your life.

'The Turks have not come yet, worse luck,' Idriess notes. 'Anything to relieve this cursed monotony and sand.'[13]

But this hell too must pass, and tonight the *khamsin* stops long enough to reveal a little touch of magic in the night.

'Fancy, a ship of the deep sea steaming across a desert!' Ion Idriess notes in his diary. 'Last night, a P & O boat glided past; we could feel her engines throbbing; the desert was so quiet they seemed like the heart-beats of a mammoth out of breath. She just glided by so close, so brilliantly lit up, that we almost imagined ourselves lounging on her deck-chairs. Some of the passengers coo-eed to us and shouted: "Go it, Australia!"'[14]

And just like that it is gone again, leaving them all alone 'neath an impossibly glittering sky filled with every constellation a man could ever want to see, bar the one he truly craves, the Southern Cross. It is a time for quiet contemplation, for taking it all in.

'The searchlights flashing over the canal sweep eerily across the desert and then melt up into the sky.'[15]

As the next section arrives to do their own guard duty, the first men are able to head back to their makeshift camp to grab four hours kip in the blessed cool of the night before they must head back again. There is no rest for the wicked or the wasted in either the whispering or the wild winds, and yet from time to time there comes proof positive that it is possible to survive long in these parts, as they receive passing visits from the natives.

'Some wild and woolly Bedouins come in from this grim desert,' Idriess records. 'My section and some En Zeds were on fatigue duty . . . when some unusually hairy camels came lurching in from the beyond. The Bedouins walked with a long, loping stride that reminded me of an emu. They were dressed in an extraordinary rough robe of goat's hair. Each wore a sheepskin water-bag slung over his shoulder. From under black cowls their jet-black eyes stared at the En Zeds as they filed silently past. You could almost hear the whites and browns say mentally: "And are you the sort of cuss we have got to fight!" The Bedouins were big men and wiry, but without boasting I feel certain our regiment could wipe out any three thousand of them, and meet them in their own country, too.'[16]

There is all but equal disdain for the Bedouin women, albeit on a different level.

'Anzacs resented the job of yarding up the Bedouin in Sinai, of hustling women and children . . .' one of the AIF padres will record. 'They were all more or less spies. The women were always prowling about our outposts.'[17]

Yes, it is the Turks and Germans who are the ones that will make the thrust at the Canal. But the threat doesn't end there. Some of the Arabs are for them, and some are against them, depending on who gives them the most gold. And the Bedouins – the nomadic Arabs, who live in the desert – make no declarations against anyone, but seem quietly to be against everyone.

The Australians regard the Bedouins as murderous, thieving bastards. They don't understand them. They don't trust them. And nor do many of the Arabs, when it comes down to it. 'They would steal horses from the British and sell them to the Turks,' Djemal Pasha would note. 'And then steal from the Turks and sell them back to us.'[18]

And the Bedouins feel the same about these latest invaders, come to these lands, *our* lands, to steal *our* water, ruin our trading routes and presume to rule simply by right of being imperial squatters. The Bedouins want all of them gone.

16 March 1916, Cairo, Chauvel runs the show

For the Troopers of the Australian Light Horse there are, in the main, just two types of officers. There are 'bad bastards' and 'good bastards'. And yes, there are 'Pommy bastards', but they are no more than a pompous variant of the first category.

General Harry Chauvel, they know, is a good bastard. Softly spoken, but firm, he projects not only sure leadership – the sense that he knows what to do, and how to do it – but, and this is the key, the Troopers feel that he cares for their welfare. Those who have had dealings with him report that he doesn't speak down to them, often inquires if they have all they need, and even asks after their families. Blokes who were with him at Gallipoli reckon that, although he can be a bit stiff in his manner, the important thing is that every action he sent them to was carefully planned and calculated to protect their lives as far as victory might allow.

So when the news breaks on this day that General Chauvel is to become the Commanding Officer of the newly formed Australian and New Zealand Mounted Division – made up of the four Australian and New Zealand mounted brigades that had been serving in Gallipoli without their mounts, but who are now riding once more – there is widespread rejoicing. (At least by most of his fellow officers. That mountain of an officer, Brigadier General Granville Ryrie, who commands the 2nd Brigade of the Australian Light Horse, had rather thought he himself might have been a better fit for the role. But, no, he had been likely considered not 'Army' enough, as war correspondent Charles Bean will put it, 'he was more successful in the field than in the training camp'.)[19]

The best thing about Harry Chauvel? He is a genuine cavalryman. Growing up on his family's vast station up Tenterfield way, he could just about ride before he could walk and trot before he could talk, and, as one so compactly constructed – nine and a half stone for five feet six inches tall – had even flirted with becoming a jockey, before joining the Army instead, where he prospered with the Light Horse in the Boer War.

The principal role of such mounted troops of the British Empire, as 1916 begins to move into its middle months, evolves and becomes ever more apparent. Of course they must continue to defend the Suez Canal, but now they also have a more ambitious goal. They are actually starting the move east across the Sinai desert itself, to push the entire Ottoman Empire back!

'We have arrived at Salhia,' Ion Idriess notes in his diary, of the small settlement, 19 miles east of the Canal, where they will be based for a month or so. 'It looks a little Eden in the desert. The ground all green under intense cultivation, a splendid grove of date-palms, the big clean village, the minaret tower gleaming under the sun and a picturesque population of Arabs, Egyptians, and Greeks. It was from Salhia that Napoleon started on his invasion into Syria. Looks as if we are to follow in his footsteps.'[20]

In fact, they will be treading in the massed footsteps of the armies of everyone from the Roman Legions to the Pharaohs, to the Persians, to Alexander the Great and the Crusaders themselves.

Inevitably that route goes mostly by the coast, as that is where most of the wells and oases can be found, but, because of the pipeline and railway initiative of General Murray, they will have a better water supply than their perpetually thirsty predecessors could ever have dreamed of!

That they are on a dangerous mission never escapes them. Regularly they stumble across old battlefields, like that of the 1882 Battle of Tel el Kebir, where British forces had routed the defending Egyptians. All around they see, 'remnants of buttons, bullets, bayonets and cartridge-cases, while yellowed skulls show up where the Khamseens have blown the sand away. The scurrying winds have uncovered odd bodies in an uncanny state of preservation . . . Several boys looked mustily young and sleeping.'[21]

Will this be their fate, if the Turks or the wretched Bedouins with their long, curved daggers fall upon them in the night? Are they fated to sleep eternally in these wretched parts and never get home to Australia? It will be their lot if they are not prepared, and don't get to the Turks and the Bedouins first!

And so a renewal of the heavy training for the Australian Light Horse begins – more long route marches, more short rote drill, more tactics enacted until each routine becomes as natural as breathing. It is for a minimum of eight hours a day and the only day off is Sunday.

While the men are not yet sure exactly what their next military challenges will entail, beyond patrolling and defending the Canal, the good news is that it will be astride their blessed steeds and so they must get both themselves and their mounts in condition. None is more keen to get at the Turks than the survivors of the shattered 8th and 10th Regiments, who sustained 372 casualties at the Battle of the Nek. It will take some time to again get up to strength with 'reinstoushments', but there is a heavy account to be settled and they want to work hard towards it.

Over coming weeks the training goes on, the Light Horse glorying in the open space, in being away from the wretched trenches at Gallipoli and once more united with their Walers – who they really do look after like silkworms, with all the grooming skills most of them had been raised on back in Australia. And sure enough, beneath the desert sun, their magnificent beasts start to regain condition, lustre and stamina. Of course the men are constantly monitoring their steeds' shape and adjusting the Australian-designed 'swivel tree' saddle accordingly so that no saddle sores develop.

By contrast, the Australian Troopers note with disdain and distress just how many of the English horses from neighbouring squadrons develop exactly those and other conditions for want of the right kind of care.

It is the surest sign of either neglect or ignorance. Don't these bastards know how to set your saddle so it is perfectly balanced, so there is no chafe, so the sand doesn't get in? Don't they know how to check with the eye, and know at the touch that something is wrong? Too many fancy lads used to a quick trot in the cold English 'sun', don't know, as every Australian does, how the heat can beat you and a horse into submission and out of use if you are not careful. On the general subject of horsemanship, don't they know how to tie down their quart pots and water bottles so they don't rattle?

No, they bloody well don't, but at least the wild colonial boys are more than happy to share their knowledge, spiced with some strong language. Sometimes the Poms listen, more often it just makes British upper lips as stiff as their saddles.

All up, when it comes to relations between Australians and the Poms, there is a strange dynamic at play. For yes, on the one hand, as the Australian flag effectively proclaims, most Australians see themselves as a British outpost in the South Seas. And, as demonstrated by both the Boer War and this Great War, 'Mother England' only has to call and Australia will send her most loyal sons across the waves to her aid.

But the instant that relationship moves into the sporting domain, all such bets are off and, as a matter of fact, we bet you bastards we can beat you motherless!

Will you take the bet, as to who is best? Ye olde English? Or the wild colonial boys?

The issue is to be decided in what will become known as 'The Desert Olympics'.

To settle the score, a competition day is arranged between the two armies. Who can represent the Australian Light Horse in the caper? Who, with his horse, is our best and brightest?

There is no discussion.

It is, of course, Lieutenant Guy Haydon on Midnight to represent the pride of Australia and the competition takes place just a few weeks after their return from Gallipoli. There are three events designed to test the ability of the horse, the rider, and the skills of the horse and rider combined.

As the Troopers from two nations gather, bets are laid, the English counting it as easy money. They *still* think it preposterous to imagine that a colonial could beat an Englishman on an English thoroughbred.

With the English lining up on one side, and the Australians on the other, the first event is a straight-out race on the sand over a quarter of a mile, a race known in the Hunter Valley as a 'Bridle Spurt'.

Is there anything more thrilling than seeing such magnificent horses racing each other close-up? The thunder of their hooves, and the way every stride throws up clods of desert! Their foaming flanks! Their manes flying as muzzles strain for mastery! The way their riders lean forward on their haunches, moving their bodies in perfect synchronicity with their mighty steeds. The way, as the two steeds round the turn for the final sprint to the line, their every muscle strains as they go neck and neck at break-neck speed, the two jockeys leaning in tight, urging their surging mounts to go faster still!

Both riders look like they were born in the saddle – it's just that the Englishman was clearly born a little late, for, after the first 200 yards, Lieutenant Haydon and Midnight are at least 50 yards ahead. Now, just as he has learnt to do in countless such races in Australia, Haydon eases back, allowing the marvellous Midnight to do only what is necessary to win, so she has as much energy as possible for the contests to come.

Oh how the Australians cheer, and throw their hats in the air as Midnight crosses the line, 20 yards clear!

Australia 1 England 0.

The next thing is a 'utility flags' event, sometimes known as tent-pegging, which sees both riders, at full gallop, using their lances to remove tent-pegs from the ground, exactly as they might if charging into an enemy camp at dawn and wreaking havoc by causing the tents of the enemy to collapse upon them before they can get out to fight.

Not only must they be extraordinarily precise, but they are also in a race against the clock. Again, the Troopers of both nations crowd close as both riders put their steeds through their paces, swirling through dust, twirling about the flags and changing directions as if their mounts were dragonflies, before whirling away once more, but it is no more of a match than last time. Guy Haydon and Midnight had been *born* for this event.

Australia 2 England 0.

Can the English at least salvage some honour by winning the event involving an 'equestrian test' of precise dressage movements, which the British thought they had cornered as this at least is a classic English event, and a staple of English riding school training. In this event the test is less speed, and more starch, as they must put their horses through a series of formal equine movements.

This time, at least, the English pair are impressive, as they move through a series of dressage manoeuvres including collected gaits, extensions, half passes, flying changes, shoulder-in, pirouettes, halts and rein backs. Lieutenant Haydon and Midnight both watch closely, and with interest, never having participated in these kinds of contests in Australia. On the other hand, what they do have is perfect communication, with Midnight able to read Haydon's desires simply by gentle pressure from her master's legs and from his faultless feel and signals on the reins.

So yes, it is a close-run thing but as the soldiers roar Haydon is able to take her through it with aplomb – and again they have their measure! *Australia 3 England 0.*

Friends? It is all over, and the Australians are the clear winners of the Cavalry Desert Olympics. Guy and Midnight are *the* heroes of the Australian Light Horse. Beyond everything else, the Poms come to see more than ever that the Walers are quite possibly the best cavalry horses ever bred, and most of the Australians who ride them have superior skills to those of the Englishmen.

In the meantime, in these hell-hot days of the approaching summer on the sands of the Sinai, the Turks and the British forces resemble two boxers in the early rounds, each probing the other for a sign of weakness – and intent.

Is the Ottoman Empire still trying to get through to the Suez, or are they content to hold on to what they still have, and dig in where they are?

For their part, are the British intent on pushing the Ottoman Empire completely out of the Sinai and even further? Or are they content to just protect the Suez?

The only way for each side to find out is to send out constant patrols, testing the other out.

April 1916, Dueidar, I love a sunburnt outpost

They call them 'Listening Posts', posted out in desert where – atop a sandhill – the primary goal is to keep your ears to the whispering winds, your eyes peeled to the northern horizon and your wits about you, always straining for *some* sign of an enemy approaching. It is cold, and no mistake. Ion Idriess must wrap himself tightly in his greatcoat, 'like a shrouded shadow that dare not move'. Right now he is three miles north of the main camp of his 5th Regiment at the Dueidar oasis – which is six miles to the east of where the 6th and 7th Light Horse are holding Romani – doing his sentry duties in four-hour stints with another nigh dozen Troopers, while another four are at the bottom of the hill holding on to their horses. Before them stretches a seeming unending sea of sand dunes.

The Troopers with him smoke, and chat quietly. As has become his practice, Idriess does the same, while regularly pausing to write bursts of observations and thoughts in his diary, on this night keenly aware of the importance of what they are doing, the whole structure that he is a part of.

'Now, the prize of nations, at present, is the Suez Canal, about ten miles behind us. So we, that is, our outpost, are really guarding that hundred miles of waterway with its load of ships and all that it means. That sounds comical, but is true. If the Turks come, our job is to detect them miles away. We then helio the regiment, which turns out to fight after it has helioed Hill 70, which phones back to the Canal Army and instantly the fighting machinery of an army is set in motion. Meanwhile our outpost fights.

'If superior numbers drive us back on the regiment, the regiment fights. If numbers are still superior, the brigade fights. If the brigade, or what might be left of it, is driven back on Hill 70, then the infantry fight. While we are fighting and holding back the enemy all we can, the army behind is rushing up reinforcements, for time means everything. If Hill 70 is captured then the whole army along the Canal fights. And if the army is pushed into the Canal, then England loses the Canal, and all her army in Egypt, and all her stores and her ships. She loses all Egypt and her prestige, and perhaps the very war. So now, England, all your might and power and the lives of hundreds of thousands of men might well rest on this sun-browned outpost gazing away out across the desert.

'So that's that! I'll have a smoke now.'[22]

General Murray is glad to have the Australians there, having already written to London a few days earlier, 'I cannot help thinking that if we had the Anzac mounted troops in the place of the Yeomanry our success would have been whole and not partial . . . They are not fit to look after themselves like the Australian troops.'[23]

•

Soon enough, a new and important base has been established at Romani in the Sinai, 20 miles east of the Canal, and Trooper Maurie Evans – who after the woes of Gallipoli, has just joined the 1st Light Horse Field Ambulance – is among those of the Australian Light Horse on his way to man and defend it.

On this day, the hot wind 'feels like a blast from the biggest furnace God ever made'[24], but there is to be no rest for the wicked and as they gaze to their purported course to the east, 'the road leads away into the distance like a great white snake wriggling in and out of the sand dunes'.[25]

Like all of them, Evans is travelling light, having left everything behind at the Suez port of Kantara bar a blanket, a shirt and three pairs of socks. He is adapting to an entirely new way of life.

'Last night I had a severe shock. I dined off some boiled meat, cold and greasy and found to my horror I was enjoying it immensely. Truly 'tis time I returned to civilization.'

But not yet.

Onwards!

'Our last stage was across pure sand heaped into every shape and position, terrible going for the horses,' Evans notes with no little fatigue, 'but really rather a pretty sight to see the long column of horsemen climbing up and down and in and out among the enormous orange-coloured sand dunes and set off by the deep blue of the sky . . . There were only those two colours as there was no vegetation or trees.'[26]

And yet it remains so *hot* neither man nor beast can focus on anything else, with both so thirsty it tends to drain any delight that the searing beauty of the desert might bring. At least the men know they will get water later this night, while their steeds only know the agony of being so dry they cannot even sweat. The thing each horse does know is where water *was*, and at one point Evans is distressed to see his horse trying to bite into his water bottle! There is of course nowt there, but the poor beast keeps nipping at it regardless, hoping a stream will gush forth. At last, at 10 pm, they arrive and the dry agony for them both is over.

For at least Romani, positioned atop a sandy plateau and surrounded by enormous sand dunes, proves to be an enormously important site for deep and bountiful wells, and the arrival of the Australians has been preceded by the arrival of the railway just a fortnight earlier.

The British also have an important outpost, even further to the east, at Katia, a rare part of the Sinai for the fact that it is something of a water-belt, with many oases scattered about the area. To hold such bases and outposts relies on the 52nd British infantry division, supported by the 5th Mounted Brigade, being based at Romani and Katia, with outposts at Oghratina and Hamisah, while the Australians of General Chauvel's Australian and New Zealand Mounted Division act as the most forward force defending the Romani base.

For its part, the Ottoman strength is based around the outpost of Bir el Abd, some 16 miles further to the east of Katia and 20 miles from Romani.

Who will make the first big push?

•

Strange, how life works out.

Back at Sydney Grammar in the 1870s, young Harry Chauvel and Banjo Paterson had been friends, of a fashion, neither having the first clue that either of them, let alone both, would achieve great fame in different fields. Chauvel, of course, is now one of Australia's most revered Generals, the man whose rise in rank and reputation in this war has been inexorable as he has gone from success to success.

But as famous as Banjo?

Not even close.

In a career that had seen him become a beloved journalist and, most recently, war correspondent, Banjo had not only written the words of Australia's favourite song, 'Waltzing Matilda', but also the country's most iconic poem, 'The Man From Snowy River', which is all about a daring horseman who goes out with recruited riders, including Clancy of the Overflow, in pursuit of the colt from Old Regret, who had got away. Who can't recite at least a few verses of Banjo Paterson's epic work, including the climactic moment . . . ?

> *When they reached the mountain's summit, even Clancy took a pull,*
> *It well might make the boldest hold their breath,*
> *The wild hop scrub grew thickly, and the hidden ground was full*
> *Of wombat holes, and any slip was death.*
> *But the man from Snowy River let the pony have his head,*
> *And he swung his stockwhip round and gave a cheer,*
> *And he raced him down the mountain like a torrent down its bed,*
> *While the others stood and watched in very fear.*[27]

Occasionally, the two men had crossed paths since schooldays and had always been *hail fellow, well met*, and *whatever happened to old Jumbo?* But here is the odd thing. In Banjo's current situation, he must salute his old friend.

For Harry is a General, the commanding officer of thousands of men, while Banjo is a mere major, in charge of hundreds of hooves, providing a fresh supply of horses for Harry's – sorry, the *General's* – mounted Troopers.

But it is one thing to get the King's horses, another to make them fit for the King's men; each horse must be ready to ride, not bracing to buck. To determine which are fit and how to mould those that aren't, well only the best breakers can do that.

As it turns out, it is precisely those kind of riders that Paterson goes looking for when he arrives. Another man might have been content to just ride out the position and do the minimum required, but Chauvel has selected him for a reason. He knows that kind of approach is not in Paterson's nature and, given the famous poet's experience in the Boer War, where he had been a correspondent, Paterson will understand better than most that the quality of horses must be the equal of the soldiers themselves, or all will be lost.

The problem is that, while the first contingent of the Australian Light Horse had boasted some of Australia's finest horses, and the second contingent some of the second-best . . . by now the stocks of fine horses are very thin indeed. It means that unscrupulous horse-traders in Australia are getting essentially wild horses, applying a little 'Barcoo polish', and selling them in lots to the Australian Army.

Barcoo polish?

Banjo will explain how it worked among those unscrupulous horse-traders back in Australia.

'He and his boy ran [the horses] into a yard and forced them through a race, one after another, and the two, between them, caught and rode a hundred unbroken horses in two days. That's a Barcoo polish. They could swear that every horse had been ridden. These men here would rather have one of those horses that knows nothing than one of these old outlaws that has been ridden till he got a sore back and was then turned out for a couple of years.'[28]

There are thousands of these unbroken horses here! How to turn them into horses that will respond to soldiers who will be relying on them to execute precise movements at precise moments?

There is only one way.

They will need dozens of rough-riders to do it – men deeply experienced in breaking horses – and mercifully, they can be quickly found. For, as it happens, the Light Horse is filled right now with frustrated riders who want to be taking on the Turks, only to find themselves back here in Cairo while other blokes get all the fun, and they are more than happy to help the great Banjo Paterson out.

All together they are put under the charge of Sergeant Major Jack Dempsey, one of the biggest Australians within coo-ee of the Pyramids – all six foot two of him! Paterson describes Dempsey as 'straight as a stringy-bark sapling and equally as tough'[29], and a rough-riding unit is effectively formed. And you can pick 'em!

No, it's not just that rough bow-legged look many of those who have spent a good chunk of their lives in the saddle possess. It is their rough melons, too, men who have been less brought up than dragged up. And their rough uniforms: riding breeches with the socks pulled up outside the bottom cuffs to keep both the dust and the scorpions out, together with always dusty shirts.

With Banjo present and correct, Sergeant Major Dempsey starts giving orders, though they are far from the usual military parlance.

'Now, you, Bill, get hold of that bay horse,' he says. The request is general, not immediate for, Banjo sees 'Men do not get on rough horses by word of command, they get on when they can.'[30]

Dempsey continues softly now: 'Charley, you take that big chestnut fellow. George, you take that black horse with the Battle Abbey brand. We'll rub some stickfast on your saddle, for they'll all buck. I was breakin' in there once, and I never struck such a lot of snakes in me life.'

The battle with Battle Abbey will be a cracker, but that's not the worst of it. Now the really bad bastards have been assigned to the best breakers, Dempsey gives his final order to the assembled motley crew: 'Now, boys, grab your horses. Get to 'em.'

They do so, when they can, as only they can, with casual authority and looking so loose you'd never guess the terrifying nature of the task that beckons and snorts. For they must relax, and project this relaxation to their proposed mounts. Banjo hears one rider begin to sing an old ballad:

'Tis of a brave old squatter, boys, his name was William Binn.
He had two gallant sons was known both near and far,
He had some outlaw horses and none could break them in,
So I went down, rough-riding, on old Bulginbar.[31]

Forget Old Bulginbar, young 'Tiger' Richards, a breaker from the Riverina, grins as he shows off his prize: 'This is my lucky day: look what I've got.' What? As far as Banjo can tell it is an old bay that looks as though it is half-asleep, but in an instant the horse sees . . . A SADDLE! And now he pulls, drags, jerks, twists and turns as if he has an actual tiger on his tail, while Richards himself is dragged hither and yon and hither again, dusting the compound with his boots as he waits for the bugger to give up: 'Come on, you silly Queensland cow,' yells Tiger. 'Do you think I'm an alligator?'

'Watch him, Tiger,' answers Dempsey. 'That cove threw Billy Waite in our show in Queensland.'

Well who the bloody hell decided this would be a good horse to send to Egypt then?

Tiger is undaunted.

'He's struck something better than Billy Waite this time then. Hit him over the rump so as I can get him in the corner and have a few words with him.'

A few words are had and lo and behold Tiger mounts the horse!

'He's mine,' yells the Tiger in triumph. The horse has other ideas and passes Banjo at full gallop. As Tiger passes at speed, he changes his proclamation and yells, 'I'm his!'

A horse and a Tiger are last seen rapidly racing towards the Nile, where they both end up 'head over heels into an Egyptian grave that had sunk below the level of the surrounding desert'. Now, falling into a grave may be taken by many as a sign, but the Tiger rises with the horse, spits sand out of his mouth and delivers his final verdict to Banjo: 'That's the cove to win the war. A million bloody Turks wouldn't stop him.'

That is by no means the end of the strife.

'In a moment the compound was full of trouble,' Banjo describes. 'Horses were bucking all over the place. A big chestnut horse, as soon as he was mounted, threw himself straight over backwards and narrowly missed pinning his rider to the ground. A waspish little bay mare refused to move at all when mounted, and crouched right down till her chest nearly touched the ground. It appeared that she was going to roll over, and her rider kicked his feet out of the stirrups. As he did so, she unleashed a terrible spring that shot him out of the saddle and sent him soaring in the air, high enough to see over the pyramids – or at any rate so he said.'[32]

Well, that bloke may not have been up to it, but most of the rough-riders are, and most of them fancy that there is not yet a horse born that they cannot master.

Bit by bit, their production of fine horses increases, and the reputation of Banjo's Remount Depot builds. Their growing, glowing renown is helped by the fact that in an open competition between all squadrons held in Cairo, it is Paterson's squadron that wins five out of seven events.

What about the Pommies, you ask?

Please.

'In the wrestling on horseback, one of my Queenslanders,' Paterson tells a friend about one of the Aboriginal riders, 'Nev Kelly, pulled the English Tommies off their horses like picking apples off a tree.'

Such is life.

They are rough-riders, riding rougher horses still, and it works – they produce *great* horses, which will enable the Light Horse to keep going after the Turk. Who knows what kind of horses the Turks are producing? Paterson knows not, but is confident that they won't be as fine as the ones he and his men are providing.

Sometimes they are visited by very senior officers and . . .

And here is one now.

It is none other than General 'Hellfire Jack' Royston, a legend among the Australians, come to visit Paterson's Remount Depot, positioned in the desert not far from the Pyramids, and right by the shining waters of the Nile River.

Jerking his thumb towards the Pyramids, the General greets the famous poet cheerily.

'From their summits forty centuries look down on us, but I don't think the pyramids ever saw anything like this. What an outfit!'[33]

Banjo makes like the Sphinx, not quite sure what the General means, but not willing to show his confusion. Yes, General. Quite an outfit. And the old hands know what you're here for. It's likely what you're always *here* for, General. The best and strongest horses just for you.

Sure enough, after watching the rough-riders put a few horses through their paces – and a few of the horses putting a few of the rough-riders on the ground – Royston gets to it.

'Where's my black horse,' he asks Sergeant Dempsey, 'the one I picked for myself?'

'I've kept him for the last, sir,' answers Dempsey. 'I think he'll show us some style. Bob Adams is going to ride him. He's an old rider but good. How are you feeling on it, Bob? Would you like me to put one of the boys on him?'

Bob Adams, perhaps the roughest of all the rough-riders, barely blinks.

'Not on your life, Jack. I'm just as likely to get hurt off a quiet old cuddy that'd fall down and break my neck. It's all in the game. If this cove throws me, the saddle and the hide'll come too.'

Very well then.

Bring out the black horse the General had specifically picked out a few days earlier, a magnificent steed, albeit so far resistant to all attempts to break him.

'There you are,' the General growls happily at his sight. 'What did I tell you? Quiet as a lamb. Best horse I've seen in Egypt. Best horse I've ever seen anywhere. You *must* keep him for me.'

Perhaps, General, but let's just see if Bob goes any better in breaking him than the others have, shall we?

Sure enough.

No sooner has Bob climbed on than it starts.

'Whoof!' Paterson will recount. 'Away he went arching himself almost into a circle like a watch-spring with his head right in under his girths. Straight ahead, sideways, round and round, backwards, he went in great bounds roaring with rage all the time and shaking and wrenching his rider at every prop and every spring. He wound up by landing, rider and all, in an irrigation canal with a splash like the launching of a battleship. Adams could hardly walk when he got off him.'

Surely now, the General understands that this horse is not for him?

'There you are, sir,' said Dempsey. 'He'll never make a General's charger. Best thing we can do with him is to sell him to the Turks. He's an old hand at the game, that fellow; no matter how quiet you get him you couldn't trust him the length of a whip. He'd be always watching you, and when he got his chance he'd set into it and he'd throw any man in the world out of one of those patent self-emptiers – those slippery army saddles.'

Royston won't hear of it.

'I can ride him,' he said. 'I can ride anything. I'll be very hurt, Paterson, if you don't keep him for me.'

Keep going. He must be broken eventually, and when he is, the General wants him first.

With which, the General heads off, with one of the rough-riders murmuring behind him.

'That's Hellfire Jack. He'd ha' been shot fifty times, only he won't keep still long enough for the Turks to hit him.'[34]

A small parenthesis here. True. Haven't you heard the story? You must be the last. It happened like this, one dark night a light can be seen. It's a fire, stoked by hungry transport workers cooking up a storm, when they hear the thunder of galloping hooves, whereupon Royston arrives at full tilt.

'What the hell are you men doing with a fire,' he roars, 'at this time of night?'

'Working all bloody day and driving all bloody night, a bloody man wants something bloody hot in his bloody guts, doesn't he?' comes the surly reply from one of the men.

'Quite right, boys, carry on.'[35]

And off he gallops.

Close parenthesis.

Easter, April 1916, Katia, Sunday, Bloody Sunday

Could there be a better day to crucify the British than Easter? What better time to launch an attack to definitively stop their outrageous push into the Sinai Desert.

Germany's most senior officer in Palestine, the man in command of the Ottoman's 'Desert Force', Colonel Kress von Kressenstein is intent on stopping the advance of the British forces. He was the one who had helped push Turkey into the war in the first place, by insisting that the two German battleships be allowed up the Dardanelles, and the pursuing British ships be fired on. He had already been at the forefront of trying to cross the Suez with the Turkish 8th Corps in early 1915, the plan that had finished so miserably.

Now, he wants to stop cold in the desert the pipeline and railway snaking out into the Sinai via Katia and Romani.

And he has already done well to assemble a force of 3500 soldiers based at Bir el Abd, supported by six guns and four machine guns.

At the garrison of Bir el Abd, positioned north of Oghratina, this force has just been dispatched by General Kress von Kressenstein in the night hours, heading for Katia, where the British forces are stretched thin and so distracted by their extraordinary task of engineering to bring water to the desert they have almost forgotten there is a war on. The rest of his forces will depart shortly, to attack at different times, and from different angles.

The desert sands muffle the press of many hooves in the darkness, they seem to glide rather than ride, so soft is the tread, so steady the movement of this cavalcade of artillery, ammunition, camels and killers. The sea fog from the Mediterranean a few miles to the west is thick, but their hired Bedouin scouts guide them with the unerring ease of a Lord Mayor walking down the principal street of his town. They *know* this world.

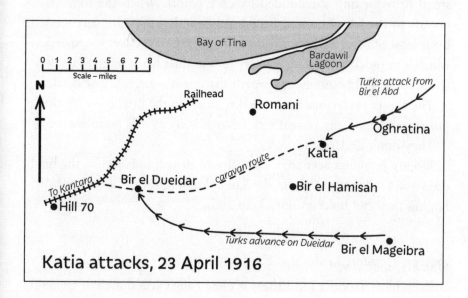

Katia attacks, 23 April 1916

Easter Sunday 1916, Oghratina oasis, death at dawn
What's that?

There is a stirring amongst the lightest sleepers of the Worcestershire Hussars defending the oasis of Oghratina. Aroused, they can suddenly hear the clear groan of the pumps on the edge of their camp being worked.

A sentry soon appears to confirm their worst fears. The perfidious Turks have not only arrived, but are right now drawing water!

Within minutes the Hussars march out for quick-fire retribution . . . only to be mercilessly ambushed in the morning mists by a far larger force. Within minutes the British are surrounded and under heavy fire, the Turks are closing in to a range of 50 yards and slaughtering them.

Under shell and shot, with the Turks getting ever closer, many of the Hussars who remain surrender or flee, and by the time the Hussars' Commanding Officer has formally surrendered, they have lost 146 men killed, with just 50-odd survivors.

And now the Bedouin skilfully guide more of Kress von Kressenstein's forces through the mist to the sandhills surrounding the oasis of Katia, seven miles to the south. Soon Turkish machine guns are aimed at the small British camp surrounded by date palms. When the fog lifts it reveals to the bare hundred British soldiers that they are surrounded by at least 600 perfectly positioned foe. Captain Michael Lloyd-Baker watches in shock as Turkish artillery fires at their horse lines; to demonstrate there will be no escape worth the name. Surrender, or battle?

The choice is obvious to the Turks, how can the British do anything but surrender, as any retreat will be as bloody as it is pointless?

They don't understand.

Bloody pointless acts are a specialty of British bravery; so the mad dogs and Englishmen fight in the dawn day sun, firing in fearless folly, hoping they can hold on until help arrives.

•

Quickly, saddle up!

Even now, Trooper Ion Idriess is one of the excited men of General Granville Ryrie's 2nd Australian Light Horse Brigade, newly returned to Kantara, soon racing to the fray. As part of Murray's reserve force, they are ready to move forward for precisely this kind of attack and it does not take long to get the Australians moving.

It had been such a short time ago that they had been laughing with the Brits who were being sent forward to these outposts, the tall, bronzed Australians finding them to be 'such pink-cheeked, decent little chaps'.[36]

But now, apparently, these same chaps at the isolated outpost of Bir el Dueidar, which is the latest Turkish target, have come under attack.

Australians to the rescue!

Soon leaving the metal road, they also leave all signs of human settlement and are heading out into the vast sea sand, a battlefield that shifts with the wind. There is enormous excitement among the Troopers. At last, hopefully, a real battle beckons, one like they have trained for, coming at the enemy on horseback! By mid-morning, the yelled order comes to the Troopers.

'Load rifles!'[37]

As they spread out in skirmishing order – well spread apart in breadth and depth so as not to present a massed target – that strange feeling comes over Ion Idriess: 'a curious exciting thrill, tinged with a deadly coldness'.[38]

Onwards they trot, towards a white horizon through a maze of drab sandhills, searching for . . . there!

The soldiers are ours, the besieged men of the 4th Royal Scots Fusiliers at Bir el Dueidar, which lies 13 miles this side of Katia. In their thick accents, made even thicker by their shock and horror, they recount being attacked the night before by the Turks, with their only warning coming from the barks of a – what else? – Scottish terrier, owned by one of their soldiers. Out of the darkness and fog had loomed a phantom figure who had crushed the head of the barking terrier with a rifle butt, only to be shot for his trouble by the sentry. Soon enough, coming out of the desert mist, were at least 500 Turks! Though there were only 100 Scots in total to stop them, they had managed to fight them off – killing 75 with their lethal Lewis gun chattering in the night – but had lost a couple of dozen good men of their own.

They went that-a-way, plans *gang aft agley*, but soon every Turk will *ken* that to cross a Scotsman is to know *nae* rest 'til death!

For of course the Scots now go after them, with Idriess and his fellow Troopers guarding their flanks as they follow the tracks of the Turks until . . .

Stop now, mon! Haud yer wheesht!

Each Scot strains his ears, and they are rewarded with a bonnie target, a faint bang-bang noise in the distance. It sounds like children firing cap-guns round a corner, but it is war in the desert and the Australians ride to the sound, faster now, 'the neddies were very willing'[39], and . . . THERE!

White tents in the distance, shimmering in the ceaseless sunlight, and camels. Curiously, the camels are in lines but the lines are not regular or clustered. One man rides ahead now, their doctor, racing to the men he can see lying in the sand, but his speed is in vain. There are two dead men. And they are Turks! The camels are nearly all dead too, the curious line they are in is simply the pattern of death.

The Tommies themselves have been through here and the run of the battle is with them.

Ride! RIDE! And there, amongst the sand dunes, the sand yields to the temporary topography of trees, palm trees and tired Tommies lying there, smiling up at them, dazed; sweating and sunburned, bloodied bandages strapped to them, and alongside them are dead British Yeomanry Horses.

But where is the battle? It has moved like a will-o'-the-wisp across the desert to the horizon and they chase it still. Idriess's horse leaps over the body of a dead Sudanese man, the corpse clutching at his crimson breast as though posed for a painting. They canter now, leaping the bodies as they come, the ones in bright yellow uniforms – some with red sashes – are the Turks; the green ones are ours. The column spreads and gallops, mile after mile, and now they see them, C Squadron, what remains of it at any rate, high and dry and eight miles past the last water.

Further north, near Katia and Oghratina, the Turks have departed. Gone. How many were there? Oh, 5000. Lord Almighty! The battle, now vanished, lasted five full hours.

The stories all the rescuers hear from the survivors are appalling.

Many of their Yeoman brethren had had their throats slit whilst in the midst of deep slumber. Some had been garrotted by Bedouins using wire twisted around their throats and pulled hard.

Wounded Troopers had been mercilessly executed by Turks sneering, 'Finish British! Turks Kantara! Turks Port Said! Turks Cairo!'[40]

All up, the British have had over 500 men killed, wounded or missing. Of particular disgust to the Australians is how poorly led those brave Brits had been by the Yeomanry officers, five of whom are English lords, travelling with everything from fine liquor to luxury foodstuffs, all now abandoned.

'They were not the right people to put at this sort of stuff,'[41] Granville Ryrie will record.

At least the Turks, happy with the attack and not wishing to over-extend themselves, have pulled back from Katia to the base they had launched from, at Bir el Abd. Clearly, however, for the British forces, the days of isolated outposts acting as a screen for the main body of troops are over.

In the meantime, the Australians must help bury the dead – most of them, both British and Turks, stripped of everything of value, including their clothing and boots, by the bloody Bedouins. Many a man swears vengeance on such scum of the Earth as could do this, who treat the dead as no more than a source of cheap booty. The Bedouins – who might guide you across the desert with infinite skill during the day before robbing you blind at night – are cursed by all of the Turks, Arabs and British. And yet, as they are a people who have mastered this desert for millennia, they are needed and used – just as they seem to have no compunction about using you when they need to.

Whatever the Australians' disgust at the Bedouins, there is general joy that they have now engaged in a major battle as actual *mounted* Light Horse and have recorded a great victory. The Turkish advance into the Sinai, threatening the Suez Canal, has been stopped.

The only question is for how long?

It is with this in mind that Major General Harry Chauvel moves quickly, and now puts the 2nd Australian Light Horse Brigade and the New Zealand Mounted Rifles Brigade straight into the dunes and gullies south of Romani, to dig in and prepare for a renewed Turkish attack. They do so, more than ever aware – by the line of white crosses over yonder – that an attack might indeed be imminent. What had been defended by just 1600 Troopers in forward posts is now defended by just under 7000.

From now, and from here, patrols will regularly go out into the desert with the specific aim of knowing at all times just where the Turks are, what their numbers are, and how likely they are to launch another attack.

It is considered . . . very likely. But no-one knows when.

•

Those lucky bastards.

Time and again as the Australian Light Horse does its training in the desert sands, they must pause as the Diggers of the Australian Imperial Force – the veterans of Gallipoli, bolstered by the 'reinstoushments' arrived from Australia – march by, on their way to the railway siding that ultimately will take them all the way to the Western Front in France!

Of the 300,000 soldiers of the British Empire in Egypt in early 1916, a staggering 240,000 of them are being shipped out to fight in the European theatre, leaving General Archibald Murray with just four second-rate Territorial divisions (the Territorials are 'weekend soldiers', home front men who have bravely volunteered for overseas service in this time of need, but Murray needs younger, fitter men to win battles) – of which only two were even up to a standard to fight a battle – and 5000 mounted troops.

Among those who leave are the Scots Fusiliers, who had fought so bravely at Dueidar. As they march out of the camp towards the station, the Scots are surprised to see the Australians of the 5th Australian Light Horse Regiment have turned out in force, and are lined up on both sides of the road.

What is going on?

Hip-hip . . .

Hurrah!

Hip-hip . . .

Hurrah!

Hip-hip . . .

Hurrah!

The Australians are giving these worthy warriors an honour guard, and cheer them to the echo as they march away, the delighted Scots vigorously shaking their hands as they march on.

Truth be told, Murray is under no little pressure to send those mounted troops, too. But he strongly resists.

'These ANZAC troops,' he writes back, 'are the keystone of the defence of Egypt.'[42]

They are, after all, as he has already explained to the British Government back in Whitehall, 'the only really reliable mounted troops I have'.[43]

And it feels like an attack is imminent.

The upside, for the troops themselves?

'This kind of warfare is much more interesting than trench fighting [on Gallipoli],' one Trooper writes in his diary. 'We do see some country and when in action we see all that is going on. Everybody is in high hopes of seeing something of the Holy Land. My horse stood the journey splendidly and is in first class nick. That is the main thing, a man is useless here unless his horse is well looked after. He might just as well come to war without a rifle as ride a bad horse.'[44]

Mid-May 1916, Tel el Kebir, charge of the tight brigade

Some things will never change.

In four days, Trooper Thomas O'Leary, from the 11th Light Horse Training Squadron, has four entries on his charge sheet. First up, at Tel el Kebir he had belted, on the side of the head, an Egyptian native he had been wrangling with.

Two Troopers are dispatched to collect O'Leary, who shouts, 'Catch me, you bastards, if you can.' Sprinting away, he is detained after being chased for 200 yards.

O'Leary promptly knocks the helmet off his arresting officer, before vainly lashing out at those charged with taking him into custody. Eventually he feigns to come quietly, before availing himself of the opportunity to kick one of his guards in the mouth – though, barefoot as he is, no injury is sustained.

The British Warrant Officer who had then remonstrated with him was called 'a gold toothed bastard'. Still not done, when hauled in front of the Lieutenant, O'Leary burst out with: 'I know those colours. You are 4th Brigade. You are a bugle blowing lot of bastards.'[45]

He is incorrigible. Well, yet one more extended stay in the stockade for him.

How can one man behave so badly?

'I was drunk at the time,' O'Leary will explain, 'in fact all that day. I don't remember anything at all that happened in the row . . . I and two others in the morning drank three bottles of whisky that I can recollect.'[46]

Being in the military stockade doesn't bother him, particularly. Having no chance to get at liquor, well, that is more than a bit bloody grim. Still, a man can always dream of liquor – unfortunately, come the dawn, that dream is shattered by the blast of reveille; the trumpet that does not just announce the start of the day but the official beginning of O'Leary's hangover.

SHUT THAT BLOODY NOISE.

The bugle blowing bastard stops, the hangover doesn't. If O'Leary could get the cell to stop spinning, he would start writing an official and obscene complaint.

•

Life is not easy in this neck of the no-woods, and in the middle of the day the temperature, if you can believe it, *would* approach 122 degrees in the shade if there was any shade to be had, which there isn't.

(Seriously, around here the Australians insist that even the *dogs* of the Bedouins squat to piss, simply for the fact they've never seen a tree in their lives!)

Instead, the men must just suffer as the wind released from the pits of hell comes complete with millions of sandflies that appear at dawn and dusk – and during the day whenever the sun is in the sky. It is only at night that the insects take pause, presumably so exhausted from sucking your blood all day they, too, must rest. (The only possible relief is to burn dried dung, creating a stench which, if it doesn't quite drive the bastards off, so stuns you that you just don't care anymore.)

Still, those flies remain only the second most shattering thing about life in the desert.

'I don't think I can stand the heat here if it gets any worse as it is sure to do,' the 'Old Brig', Brigadier General Granville Ryrie, writes to his wife. 'It was 120 in the shade the other day and I think I told you 100 of our men and the New Zealanders went down with sunstroke and heat exhaustion . . . I hate this infernal desert, it makes me tired to look at the sand, and it is everywhere.'[47]

And still – even as many collapse from the blaze just above – they yearn for action.

'The Turks have not come yet, worse luck,' Ion Idriess notes. 'Anything to relieve this cursed monotony and sand.'[48]

Mercifully, the *khamsin* comes only infrequently, but just as it always begins with just a few filthy flurries of wind, so too, now in this late spring, is there a growing sense that Jacko the Turk is building up to unleash an almighty storm of his own upon them . . .

CHAPTER FOUR

HORSEMEN FOR THE APOCALYPSE

The men of the Light Horse straddled two ages. They carried the abilities of the frontier Australian into modern warfare with an ease that fascinated and baffled observers. They formed a fighting machine of an efficiency and audacity that staggered an enemy with a desert cavalry tradition of centuries. They matched the Bedouin in their ability to survive and thrive in the deserts and drylands. They fought with terrible efficiency. But they remained gentle men.[1]

Ian Jones, *A Thousand Miles of Battles*

We never had a leader like him. He often got us into trouble, but he always got us out.[2]

Brigadier M. W. J. Bourchier on 'Hellfire' Jack Royston

July 1916, Romani, mightier than the sword

It is a strange condition of modern warfare, that the primary task of its masters at any given moment is close to the most unaggressive activity imaginable – paperwork. There are reports to read, reports to file, orders to compose, orders to sign, literally hundreds of signatures required for everything from the requisitions of Quartermasters, to confirmations of injuries borne, to intelligence briefings far from brief in their anxiety to exhaust every contingency imaginable. And for Harry Chauvel, in command of the Anzac Mounted Division, it has rarely been more intense than now as the sense grows that the Turks are about to strike and that it is his own men who are likely to be in the firing line. True, the Bedouins in their employ have assured them that there is no force of Turks in the area, but Chauvel has learnt to take all the Bedouins say on such matters with at least a grain of salt and a few peppery remarks.

It is with this in mind that he puts the two brigades he has on hand, the 1st and 2nd Brigade Australian Light Horse, on daily rotation from the defensive line established some miles to the east of Romani.

Each morning patrols head out seeking Turkish contact. If the enemy is weak, they push forward and do damage. If the enemy is strong and inclined to attack, they fall back. Relieved by their brother brigade, the same process is pursued by them, until they are relieved in turn. It means the enemy is constantly harassed and Chauvel is able to get precise intelligence of just where they are and what their strengths are.

Clearly their force is large. What is not clear is their timing. It seems certain that they intend to make a big push on Romani – but when? Reading report after report, calling on his vast experience, he comes up with an answer: soon.

Chauvel, a master of cavalry tactics, insists his men have positions prepared well before Romani that are most easily defensible, the idea being that the Turks could be induced to actually attack them *en masse*, whereupon the Light Horse could fall back on Romani where the infantry is garrisoned, and the artillery batteries could see for themselves just where their shells are landing among the Turks.

With just a small posse of Troopers for protection, Chauvel personally reconnoitres the approaches and works out the two best spots of thick sand and high hills for his forces to make a stand – one where the Turks could be delayed and weakened, and the other where they can be stopped. Guessing the Turks will try to come around his right flank to attack from the south, he has his men dig in on the line he sets out, with orders to hit the Turks hard when they cross this *actual* 'line in the sand that shall not be crossed'.

•

The German Commander, Colonel Kress von Kressenstein, is indeed intent on striking a decisive blow on the British, and has already issued his Turkish troops with orders to 'drive the English into the sea, as at Gallipoli'.[3]

Rather than merely baiting them in open battle, he wants to destroy their railhead and as much of their pipeline as he can get to. Beyond that, capturing Romani will give his forces a secure base from which they can launch an attack on the Suez Canal, just 20 miles west of Romani.

To do the job he is putting together a force 16,000 soldiers strong, which he will personally command, composed of the Turkish 3rd Division, supported by machine-gun companies and both German and Austrian heavy artillery batteries. It is getting the heavy artillery forward that is taking the time – on soft sand, having to put planks beneath the wheels, rolling it forward, putting another plank down, and so forth.

But they are getting there . . .

Screening patrols are sent out ahead, to ensure that the British cannot discover their bulk, before they are actually destroyed by them. And so each side engages in their bluffs, waiting for the battle that is coming.

There are occasional clashes between the two forces, but a certain decency prevails.

After personally going out with one of his Light Horse patrols and clashing with the Turks near Katia, Chauvel writes to his wife on 10 July.

'I have just come back from a stunt. We had to leave two [Turks] who were too badly wounded to shift. I hope their mates will come for them. We built a little shade for them, and left them a water bottle each and that was all we could do.'[4]

25 July 1916, just to be clear

'Taubes!'[5]

As ever, at the sight of the German planes overhead, the Australians either reach for their guns, or run for cover knowing that they risk being either sprayed with machine-gun fire or having bombs dropped on them.

On this otherwise sleepy afternoon, Trooper Maurie Evans is with his stretcher, ready to move whenever the cry goes up that one of the men has been wounded.

To his amazement, however, instead of bombs comes a single message wrapped around a rock, with red and black streamers – the colours of the German flag – trailing from it. The message lands right at the door of 1st Brigade HQ and is quickly opened.

'Refrained from bombing,' it reads, 'as hospitals too indistinct.'[6]

Trooper Maurie Evans is impressed.

'Likely it was a bit of boasting. Very probably he had no bombs on board . . . but anyway it was very decent of him to give us the warning.'[7]

Late July 1916, east of Romani, Bedouin breakfast

Hush!

There are noises in the night, just near their observation post.

With Lieutenant Ernest Stanfield and Sergeant Paul by his side, Ion Idriess risks a very quick looky-see over the sand dune and there they are!

Armed Turkish soldiers are crawling towards them, perhaps a quarter mile away. With a nod from Lieutenant Stanfield, Idriess silently adjusts the sights on his rifle to 400 yards, and brings it to bear on one of three big Turks he can see actually standing up at the base of the dune. He is just about to fire when, from just 30 yards, he suddenly sees movement in a nearby bush. First appears 'black cloth, an elbow, then the rifle muzzle, then slowly and carefully rose the head of a Bedouin'.[8]

On the reckoning that a Bedouin in the bush is worth three Turks on the plain, Idriess adjusts his sights, swivels his aim, narrows his eyes, bites his lip, and focuses intently on the Bedouin's head . . . even as he tightens his finger on the trigger.

Bang! Bang! Bang! Bang! Bang!

Five shots ring out in the space of three seconds and Idriess has the satisfaction of seeing the Bedouin fling out his clenched hands to both sides, even as his head – or what remains of it – hits the sand.

Got him.

'On your horses, boys, quick,' shouts Lieutenant Stanfield, 'ride like the hammers of hell.'[9]

The three Australians do exactly that, and are soon thundering back to their own lines, their heads down to present smaller targets as shots ring out behind them. Yes, this is just another Turkish patrol they have stumbled upon, but the point remains. They're not only out there, they're getting closer, and ever more numerous. A full-blown attack cannot be far away. Men, munitions and weaponry are pushed forward to Romani. The last includes, wonderfully, new Hotchkiss machine guns.

Made by the French, the Hotchkiss is so powerful it is unbelievable, firing 8-mm Lebel rounds at the rate of 450 a minute. The best thing though is how light it is. A single packhorse could carry the gun, a spare barrel and just under 1000 rounds!

The storm is coming – and the Australians can't wait.

'Dear Mother and Father,' one Trooper writes. 'The enemy are showing great activity here . . . our spirits are very high on the anticipation of a scrap. According to reports they are there in large numbers and mean business. So do we. It is what we have been waiting for, for 5 long weary months of heat and flies. You can bet your life we will give them some "hurry up" for keeping us here so long.'[10]

Night of 3 August 1916, Romani, shifting sands

Never say anything on the water that you're not happy to have heard on the shore, they say, as it is extraordinary how far sound travels.

Much the same applies to the desert, as the Troopers on duty here in a sea of sand know, it is extraordinary to sometimes be able to hear things – rifle shots, cannon fire – that they know must be coming from *dozens* of miles away.

It is why, when the men of the 1st Australian Light Horse Brigade out on picket duty east of Romani hear shots in the distance on this mild, still night, there is not undue alarm. Yes, it might be trouble, but it also might be someone else's trouble from many miles away.

Still, the sentries are particularly alert, and all the more so when they suddenly spy a light from the direction of Katia – the direction of the enemy. The light vanishes and reappears four times; not just a brief flash, it comes on for a period of ten seconds, and ten only – like a lighthouse of battle, warning them where to find trouble in this night.

Nearing midnight, another flash in the night, this time it is a news-flash carried from a post further ahead, there is movement in the desert, coming from the south-east – a large body of men, heading this way with intent.

Via the telephone lines that have recently been laid, on General Chauvel's insistence, a call is quickly put through to the Australian and New Zealand Mounted's Divisional HQ at Romani.

Trouble. Bad trouble. They're here.

Chauvel is not panicked. Immediately advised of the situation, he in turn alerts Brigadier General 'Hellfire' Jack Royston who – in the absence of Granville Ryrie, who, to Chauvel's deep chagrin, is on six weeks leave in England to attend a parliamentary conference – has taken command of the 2nd Brigade, that he and his men will soon be required.

Should we go immediately?

No.

Chauvel is certain that his well-trained men and officers of the 1st Light Horse Brigade can hold them, and it will be better to throw in Royston's 2nd Light Horse Brigade as a fresh and completely intact reserve at first light the following morning, when the situation will be literally clearer. Chauvel has little faith that the British garrison at Romani itself would be able to fight the Turks off, *or* come to the aid of the Anzac Mounted Division if they get in trouble as – like most British units – their own Generals are in faraway Cairo, and passing requests and orders back and forth is always lengthy. He is under no illusion. The Anzacs must stand in the sands on their own two feet – four if mounted.

The importance of controlling Romani cannot be overstated. It's the only sure large supply of water for miles in any direction, and if the Turks are to make any mass move on the Suez Canal then Romani is the only place they can launch from. If they get their heavy guns a dozen miles beyond Romani they could even destroy shipping in the Suez from that position.

But if they don't secure the water of Romani?

Any large army would be simply stranded in shimmering sands and temperatures of well over 110 degrees, and have no choice but to retreat.

Chauvel is not yet sure how, with just 1600 men from his two brigades up against as many as 16,000 of the enemy, he can hold them back, but he has at least been assiduous in his preparations. Based on his previous reconnaissance, each brigade, when on duty, has its 800 Troopers strung out for four miles along a particularly high dune, meaning when the Turks get close enough the Australian defenders will initially be firing from on high upon an enemy that cannot rush them.

For all that, the Australian Troopers have also been ordered by Chauvel: do *not* try and make a last stand out here.

Rushing will mean massacre. Don't forget our intelligence has established that the Turks are backed by a serious German force, code-named 'Pasha I', which includes a machine-gun battalion of eight companies.

Make your first stand instead, with an eye on your second. Yes, the key is to engage and withdraw, engage and withdraw, engage and withdraw. The Australians must engage and ensure a series of firefights where the Turks and Germans never know from which sand dune they are about to be ambushed. Keep pulling back towards Romani. Hold them up, slow them down, weaken them, as they move further and further from their own water supply – as we get closer to our own water, our infantry and our newly reinforced artillery. Draw it out, draw them in, draw on all your resources and tomorrow's blistering sun will be fighting on our side.

Now, those who had been in the outposts fall back to their regiments and give the news: there really are thousands of them, coming this way! It is Turkish and German infantry, hauling heavy artillery across the soft sands. The Anzacs know what that means, for they have done that hauling themselves – it is slow, cumbersome work. It means they indeed have time to prepare for the infantry's arrival.

Rifles are loaded. Bayonets sharpened. Ammunition is checked, passed by palms suddenly sweating even in this cool evening air; the fight is coming.

•

There they are!

They are the dark phantoms of the night, moving stealthily across the desert in the moonlight. Armed. Dangerous. Committed.

The Australians watch them carefully, barely breathing, just looking down their sights and waiting for the first shot, at which point it will be open season.

A single shot rings out across the line, followed by a fierce volley as 800 Troopers of the 1st Australian Light Horse Brigade unleash their best.

'Up and down the line,' one Trooper recounts, 'comes the crackle, crackle of rifle fire and the rip-rip-rip of machine-guns.'[11]

Many of the phantoms fall. Many go to ground and fire back, the flashes from the muzzles of their guns providing more good targets – though suddenly the Australians atop the ridge are themselves under heavy fire.

From out of the night, over the chattering fire, comes the unearthly cry of 'Allah! Allah!'[12] as the Turks call upon their God to protect them and smite their heathen foes even as, with extraordinary bravery, they charge forward.

'Allah, you bastards,' the Australians cry back, firing straight into the phantom forms coming at them, 'we'll give you Allah!'[13]

In the darkness all is soon catastrophic confusion as the two forces get ever closer to each other, the Turks and Germans struggling up the dunes in their thousands, the Australians continuing to fire even while using their bayonets on those who get close enough, and yelling at those who fall back, 'Try it again!'[14]

'Both sides blazed away point-blank at one another's rifle flashes, which when the quarter moon had set made the intense blackness seem aflame,' Idriess will recount.[15]

'Up steep slopes comes the Turk infantry,' records another, 'withering away under our steady fire, but always coming swiftly on.'[16]

Inevitably the Turks and the Australians come together like crashing waves on a stormy night of death, the hand-to-hand fighting vicious as some of the Australians fall back, only to lie in wait to become, in turn, 'shadows that arose from the night and annihilated the Cossack posts'.[17]

In fact, there are many such Australian shadows, who after falling back just a little, materialise from nowhere to ambush the attackers and bring the darkness of death before dawn. Yes, the Australians are shockingly outnumbered by the 16,000 Turks and 500 Germans, but the only backward steps they take are strategic, not panicked, as ever more blood flows.

'The Turks charged and I could hear them yelling "Allah! Allah!" and "Finish Australia!"' one Trooper will record, 'but we simply poured rifle and machine-gun fire into them and beat them off.'[18]

The beating is immeasurably helped by the Troopers of the 3rd Regiment now making a co-ordinated charge straight at the Turks, to use their bayonets with great effect.

It is at this point in the murderous madness that four Troopers charge so far 'right through' the Turks – protected only by 'brilliant starlight'[19], and shooting the infantry on the way through – that they become isolated. Turkish soldiers further back bayonet their horses, leaving four stranded Australians in the night, fighting to stay alive behind Turkish lines.

Things are crook in Tallarook, and not much better in the desert just outside of Romani.

Bullets are flying and shells are exploding as the 1st Brigade's own artillery – which has been held back until a firm front line has been established – comes into play, and the swirling dust alone could kill a brown dog.

Meanwhile, the four stranded Australians are on their last legs, surrounded by dead Turks, their ammunition finished. Though they have not yet met their Maker, all could be forgiven for preparing their opening remarks. There is no way out.

But now comes some wild snorting from behind. A horseman!

Surely, in these Biblical parts, it must be one or all of the Four Horsemen of the Apocalypse: Death, Famine, War and Conquest?

No, actually, it's the *Fifth* Horseman!

For it proves to be none other than Major Michael Shanahan on his mighty chestnut steed, the biggest in the regiment, Bill the Bastard!

'Get up on him!' Shanahan roars. 'One on each stirrup, and two on the back!'[20]

It is no easy feat, as the bullets and shrapnel continue to fly, even as through the desert howl of the swirling dust they can see the Turks surging forward, but it is shortly done with Shanahan now the principal anchoring point for all four grasping him. The Major drives his heels into Bill the Bastard's sides and they are soon heading back, Bill's every step plunging deep into the sand, but somehow he keeps his feet and keeps moving. Minutes later, Shanahan can drop all four men in a position of relative safety, before he heads back to see who else might be saved.

Inspired, one fearless Queenslander seeks to emulate the feat; spying a lost soldier in the starlight, he too leaps over the Turkish line, scoops up the fellow onto his horse and gallops back to safety! Unbelievable! Even more unbelievable? He has just 'rescued' a Turk; who is absolutely stunned that this is how Australians take prisoners! His fellow soldiers are still howling with laughter at the Queenslander's fury; it's like crossing the tryline triumphant and then realising you've just scored for the opposing team.

Elsewhere, the carnage goes on, and other Australian Troopers are not so fortunate as to be saved by a miraculous steed at their time of greatest need. Some are caught in powdery sand, unable to get away as the Turks either run them down or simply line them up in their gun sights and gun them down – rarely missing such slow-moving targets. Some of the canny Turks kick off their boots, knowing it will allow them to move over the sand traps more quickly and allow them to simply bayonet the Australians.

Still the Australians manage to follow Major General Chauvel's plan and fall back to their next prepared line before turning to make a stand – 'Sections Mount, and turn!' – on a large sand dune known as Mount Meredith, and at 2.30 am the Turks and Germans begin to struggle up it.

'Allah, Allah, Allah!' comes the cry, as some 800 Turks surge forward, with cries like a terrible scream, their bayonets glinting softly in the night's glow.

In the dark night, lit only by the brilliant stars, these 'shadow men', just silhouetted against the white sands, are easy targets and the Australians – now supported by the blessed Kiwis who have just arrived as reinforcements – are without mercy.

'They shot the Turks down like wallabies,' Ion Idriess will note, 'and they rolled over and over and over down the walls of sand.'[21]

Still the Turks keep surging forward, and as recorded by one Trooper, 'the bullets were like hail all the time. You could feel the wind of them as they went past your ear.'[22]

Not all of the bullets miss, and sometimes the reaction is unexpected.

'One of the chaps who was hit close to me,' one Australian Trooper will recount, 'suddenly jumped about six feet in the air yelling with delight. "Hurrah!" He shouted out almost a dozen times. "Couldn't have ordered a better one".'[23]

What is going on?

Well, it is simple. Despite being covered in his own blood, as it continues to pour from the wound in his shoulder, it is not a fatal shot, and he should shortly recover. '[But he] was so carried away by the thought of a holiday as to be utterly heedless of the thousands of Turkish rifles potting away at him.'[24]

On the Western Front they call such wounds a 'Blighty', something that will get you back to Old Blighty, England. But, here, it is known as a 'holiday wound', and the Trooper is thrilled to have one.

Still, it is one less rifle in the service of the Australians, as the Turks continue to press on this massive sand dune of Mount Meredith.

'We held them for three hours until it was impossible for human flesh to stand more,' a Trooper records. 'We had to retire over bullet-swept ridges.'[25] It is a second retreat, but there are still enough of the 1st Brigade left and firing that the Turks can't simply charge forth and take Romani. Still, how long can it, and they, last?

Where is the 2nd Light Horse Brigade? Surely, they must arrive soon?

•

It is a strange thing to suddenly have a limb nearly severed – the strangest of all being that the first feeling is not of agony, but shock.

For Major Shanahan is again at the front lines atop Bill the Bastard and in the thick of it all, when a bullet hits his left leg amidships, gouging the flesh and shattering the bone.

One moment Shanahan is surging forward on Bill, the next he looks down and his left leg has become a veritable drainpipe from which blood is pouring. Shanahan, grievously wounded, and now faint, slumps forward. He has only one chance, and he knows it. He must hold as tight as he can to Bill the Bastard, and count on him to turn and get back to their own lines.

Bill, his flanks bathed in fresh blood, turns of his own accord. *Gallop!*

•

In that first dull glow of dawn, the Troopers of the 1st Light Horse Brigade are just holding on, like cats to a curtain. To wait for reinforcement is to realise the eternity of a minute. The minds of the men have but one thought: 'Where are they?'

They know armed comrades are near, but for whatever reason – exhaustion, fear, death – they fail to appear.

But now . . . *look*.

A dust cloud behind them reveals movement!

Look there! Look there!

Just above the heads of the leading troops they can see the fern leaf with boomerang flag, the symbol of the Anzac Mounted Division, and the cherry red pennant of the 2nd Australian Light Horse Brigade.

Of course, it is Chauvel himself in command of the Anzac Mounteds, with Royston and the mighty 2nd Australian Light Horse Brigade, assisted by the Wellington Mounted Rifles Regiment – flint-hard Kiwis like Grandpa used to make, who are fine soldiers and horsemen. They are arriving in just the nick of time: fresh, furious and desperately relieved that there is still some fight left over for them. As they get closer, just the sight of their slouch hats with emu plumes – for by now the practice of wearing those plumes has become the signature of the Australian Light Horse from all states, not just Queensland – is enough to lift a man's heart. (Those plumes have also impressed the local population who refer to the men of the Light Horse as the 'Kings of the Feathers'[26], while the men of the Light Horse have been happy to tell the Pommies who ask what bird they originate from that they are 'kangaroo feathers'.)[27]

And now the first light begins to glow, an ember, a sliver of sun revived, and all cover is gone for the desperate Turks.

'The slopes were like long golden sheets faintly alight, the Turks climbing up distinct as coal-black shadows.'[28]

The phenomenon soon makes them no less than shadows in the valley of death – dispatched by crack shots as the day deigns to appear. But *still* more Turks appear, and the sweat flows as fear fights the order to stay.

It falls to the Wellington Mounted men, together with Lieutenant Colonel George Macarthur-Onslow's 7th Light Horse Regiment, to remove them.

Leave your horses behind, line up, fix bayonets, and get ready to charge at the Turks in front . . .

And GO!

Endeavouring to match the Wellingtonians, the Australians 'raised a coo-ee and charged'.[29]

Macarthur-Onslow himself is quickly running in the lead, less as a matter of leadership than simply physical vigour and eagerness to get to it, with three Troopers right behind him, and the rest 20 yards back. All of them have their legs pumping in the soft surface, their lungs soon burning like the sand itself with the effort. Yes, courageous. In fact, such valour is nothing less than extraordinary. And the Turkish soldiers are impressed, even as they bring their Mausers to bear, and aim at those leading the charge.

The shots ring out, and – *oh, Christ!* – the valiant Macarthur-Onslow goes down hard, soon followed by the next three Troopers, only for the Australian tide to roll on, and over the Turkish defenders.

Among the stretcher-bearers who get to Macarthur-Onslow – he is alive, but with blood pouring from his legs and in danger of bleeding to death – is Private Maurie Evans of the 1st Field Ambulance. With valour all their own, the stretcher-bearers gather the fallen officer, and the other wounded, and 'we beat a hurried and I fear somewhat ungraceful retreat . . . for myself I haven't been so mortally frightened since Sari Bair [at Gallipoli] this time last year. In future I shall spend the first week of every August safe in bed I think.'[30]

Behind them, however, the Wellingtonians and men of the Australian Light Horse continue savaging every pod of Turks they can find, first firing and soon thrusting bayonets into the defenders,

It is a bitter battle under the rising sun, with gallons of blood soon flowing into those timeless sands, much as they have for ages past.

In short order, however, they are back to it, as Chauvel throws in two fresh regiments of Light Horse on the 1st Brigade's right flank, with orders to pivot: swing back to protect our own flank and steer the enemy to the soft sand that has been picked out for their destruction.

Within the fresh forces, the Wellington Mounted Rifles Regiment are to the fore, fully engaged with the Turks, firing, bayoneting, charging, cutting, falling back.

One German officer observing the display cannot help but be impressed. 'The Australian Cavalry fought in a most exemplary fashion,' he will note. 'Many a time we cursed those active and agile horsemen in their big soft hats.'[31]

The Australians themselves are now under more pressure, for, as recounted by one Trooper, in that 'fatal tinge of dawn, [came] the bark of a mountain gun and the whine of the shell followed by the white puff as the shrapnel bursts over the stubborn line'.[32]

And now both Turks and Troopers fight in the light.

'The Turks were coming up the gully in their hundreds,' one of the Light Horse will recount, 'and the closest were within 100 yards of us when we opened fire and they charged yelling "Allah!" "Allah!". But Allah deserted them that day and they fell thick and fast.'[33]

However, the enemy surge proves overwhelming and the defenders are forced to retire slowly from the ridge, to pull back and regroup, the battle breaking as the morning does.

Of the 2nd Brigade, few are busier than Hellfire Jack Royston, who – as is always his manner – is constantly on the move, exhorting and encouraging his men to ever greater efforts. Not for nothing is Royston described by Banjo Paterson as being 'by instinct a bandit chief and by temperament a hero'.

Go on, Banjo?

'[While it is] altogether an admirable thing for a general to set his troops a good example by showing a contempt for danger, it must be admitted that Royston rather overdid it.'[34]

Hellfire Jack is, after all, nearly 60 years old, and 18 stone if he's a pound!

Neither fact appears to bother him, though there is no doubt the latter bothers his horses as he continues to wear them out as he charges back and forth.

'That's it, boys,' he would roar, 'Pump it into 'em!'[35]

His men, mutter back *sotto voce*, 'Get out of that, you old bastard . . . You're drawing the fire on us!'[36]

But the fact that Hellfire does not blink is in itself inspirational, as he continues to roar, 'Keep your heads down, lads. Stick to it, stick to it! You are making history today!'[37]

Even more important than the fire brought by the 2nd Brigade, however, is the fire the Turks are now lying on, as the sun beats down on one and the same hot sands that Chauvel has steered them to, and continues to burn their very souls. And yes, the same goes for the defending Australians, but their water supplies are just some miles behind them, and some supplies have been brought forward on camels. The Turks, for their part, *and* their horses, have been without water for many hours and are not just in the fight of their lives with the Australians, but fighting *for* their lives for lack of hydration.

By mid-afternoon, Chauvel's plan comes into full effect as the German and Ottoman forces are helplessly stuck in the powdery sand lying just to the south of Romani – within range of the heavily entrenched infantry of the 52nd Division, who exact a terrible toll, together with their artillery.

And yet, such are the numbers of Turks swarming forward, the Australians do risk being overwhelmed. Where are the promised British reinforcements, to go with the mounted Troopers? Again, eyes go back to Romani, hoping the Brits are on their way. In the meantime, fight on!

'Blood was everywhere and at last we knew what war meant,' one Trooper will recount. 'The next hour was agony for us, the shells burst in front, on both sides and behind, it was hell let loose . . . Five of [our] men came from the Echuca district and lay side by side on the ground . . . another shell came over, it caught the five and made a terrible mess. One seemed to have his arm torn off, one his side torn open, and [one] got the full benefit in his head . . . one look was enough to prove he was past human aid.'[38]

The Australian stretcher-bearers are nothing if not busy.

'We clapped our spurs in,' Private Maurie Evans of the 1st Field Ambulance will recount, 'and went hell for leather over the ridge into a little dip . . . The carts [for the wounded] rolling and ploughing up sand like ships in a heavy sea . . . The enemy evidently spotted these and began to put shrapnel systematically into this hollow. It was really marvelous how well the horses stood it for the shells were bursting only a few yards overhead or to the side. We filled up one cart [with wounded] and it went back.'[39]

And now, just as the British infantry who have been rushed forward from Kantara begin to arrive, the Turkish attackers gain the top of a massive sandhill known to the troops as 'Mount Royston' in honour of the great man.

Who can dislodge them?

It falls to the men of the New Zealand Mounted Rifles Brigade. Charging right to the base of the hill, they dismount and, with no cover, begin their assault.

'It was a chance and a big gamble . . .' ran one eye-witness account. 'The brigade mounted and galloped for Mt. Royston – such a sight I have never seen, it was too wonderful for words . . . '[40]

Machine guns chatter, rifles fire, men die. One man wounded is none other than Hellfire Jack himself, as a bullet buries deep in his right calf. Reluctantly, Royston has the wound seen to, but even before the medic has finished, he – of course – gallops off, trailing a bloody bandage behind him. There is a battle to get back to, and he must not tarry.

Chauvel will not have it.

'The old beggar would not have his wound attended to,' he will recount, 'and it was not till I personally chased him and ordered him to do so that he went to a field ambulance to have it dressed.'[41]

Not that it lasts long, as Royston is soon observed to return to the fray.

In fact, Chauvel himself now throws caution to the winds as one impressed Trooper writes in the next letter home.

'I saw him riding backwards and forwards under heavy fire . . . and it seemed he did not know what danger was.'[42]

Not everyone is so brave.

Trooper Oliver Clarke of the 2nd Light Horse Brigade is just a few feet away from a bloke who is no sooner shot than he sits up and cries out for stretcher-bearers, insisting, 'I have been shot through the heart!'[43]

Clarke can't help himself, and roars with laughter – being shot through the heart is usually a touch more fatal than this.

'Can you walk?'[44] the stretcher-bearers ask, when they arrive.

'Walk?! Lord no!'

He has a bullet in his heart, did he mention?

Well, in that case . . .

'Drag yourself down the hill.'

He has gone only a short way when a Turkish 18-pounder shell lands not far away, sending shrapnel scything past in all directions. Everyone keeps their head down, and mercifully no-one is wounded. Quite the contrary – for when the dust clears, the fellow who has been 'shot through the heart' is at least 150 yards away and 'disappearing in a cloud of dust'.[45]

A new miracle! And they are not even in the Holy Land yet!

And now for a real miracle, for it is Hellfire Jack Royston, still alive, still red-hot keen to make his mark, despite the bloody bandages that he is unwittingly trailing behind him. He arrives to find one regiment standing by as they wait for their absent colonel to return from a briefing.

Without hesitation he gallops up, cries out, 'Come on, boys!' and exhorts them to follow him into the attack.

'We are winning now,' Royston roars, 'they are retreating in hundreds!'

Really?

'I poked my head over the top,' one Trooper will recall, 'and there were the blighters coming on in their thousands!'[46]

Never mind. Royston has faith, and the men flow forward in his sandy wake.

Later, one of the British officers rides up to Royston and anxiously asks, 'Can you hold them, Colonel?'

Royston doesn't hesitate.

'If they can get through that crowd,' he says, pointing the end of his pipe at his men, 'they can have the camp.'[47]

And yet elsewhere in the battle it is the Turks on top and the only way for the Troopers to survive such withering fire from on high is to dig into the sand and fire back, but the casualty rate remains fearful as they become bogged down. It is only when they are joined in the early evening by a force of British Yeomanry that they are able to surge forward once more.

Without hesitation, the Gloucester Hussars and the Worcester Yeomanry gallop forward to gain the southern spur of Mount Royston before surging even further forward.

'The top was gained – huge excitement – and hundreds of white flags went up. The Turks saw that they were cut off [and] we stopped firing. They had dropped their rifles and put up their hands. The sight was wonderful . . . A wonderful day for the mounteds – we had waited for two years for this to come off.'[48]

In all, the defenders take just over 500 Turkish prisoners on the day, and – despite their own heavy casualties – have caused staggering losses among the enemy, with mangled corpses from both sides littering the desert.

'The sun is fast disappearing over the horizon,' one Trooper records, 'as if ashamed to shed this glorious light on such a ghastly scene as this.'[49]

By dusk it is not quite a stalemate, but at the very least both sides must pause from sheer exhaustion. No, they won't really get sleep, but in the time when they are spared full-blown battle they can dig in, shift the wounded back, and the *materiel* forward.

In a night thus filled with moving phantoms in the moonlight, all of them exhausted, Chauvel still remains confident. In this position, even a stalemate is a victory. His forces only have to hold the line and, denied water, the attackers simply *must* retreat. (After all, the defenders themselves have completely had it, and that is with more water than the attackers have had! 'I never felt so done in all my life,' a Trooper of the 6th Light Horse records. 'I could no more run than I could fly and I don't think I cared whether I got hit or not. My tongue and mouth were so swollen I could not chew a biscuit.'[50])

The good news is that, just after dark, a report comes in to Chauvel that his forces have captured from the Turks a notably significant sand ridge that lies just before Romani.

Alas, alas, as day dawns so does the realisation that they only control a part of it, and the Turks, together with the Germans of Pasha I, are in fact occupying what will soon be known as 'Wellington Ridge', and for good reason.

The Turks are exhausted, hungry and *thirsty*, acutely aware that their only sure supply of water in this shimmering heat is a long trek behind them, back to Katia. Or just a mile ahead if they can take Romani!

•

Their mouths are becoming ever drier, the saliva thickening, the tongues beginning to swell and sticking to the roofs of their mouths. Sparingly, they sip on whatever drops are left in their canteens, and no man dies whose canteen isn't instantly claimed. Still – despite having marched and fought for most of the last few days with little sleep or replenishment – they fight mightily and exact punishment.

As the battle ebbs and flows, the Australians are mindful to leave none of their wounded behind and . . .

And who's that?

Still up on the ridge, it looks to be Trooper Fred Cox, unmoving and almost certainly dead as a doornail.

Christ. Just to be sure, his mate Trooper Scotty Duguid crawls forward, inch by inch, 'every moment expecting a bullet, for they were as thick as flies . . .'

Finally, he reaches Cox and grabs him by the ankle, ready to drag him back.

'Like a flash of lightning,' Trooper Verner Knuckey will record in his diary, 'the "dead man" sprang to his feet and rushed down the slope to safety leaving poor old Scotty up there . . . we roared with laughter. Fred had gone to sleep.'[51]

Still, the battle rages as the sun starts to make the sand shimmer and the Turks begin to take heavy fire. One of those firing the machine guns is Lieutenant Ross Smith, originally a warehouseman from Adelaide.

'It was exciting to say the least of it,' he will recount. ''Tis a blessing that Nature bestows a thing called "fighting madness" upon us at such a time . . . All fear of danger seems to vanish. One gets worked up into it and I wish I could describe my feelings as I sat at that gun with my thumbs on the firing button and pouring out 600 bullets per minute into living targets. The savage satisfaction too, as you see them drop.'[52]

Finally, the Australians see it.

The Turks are pulling back, *en masse*!

Desperate for water, unable to break through the Australian wall, and now planes dealing death from the skies, they simply have no choice: retreat or die. With his sagacity matched by his brevity, Chauvel notes, 'It was the empty Turkish water-bottle that won the battle.'[53]

There is truth in it, but it had been Chauvel's strategy, tactics, battle-plan and men that had allowed the water bottle to have such extraordinary effect. With just two brigades of Light Horse, Chauvel had held up a large force of Turks on a waterless ridge for 18 hours.

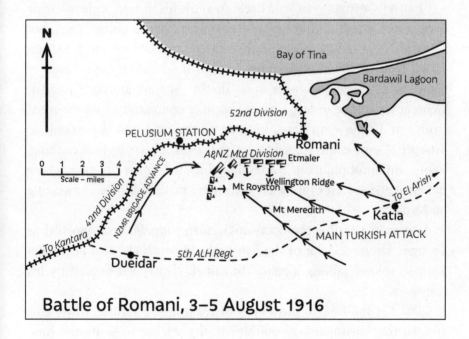

Battle of Romani, 3–5 August 1916

For the moment, the Empire is saved, and the Turkish tide has been turned. For the mounted Troopers it has put a spring in their step and ever more bullets back in the breeches of their rifles – *once more unto the breech, dear friends, once more*. For now the Australians and those wonderful Wellingtonians – New Zealand's finest – sweep down the other side of the ridge in hot pursuit. Another 1000 Turkish and German prisoners are soon taken, and marched back to Romani. The Turkish survivors that get away will have a tale to tell, of these mounted Troopers, many of them with curiously sloped hats with a strange feather poking up. And so too, the German officers with them.

'The Australian troops showed such courage as I had never seen since the beginning of the war in France,' one of them, *Kapitän* Heinrich Romer-Andrea will write. 'They fought without any regard for cover, or personal losses.'[54]

The question is, how hard to follow up, now that the Turks are in retreat? For the Allies are not without their own losses, with over 200 Troopers and soldiers killed, and nearly 1000 wounded. Their numbers include a badly bleeding and nearly unconscious Major Michael Shanahan, brought back to safety by Bill the Bastard.

Chauvel's instinct is to hold back, to allow his men to replenish their own water supplies, and gather themselves, before going again, but General Herbert Lawrence, the British commander of No. 3 Section Canal Defences – who presumes to lead the battle though based at Kantara, 20 miles away – is in no doubt. At 6.30 am on 5 August, General Lawrence orders Chauvel to take command of all mounted troops and follow up hard, keeping to the trail that is marked, as Trooper Maurie Evans records it, by 'the desert . . . strewn with clothing, boots, ammunition, camels abandoned by the Turks . . . everywhere the eye could see over the desert there were mounted troops advancing on Katia'.[55]

Also on the trail is the occasional Turk, some far from hostile, as Trooper Oliver Clarke of the 7th Light Horse finds out. He sees a Turkish soldier pulling a reluctant camel, clearly left behind by his comrades.

Clarke is the first to grab hold of the surprised Turk, who turns and, to the Australian's astonishment, throws his arms around him, and kisses him!

Friedrich Kress von Kressenstein. Responsible for Turkish operations in the First Suez Offensive in 1915, he later took over command of the Ottoman Eighth Army in Palestine. (Wikimedia Commons)

Colonel T. E. Lawrence – Lawrence of Arabia – dressed in traditional Arab robes. Lawrence became famous for supporting the Arab Revolt against the Ottoman Empire. (Wikimedia Commons)

Captain Andrew Barton 'Banjo' Paterson (right) of 2nd Remounts, Australian Imperial Force, inspects a sulking horse. (AWM P00269.001)

Studio portrait of Trooper Ion Idriess of the 5th Light Horse Regiment. Idriess was wounded at Gallipoli and in Palestine. After the war, he became a celebrated author. (AWM PO8584.001)

Men of the 12th Light Horse Regiment in training at Holsworthy Camp near Liverpool, NSW. (AWM A03315)

Katia, c. August 1916. Australian Light Horsemen watering their horses at a well in the desert. At left, wearing a feathered hat, is Major General Harry Chauvel. (AWM P00859.018)

Brigadier General Granville Ryrie on 'Plain Bill', a horse selected especially to carry a man of Ryrie's great weight and stature. (AWM B01681)

Portrait of Lieutenant General Sir Harry (Henry George) Chauvel, Commander of the Desert Mounted Corps, c. 1918. (AWM B01484)

A mounted member of the 1st Australian Light Horse Regiment practises bringing in a wounded comrade laid across a horse. (AWM P00153.014)

Bedouins, suspected of giving information to the Turks, brought into Romani by the Australian Light Horse. (AWM J02878)

View of the 1st Australian Light Horse Brigade watering their horses in the Wadi Ghuzze. (AWM A02396)

Troops of the Australian Light Horse moving forward during the Second Battle of Gaza, April 1917. (AWM J01122)

Turkish soldiers at Gaza in trenches with rifles at the ready. (AWM P02040.012)

How good is it to be out of this eternal, infernal war?

'Yes, well and truly kissed me, and got in a good couple too, before I was sufficiently recovered to punch him.'[56]

Lone comrades are found too, including the discovery of one Australian Trooper of the 8th Light Horse who, Trooper Verner Knuckey will recount, 'had been shot in both legs and lay out for three days and nights'.

When the Turks had found him they had, 'made him as comfortable as possible and left a bottle of water beside him. That water saved his life . . . Any dirty action done can I think be traced to the German and Austrian officers in charge of these Turks.'[57]

It is not just the Australians who are angry at the Germans, however.

'We have quite a number of German prisoners,' Maurie Evans writes, 'mostly officers and machine-gun crews. The Turks fought well, but say the Germans turned the machine guns on them when they started to retire or surrender.'[58]

Ion Idriess's 5th Australian Light Horse Regiment men are at the forefront of those troops pursuing the Turks, with strength undaunted for the task. Atop one sand dune in a spectacular rosy dawn they look back and see 'a grand sight all lit up in pink and grey and khaki stretching right back . . . a winding column of New Zealanders and Australian mounted troops'.

Onwards! The 5th Light Horse know they are getting closer when, instead of passing the detritus of the Turkish kit, they pass actual Turkish corpses, at first in singles, then in handfuls. And now a dozen pooled Turkish stretchers are passed, each carrying a bloodied corpse – perhaps their stretcher-bearers simply abandoning the dead weight to save themselves. Next to the corpses, more often than not, is an empty bottle of booze, strictures against alcohol seeming to be loosened in the desert in a time of war.

They 'drank to the day,'[59] left with liquor, slipping into the other world with a final toast to fate. Rifle fire now, the odd bullet whistling past, the Australians pass an oasis that has become a tip for shell casings, and all feel that strange mingling of fear and excitement; it can't be named, just shared. 'I wonder if my ancestors experienced it when they advanced with club and spear.'[60]

Such thoughts are interrupted now by a yell: 'HALT! HALT! TAUBE! TAUBE!'[61]

All stop, stock still, as the plane roars above them and they watch as the pilot drops bombs, by hand, from on high. And they watch the bombs fall and explode into the sand – often burrowing too deep to do any real damage, and too far away to bother them.

The German pilot can spot the enemy, but mercifully throws like somebody who can't make the 3rd XI. No, if the men below are going to die today, it will be in an old-fashioned way; death from above is still being developed. The top of a ridge is reached, and the men watch on horseback as the officers confer in a cluster on foot. Shrapnel increases along with their sweat, as a Colonel finally steps forth and points to a dot of blue in the distance:

'A battery of heavy Austrian guns have been located in that oasis!' he says, not loudly, but quietly, for he knows every ear is straining to hear him. To out-yell the cacophony of war is impossible; the first to hear the word will pass it back.

'We have to charge and take the guns.' And now his voice rises: 'Regiment – fix bay'nets.'[62]

No fewer than 500 bayonets of the 5th Light Horse Regiment flash, the steel wielded into the air, the click of the weapons coming as one. Now they ride, straight ahead, at a trot so brisk it could be called a gallop in a second. The Colonel leads and they follow.

As they do, Idriess notices a strange portent: two men are laughing as they ride, side by side; the regiment's doctor and their padre! Is it hysteria or just a damn good joke?

Ride on, but hold back, the horses are excited, so are the men, but they must keep their energy and their nerve. They ride close, so close, knee to knee, they can feel the heat of the mass of flesh drawn together, their sweat is nearly dripping on each other as they quickly move into a gallop, going pell-mell and damn the hellfire coming at them. They are riding so fast that the oasis seems to be rushing at them, and they'll be drowning in it soon if the Turks don't do something! They can see the Turks, well a few of them, but they can't see the guns? Where are the bullets? Are the Turks frozen in terror? Is their fire spent? The horses reach the oasis in a leap, the curious Colonel ordering a halt in front, it has been . . . easy. Too easy. For now the thuds begin, bullets hitting horseflesh, and they realise where the guns are: in the palm trees above them! No, it is not bullets striking, it's . . . *dates!* The Turks are hiding in a different oasis, their machine guns are hitting high and they are shooting the bloody palm trees!

If the Colonel had pointed to a different speck of blue, just a little left, they would have been mown down on the sand plains. As it is, they live, and what is more, they know where the Turks can be killed. Meantime, the Colonel's horse is hit, occasioning what is always much the same horror.

'We'd hear a heavy smack,' Idriess will recount of the experience, 'and know a horse had been hit. The poor brutes were mostly hit thru the stomach. Some of them did not even move, others shook themselves a little. The owner of a horse shot through the stomach would take the saddle off immediately for it was always a [fatal] case. The horse would nose around a little among the other horses, shake himself, and five minutes later roll on the sand. It was the beginning of the end.'[63]

On this occasion there is no time to make the dying horse even comfortable. For there is work to be done.

The men leap off their mounts, all racing not to be one who holds the horses – almost like when they were kids charging at dams, shouting 'last one in is a rotten egg', except this time it is 'last one off, misses the fight'. Damn! Morry loses the race and will be the horse holder. Morry pleads with his comrades that one might take his place, but there are no takers. They move off, an encircling movement to the right, the target is the oasis where the Turks lie now, picking off any man who dares to break cover. Some En Zeds – as the Australians often refer to them – spot a couple of snipers but as they run towards them, the Turk snipers simply stand up, holding a white flag! The bloody cheek.

'It would have served them jolly well right if they had been bayoneted,'[64] thinks Idriess, but that would not be cricket.

Forward they charge in the oven-like conditions, the searing heat hitting them nearly as hard as the Turks, not sure if you are to kill, or be killed – by either a bullet or through dying from thirst.

Onwards!

'You saw a Turk's head in a bush, you saw his moustache, you saw his eye glaring along his rifle-sights. You fired too, with your breath in your belly, then rushed forward screaming to bayonet him, to club him, to fall on him and tear his throat out and he met you a replica of the berserk, frightened demon that was in yourself.'[65]

The air hisses with bullets as the Australians rush forward, yards feeling like miles, seconds feeling like minutes. Spying a clump of sand that offers scant cover, Idriess throws himself behind it, only to see the soldier who was running right next to him just seconds ago come crashing down beside him, fighting the death that is just seconds away after a Turkish bullet has taken him in the guts. At least the Katia oasis is just up ahead and the Australians are able to fight their way into it, pushing the Turks back, before a welcome yell goes up: 'A well! Boys, here's water!'[66]

And not just water, but cold, sweet water! They dip their bottles in again and again, all while looking at the dozen Turkish water bottles that have been left behind, just a minute ago. How thirsty are the Australians? So thirsty that when one of the retreating Turks fires a Parthian shot which hits one of the Australians in the temple, killing him, his mates pull his body from the well and keep drinking – just a little more carefully.

A fierce fight breaks out, with both sides racking up casualties.

Again, the Turks are noted to be decent to the wounded and those who care for them. When one of the Australian wounded can still walk with the support of a mate it is noted that the Turks do not fire at them as long as it is a mission of mercy. But the moment you drop your human load and try to head back, the bullets hail without fail. It is a courtesy that is telling; nobody would call this war civilised, but there are civilised men fighting it.

Of course, as the battle rages out into the desert, neither luck nor decent Turks can save some Troopers.

Like a fellow from A Squadron of the 1st Light Horse, a popular soldier by the name of Nobbs who has his arm nearly severed by Turkish shrapnel. His mates get him a cart and start to get him back, but can do nothing to stem the flow for this only son in a family of eight from Parramatta.

'It is,' Nobbs says, through grey lips, 'the fortune of war.'

And dies.[67]

Finally the battle is over through sheer exhaustion from both sides, and, to distant cries of 'Allah! Allah! Allah!'[68], the Australians leave it all behind to head back to where it all began: Romani. Through the night they ride, the end of 60 hours of battle, the end of many friends and too few enemies, through to the end of the night, as sunrise beckons and 'we rolled out of our saddles at Romani and fell fast asleep on the sand'.[69]

Not far away is Chauvel himself.

'Chauvel was as weary as any trooper,' it will later be noted. 'For days he had not changed his clothes and he had slept in the sand without so much as removing his boots.'[70]

True, the whole place is beset by the overwhelming stench of dead horses, but officers and Troopers alike are just too tired to care. After days of battle, both sides are back where they began – less the men who have been killed.

And the horses.

The most extraordinary thing had been the composure of the surviving horses.

Idriess has long marvelled at how well their horses cope with the 'infernal row' of war. 'I had thought our horses would go mad when under shrapnel, but here they were, shrapnel fair in amongst them, our own guns blazing away under their noses and only the lifting of a few startled heads, a little uneasiness.' And so it proves once more today, the deeds of these steeds are simply extraordinary![71]

Meantime, despite the bitterness of the battle, among the Australians there is renewed respect for their enemy, at least in a highly begrudging way. Jacko is a decent enemy.

If not quite 'good bastards', they are at least 'not bad bastards'.

They are better than the Germans, and a *long* way better than the nomadic locals who so often show up against them.

'Bedouins frequently dug up our dead.'[72]

Jacko would never think of such a thing, and fights fair.

Heading back to Romani themselves, many British soldiers had been staggered to see exhausted, shattered, Turkish prisoners atop Walers, while their Australian captors walk along beside them, holding the reins.

This was not unusual, as Chauvel writes to his wife:

'[The Turks] have the time of their lives when they get into our hands, the men crowd around them and give them cigarettes and share their water and rations with them and put them up behind them on their horses to bring them in because they are footsore.'[73]

The Australian commander is deeply satisfied, writing from an improvised shelter of two Turkish ground sheets and some date palm leaves, that, 'We have fought and won a great battle, and my men put up a performance which is beyond all precedent . . .'[74]

•

Where have the Turks retreated to?

It is not hard to find out, once the next big push out into the Sinai takes place.

'We pushed on and all around us were tracks, tracks, a few horse tracks, countless camel tracks, tracks of men barefooted,' Ion Idriess documents of the days and weeks that follow, 'tracks everywhere. A great wide space of tracks running into the desert, the tracks of the retreating Turkish army.'[75]

The Australians, once restored, heading out after them into the grim desert wastes, engaging in endless skirmishes against the rear-guard of the Ottoman Army.

How to survive in the desert, when between oases, on the very stretch of desert that came very close to destroying Napoleon's army?

The British are surprised to learn just how from the colonials.

These men born beneath the Southern Cross use 'spearpoint pumps', a long tube with a sharpened end and a perforation above the point that you could quickly knock into the ground to seek for a hidden water source. Just as it had worked back home in the outback, you look for the low point of dry watercourses, particularly where there might be palm trees around, and start bashing it down. If no luck, withdraw and bash again. Keep going until water is found, whereupon it gets even easier. You don't dig, you pound down to the water strata and then use a normal pump to bring it up the tube – *hey, ho, and up she rises!* – and into a portable canvas trough. Inevitably, once observed, it takes just a few weeks for this improvised trick to become a British approved institution. (It is sometimes a little more difficult for the high-pedigree English horses to follow the same lead. While the Walers have a high tolerance for even heavily brackish water, M'lud's horses can oft not tolerate it. The Australians are determined their horses learn to thrive, not just survive like the British steeds.)

It is a trick good enough to keep small patrols alive, even when many miles from a confirmed water source, and General Murray will note in his report to London, 'the Anzac mounted troops . . . have a genius for this desert life'.[76]

Now, there is next to nothing to hunt, but mercifully the strength of the Walers means that beyond carrying the Troopers themselves, they can bear the burden of their rifles and 150 rounds, on belt and bandolier, the haversack food rations and a two-pint water bottle. Then there is the night-gear and equipment needed for the horse itself. Hanging from the heavy saddle is a greatcoat, blanket, bag with spare horse-shoes and nails with hammer; eight pounds of grain in a nosebag, and often across the horse's neck is a sandbag filled with 25 pounds of extra grain. It means the horse is often carrying at least as much weight again as the Trooper.

The British, observing these mounts going as long as 36 hours in the desert without water and still performing, are in no doubt that they are the best cavalry mounts in the world.

One by one, the Turkish outposts fall as Kress von Kressenstein's *Wüstenkraft*, 'Desert Force', continues to wilt in coming weeks, and the forces of the British Empire get ever closer to the Holy Land.

As they enter the oasis of Bir el Abd, one section of the 8th Light Horse Regiment is of particular interest. For this section is composed of the oldest Trooper in the 8th Light Horse, and his three sons. For this attack it is the father who holds the horses while his lads go forward . . . only for one of the last of the shells fired by the retreating Turks to land just a few yards from him and explode. When his sons race back they find the pieces of three dead horses and . . . their father, completely unhurt but very annoyed!

Bir el Abd has indeed been abandoned by the enemy, and the new arrivals are impressed to see that at least some among the enemy had been thinking of their welfare. For there, right beside the principal well, is a large noticeboard on which is marked:

> *Notice Cholera.*
> *Kind wishings and greeting from*
> *a German Field Ambulance.*[77]

Kind wishings to you too, *mein herren.*

At least around here it is easier to get supplies coming in by sea.

'A wet canteen has just opened at the brigade,' Maurie Evans records in his diary, 'the result being of course that the first day was a positive saturnalia, three parts of the brigade were paralytic and the remainder looking for a fight.'[78]

Sobering up again, the Australians and Kiwis push on, brothers in arms, on horses. The fraternity between them all grows ever wider and deeper, as does the sense that they are on the mission of their lives and that the survivors will treasure it for the rest of their days.

'The desert all around the oasis was a great dark brown cloth of horses and men . . .' Trooper Ion Idriess will write in his diary at one camp. 'The men whistling and singing, laughing and joking, the horses pulling at their bits in the fierce desert heat. And again on a high hill we looked behind us, and what a great sight, squadron upon squadron, column upon column, regiment after regiment. A grand array of Australian and New Zealand mounted fighting men, all in their shirt sleeves, hardy, laughing fighting men . . . It was great to feel a man was a member of such a fighting force.'[79]

It is a force not just to be reckoned with, but a force that is actively seeking a final reckoning.

CHAPTER FIVE

POMP AND CIRCUMSTANCES

The Australian Light Horse ... was in body and spirit the true product of the wide Australian countryside ... Looking back upon that throng of great-hearted country-men riding in to enlist for service overseas, one ceases to feel astonishment at the war deeds of the Australian light horse-men. For these men were the very flower of their race.[1]

Official Historian Henry Gullett, *The Australian Imperial Force in Sinai and Palestine 1914–1918*

Most remarkably, each man and his horse were a fighting unit which could operate independently or mesh in with section, troop, squadron or regiment. It seemed strange that men who thrived on isolation could team so effectively – until you looked more closely at the way they had lived and worked.[2]

Ian Jones, *A Thousand Miles of Battles*

1 September 1916, 'An Oasis in the Desert', baby blues

Under a palm tree, Guy Haydon is frank in a letter to his mother.

Dear Mum,

... Your remarks about little Patricia make me more anxious than ever to see her, it is hard luck to own a kid about 6 months old and not have seen her, anyway she will be just at her most interesting age when we get back. I wonder if there is a hope of the war ending this year, it seems almost too good to think about . . .[3]

There is no time to think about it now, it is time for patrol. The second one today, the first drew distant fire, this one shall see Jacko get some in return. The letter is sealed and a rider bears it in a haversack with the other mail, its destination half a world away.

•

Half a world away, at *Bloomfield*, Bon Haydon's every waking thought is of Guy. *He's not here. He is so far away. Is he still safe?* And yet his presence in her life is constant, given that she is living with his parents on the glorious stud he grew up on and will hopefully return to, and her world is their daughter, Patricia, five months old and queen of the whole farm. Pat has her father's eyes, if only he could be here to see her, and hold her. Every day she waits hopefully for a new letter from him, but on this morning a different type of message arrives, far faster than a letter. It is a telegram, delivered by a grim-faced postmaster who has no sooner handed it over than he touches his cap, and is gone in a cloud of dust. Hastily, Bon opens it, her eyes devouring the contents as her heart races, and fastens on the one sentence that matters:

GUY KILLED IN ACTION[4]

Bon Haydon, holding the babe Patricia, falls to the floor. She weeps as baby Patricia wails; crying for a reason she does not know; for a father she never will know. Their world ended, from a message tapped out half a world away.

•

In England, the Australians flying for the Royal Flying Corps against the Germans in France continue to excel to such a point that Whitehall actively pursues more of them.

So much so that the Secretary of the War Office formally writes to AIF Headquarters in France, noting that, 'in view of the exceptionally good work which has been done in the Royal Flying Corps by Australian-born officers, and the fact that the Australian temperament is specially suited to the flying services, it has been decided to offer 200 commissions in the Special Reserve of the Royal Flying Corps to officers, non-commissioned officers, and men of the Australian Force . . .'[5]

Though serving with British forces, not Australian, Lieutenant Alaric Boor makes his third application to fly. Twice his Commanding Officer has declined to allow him to leave, on the grounds that he was too valuable to the war effort here. And he has a point, for Boor, both at the Western Front and then stationed at Salonika, had more than done his duty and continues to fight despite sustaining quite a serious wound to his arm in Greece. But, the chance to fly, to be a cavalier of the sky?

British Prime Minister David Lloyd George will sum up the spirit of it all, singularly well. 'The heavens are their battlefields,' he will say of these pilots. 'They are the cavalry of the clouds. High above the squalor . . . their daily, yes, their nightly struggles are like the Miltonic conflict between the winged hosts of light and of darkness.'[6]

It is simply irresistible for the young Australian and he quickly fills out his application.

His new Commanding Officer calls for him a short time later.

'I do not want to lose you,' he says frankly. 'But I will not stand in your light. I will let your application go through.'[7]

Hurrah!

Within days, he is out on the grassy field of the Salonika aerodrome just to test how he will react to being in the air.

He is not long in finding out.

The earth falls away, even his stomach does flip-flops and the howling wind stings his eyes and tugs at his shirt, and . . . and . . . *and oh God, what now?*

Just as Alaric is starting to settle down, the bloody pilot 'banks' the plane. The young Australian would vomit but the bastard in front might bank again and it would go straight back in. Flight theory is one thing; the lunge and plunge of actual planes another.

'I was not expecting it,' he will write to his parents, 'and when I saw the wings almost at right angles to earth, I thought very heavily and was looking for a soft place to drop . . . I was very sick, although I swallowed my heart a few times, especially in the first "bank", and when we raced to earth from 4000 feet at a rate of 72 miles per hour, I was up for 35 minutes. I was slightly deaf when I reached earth, but it was due to the sudden change from 4000 feet at the rate of 72 miles per hour . . .'8

It is terrifying, it is disorientating, it is . . . wonderful! He quickly signs up for more.

•

Could Guy Haydon be the modern day's answer to Lazarus? For he has risen again! It has taken some time to sort out; and enough confirmation cables to sink a U-boat, but Guy is alive!

That terrible telegram that made his bride faint? Well, it turns out the name GUY was supposed to be the name GERRY. Who is Gerry? Gerry is the now dead brother of Guy's sister-in-law, Grace, who, sobbing in grief, had sent a telegram to Bon Haydon and transposed the similar names! Death by typo is very rare, but the victim can be revived by a stroke of the pen!

Bon's relief, and that of the Haydon family, is bountiful – while being keenly aware that while correcting the error has magically brought Guy back to life, the Aplin family is plunged into precisely the misery from which they have escaped. Gerry Aplin, Grace's brother, had paid the ultimate price in the first burst of the Battle of Poziéres on the Western Front. Guy lives today, but another battle may come on the morrow.

23 October 1916, the Hejaz, Lawrence leans Arabic

For Captain Thomas Edward Lawrence, things have moved with remarkable speed, and a genuine Arab rising has arisen in part from his artful advocacy, a collusion of causes, and the longing of centuries married to the instant British desire to beat the damned Turks. The key had been to convince Sharif Hussein, the Emir of Mecca, to put his weight behind it. It began with a solid British promise of support for an independent Arab state under Hussein's reign, based around Syria, Hejaz and Mesopotamia. 'King Hussein' – as Lawrence always refers to him with his own British masters, to capitalise on their natural predisposition to bend their knee to kings – had agreed and made it known that he wishes those loyal to him to join this uprising against the Ottoman Empire. He helps raise the armed Arabs that Lawrence needs to join his rising band. In fact, King Hussein had signalled his support for the Arab Revolt in iconic fashion, going out onto his balcony in Mecca with his rifle and firing a single shot into the air, the agreed symbolic signal that the revolt had begun and that the King himself had fired the first shot.

The British Intelligence officer has been intimately involved from the first, transforming himself from detached British ascetic to passionate Arab in name and garb, and after intense negotiations not only had a written British guarantee been forthcoming – promising that all the desired lands bar the Holy Land could be under King Hussein's rule – Lawrence personally acts as a liaison between the Arab rebels and the British forces, although which one of these he is loyal to at this point confuses even him. His greatest breakthrough has come on an intelligence-gathering mission to Hejaz, the desert region around the holy city of Mecca that is a province of the Ottoman Empire with 4000 Turkish soldiers garrisoned there to make sure it remains so. And yet it is here that Lawrence determines that it is King Hussein's third son, Prince Feisal – a 38th generation direct descendant of Muhammad himself – who is the best man to lead the revolt. (Mecca itself fell to Hussein's men in just six days, what better auspice can there be to smite an Empire, than that?)

The young and charismatic Arab prince proves to be that rarest of things, an aristocrat with ambition. Prince Feisal will not rest on the vagaries of succession, he is determined to forge his own fate. Lawrence sees at once that this is a man who would be king and could be, with a helping self-interested hand from the British Empire. A deal is struck, one of the blizzard of promises that Lawrence makes and is determined on his honour to fulfil. Lawrence will organise the delivery of weaponry, ammunition and money for Feisal, in return for a role as 'adviser' on just which part of the Ottoman Empire is attacked to serve British interests. Once they have defeated the Turks and the Ottoman Empire falls, the new Arab state will be established, with Damascus as its capital!

And one more thing – Lawrence is to ride with Feisal and his men, and actually participate in the attacks himself. It is unheard of for an

Englishman, but none have ever seen or heard of an Englishman like Lawrence, five foot five inches of English eccentricity and effete energy.

In short order, 'Lawrence of Arabia', as he will become known, is able with Feisal's leadership to turn muttered and muted Arab ambitions into the open as a raging 'Arab Revolt' takes form.

'I believed in the Arab movement,' Lawrence will note, 'and was confident before I ever came, that in it was the idea to tear Turkey into pieces.'[9]

Their job now is to continue uniting every Arab tribe they can reach that is willing to take on the Turks, and turn them into a real force – striking their oppressors from all angles when they least expect it, before melting back into the desert. The Turks have always relied on the Arabs to fight each other, now quarrels are put aside to vanquish a foe, a victory that will restore the birthright of their ancestors.

'Going native', Lawrence dresses like the nomadic Hejaz Bedouin, rides camels with them, eats like them (using his right hand only), acts like them, and is *of* them. The English have a centuries-old practice of standing apart, of behaving as though they were still in Britain no matter how far the Empire has flung them. Lawrence is a man apart from the British, determined to join with those he is sent to observe. As one who has been studying and working in these ancient lands for the last six years, he already speaks Arabic, but now embarks on total assimilation, and for good reason.

'If you can wear Arab kit when with the tribes you will acquire their trust and intimacy to a degree impossible in uniform,' he will advise other British officers attempting the same. 'It is however dangerous and difficult . . . You will be an actor in a foreign theatre, playing a part day and night, and for a dangerous stake. Complete success, which is when the Arabs forget your strangeness and speak naturally before you, counting you one of themselves, is perhaps only attainable in character.'

And it requires more than a half-hearted effort.

'If you wear Arab things at all, go all the way. Leave your English friends and customs on the coast, and fall back on Arab habits entirely.'[10]

•

The response of the Turks to the Arab revolution is a cross between rage, dismay and distress, starting with, as Djemal Pasha would call it, 'the secret betrayal of Sherif Hussein (who thereby committed an unforgiveable sin against the Mussulman world) ... [and] divided the two Mussulman brother nations, Arabs and Turks; he made the former the slave of the English and French and forced the latter to fight a hopeless fight against the most pitiless foe ... The rising was a serious blow to the campaign against the Canal.'[11]

To fight this kind of ancient war against those they have repressed for so long, even while fighting a modern war against powerful enemies who seek to repress *them*, is every bit as draining as the British hoped it would be. This Great War will spark more than one revolution. The question for the Arabs is whether they can turn this current revolt into an actual revolution and achieve genuine freedom and independence – such is the promise of all revolutions at their beginning.

Winter 1916, London, *Daily Mail* fail

It is a reflection of both the times and the weather closing in that – so well has the Light Horse been doing under his command, even as the coming rains of November will make movement in the desert imposs- ible – General Chauvel is able to head off to London on six weeks leave to see his wife and children.

True, it is a trip that displeases Granville Ryrie, who writes to his wife, 'General Chauvel has gone on leave to England and Chaytor has got command of the division for that time. If it comes to a permanent command I will protest. I have no chance of promotion as long as Chauvel keeps his position and he is an awful old woman.'[12]

But never mind. The visit proves to be a delight, and for Chauvel being with his family is a reminder of what they are fighting for in the first place.

The shock comes during the return journey while on the train from Paris to Marseilles, where a frigate awaits to whisk him and some fellow officers across the Mediterranean. For, what's this? It is a copy of the *Daily Mail* and it contains a report from the British Commander-in-Chief in Egypt, General Archibald Murray, exulting – rightly – the victory registered by his forces at the Battle of Romani, four months previously.

There is one problem, and it is rather galling.

General Murray barely mentions the Australian and New Zealand Mounted Division, when they had suffered 90 per cent of the casualties, and done most of the heavy lifting! And, not that Chauvel is remotely vainglorious about these things, but equally he can't help but notice that while the same article lists honours accorded to officers for their involvement with the battle, there is no trace of one 'Harry Chauvel', while dozens of British officers who had not been remotely close to the action are being *showered* with medals.

'I cannot understand,' Chauvel writes to his wife, 'why the old man cannot do justice to those to whom he owed so much. The whole thing is so absolutely inconsistent with what he had already cabled. I am afraid my men will be very angry with what they see.'[13]

He does have one theory, on the quiet.

'It is because the men do not and will not salute,' he will tell Henry Gullett, the Official Historian. 'They make enemies of headquarters officers who are responsible for communiques.'[14]

After all, Murray had already acknowledged the truth, officially – in messages of appreciation to the troops – that the bloodiest of the Battle of Romani had been done and won by the Australian and New Zealand Mounted Division.

That is certainly the view of his men, who are equally appalled when they read similar accounts. 'We never realised what mistakes a paper could make until we read the report of the latest stunts,' Trooper Rupert Fenwicke of Gunnedah writes home. 'I'll never take any notice of them in future.'[15]

After all, the casualty numbers bloody well speak for themselves!

In a total British and Dominions force of 14,000 there had been 1130 casualties at Romani, of whom 930 had come from the Anzac Mounted Division. There can be no argument with numbers like that.

And the English General has sent a report to Australia's Federal Cabinet, heaping praise on both Chauvel and his Troopers: 'Its commander and all his officers and men have every right to be proud of their achievements. They have the satisfaction of knowing that for each one of their own casualties they accounted for ten of the enemy. I wish to place on record my warm appreciation of the services of the Commonwealth dominion troops.'[16]

Fine words, but Murray's private mail reveals a generally low regard of the Australian soldiers as people, having already written to Sir William Robertson, Chief of the Imperial General Staff, that the Australians are 'from a physical point of view a magnificent body of men' but they have 'no idea of ordinary decency or self control'.[17]

The Australians have an equally low opinion of him, at least the few that actually deal with him. There is a pomposity about this British officer that grates; an air of superiority that might be all right for a man who has brought up 100 runs on the board before lunch in a Test match, but for the life of them they can only recall 20 runs scored; most of them from sneaky, streaky French cuts.

All up, after Romani, Murray is on the nose with all Australians and New Zealanders for starters: regarded as just another Pommy who sees them as workhorses destined for the knackery, while giving awards to his own English show ponies.

The award-less Australians and Kiwis keep pushing on into the Sinai, side by side with their brassy British brethren, and are now bound more tightly than ever by the formal formation of 'Desert Column', a newly created formation under the command of the generally well-regarded General Sir Philip Chetwode, who has just arrived from England.

General Chetwode is the commander of this force of massed mounted advance units of 10,000 Troopers of the Egyptian Expeditionary Force and their horses, together with two divisions of infantry. Following the lead of Napoleon's realisation that camels are superior for moving men and supplies over long distances in the desert – they can go five days without water, walking up to 40 miles a day with a load of 350 pounds. Also, they are a lot less frisky under fire than horses, perhaps from stupidity, meaning that when the unit dismounts one man can handle a dozen camels, allowing more men to fight. It is for this reason an 'Imperial Camel Corps' has been formed, made up of British Empire soldiers not only familiar with those difficult animals but happy to work with them, including more than a few Western Australians.

Prime Minister Lloyd George has taken over from Lord Asquith, and he is determined to push into the Holy Land to boost British morale, soak up more Ottoman resources and fracture German focus. Chetwode's job will be to lead that charge. His Desert Column is composed of those units within the Egyptian Expeditionary Force best equipped to tackle the challenges of the desert, including Chauvel's Anzac Mounted Division, the 5th Mounted Brigade (Yeomanry), and the 42nd and 52nd Infantry Divisions, the Camel Corps and the Royal Flying Corps 5th Wing. (Indeed, with both camels and aeroplanes in the mix, the tactics and technology span millennia and continents.) There is also an Australian-manned Light Car Patrol – six Model T Fords with Lewis guns mounted on them.

No sooner has Chauvel returned to his troops than he and they are at the pointy end of Desert Column's spear pushing into the Turks' lower rump in the Sinai.

In short order Chauvel is to be found sitting beneath a palm tree with Brigadiers 'Fighting Charlie' Cox of the 1st and 'Hellfire Jack' Royston now heading the 3rd, planning their next move, on how to take the large coastal settlement of El Arish, just 15 miles to the east. There are just three officers sitting comfortably going over the map, but four living beings sipping water as they do so. For the fourth is Royston's current horse, who helps herself every now and then with a languid tongue to get some precious drops. Royston does not mind at all.

Clearly the horse agrees – we need the water supply at El Arish, sooner rather than later. There will be no argument from Hellfire Jack, for there never is when it comes to possible attacks. And there will equally be no argument from 'Fighting Charlie' Cox, who earned his nickname for equally aggressive instincts during the Boer War.

As it happens, there will be no Battle of El Arish, as the Turks have abandoned it by the time the Desert Column – after a long night-march – descends at dawn on 21 December 1916. The Turks have left seemingly just one stray dog to hold the fort.

It proves to be a 'fairly large town built of limestone bricks in the Egyptian style'[18] and its previous 2000 defenders – it is soon revealed to Chauvel by a report from his aerial reconnaissance men – have escaped to build up the defences of the Turkish outpost of Magdhaba some 25 miles inland.

Today, at least, there is the Levant's most precious commodity to enjoy, in abundance. At the nearby ocean, both the Troopers and their weary horses can bathe with delight. And when it comes to drinking . . .

'Water of the best variety is found at a depth of three to five feet,' one Trooper notes, 'only 100 yards from the sea. It is remarkable that such fresh water is found so close [to] the briny. It is so sweet the troops prefer it to the inferior water we are issued with.'[19]

December 1916, El Arish in sight, big nobs and broomsticks

As soon as the following morning, 22 December 1916, General Chetwode, having rushed forward by ship from Port Said, arrives on the beach at El Arish at 10 o'clock to consult with Chauvel, and together they decide on the next plan of attack.

A formal kind of chappie is this Chetwode, at least from the Australians' point of view. If he could be an inanimate object, he'd be a starched white shirt. Chetwode has never met a formality he did not like, a protocol he did not minutely observe and is in all things the very model of a modern stickler general. All of which means he is perfectly constructed to be an object of fun for Australian Troopers, who, as a breed, eschew formality with an enthusiasm only to be matched by the way they chew protocol and spit it out. On this fine blazing morn, Chetwode happens to preen and prance past some sons of the Southern Cross.

'Where did you learn to ride like that, mate?' one Australian Trooper calls out cheerily to him as he passes.

'What do you mean?' the General replies, gobsmacked at the colonial's infernally familiar approach.

'Nothing, just that you and your horse look like you've got broomsticks up your bums.'[20]

What can the Englishman do? Neither he nor his entourage could chase the brute down, as he would quickly disappear into the maze of Australian tents. Nor could they give him the satisfaction of loudly remonstrating, as it would only demonstrate their impotence. All they can do for the moment thus is glare and ride off.

But it is not just this Trooper's words. As a breed – or is that half-breed? – the Australians are a real problem whenever he rides about their camps, inevitably followed by – as the Official Historian will record it – his 'mounted orderlies whose smart dress and precise and stiff horsemanship were in strong contrast to the appearance of the casual and desert-worn Australians'.

It does not take long before he decides he must take action.

'Not only do your men fail to salute me when I ride through your camps,' he protests to General Chauvel, 'but they laugh aloud at my orderlies.'[21]

The horror. Will the formal charge be 'Giggling' or should the more severe 'Snickering with Intent' be used?

Chauvel makes the right noises, and keeps a straight face, but is not particularly fussed, most particularly when it comes to trying to get his Australians to fit in with everything the English officers want.

(Back in the Boer War when a senior British officer had tried to get his men to wear khaki helmets just like their English counterparts, Chauvel had declined in forthright fashion, 'We have quite lost our individuality – and our interest in further proceedings.'[22] In sum, we are a different breed, and do things a little differently, in this case diffidently.)

All that Chauvel truly cares about is his charges' fighting ability, rather than their saluting or sartorial elegance in martial wear. It is the Australian way, particularly in these parts, to have torn shirts, dirty shorts and not be particularly careful about saluting.

But, yes, General Chetwode, I will do what I can.

Later that night, the soldier most responsible turns up at Chetwode's grand tent with a bottle of liquor to say sorry, but Chetwode refuses to accept either the apology or the liquor.

A strange cove, did we say?

A little bemused, Chauvel writes to his wife that, while there was 'nothing wrong with the idea, [the Trooper] just picked the wrong tent'.[23]

Differences over formalities will remain, but Chauvel and Chetwode are happily of one mind when it comes to action: they will attack Magdhaba on the morrow, and the port town of El Arish will become the new advanced base. As Magdhaba has one of the key water supplies between here and Palestine – and even skirting them they can hardly leave 2000 Turks to the rear, ready to attack them – it is essential that it be occupied.

(One who is not impressed with all the movement, all the comings and goings or men and munitions in this exotic place by the Mediterranean is an ancient Sheikh, who through an interpreter says it reminds him of the time when he was no more than a toddler, back when Napoleon and his men had passed through in much the same manner – something that impresses those who don't do their sums enough to work out that his age would have to be nigh on *six* score years and ten for that to be the case!)

The orders go out, and immediately there is movement all around. The chance to finally push the Turks completely out of the Sinai is at hand, and the Promised Land is just ahead!

Within the hour, carts are being loaded, horses fed and watered till they can be fed and watered no more, and Chauvel's forces are on the move, carefully following their scouts, who are steering by the stars – thankfully in plentiful supply in this extraordinary land.

(Left behind of the Australian forces are the 2nd Light Horse Brigade, their commander General Granville Ryrie reporting to his wife, 'Darling Mick', that, 'we are all very wild about it'[24].)

The Australian and New Zealand Mounted Division, accompanied by the Imperial Camel Corps Brigade, 6000 men in all, move through the night, along the dusty white clay floor of Wadi el Arish, with luminescent white cliffs on each side that capture the moonlight. As they have learnt to do when travelling long distances, they ride for 40 minutes, lead their horses for 10, rest for 10, and go on. While riding they are observed to engage in a 'continual concertina motion'[25] as the Troopers expand and contract on one another; tiredness and terrain the two main culprits. Behind them come the straining crews of the Somerset and Inverness Artillery batteries together with the Royal

Horse Artillery, the Hong Kong and Singapore Artillery, their horses dragging their 10-pounder guns.

Dawn finds them more weary than ever, but at least arriving on the fringes of Magdhaba, with Chauvel quick to climb a knoll on the northern outskirts of the settlement and bring his field-glasses to bear, particularly on the small fires which surely mark the Turkish outposts. The sound of a dog barking in the distance perhaps indicates at least one being is aware of their presence, but otherwise all is quiet in this desperately dusty dawn as the smoke generated by the fires in Magdhaba covers it in a low blanket.

But Chauvel can clearly see it is protected by six heavily manned 'redoubts' – the small forts of stone, brick and earthworks that the Ottoman Empire specialise in, usually as their first line of defence before the larger fortifications. Those redoubts are connected by deep trenches, which allow the Turks to move from defensive point to defensive point without ever exposing themselves to fire.

At least in working out how to crack this citadel, Chauvel is blessed to have one thing that no previous army commander has had in taking this ancient territory; eyes in the sky, one of whom used to be a Light Horse Trooper.

Flying Officer Ross Smith, the warehouseman from Adelaide who had done so well with the machine gun for the 3rd Light Horse Regiment at both Gallipoli and Romani, had changed course upwards from the days when he was a Trooper. Just qualified as an observer, and on his way to being a pilot, he is excited to be flying on this day with the newly formed Australian Flying Corps' No. 1 Squadron.

Soaring over Magdhaba at 6.30 am, the airmen serve a dual purpose. Not only can they spot where the Turkish defenders are concentrated, but their planes draw the enemy's fire, exposing where their artillery batteries are positioned. Smith's pilot on this morning is his mate, Flight Lieutenant Eric Roberts, who expertly manoeuvres their bird as close as they dare – while both taking fire and giving it – and now Roberts is able to use the new-fangled radio connecting him to the ground HQ for the first time, to report: 'The bastards are there all right!'[26]

After a few more fly-overs, Roberts and Smith decide to give a detailed report in person and soon land on the desert floor, to borrow horses and ride to Chauvel. As one Trooper notes, 'It was a queer sight to see the airmen in their flying togs galloping about on horses for a change.'[27]

After Flight Lieutenant Roberts personally informs Chauvel of the disposition of the Turkish troops, the Australian commander gives the orders. Royston's 3rd Brigade will link with the New Zealanders and attack from the north, while Brigadier General Charlie Cox's 1st Brigade and the Camel Brigade will move in from the north-west and west respectively.

Attack!

The artillery – again for the first time, being informed by wireless from the planes of where to direct their fire – opens up and, before the billowing smoke and dust has even had a chance to drift, the men of the 1st Light Horse Brigade are the first to charge in, fire, and work in ever closer until they can dismount, racing forward and bringing their bayonets to bear.

Artillery booms, the machine guns ceaselessly stutter, the rifles fire and the air is filled with smoke, dust and shouted orders and imprecations.

Still positioned on his high knoll, Chauvel is able to closely follow the slow progress – for in truth, the enemy is well dug in and are exacting a heavy toll from the attackers – and gives orders accordingly.

When one of the planes reports a body of Turks getting away to the east, the acting Commanding Officer of the 10th Australian Light Horse Regiment, Major Horace Robertson, all of 22 years old, is ordered by Royston to take some of his best men to cut them off. Off they gallop in a wide sweep, and indeed descend on the 300 fleeing Turks like the wolf on the fold.

Completely dismayed at the youth of his principal captor, the commanding Turkish officer seeks confirmation that the unshaven Robertson, covered from head to toe in dust, and without a ribbon or a sign of rank upon him, is actually in command.

Assured by all the grinning Australians that is the case, the Turk, it is reported, hands over his sword 'with the air of a man resigned to a violent death at the hands of savages'.[28]

It has really come to this.

Meanwhile, the 1st Brigade under 'Fighting Charlie' Cox have now pushed to the fore. The Troopers get to within two miles of the enemy's defences before coming under artillery fire, whereupon, following Cox's hand-signals, his Troopers move into artillery formation – far more spread out than before, but now moving at full gallop to present a difficult target. Geysers of sand shoot up all around them, and shrapnel fells a few, but after another half-mile, the rifle and machine-gun fire is so thick it is time for the attack to change tack.

'No cover being available for horses on my front,' Cox will recount, 'I swung the Brigade to the right and gained cover in a rugged, blind Wadi at a point about 1900 yards north-west of enemy redoubt.'[29]

They don't call him 'Fighting Charlie' for nothing.

Barking orders, Cox drives his Troopers forward, using whatever cover they can from the wadis and dissolute dunes, while also bringing his machine guns into play, even while the big guns of their accompanying battery start to rain shells down on the Turkish defenders. His men hit the desert floor and bring their rifles to bear, though the sand is so hot in the midst of this shimmering day that it blisters their elbows.

The machine guns chatter, the shells explode, shrapnel flies and men die, even as the Australians push ever closer, able to bring ever more fire. Just before 2 pm, Redoubt No. 1 falls to Cox and his men, with nearly 100 prisoners taken!

In the meantime, however, the 2nd Light Horse Regiment are making heavy weather of subduing No. 2 Redoubt, and they are running out of time.

For the key problem is water.

None is readily available.

The fact that the Army engineers had failed to find any at the nearby settlement of Lahfan – for those wells had been destroyed by the Turks – makes the situation urgent, as the nearest water is now back at El Arish, on the coast.

Does General Chauvel have any choice?

He does not, and so shortly after 2 o'clock in the afternoon he gives the order to his three brigades.

'As enemy is still holding out and horses must be watered, the action will be broken off and the forces withdrawn. Each brigade will be responsible for its own protection during the withdrawal. Hour of withdrawal to begin at 1500.'[30]

The order comes to Cox just as he and his men are about to launch a do-or-die bayonet charge on Redoubt No. 2.

'Take that damned thing away,' says Cox[31], 'and let me see it for the first time in half-an-hour.'[32]

What a risk he is taking!

But Cox is backing himself and his men. He senses victory is possible, and after grimly giving the order – 'Fix bayonets!' – launches his troops forthwith, together with those of the Imperial Camel Corps who have come to the fore.

It is brutal, it is bloody and above all it is brave. With the bit between their teeth, Cox's men charge forward and are quickly engaged in hand-to-hand fighting with the Turks who are overwhelmed – in both senses of the word.

Within 30 minutes Redoubt No. 2 has fallen – with 130 soldiers and seven officers, including a shattered Kideir Bey, the commanding officer of the garrison – taken prisoner.

'Now,' Trooper Roy Dunk will write home, 'when you are in a show like this and being fired on at point blank range and there are fellows falling after being shot – perhaps your best mate – you don't feel like kissing the enemy when you get there even if they have got their hands up; but that is almost what happened on this occasion. Within seconds of reaching the trenches our blokes were shaking hands with the Jackos and handing around their cigarettes. The Turks got the greatest surprise they had ever got because they thought they were about to be killed.'[33]

Shortly thereafter, in part due to 'savage' Major Robertson and his men of the 10th Light Horse launching their own savage charge on the next redoubt along, the rest of the defences begin to unravel.

Not to be outdone, Hellfire Jack Royston is in the thick of it with the best. Nothing can stop him and it will be officially recorded that, even when galloping up to a Turkish trench to find himself covered by five enemy rifles, Royston does not blink, but only roars:

'Lahla izibhamu zakho futhi uzinikele, noma ngizodubula!'

'The old fighter excitedly raised his cane and, knowing no Turkish, shouted at the riflemen in Zulu; whereupon the Turks, impressed with the demonstration, dropped their rifles and held up their hands.'[34]

The remaining garrison of Magdhaba surrenders . . . together with their precious water.

The whole battle is all over at 4.40 pm, with 1280 Turkish prisoners taken.

By dusk the Australians have the settlement secured, their prisoners under guard, and their own wounded made comfortable in mud huts, warmed by fires and with ambulance men and a guard around them, ready to be taken by more men of the Ambulance Corps tomorrow. The rest of them must now head back through the night – for while there is some water indeed at Magdhaba, there is not enough to sustain another 6000 men, with their horses.

But oh, the exhaustion!

Riding back from Magdhaba to El Arish, the Troopers of the Australian Light Horse are enveloped in such thick dust, while so deprived of sleep and so shattered by riding 90 miles . . . that strange things happen.

'Hundreds of men saw the queerest visions,' Ion Idriess will chronicle, 'weird looking soldiers were riding beside them, many were mounted on strange animals. Hordes walked right amongst the horses making not the slightest sound. The column rode through towns with lights gleaming from the shuttered windows of quaint buildings. The country was all waving green fields and trees and flower gardens.

'Numbers of our men are speaking of what they saw in a most interesting way. There were tall stone temples with marble pillars and swinging oil lamps – our fellows could smell the incense – and white mosques with stately minarets.'[35]

For some of the veterans who had arrived on the first slew of ships from Australia, it is all reminiscent of the 'ghostly desert town'[36] they had seen – complete with spires and big buildings, just kind of floating on the shimmer of the far horizon – when first they had ventured into these strange and ancient lands, heading up the Suez Canal. This time they have visited it up close, only for it to disappear once more. Again their collective feeling is confirmed – they are in a strange part of the world, a world that is . . . unworldly.

In the wee hours, a lone horseman charges to meet them, bursting with excitement. It proves to be none other than General Chetwode.

'Oh, you beauties!'[37] he cries, shaking the hands of some of the Australian Troopers within reach.

'The mounted men at Magdhaba,' he will note, 'had done what we had never known cavalry to do in the history of war: they had not only located and surrounded the enemy's position, but had gone down to it as infantry and carried fortified positions at the point of the bayonet.'[38]

The General's enthusiasm and gratitude is appreciated at the time, but not as much as what happens when they arrive back in camp at El Arish, as the Scots, who have just arrived, get up to pump water for the horses, allowing the victors of the Battle of Magdhaba to fall into their swags and sleep.

It is the day of Christmas Eve, they and their stunning steeds can at last rest; with Chauvel in awe of both man and beast. Of the latter, Chauvel will soon write to Australia's Minister for Defence: 'I have never ceased wondering how Australia has produced such a splendid lot of horses. During the fighting at Romani in the hottest month of the year, the horses of one regiment were without water for fifty-two hours . . . and during the raid on Magdhaba most of them were without water for thirty-six hours, having done fifty miles and been under the saddle all the time.'[39]

As to the holy day itself?

'And this is Christmas Day!' Ion Idriess exults. 'Caesar! Great Caesar! Which reminds me: we are very near to the land which gave Christmas to the world.'[40]

The good news is that, whatever happens from here, they will be better supplied, with Maurie Evans noting of all the *materiel* being brought in by landing craft coming from big ships, 'The place will soon be like Anzac.'[41]

And at least from now, the country will be a little easier on both the Troopers and their mounts.

For with the fall of the last of the Turkish strongholds and outposts in the Sinai, the forces of the British Empire move forward *en masse*, to the edge of the Holy Land – in fact to the border that separates Africa from Asia – and start to notice things are . . . different?

All day they have been going east, and, as they now push past one of Cleopatra's old camping grounds, they realise that instead of pushing through sand, they can actually make it shake with 'the rumbling of chariot wheels – eighteen pounders! The desert became harder.'[42]

Now that is a good sign, if the desert is harder that means sand is melding more with dirt, and their sinking tread may, might, no, dammit, *will* soon be a memory. Today's riders are a deputation of the Desert Column, the 2nd Light Horse Brigade and the New Zealand Mounted Rifles Brigade, accompanied by the big guns. A shout is heard ahead and each hand springs to its place on its rifle and awaits what must come: shellfire, a machine gun, a Turkish charge, but no, the only further sound is another yell and they can see the riders in front rise in their stirrups and point in delight. What on earth? It is not on earth, it's in it, now they can see.

'Scarlet poppies! Wild flowers and scarlet poppies. They might have been born of the very love of Antony and Cleopatra; we thought them as wonderful as if they had been.'[43]

Oh, but there is still more.

'At dawn we found ourselves in fine undulating grassy country,' another Trooper will recount. 'It was beautiful. Thousands of Light Horse and infantry practically bare of trees but covered in grass about a foot high with here and there patches of poppies, daisies or butter-cups . . . On the gentle slopes were flocks of sheep and herds of cattle as in days of old.'[44]

Their joy is transcendent, and is accompanied by the most perfect music imaginable – larks singing!

Those flowers and that grass, let alone the herds upon them, mean the endless desert must be at an end; it means water, it means solid ground, it means their horses are soon munching on the first fresh grass they have eaten since Australia. And here now, as they push on, is a patch of shade from an actual tree, and soon *trees*. Yes, the endless monotony of the desert is no more.

'A paddock of white daisies suddenly came into view ... what a relief after the everlasting sand to see grass, barley and wheat; these crops were almost ripe at the time.'[45]

In short order they see a stone wall! A house! Date palms! A lake! A bloody awful-tasting brinish mess of a lake, but it's water and their mounts won't quibble with the taste as they gulp it down.

In the words of 'Fighting Charlie' Cox, 'The hard going for the horses seemed almost miraculous after the months of sand, and as the shoes of the horses struck fire on the stones in the bed of the wadi, the men laughed with delight. Sinai was behind them.'[46]

Shortly after, a battle takes place some 10 miles to the north, right by the border town of Rafa, and for the first time it really looks like a place *worth* fighting for.

'At Rafa the whole countryside is one big barley field,' one Trooper records. 'The country is like a Garden of Eden after the desert ... There are miles of orchards [and] pomegranates, dates, figs, almonds, peaches, apricots, guavas, grapes, water melons and other fruits are all prolific.'[47]

And even chooks!

'We are beginning to think what with grass and floods and hen's eggs,' Ion Idriess notes, 'that we will soon be entering the land of "milk and honey".'[48]

The Desert Column begins its move on Rafa in the late afternoon, marching through the night to launch a surprise attack at dawn, before also moving forces around to the other side. Colonel Charles Mackesy, the commanding officer of the Auckland Rifles, is the first to cross the border, and does so alone, savouring the moment and piously thanking the Lord for allowing him to enter the Holy Land on such a mission as this.

And yet the Lord's presence is not apparent in the first instance. Part of the plan in sneaking up on the Turks in the ancient fortress of El Magruntein – surrounded by trenches and small redoubts – requires going through the actual village of Rafa. So far, so softly, softly, silent. But now the soldiers are spotted by some of the village women – many of them pregnant to Turkish soldiers, it will turn out – and a lot of the women begin ululating, as an unearthly, high-pitched, trilling howl dashes the dawn.

In the first action, the New Zealanders are able to storm and then swarm all around a trench, to capture both Turkish soldiers and a few stunned German officers. The most senior of the latter tells Mackesy in passable English that while the Kiwis are impressive, not even they will be able to finish the job and overcome the heavily fortified position.

'Huh, all right, we'll see,' Mackesy replies, bemused. 'We're going to have a go – tell you later on.'[49]

True, it is not quite Henry V's St Crispin's day speech, but it is the Kiwis' understated way of going about things. Just get on with it, and we can chat later.

Sure enough, as the battle proceeds throughout the day, the New Zealand Mounted Rifles Brigade – encompassing the Auckland, Wellington and Canterbury Mounted Rifles regiments – is outstanding. Still, late in the afternoon, things seem to have stalled. After galloping around the entire perimeter of Rafa, not even Hellfire Jack Royston can see an opening, and with a scouting report that a large troop of Turkish reinforcements has been spotted coming their way, General Chetwode gives orders for the attack to be abandoned and actually heads back to El Arish himself, leaving at 4.25 pm.

Major Henry Whitehorn of the Auckland Mounted Rifles doesn't care to hear that and, rising out of the line and yelling for his men to follow him, charges forward. Two of the men who follow, Captain Herrick and Corporal Ben Draper of the Wellington Mounted Rifles, have a Lewis gun which they use in novel fashion. While Herrick concentrates on firing it, Draper uses it like a hose, spraying along the entirety of the key Turkish trench.

Royston can bear it no more, yelling to his own troops of the 3rd Light Horse Brigade, 'Attack at once or those NZ bastards will take the lot!'[50]

The 9th Australian Light Horse Regiment are immediately to the fore, as Chauvel shuts down the artillery for fear of hitting his own men who are now getting to grips. 'It was a marvellous sight to see them. With bayonets fixed and cheering like mad, rush the position.'[51] This redoubt too soon falls, as the Turkish resistance can resist no more, while the cameleers continue to attack from the south.

Rafa falls just before dusk, and the same German officer asks Mackesy how they had done it!

The short answer is . . . they had a go.

With the fall of Rafa, Egypt and its Sinai Peninsula is all but free of the Turks for the first time in 400 years. The forces of the British Empire are now on the doorstep of the Biblical land of Palestine, and General Murray has discovered, as he puts it in his report to London, 'In this mounted force we have a magnificent instrument.'[52]

The obvious question begs.

'Are we to invade Palestine?' Ion Idriess and his fellow Troopers ask themselves with rising excitement. 'With the taking of Rafa, we have cleared Egypt and the Sinai of the Turk. So what next? Only the desert answers, which seems all whispers in this land which was ancient when Christ was a child.'[53]

This is, in fact, the very question being examined by their political masters in Britain at the War Cabinet: just how far should they keep going? Might it even be possible to take back the whole Holy Land, including Jerusalem, and push on to take the second most important city of the Ottoman Empire, Damascus?

In the meantime, there is something else new under the sun. When some suspicious Bedouins are taken prisoner – you can never tell which side they are on at any given time, so best to arrest, and sort out later – it is discovered that one of them is carrying a newly issued proclamation from the Turks bearing a warning: 'The Sharif of Mecca [Hussein] has revolted against the Turks, and taken the town of Medina and gone on the side of the Christian dogs. All true Mussulmans must fight against the Christians lest they overrun the land and kill all the Bedouins in the hills.'[54]

Some of the Troopers have heard of the Arab Revolt. This is the first sign that it is having some effect.

●

The picks swing and the men sing. More than 10,000 labourers sweat freely in the blistering sun as the pipeline they are building slowly pushes its way north across the shimmering sands of the Sinai, accompanying the railway line that keeps pace beside it. For obvious reasons, it is the pipeline that sets the pace and not the other way around – for like everything else in the desert, water wins, thirst dies.

Dig faster! Everything must be ready for when we make our big push on the Turks in the summer.

(In the wake of our defeat at Gallipoli, it has become clear that the Turks – with 100,000 soldiers free to move elsewhere – are feeling newly aggressive, and are likely to make a renewed push on the Suez Canal. The Turkish leader, Enver Pasha, has even stated, 'The conviction resulting from this enterprise, is that the campaign against Egypt will take place.')[55]

As officious as he is efficient, Chetwode is not just Old School, but a little superior about it, given that his old school is Eton, and his aristocratic family has a history of high military service dating back centuries.

He looks both distinguished and sad, rather like a man who is perpetually winning second place in Lord Kitchener lookalike competitions, and for the life of him cannot work out why, particularly with his imposing moustache. Despite his pomposity, however, Chetwode at least leads by example and displays an endless enthusiasm for getting things done, mixed with a relentless rigour in insisting that they are done *right*.

The task of bringing water to the desert obsesses him, as he rides and strides the sands each day, a one-man train of enthusiasm, egging each man onwards with the rail-line they are laying, the railway competing with the pipeline as to which can snake further into the desert.

•

The issue of the approach taken by Australian Troopers to British officers has not gone away.

'We are getting it hot about not saluting officers,' Ion Idriess records in his diary. 'A man would need an automatic arm. We have been told, too, that the disgraceful Australian soldiers will not be allowed to go to France if they do not salute officers in the streets. Bow-wow!'[56]

But, truly?

It's not just the Troopers of the Australian Light Horse who are disinclined to show deference to their English betters. Sometimes it seems the Walers feel much the same.

On one excursion to a Pommy camp, on escort duty, Trooper Chook Fowler ties his Waler to a post where one such thoroughbred is also tethered, only to have a Yeomanry Trooper running after him, yelling with some anger: 'Do you want your horse *killed*? That's the Major's horse and he will kill anything tied near!'

'Don't worry,' Fowler replies, 'that pony can look after himself.'

There is a commotion behind them.

Sure enough, the Major's horse has lined up the Waler and is now lashing out viciously with both hind feet. Like a middle-weight boxer bemused by the wild swings of a heavyweight blow-hard, the Waler comes up on his hind feet and easily sways away from the lashing feet, before he comes in 'like a screaming stallion and with his teeth inflicted a gash in his opponent's side, at the same instant he swung around and planted both hooves in the same place'.

A lucky strike? Maybe, but when the English thoroughbred, with blood gushing from its side, tries again, it is for the same result!

'Like lightning he swung away and again missed the hooves of the major's horse,' Fowler will recount. 'My pony instantly reared up and repeated the process with teeth and hooves . . .'[57]

Beaten, the Major's horse retreats to the end of his *actual* tether.

'See what I mean?'[58] Fowler says mildly to the ashen-faced groom, and goes about his business. He loves that horse.

•

More eyes in the sky?

These ones include Australian eyes, those of Flying Officer Ross Smith, whose pilot for the day is already a legend of the Australian Flying Corps' No. 1 Squadron, Flight Lieutenant Frank McNamara, as they head out on an initial sortie to the Turkish outpost of Beersheba. An attempt that morning had failed because of too much cloud, but this afternoon the way is clear and, in the company of seven other planes, they are able to swoop over the outpost and drop bombs, watching closely as the Turkish troops below dive for their trenches. For Smith, who had been in the thick of the action at Gallipoli and then Romani as an unmounted Trooper of the Australian Light Horse, there is a certain savage joy in causing such havoc, a confirmation that he has done the right thing joining the Flying Corps. Beersheba itself looks . . . isolated, an exceedingly small and ancient settlement right out there in the desert. It is a relief when McNamara turns the BE2c – a two-seater biplane – back to their base at Mustabig, and they see the green of the coastal strip around Gaza again.

•

Well, it's something.

After the outrage of General Archibald Murray's lack of recognition of the Australians at the Battle of Romani, and the battles since, there had been speculation that General Chauvel himself would be recognised in the New Year's Day Honours List. That had not happened, but with the rumbling growing from Australian quarters now comes a letter from the English General.

19 January 1917

To : General Chauvel

I am glad to inform you that your services and the gallantry of your division at El Arish, Magdhaba and Rafa should be recognised by appointing you a K.C.M.G.

I send you and your division my sincerest congratulations

Archibald Murray[59]

Strange, that there is no mention of what they had done at the Battle of Romani? No concession that Murray had been wrong to so slight Chauvel's men as to barely mention them in his public pronouncements?

Still, it is at least something to be knighted, and Chauvel takes it as belated recognition of himself and his Troopers.

•

The first reports are bad, and the detailed reports are worse.

Djemal Pasha and Colonel Kress von Kressenstein are now alarmed to see just how extraordinarily quickly the English are constructing their railway and pipeline. It seems unbelievable, but the photos are undeniable. Aerial reconnaissance photographs show both the tracks and the pipeline advancing towards Gaza by 'two kilometres almost every day'[60], like a menacing snake slithering through the desert sand to get in striking distance of its prey.

With the blessing of Enver Pasha, who visits the Palestine Front in mid-February 1917, Djemal Pasha decides to withdraw the Ottoman forces to a defensive line stretching from Gaza on the coast, south-east to Beersheba in the desert, which he views as 'the natural frontier between the desert and the inhabited regions'.

His reasoning is straightforward.

'I decided to hold that front and prevent the English from breaking through at any cost by concentrating all the Turkish forces there. The greatest advantage of this position was that it could not be turned, as the right flank rested on the sea and the left on the desert. Moreover, as long as we were holding these defenses, the English were compelled to remain in the desert, while we were in a region which could be described as cultivated.'[61]

Djemal Pasha orders Kress von Kressenstein to 'defend this position'[62] at all costs. Keep the enemy in the waterless sea of sand.

February 1917, Huntingdonshire, England, with the 20 Training Squadron, escaping the surly bonds of Earth

It is, of course, one thing to be selected to train as a pilot with the Royal Flying Corps and another to be judged as being made of the right stuff to actually be given a licence to command a plane. This much is quickly made clear to Cadet Alaric Boor on his first day of training, as he and fellow cadets are obliged to stand to attention before the bristling Commanding Officer of 20 Training Squadron on this freezing winter's day.

And so begins several weeks of studying everything from aviation lore to military law, from high altitude flying to hygiene, from topography to types of German aircraft, and infantry training.

They are to be prepared as 'officers and gentlemen', and, after being issued with their cadet uniform, featuring a double-breasted tunic and a Glengarry cap with white puggaree, they at least look the part. If only Ida Rawlings, who has recently become his fiancée, could see him now!

Just a few weeks into training, the great day comes as, in the soupy morning light, Alaric Boor prepares to takes his place in no less than a BE2c training craft, for his inaugural flight. Walking with him across the big flat green field is his instructor, who climbs up to take his place in the for'ard seat, with the Western Australian carefully tucking in behind him.

Flying helmet fastened. Gloves on. A waggling of his joy-stick to ensure that all is as it should be, and the instructor waves to a mechanic hovering near, who comes and grips the huge, four-bladed wooden propeller.

'Switches off,' the mechanic calls.

'*Switches off,*' the instructor affirms.

Now, as the pilot pushes the throttle lever one-third forward, the mechanic pulls the propeller backwards a few turns, to suck petrol vapour into the combustion chamber.

'Contact!'

'*Contact!*'

With which, the mechanic grips the propeller with both hands and with a huge heave starts to turn it in the clockwise direction – which it grumpily resists, and stops. He tries a second time for the same result. But on the third attempt there is a small cough, a throaty gurgle, and now . . . the engine catches! In seconds the motor is roaring like a lion with a thorn in its paw, blowing angry blue-white smoke out of its nostrils as it positively shakes with restless energy. Behind, RFC Cadet Alaric Boor and his instructor are suddenly awash in the gusty gale sent their way by the whirling propeller. Still the pilot instructor lets the engine warm up, idling slowly, until the temperature gauge gets to 120 degrees Fahrenheit. And now, with a nod from the instructor, the ground crew removes the chocks from in front of the wheels, allowing the plane to do what it so desperately wants to do. First it trundles out onto the field, and, as the pilot pushes the lever forward to full throttle, it surges forth, getting ever faster, with the propeller whirling and flashing in the morning sunlight and the air flowing over the wings with such speed that they begin to vibrate, and hum, and *sing*, and . . . and now comes the moment.

Just as it seems like their life is about to end courtesy of hitting the trees at the end of the runway, the nose starts to lift! And now the endless bumping, rattling and unseemly shaking simply stops as they lift off! Most magical of all, Boor looks down to see the earth itself falling away as they start to move with the gods themselves. Even as the savagely cold wind slaps his face, his ears pop, his eyes stream, and the sides of his loosely strapped helmet stream behind him . . . they are . . . flying.

Flying!

Flying!

Good God Almighty.

This life has delivered him extraordinary experiences, great sensations, thrills that will warm the cockles of his soul forever more, but never anything like this. To enter the world of billowing white clouds, to see the sun shining more brightly than he has ever seen it, to look down and see a moving mosaic of fields, farms, towns and tiny laneways, where houses are tiny squares, and forests patches of moss, a vast map upon which seemingly little earth-bound ants called people are making their way . . . is like nothing he has ever known. And he wants more of it.

•

Things have moved quickly, and now Lawrence of Arabia is right beside the son of King Hussein, Prince Feisal, at the head of a band of a hundred Arab tribesmen. They have been continually harassing and attacking Turkish military interests in the desert of Hejaz – on the eastern shores of the Red Sea to the south of Damascus – and most significantly boasting the Holy Cities of Medina and Mecca. Their principal target is the Hejaz Railway, an attempt by the Ottoman Empire to bind its far-flung empire closer together, starting with connecting Damascus to Medina by rail – along the pilgrims' route – a thousand miles to the south.

On this day, Lawrence gets to the edge of a large sand dune just in time to see 50 of his horsemen charging down a slope straight at the Turks at the bottom. Of course the Turks fire back, and two or three of the Arabs go down but, as Lawrence will recount, 'the rest thundered forward at marvellous speed, and the Turkish infantry . . . finally broke before the rush'.[63]

'Come on,' Lawrence's companion screams at him and the two charge down their own sand-dune slope after the fleeing Turks, Lawrence astride his camel, a racer, Naama. In fact, so fast is Naama that Lawrence is soon ahead of the others and coming at the Turks from their flank. Lawrence uses his revolver to bring some down, 'when suddenly my camel tripped and went down emptily upon her face, as though pole-axed', which sends Lawrence flying, landing with a heavy thud.

'I lay there, passively waiting for the Turks to kill me . . . I sat up and saw the battle over, and our men driving together and cutting down the last remnants of the enemy. My camel's body had lain behind me like a rock: and in the back of its skull was the heavy bullet of the fifth shot I fired.'[64]

The blooming *bad luck* of it!

Still, Lawrence is learning fast, and will soon become so proficient at blowing up bridges along the railway, he will even develop a methodology whereby, while they are 'scientifically shattered', they remain standing – meaning it will take even longer for the Turkish engineers to first totally bring them down, then clear them away, then rebuild. It is ingeniously difficult, much like Lawrence himself. It is the start of an embrace of guerrilla tactics that will come to dominate battles and shake an empire; the unconventional Lawrence married to the unconquerable Arabs. It is a reckoning that has just begun to be realised and on it rolls at a pace.

CHAPTER SIX

DEFEAT IN VICTORY

When thou goest out to battle against thine enemies, and seest horses, and chariots, and a people more than thou, be not afraid of them: for the LORD thy God is with thee, which brought thee up out of the land of Egypt.

Deuteronomy 20:1

The Australian Light Horseman was generally very quick in summing up a situation for himself. No doubt his early training in the wide spaces of the Australian bush had developed to an extraordinary degree his individuality, self reliance and power of observation; and the particularly mobile style of fighting he was called upon to take part in suited him and brought out his special qualities far more than any trench warfare would have done.[1]

General Sir Harry Chauvel, in his introduction to
The Desert Column by Trooper Ion Idriess

Late February 1917, Deir el Belah, time to pay the piper

What is the stuff of empire?

It is to expand, the very *sine qua non* of being an empire in the first place. In the same way that nature abhors a vacuum, so too does an imperial power inevitably look covetously upon valuable neighbouring territories occupied by lesser empires and begin plans to take it. For, after successfully pushing the Turks out of the Sinai and making the Suez Canal safe from Turkish predations, the attention of General Sir Archibald Murray and his senior officers inevitably turns now to the ancient port city of Gaza, currently an Ottoman stronghold that lies just over the border to their north, in Palestine.

Established well over 3000 years ago, the fiercely fortified town is built atop the plateau of a 200-foot hill upon a coastal plain that abuts the Mediterranean two miles to its sandy west. Surrounding the better part of it on its lower ramparts, the Ottoman Army has constructed trenches and redoubts, manned by soldiers with machine guns and further protected by rolls of barbed wire – and there is little cover in the approaches.

To the east of the town is a ridge that runs north–south, boasting a 300 foot knoll as its peak, Ali Muntar, which towers over the town. Atop Ali Muntar are the large tomb of a Sheikh, and a garrison of soldiers and artillery observers given a bird's-eye view of precisely where to direct the batteries of Gaza upon all who would seek to be kings of this castle. Ali Muntar is the key defence of Gaza and its 40,000 residents against all those who would attack from the south and east – which is precisely where the troops of the British Empire intend to attack from. It will have to be subdued.

(Unless, of course, Jacko might strategically abandon the place without a fight, as they have done several times before? Alas, when one of Royston's patrols captures three Turkish officers and brings them back for interrogation, the response of one of them when this view is put is instructive.

Delicately touching his fez with one hand, he uses the other to point at Ali Muntar, glowering in the distance, 'Pardon, sir. I do not think so. We gave you Rafa, but we will not give you that.'[2])

All around Gaza are the cultivated fields which have provided the town with its food for millennia, each fertile field ringed by thick and prickly cactus hedges. It is a strange thing for some of these British officers to gaze upon it, as before the war, as some of the Oxbridge types know, barley imported from the fertile fields of Gaza was used to make their whisky.

Any attack on the town will inevitably have to get through that cactus, before getting to grips with the Ottoman garrison, thought to be manned by around 2000 Turkish soldiers, and – according to intelligence – backed by no fewer than *seven* artillery batteries, including one from Germany and two from Austria.

Coming from Rafa, the Gaza approaches are glistening green, shaming the sand surrounding them with orange groves, eucalyptus trees – yes, real gum trees that seem to have been brought from Australia and planted as saplings, decades earlier – and various settlements having got a toe-hold on this rare patch of arable land. Just five miles south of Gaza lies the Wadi Ghuzze, the enormous gulch of an ancient riverbed – which is still impassable with the winter rains, and at dry times still acts as a defensive bulwark to all those who would attack the town from that direction.

Getting a mass of men and supplies across it, not to mention heavy artillery and munitions, will be no easy task. But at least, to many of the Australians, the land seems strangely familiar, which can only help things.

'You know the country here looks just like the Queensland Downs,' one Trooper writes to his father, 'but it has this difference. It has deep washaways and creeks cut here and there.'[3]

Gazing at his maps once more, Chauvel notes that to the east of Gaza's Ali Muntar there is mostly arid desert for miles, bar a scattering of ancient wells, most of which have been blown in by the Turks, though they have kept them intact at a town where they maintain a strong garrison, here: Beersheba.

The deeply religious Harry Chauvel recognises the name at once. Beersheba. Isaac, yes? Now he thumbs the Book of Genesis and finds it:

> And they rose up betimes in the morning, and swore one to another: and Isaac sent them away, and they departed from him in peace. And it came to pass the same day, that Isaac's servants came, and told him concerning the well which they had digged, and said unto him, We have found water. And he called it Shebah: therefore the name of the city is Beersheba unto this day.

Unto this day too, and Chauvel reads on, marking each time the name occurs. Ah yes, when Abraham's slave, Hagar, is cast into the wilderness with her illegitimate son, she finds the well that saves them both. How strange it is to think they may drink from that *same* well, although the Turks will be doing their best to keep the Australians parched. Even Abraham himself journeyed to Beersheba to plant a tamarisk tree. In these lands, you are not just walking with history, you find yourself drifting in and out of testaments.

Since those times, Babylonians, Assyrians, Philistines, Ottomans and Bedouins have fought for water at Beersheba. Water is gold in the desert, the prize of Beersheba glitters to this day.

In fact, Murray and his senior officers briefly look at attacking Beersheba first, but that is quickly rejected.

'I decided,' Murray will recount, 'that it would in any case be unwise to make an attempt on Beersheba, since by so doing I should be drawing my line of communications parallel to the enemy's front . . .'[4]

And so an attack on Gaza it must be.

With that decision, the forces of the British Empire are moved up, *en masse*.

In late February the 2nd Brigade arrives at a coastal settlement not far from Rafa. By what name?

'Sheik Zowaid.'

A person or a place?

Both, for now the Sheikh himself arrives, riding forward to greet the Old Brig, Granville Ryrie. And the local looks like 'a proper Sheikh too'[5] – all flowing white robes, red head-dress, and curved, bejewelled daggers dangling from both hips, cut out of the *Arabian Nights* and now salaaming in this beautiful dusk. The Sheikh is graceful and smiling to them, but they note he has been the same to the recently departed Turks. There are oil engines and pumping-plants built here for the Sheikh by the Turks. You do get the distinct impression that all foreigners are just accessories to the oil, the good oil being that all alliances and friendships here are temporary. Ah well, the temporary will do for the present, and – after placing guards around the settlement to ensure that no-one from here will move forward to tell the target of their next intent – they have an evening of peace and rest, girding their loins for the big battle they know is to come.

17 March 1917, Mildura, for whom the Bell tolls

The hell with it.

Wee young Harry Bell has simply decided he can wait no longer. For *three* years he has continued working on the family farm, always aching to join up, and badgering his father to let him – for always the same answer.

'NO.'

His brother Samuel had joined up the year before and is now seeing service with the 57th Battalion on the Western Front, whatever that is. And he is left here, rotting in his stead at the homestead.

Maybe there's another way?

On this day he is going to give it a try.

After telling his parents that he is going to try his hand droving in Queensland, he instead heads to Mildura, just 80 miles away, and goes straight to its recruiting centre. He gives his name as 'Harold Thomas Wickham', the surname being his mother's maiden name, and his age is now 21. (If you are going to lie, there is no point in small fibs, wild whoppers paradoxically having more credibility.) Next of kin? He offers up his 'uncle', Thomas Bell, of Walpeup – in reality, his father.

The recruiter looks him up and down.

Can this lad, all of five foot four inches tall, and weighing in at 114 pounds – just over eight stone, wringing wet – *really* be 21?

Well, he says he is, and there is no-one to say anything different. There is a war on, you know. Young Harry is accepted and – as an excellent horseman – soon makes his way into the Australian Light Horse Reinforcements.

20 March 1917, Mustabig airbase, a wing and an effing prayer

Another day, another bombing raid, this one by seven planes from the Australian Flying Corps' No. 1 Squadron. One after another, following their Squadron leader, Major Richard Williams, they dive down and drop their 'eggs' from as low as 50 feet on the Turkish railway junction Tel el Hesi, just seven miles north-east of Gaza. With the dearth of the usual bombs, the Australians have adapted ingeniously with fencing wire, elbow grease and timers to drop instead specially modified 4.5-inch howitzer shells.

Alas, things don't go according to plan.

Just after Flight Lieutenant Frank McNamara drops his fourth bomb – timed to explode 40 seconds after being dropped – the release mechanism is momentarily hit by a strut, and it explodes just beneath the plane, sending shrapnel into the pilot's legs and buttocks. Bleeding badly, with a damaged plane, McNamara hauls on the joy-stick and steers his Martinsyde back towards their base at Mustabig, west of El Arish, only to see that one of the other planes has come down in a rough part of the desert, criss-crossed with wadis, but just enough space to make a landing. It is his mate, Squadron leader Captain Douglas Rutherford, beside the BE2c he has just brought in for an emergency landing thanks to an engine that has gone on the blink.

Christ Almighty!

The fate of downed pilots at the hands of either the Turks or, worse, the Bedouins, is grim – more often than not, stripped naked and hacked to death. On the distant horizon McNamara can see a Turkish cavalry unit heading towards where they can see that Rutherford has come down. Despite feeling faint from loss of blood, McNamara brings his own plane down beside Rutherford and calls for him to climb on . . . *climb on* . . . CLIMB ON!

The only problem with this order is that the Martinsyde is a single seater! Rutherford can only 'climb on' to the lower wing, sprawl across the engine cowling, grab a strut and pray. He does so and McNamara guns it – only to find that, through the imbalance of the plane and the inability of his right foot to push the pedals, they veer into a gully at 30 miles per hour, tearing off the undercarriage. Oh and the Martinsyde is now on fire. It's clearly time for plan B.

Back to your BE2c, Rutherford. After all, how bad can that engine problem be? At least it's not on fire, yet. The duo limp away to their new supposed salvation, Rutherford helping the weakened McNamara, even as the dust cloud of the approaching Turkish cavalry looms larger.

Now, Doug, we have all known mechanics who like to take their time, yes? NOW IS NOT THAT TIME. Feverishly, Douglas Rutherford takes spanners in hand and starts to repair the engine like his life depends on it, which is easy under the circumstances. Meanwhile, McNamara opens fire on the Turks, who are now within range. If all the Turks charged at once, he and Rutherford would be overwhelmed, but it is equally true that the first Turk in the charge will likely be brought low, and so the Turks dismount, and approach in small rushes. McNamara fires anew, and is delighted to see fire supporting him from the sky! Thank Christ, two of their fellow pilots from No. 1 Squadron,

Lieutenant Roy Drummond and Lieutenant Alfred Ellis, have spotted them, and are now strafing the Turks, stopping their advance for a couple of cautious minutes at least.

Quickly, Doug, QUICKLY!

Rutherford has given it his best shot. He throws down the spanner and gives a yell, McNamara climbs into the cockpit, Doug rushes to the propeller and hauls on it.

It doesn't start.

He hauls again.

It *coughs*.

It STARTS!

It bloody ROARS!

Rutherford jumps on board, and McNamara guns it. They are in the air! But McNamara can feels himself blacking in and out of consciousness. Please God, let me not black out now. With the other two AFC planes riding shotgun, they make their way west and, amazingly, astonishingly, land alive back at the Mustabig base. Doug yells with delight and McNamara retains consciousness just long enough to swear very loudly, to the delight of the ground crew.

They made it. *They bloody made it!*

There have been a thousand miracles in this spiritual land. This feels like one of the greatest.

As Flying Officer Ross Smith will note in his diary that evening, 'It was a jolly fine stunt on Mac's part.'[6]

Later on, one of the mechanics of No. 1 Squadron, Private Bull, will also be pleased, as he notes in his own diary, 'Got half day off. Lt McNamara has been awarded the VC which is the first one to be awarded in Egypt during this war.'[7]

21 March 1917, Rafa, far laps

Oh, the sheer fun of it!

Formally known as the 'Desert Column's First Spring Meeting', and unofficially the Rafa Races, today is the day for all the Mounted Brigades who are part of the Desert Column – the Yeomanry, Australians and New Zealanders – to gather and race each other. (The fact that it falls on the same day that the railhead arrives in Rafa is no coincidence. It is a day to celebrate!)

Listen, if you drink enough, and squint just right, and pretend the sand is grass, well . . . it is still a stretch to think it looks like a real racecourse, but who cares, for down the stretch they will come today and we are ready for a punt.

Soldiers who are bookies back in Australia have set up a totalisator enclosure to take bets – and there is even a race program and trophies brought all the way from Cairo! Better still? The Scotties have put together a pipe-band, playing a new composition, 'The Battle of Romani'. To some the bagpipes sound, as ever, like cats strangling each other, but to most it is sheer music to their ears in a rare day of rest and relaxation when anything that doesn't sound like guns and cannons firing sounds great!

All set to go . . . *raaaaacing* now? Good God, the British start to get a real feel of what Australians can accomplish when it comes to pursuing their genuine passions. For there is *nothing* 'forgotten in the way of conveniences, saddle cloths, arm bands, weighing scales, the cups for presentation, a small field hospital in the centre of the course; a band of pipers, and a brass band supplied the music; individuals supplied their own liquor'.[8] As a matter of fact, many have been supplied at least eight times before the races even start.

And now look at the 'saddling paddock', the 'parade ring', the 'stewards stand', and the 'officers enclosure' – all of them just like back home, except that instead of being formed by white fences, here they are constructed from barbed wire; as are the totes. An extraordinary 20,000 quid is laid down in bets for today. The fact that you might die tomorrow makes every man Diamond Jim when it comes to laying bets at this most unusual racecourse.

Those who look at the track will notice another unusual feature: the steeplechase jumps are built of sandbags! They are three foot six inches high and three foot wide, 'brushing up' to four foot six inches as the challenge increases, and all together they make 'a splendid obstacle'.

Look, cobber, all up it's not often you get time to stop and reflect in this war, but today, as they wait for the races to begin, is the exception. And the reason it feels like it was just last week they were fighting on this very ground? Because it was! Shrapnel is still scattered like confetti all over the ground, including the nominal 'racetrack', while the graves of both their enemies and their comrades are in the sands just beyond. Inevitably as grog starts to flow, the punters reminisce.

'Do you see that rise over there, Bill? That's where we got such a grilling.'[9]

Bill sees it.

'Jim was killed just where that fellow on the grey pony is standing.'[10]

So he was. And look!

'There's poor old Joe's grave over there by that brush. I wonder if he will hear his own horse galloping past today?'[11]

The races are many and wild, and they included the Rifle Cup and the Syrian Derby, the Anzac Champion Steeplechase, the Sinai Grand National and the Promised Land Stakes. For fun, there is a race called 'The Jerusalem Scurry', where only 'Arab stallions', otherwise known as donkeys, are allowed.

Ah, how they laugh, drink and bet.

The races are as full-on as they are many, proper wild Australian dashes, with heedless risk compulsory, just 'neck or nothing' as the saying goes! 'The Rifle Cup' race, particularly, would do the Geebung Polo Club proud: – *But their style of playing polo was irregular and rash / They had mighty little science, but a mighty lot of dash*'. It is won by 'Young Bax', a South Australian jockey riding a horse rechristened Fatima for the day. Young Bax says, after what was practically a mid-race jockey-brawl, 'I had just as rough a cross going over the flat as I did during the battle!'[12]

But there is a protest! Claims are made that at least three horses ran inside one of the racecourse posts, which would normally see instant disqualification. The stewards agree that three horses did precisely that, but let the results stand on the grounds they can't quite remember which ones they were.

NO! More protests.

The stewards will not be swayed, at least not in their legal opinions, though physically it must be said they are indeed swaying a little as the booze continues to make its own race round the turns and through their bloodstreams.

Controversy again rears its horse's head in the Syrian Derby, a race distinguished by the fact it is restricted to only Arab horses. For this time, one of the stewed stewards insists that something is rotten in the state of Denmark, and here too. That horse there, the stocky, white, breed mare – does not look like an Arab purebred! The trainer in question, a Digger, gazes back at the steward with 'a face that was childlike and bland'.[13] Close examination is made nevertheless, and it is established beyond doubt that this particular animal is about as Arab as a wombat with a dirty snout, and every bit as Australian as the same. But the trainer remains the very picture of innocence, insisting that a terrible error has occurred: 'I do not know much about horses and as she was very white and had a long tail I thought she was an Arab.'[14]

Yes, well. The stewards accept his explanation, even as other punters yell out that back home this Digger/trainer is one of Australia's foremost steeple-chase jockeys, as expert in horses as he is in . . . race-fixing. As for the 'Arab' mare, the trainer had ridden him in Australia so either he's a bloody liar or shell shock must have affected the poor man's memory.

Either way . . .

'The Australians,' it is chronicled, 'won five out of the six races they were allowed to start in.'[15]

Drink up, boys, for tomorrow we . . . at least prepare to go to battle. And they really do.

For as they are all now aware, tomorrow begins the big push on Gaza, the first part of which is moving the 30,000 men of Desert Column, their guns, and their water supplies as far forward as they dare, up around the small native settlement of Deir el Belah, right on the edge of the coastal sand dunes fringed with palm trees and within 10 miles of Gaza.

It is a massive exercise, given that, for the first time in the entire campaign, the attack on Gaza will be 'all arms', infantry, cavalry and artillery, operating together as one.

To help move the men and *materiel* to the ramparts, the Egyptian Camel Transport Corps has also been brought forward – each camel is capable of moving as much as 900 pounds in weight – and they are backed by horse- and mule-drawn wagon trains.

How can such a well-entrenched garrison be taken?

The newly installed commander of 'Eastern Force', Lieutenant-General Sir Charles Macpherson Dobell, who has carriage of the battle, lays it out for his commanders.

We will move forward under cover of darkness to get into position, unleash an artillery barrage at dawn, followed by the Welsh infantry of General Alister Dallas's 53rd Division storming forth, and they will be backed by a brigade of the 54th Division.

Meanwhile, the mounted forces will move around the other side. Chauvel's Anzac Mounted Division will base themselves north of Gaza, blocking both escape and reinforcement, ready to attack. Major General Henry Hodgson's Imperial Mounted Division will do the same from the east and north-east.

For his part, General Dobell is so confident of success that plans are put into place so that once the Turks retreat, the mounted cavalry can pursue them, cut them off, and then cut them down.

Just under 50 miles to the south, General Murray has his HQ established in a railway carriage at El Arish and, after being satisfied that all is as it should be, gives the order to Dobell: you may proceed.

Brigadier General Granville Ryrie is not quite the student of the Bible that Harry Chauvel is but even he knows a little about their current target, writing, 'Gaza is very interesting; it is where Samson pulled down the house, and his tomb's there.'[16]

Let's hope our own tomb is not there soon.

•

From His position on high in the sky on this early evening of 22 March 1917, Horus the falcon-headed Egyptian god can now observe something as old as the Pyramids.

It is the sight of soldiers moving forward on Gaza, filled with hope of at last subduing it.

In this case it is the men of Eastern Force beginning their staggered forward ride to Deir el Belah. In the fading light they race the night, a burst of energy and nerves as they fling themselves across the sand. Why such haste as the day ends? It is because their day has only begun. It is impossible to escape detection during daylight with so many German planes constantly flying overhead observing – all but unchallenged by the British planes, which are incapable of climbing to the altitude of the Taubes, making them like starlings trying to get to eagles – so they *must* move at night. The best they can, the advancing troops try to have their day-time resting places concealed in either dry wadis or the troughs formed by tight sand dunes, meaning the Taubes would have to fly directly overhead to detect them.

Dawn on the twenty-fifth of March brings caution with sight, as every Australian eye scans the horizon, searching for Bedouin or Turk, the glint of a gun or shine of a sabre in the shimmering distance. For the 3rd Australian Light Horse Brigade is advancing into Turkish defences this day, carefully moving forward in a probing manoeuvre, trying to determine exactly where Jacko's defences lie on the southern approaches to Gaza and what they are. Arriving at the first major obstacle, the vast Wadi Ghuzze, the advance working parties determine the best places to descend the 40 feet down the banks of sandy clay to the wadi floor to ford the thick stream that lies there, before getting back up the other side. And now they use picks, shovels and planks to quickly build something resembling a rustic thoroughfare.

Still the 3rd Light Horse Brigade push further, constantly expecting some kind of enemy ambush. For the moment though, there is stone-cold motherless nothing and they are able to push up right to within close view from the south-east of Gaza, and staff officers take careful notes on the contours of the landscape over which they will be attacking on the morrow.

The main thing to see is that the Turks are not there! Clearly they have taken the view that, rather than sacrifice troops by putting them in preliminary defences that will inevitably be overwhelmed, it is better to strengthen the town and bring whatever force they can to bear from on high to all those who approach on the low ground.

All seems in place for a successful attack and General Dobell estimates that, based on their best intelligence, Gaza is defended by no more than seven battalions of infantry, comprising 3000 soldiers, supported by two Austrian howitzer batteries, a German artillery battery and a squadron of cavalry – the whole citadel under the command of a German officer, Major Ernst Tiller.[17]

Will he be up to mustering sufficient resources to mount a strong defence of Gaza?

Not on your Nelly, or mine.

'It is believed,' General Chetwode sends out in his final communique to his senior officers of Desert Column, 'that Gaza is not strongly held, and it is therefore intended to push the attack with great vigour.'[18]

As darkness finally falls after this restless day, the last of the Troopers of Desert Column move forward to Deir el Belah, where they can get what rest they can.

And hark!

What is that?

Music. Coming this way.

And men. Marching.

> Far and near and low and louder
> On the roads of earth go by,
> Dear to friends and food for powder,
> Soldiers marching, all to die[19]

Idriess can scarcely believe his eyes or his ears, but in those minutes after the sun has set and the dusk retains that golden glow, a tune floats towards them mixed with the ceaseless tramp of feet.

This is no ancient chant, no market flute, no nuttin' that belongs anywhere near this part of the world. For, Christ Almighty, it is, yes . . . *a bloody brass band!* Yea, it is verily written that Joshua felled the walls of Jericho with trumpets, but he certainly didn't march there in Oompah 4/4 time. Of course there is only one race that imports the incongruous with such complete indifference to sense or custom, let alone the idea that when moving forward for a surprise attack, it might be a good idea not to play marching tunes while doing so. Yes, it is the British, the men of the 53rd and 54th Infantry Divisions also on the move – some 30,000 soldiers in all!

As one, stunned by the spectacle, the Desert Column scramble to the small crescent hills to view the spectacle of these brave men, marching to death or glory.

'Bands! Masses of horsemen! Then infantry! Brigade upon brigade, battalion upon battalion, column upon column, growing rapidly, spreading rapidly all over the plain.'[20]

To the eyes of Idriess and his mates – themselves blackened by the sun, wearing little more than khaki rags after months of this campaign – these fresh arrivals look clean, shining, and 'altogether splendid', as if they have stepped out of a painting instead of out of the desert. Their horses look smarter than any Walers, with even their harnesses shining, glinting in the golden glow. And now come the guns. And guns and guns and ever more guns. Idriess has seen guns before, but, as opposed to their 'own precious little guns', well, 'these – why these were GUNS!'[21]

Such a display of power pure, in such numbers, makes the Australians feel like they have been fighting with bows and arrows, as still more brave battalions march before their eyes.

The Desert Column yell down 'Hellos' and 'G'days!' to the marching men; who look like fresh-faced boys for the very good reason that they *are* fresh-faced boys. They talk like them too.

'Are there any Johnny Turks out this way?'

'Yes. And the beggars are waiting for you too!'

A thick British accent answers, 'They won't have long tu wait, choom.'

'Good lad!' yells the Australian Trooper.

'We'll wipe 'em right off the map!'[22]

But, truth be told, or rather whispered to yourself – as bringing up the rear of the Brits is their white canvas–topped ambulance carts, catching the very last of the sun, before they too disappear and all falls quiet – it is the Desert Column that feels as if it is wiped off the map at the moment. Idriess speaks what he knows the others are thinking.

'What of the Desert Column? Are we to lose our individuality in this bigger army?'

Just a day ago they were formidable, now they feel an asterisk forming above their names.

'There is grim regret in the thought. For we are the Desert Column.'

They are, and they will be underway themselves shortly. Idriess writes rapidly in his diary, packing up his impressions as soon as they are recorded; and as he closes it, he thinks, 'Will I ever write in the old diary again?'[23]

Who knows? If he does not, the past is recorded. Somebody may read it, someday.

For now, the Desert Column Troopers snatch what little sleep they can as they lie secreted in wadis, palm groves and orchards around Deir el Belah, before being roused at 2.30 am, with a nudge and a grunt. In short order the men are eating cold grub for breakfast. Today, they will be travelling light – carrying supplies for just 24 hours – moving fast, and attacking mercilessly to conquer Gaza in that time and help themselves to the town's water and supplies. If they cannot crack the town's defences by then, there will be no alternative but to retreat, all the way back here to Deir el Belah, which will be their nearest source of water.

The horses whinny lightly in the moonlight. Troopers mount their horses and form up by Squadron, soldiers form up in Companies and broadly together they all begin to move. They head off silently in the night, at least in the sense that no-one is talking. It is a little harder to order a squeaking mass of artillery to keep it down as an entire army crosses the sands. Major General Hodgson's Imperial Mounted Division will depart 30 minutes behind the Australian and New Zealand Mounted Division, all of them heading for the Um Jerrar crossing of the Wadi Ghuzze just over four miles away.

In the silence, so many small sounds grow great, as Ion Idriess notes: 'The murmuring of thousands of hooves, the snort as a horse blew dust from its nostrils, the jangle as a packhorse shook itself, the straining of an ambulance team, the rumble of guns, the whisper of thousands of feet.'[24]

As it happens, the Desert Column, together with all the British Divisions, find themselves in a fog so dense that progress can be at best stop-start, but mostly stop. This fog of war is no metaphor, it is real and it would do justice to a December morning in London. With just one step forward, your horse's muzzle hits the rump of the horse in front and stops, meanwhile the muzzle of the horse behind you hits the rump of your horse, rinse and repeat. There is no talking, which is fine, and no smoking, which is hell. Dare you risk a puff or two and trust in the fog to hide your light? No, you don't. For it is so strangely quiet now, the hooves muffled, the men quiet as the graves they dread filling, that striking a match would sound like a shell bursting. The silence is no ordinary absence of noise, it is, 'the expectancy of a volley – the feeling of unseen life all dense around us everywhere'.[25]

Where the hell are they? Somewhere. The horses step into the night and all the riders can do is lean back in the saddle as they pitch down-wards in the dark, daring 'ravines so precipitous that they never could have faced them in daylight'.[26] The night acts as a giant blinker for the horses, the riders are the ones who tremble with fear. The men hold their breath, the horses snort and . . . stop. At the head of the column, the two lead horses refuse to budge a step further. Now what do they know that we don't? Their riders leap off and tread, carefully mind, just ahead and find their feet stepping on the edge of a bloody precipice 'dropping sheer into the Wadi Ghuzze'.[27]

Right. So not that way then? Apart from this, those divining direc-tion do a divine job, they seem to split the passage between Gaza and Beersheba perfectly, the fog acting as their cover even as the compass is their guide. The fog defeats the sunrise, they sense white light, then see it, but the morning cannot make its way through the atmosphere to their eyes. The fog is still so thick that you only have to lean back and you can't see your horse's ears twitching. Mercifully, the scouts out the front have been issued with luminescent prismatic compasses which help keep them on track regardless.

Off in the distance, to the south-west, they can at least hear that the British artillery barrage on Gaza has begun, as some 80 field guns rain down shells, hopefully, on the enemy's trench system on the south-east side together with Ali Muntar – though there will be no way of knowing, as the fog will be preventing the artillery observers from assessing accuracy and damage.

The Troopers of the 2nd Australian Light Horse Brigade keep moving, carefully, until finally at 6 am the fog lifts and here they are!

The light brings location and history rushing at once to the Desert Column, for this ancient desert now has many features. Naked hills, plunging valleys and the shining green of the Plain of the Philistines, an aptly named stomping ground for perhaps, some of the Australians, who view learning with suspicion unless it involves women, horses or liquor. To the left of them they can see the dark hills of Gaza, trees hidden between roofs, a city waiting, as it has for so many centuries, to defy brazen intruders. The town itself is beaten in beauty by the villages that surround it, themselves encircled by lemon and olive groves, almond groves, fig plantations and beautiful trees that keep trying to trick you into thinking you are back in Australia.

Alas, now that they can see, they can also be *seen*, and the stutter of Turkish guns begins, with even the odd shell landing within coo-ee. With more reason than ever to press on, Brigadier Granville Ryrie and the 2nd Light Horse Brigade – with the rest of the Anzac Mounted Division coming behind – are now in open country, so they sweep across the land in a wide front, quickly quelling every Turkish outpost they come across with their overwhelming numbers.

The Turks, taken completely by surprise and only just awoken, are no chance against these wild colonial boys from the other side of the world, who no sooner see them than come charging straight at them. Yes, Chauvel must leave a few men behind to take in hand so many prisoners, but it is a small price to pay. Crossing the broad, white Gaza–Beersheba road soon after dawn, Granville Ryrie's men of the 2nd Brigade – in the vanguard – pause only to cut the telegraph wires with a satisfying snip and keep going.

•

In Gaza, an alarmed Major Tiller has been in regular contact with General Kress von Kressenstein at the Turkish Desert Force HQ at Tel el Sheria since the beginning of the barrage as they try to determine how seriously the British are attacking, and just what must be done. The answer to the former is soon obvious: this large a barrage can only precede a serious attack, and the fact that Australian Troopers have been spotted moving fast, east of Gaza, confirms it. The key to the latter is calling in reinforcements, quickly. The closest to hand is

the Ottoman 53rd Division, marching to Mejdel, 13 miles north-east of Gaza, and they must immediately . . .
(*Click.*)
The line has gone dead.

•

As the sun finally shines, it finds the Australian mounted forces moving fast, deep into enemy territory, and never happier.

'[They are] a long, slight, swiftly-moving column, ignorant as yet whether the other mounted brigades and the infantry had succeeded in penetrating the fog, but, in the excitement of the morning's sport, as careless as they were ignorant.'[28]

Inevitably at the head of his troops 'the old Brig', Granville Ryrie, and his escort of Troopers in the advance guard of the two mounted divisions – what he will describe as 'the post of honour'[29] – suddenly hear the roar of engines above, just as the last of the fog lifts.

Taubes! Two of them, and they are coming right for them.

Scatter.

With no ack-ack from anti-aircraft Archies about, the Germans have relatively free rein to swoop low, meaning those below must flee. The key in such matters, as they have learnt, is not to present a massed target. They quickly disperse, rather in the manner of the fictional Lord Ronald, who famously, 'flung himself from the room, flung himself upon his horse and rode madly off in all directions'.[30]

Within seconds, Ryrie's advanced guard are doing exactly that before dismounting and, following his orders to 'Fire!'[31] – using their own horses for cover – are able now to bring such withering fusillades on the two swooping Taubes that the planes must disengage. There is no damage done, at least not to Ryrie's advanced guard, and they press on to the next adventure.

Up ahead! It proves to be *another* two German Taubes about to take off, and already taxiing, while the ground crew scramble out of the way.

Ryrie's men charge forth, but are too late, as the planes leave the ground just in time, and quickly return to strafe the column! Mercifully, the planes take enough fire from the ground that they do not tarry.

Onwards!

And yet?

And yet the thing that strikes all of the Australians of the Mounted Divisions, as they continue to skirt Gaza to the east, is . . . where are the British infantry? Surely they have not been lost in the fog? Surely, by now, we should hear the sound of the infantry battling their way towards us?

But there is nothing, beyond the distant, haunting sound of Turkish bugles carried in the mist – a sign that the enemy's defences, at least, are active, and men are being moved into position. Whatever the British infantry is doing, it is neither sending fire, nor drawing fire – meaning the Turkish snipers in the high citadel of Gaza, above the fog, can devote their attention to us of the Desert Column alone.

For as we continue to flank, Gaza begins to be flanked by horsemen, each looking for the point the Turkish garrison will spill out from; but the enemy is not to be seen in number. The silence is eerie, only broken by the occasional '*crack! plip plop*'[32] from one of the snipers yet to be rounded up or dispatched by a bullet themselves. Well, time to break the silence then, with the guns they have, and add a bang to the whimpers! Idriess records the strange symphony unfolding:

Crack! CRACK! crack. *Rut-tut-tut*, SH-SH-SH-SSHSHSH!

Turkish troops indeed start running, but they are isolated men in an outpost – seeing the galloping troops coming towards them, they have tried to make it back to base, only to become prisoners in a moment. Usually, capturing prisoners has a finality to it, but here and now it seems like a temporary gesture, the wave of battle could flow and free these men in minutes. Like a dog chasing an army truck, the Desert Column have caught a town and have no idea what to do with it. They gaze up at the odd square houses built into the hills, roofs jutting out in jumbles and there, just above them, is . . . a minaret. Beautiful. Like something from a fairy-tale, or rather the *Arabian Nights*.

'I bet the Turkish Artillery Observation officers will be up there!'[33] jokes one Australian, only for the jest to suddenly turn deadly. For that's exactly where they are, and now is exactly what they have been waiting for.

From a distance comes the familiar sound of rolling thunder, a BOOOM that soon engulfs the men, followed by the wailing whine of an approaching shell, which now explodes, screaming into fragments as red earth springs up around them, and red blood falls to the earth.

'Where will the next land? There! black smoke and earth right before the column.'[34]

Ion Idriess finds himself shivering in fear, you can act as brave as you like, and you will, but your body knows, the hairs on the back of your neck know, and the truth is that a cold sweat breaks out in the heat of the battle every time. Dammit, you'd think you'd get used to it, but you never do; being under fire remains bloody disconcerting. They tend to leave that bit out when writing accounts of glory, the fact that fear still envelops you even as your training kicks in; your primal instincts accompany the ones the Army has taught you and they won't go away. Of course, there are always the lucky buggers who seem to treat the whole thing as a walk in the park, and the Old Brig is one of them. Ryrie puffs on his pipe as the artillery flies, before turning to the troops and taking a break from his smoko to call them on with the pipe itself!

Follow the direction of the smoke, boys! Right now, in formation . . . *what the hell has happened to the infantry* . . . and they ride across the plain towards the guns. Ryrie leads the pack and the whistling of a shell turns into a CRASH and the Old Brig vanishes into earth and smoke. Idriess's mate Morry is the one who gives voice to it: 'My Christ! It's got the Old Brig!'[35]

And this one doesn't look like it might have got him where 'the chicken got the axe' either – but has more likely completely blown him apart.

Yet, stunningly, once the smoke clears they can clearly see . . . smoke! Still coming from Ryrie's pipe! That bugger has the luck of the gods as well as their nerve. Even Ryrie's horse, Plain Bill, is entirely unruffled and charges ahead once more! Talk about leading by example; Ryrie's example is a trotting miracle, but it is bloody inspiring. *Come on, boys! Into it! After it!*

This is, and no mistake, as Ryrie will write to his wife, 'a big affair. I mustn't say how many of our troops were employed, but about 4 or 5 times as many as there are sheep in Michelago'.[36]

(Let any German interceptors of this letter try and break *that* code! It will surely put them to sleep.)

For their part, the 6th Australian Light Horse Regiment heads off to block any Turkish reinforcements who might head down the Jaffa–Gaza Road, while the 7th and the 5th ride with Idriess and his section in the thick, turning in behind Gaza. On they go, 'hell for leather', at the sight of Turkish troops in the distance, but the closer they get the more curious the sight; for it is a cavalcade, not a company of the enemy that awaits! Two curious carriages, not even that; 'two funny little coaches that might have come out of Queen Anne's reign. There was a bodyguard of Arab cavalry all done up like wedding cakes.'[37]

What on earth have we here? Lieutenant Colonel Macarthur-Onslow, the Commanding Officer of the 7th Light Horse – wounded at Romani, but now well settled back at his post – is stunned to discover the answer. It is a ceremonial arrival of a Turkish divisional commander, with his senior officers, servants and bodyguards! But let's not stand on ceremony, the commander becomes prisoner before he even enters his city. His bodyguards fire no weapons at all, surrounded by snorting horses and serene Australians, trying not to giggle at the absurdity of this seeming fancy-dress procession in the middle of the desert. The Australians are mightily amused, the Turks terrified. For, oh yes, the Germans have told them many stories of the wicked cruelty these strange beings from the other side of the world are notorious for visiting upon their prisoners.

Perhaps some Turkish delight might allay their savagery?

For it is surely with this in mind that, with some ceremony, the Turkish General theatrically produces a glistening gold cigarette case and – *noblesse oblige* – offers elegant and tailor-made cigarettes to these mounted barbarians. Not to be outdone, and with similar theatricality, albeit of more rustic bent, a Trooper from New South Wales takes the proffered fag, before digging deep into his own dungarees and hauling up half a bedraggled fag from his own pocket which he reverently offers to the fuming General, as his mates fall about laughing.

The Turkish General does not join in – appalled at their discourtesy – and the punctured popinjay glowers in his storybook carriage, as his captors laugh all the harder. *Oh, Gawd, they'll never believe this at home!* It is with that in mind that several Brownie Box cameras come out.

The 'Kaiser Bill' moustache of the captured General twitches in fury as – this will teach the Australians! – he turns his head to spoil the snap. At least the General's bodyguards are more obliging, and with amazing poise, pose with due solemnity. But the Turkish General is not done, and is quick to make the first of what will be many forceful requests to Brigadier General Granville Ryrie.

'I demand at least some of them should be shot!'[38] he says.

Unfortunately Ryrie cannot keep a straight face.

'It *was* damned funny, though wasn't it?'[39] he offers.

No!

Clearly, the Turkish General makes a mental note of the Old Brig's name to be added to the list of those to be put up against the wall when this war is won. The General and his entourage are taken back behind British lines, with the infuriated Turkish General being seen to 'stride on behind his carriage twirling his walking stick, twisting his moustache furiously, and frowning very hard'[40] while Brigadier Ryrie, Lieutenant Colonel Macarthur-Onslow and their Troopers keep moving as the vanguard of the Australian Light Horse, which is pressing behind them.

Pausing only here and there to water their horses from the farm wells that abound all around Gaza, as do pools and puddles found in deep wadis, Chauvel's men of the Australian and New Zealand Mounted Division are soon in position north-east of the city. Cable, helio and wireless communications are speedily set up so Chauvel can command his forces.

Meanwhile, Ryrie's 2nd Light Horse Brigade pushes further on, and is soon positioned north-west of Gaza, with those on the extremes able to see the Mediterranean!

The Imperial Mounted Division under General Hodgson – an efficient, steely British officer of great experience, who finds a way to get things done – has likewise crossed the Wadi Ghuzze, and is now positioned east of Gaza, with the Imperial Camel Corps Brigade blocking the road and railway line that runs south-east from Gaza to Beersheba. Gaza is surrounded and sealed off. It is now for the British infantry to penetrate the perimeter and overwhelm the defenders.

•

Trouble?

Yes, trouble.

Sixteen miles north-east of Gaza, Colonel Kress von Kressenstein at Tel el Sheria – 'the mound of the drinking place' – has just received an alarming report dropped from one of the reconnaissance pilots of the *Deutsche Luftstreitkräfte*. The clearing fog has revealed that two divisions of British infantry are closing in on Gaza from the south, while 'some three cavalry divisions' had broken through the line between Gaza and Tel el Sheria. Kress von Kressenstein's eyes flash with anger, his monocle magnifying that spectacle to his watching staff as he lifts the telephone line to the highest-ranking German officer in Gaza, Major Ernst Tiller, only to remember the line is dead!

Raising Tiller on the wireless at least, the report is confirmed. There are now formidable forces arrayed against Gaza in the south, east, and north-east.

Kress von Kressenstein rises. Major Tiller is ordered to hold Gaza, 'whatever might happen, to the last man'.[41]

•

The tension is thick, and getting thicker.

Just after 9 am, General Chetwode receives a report that a large cloud of dust has been seen on the road from Beersheba to Tel el Sheria, heading towards Gaza, prompting a message to be urgently dispatched to General Dallas:

THE GENERAL OFFICER COMMANDING, WISHES ME TO PRESS ON
YOU THE EXTREME IMPORTANCE OF THE CAPTURE OF GAZA BEFORE
REINFORCEMENTS CAN REACH IT. HEAVY CLOUDS OF DUST ON ROAD
FROM SHERIA. [42]

Alas, there is no reply.

Again, a message is sent, with Chetwode insisting that you, General Dallas, must 'push [your] attack vigorously'.

Alas, for some reason not understood, they cannot raise General Dallas, the only explanation being his HQ can have no staff officers in it?

All around, there is confusion, and it will take some time for an explanation to emerge, that – after severe delays to their allotted schedule, caused by the heavy fog – Dallas, with his senior staff, have gone forward to the HQs of one of the 53rd's brigades, leaving his Divisional HQ abandoned.

It is with some fury, thus, that at 11.30 am – and with the 53rd Division *still* not moving – that Chetwode sends a new cable to Dallas:

```
NO MESSAGE FROM YOU FOR TWO HOURS WHEN ARE YOU GOING TO
BEGIN YOUR ATTACK? TIME IS OF VITAL IMPORTANCE. NO GENERAL
STAFF OFFICER AT YOUR HEADQUARTERS FOR TWO HOURS. 43
```

It is unconscionable!

Already the 53rd Division is five hours behind schedule, meaning that the entire plan to take Gaza is badly thrown out.

Who, and what, can save the day, *before the end of the day*?

It is obvious.

Chauvel can take command of the forces positioned to the north and east of Gaza and look to launch a successful attack from there, even if the trenches to the south have not been quelled by the 53rd.

Orders are issued at 12 o'clock, by General Chetwode, for the two mounted divisions – the Australian and New Zealand Mounted Division and the Imperial Mounted Division – 'to reconnoitre immediately, with a view to closing in on the enemy at Gaza to assist the infantry if ordered'.44

In the meantime, Dallas's men of the 53rd Division have at last launched their attack, and are now going in hard.

And doing it tough . . .

With little artillery cover, the Welshmen must struggle in searing sunlight over soft sands against an entrenched enemy who are firing artillery, rifles and machine guns at them from on high, much of it direct from Ali Muntar.

Somehow, extraordinarily, they do not falter as they approach. The Australians and New Zealanders of the mounted regiments watch with a mixture of awe and horror as, for the first time, they see the approach of the British forces in an open action like this. On the one hand, it is inspiring to see the discipline they display, how they keep on in serried ranks, 'little toy men . . . plodding in waves towards the grim fortress, suffering under its machine guns',[45] and keep going no matter how the fusillades of bullets and shells landing among them regularly knock out dozens at a time. If only they had moved sooner, the fog would have provided a wonderful blanket of cover!

'The Little Tommies went at it bravely,' one Australian Trooper will recount, 'and for hours fought in perfectly open country . . . it looked and sounded very dinkum.'[46]

But on the other hand . . . it seems like madness? Surely there is a better way than this military practice, with its roots in a time when massed cannon could not fire from miles away? What is wrong with their officers that they so insist? Still the Brits keep coming for another two miles.

By the time Dallas throws in the last of his reserves, it is obvious to both Dobell and Chetwode – now installed in the Advanced HQ of Desert Column and Eastern Force at In Seirat on the Deir el Belah side of the Ghuzze – that the 52nd, 53rd and 54th infantry have little chance of accomplishing the task set them.

It leaves them with just one option left to get Gaza before nightfall.

•

It is 3 pm, and General Chauvel must be raised on the cable phone and . . .

And what now?

Really?

Must he be petitioned *right now*, by a Turkish General as short in stature as he is of fuse, insisting – despite being a prisoner – that Chauvel personally escort him back to HQ, as his Australian Troopers who are meant to be simply guarding him, keep wanting to take his photograph and have photos taken with him inside his fancy carriage. The Turkish General had declined, whereupon his captors simply replied, 'Aw, go on, be a sport, General'![47]

General Chauvel musters as much sympathy as he can, but insists that he is too busy to do as requested at the moment – what, with the war and all, and this ongoing battle? – but wishes him well. The only thing Chauvel can give him is a wan smile, which infuriates the Turkish General even more. Taking his hat, his medals, and his umbrage – while leaving only his carriage and his dignity – the Turk departs in a huff.

Only a few minutes later, Chauvel is handed a second urgent message from the Commander-in-Chief of Desert Column, General Chetwode, now confirming what had only previously been raised as an option.

THE SUCCESS OF THE OPERATION AT GAZA, DEPENDS LARGELY
ON THE VIGOUR OF YOUR ATTACK. IT IS IMPERATIVE THAT THE
POSITION SHOULD BE OURS BEFORE DARK. [48]

•

At their HQ at In Seirat, just eight miles south from Gaza, the Generals Dobell and Chetwode remain desperately worried. The day is ebbing. It seems obvious that with the five hours lost by 53rd Division, the whole attack has been thrown out of kilter, which means the likelihood of enemy reinforcements arriving to turn the whole tide of the battle is greater than ever.

•

It has taken two hours. But General Chauvel now knows that all is in order, and so can give a key order of his own: 'Advance.'

Astride their horses, the men of the 2nd Light Horse Brigade begin to close on Gaza with Macarthur-Onslow's 7th Regiment in the lead, while to their left the New Zealand Mounted Rifles Brigade, equally, start to advance, approaching the city from the north-east and east. What both the Australians and the Kiwis see as they get closer to the ramparts of Gaza is curious.

They are not just cactus hedges, which they know about, but gargantuan ones!

Just how to get through them is not immediately obvious, and making matters worse, those few Turks still holding out atop Ali Muntar are also firing down upon them, causing carnage.

Suddenly their world is one of shattering shells and scything bullets as the great plain before the cactus becomes soaked in blood, even as clouds of smoke drift across and survivors drive their horses forward. Screams of agony compete for dominance with the sounds of battle, barked orders and war-cries. They *must* break through this natural barrier.

'I'd rather,' one Trooper will note, 'face barbed wire.'[49]

Jumping off their horses, the Troopers start slashing a way through, teaching those bloody cactuses a lesson they will never forget, all while the Turks take more pot shots, as 'from tiny holes were squirting rifle puffs, in other places the pear was spitting at us as the Turks standing behind simply fired through the juicy leaves'.[50]

Upon penetrating to the other side, Idriess finds the Turks waiting for him; six Turks to be precise. They look at him, he looks at them and then he springs and thrusts his bayonet through flesh instead of plant and a howl yowls like a siren to begin this next stage of battle; close, mad and brutal: 'the grunting breaths, the gritting teeth and the staring eyes of the lunging Turk, the sobbing scream as a bayonet ripped home'.[51]

The fight is a frenzy, the Turks shocked by the ferocity of their foe; the Australians just as surprised to see so many bodies fall. Idriess cannot believe it, they are supposed to be the underdogs!

'Amateur soldiers we are supposed to be but, by heavens, I saw the finest soldiers of Turkey go down that day.'[52]

Brigadier Granville Ryrie agrees, and will write to his wife: 'I never saw anything like it. We had to attack through a perfect maze of narrow lanes and high cactus hedges ... I saw our men and Turks firing at each other through the cactus not more than six feet apart and some of our fellows were shooting off their horses, like shooting rabbits. They said they could see them better from up there. [Then] they charged the Turks with the bayonet and killed a great many.'[53]

For those Troopers who remain on their horses and are getting among the Turkish infantry, it is a revelation.

'Horses are better than foot soldiers because we galloped right into them and within a few short minutes the individual Turk was terrified, fighting for his life against our steel and he went down paralysed with horror at the madness of our rushes. Even their biggest men were like schoolboys against us when we got amongst them.'[54]

In all of the murderous mayhem now that the Australians and New Zealanders are through, there is little mercy. 'Man after man tore through the cactus ... It was just berserk slaughter ... The Turkish battalion simply melted away: it was all over in minutes.'[55]

Victory isn't here yet, but it looks like Gaza soon will be. It's just a question of time. The day is theirs, will the town follow before evening falls?

It will if the Canterbury Mounted Rifles Regiment can keep up their terrific pace, racing along the ridge from the north-east, attacking Ali Muntar.

The Turkish citadel has not yet fallen to those marvellous Kiwis, but at the very least the Turkish regiment atop it have their hands full just defending their own position, and can no longer bring withering fire upon all and sundry attacking Gaza.

•

And help is coming from above. Not the Lord, but better. It is the men of the No. 1 Squadron Australian Flying Corps, and if one pilot is calling in artillery with particular intensity it is because only he knows their agony.

Flying Officer (Observer) Ross Smith, who had served with the 3rd Light Horse Regiment at the Battle of Romani, calls in gun after gun on those doing so much to hurt his own – dropping smoke bombs on the Turks, so the British artillery can know exactly where the brutes are.

'I got a 60 pounder battery on to a big lot of Turks ...' he will recount. 'It seemed very inhuman to be shelling men who must be half mad with thirst, but I soon got over those sentiments when I looked around and saw our own men laying dead up towards Gaza.'[56]

Flight is a modern miracle; but to be able to see so many of your comrades dying at the same time with crystal clarity from the sky – that is a fresh horror.

•

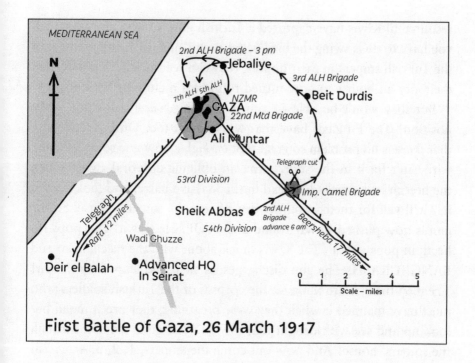

First Battle of Gaza, 26 March 1917

In full attack now, Chauvel's forces continue to outdo themselves. Just being within coo-ee of Gaza 'with its towers and minarets and white houses showing clear on the hill above the dark plantations, seemed, after the wilderness of Sinai and the hovels of the coastal villages from El Arish to Deir el Belah, a civilised place greatly worth winning',[57] energises them.

And now – even as the night comes falling from the sky with stunning rapidity, as it is wont to do in these latitudes – Chauvel's men are indeed able to penetrate the perimeter of Gaza *en masse*, and are soon running down the cobbled streets searching for any still willing Turkish defenders to take on.

Gaza proves to be still full of snipers, hiding in houses with rifles at the ready. No, make that machine guns at the ready, one house down the street blazes forth with fire so rapid the sound ricochets into itself as the bullets stream.

Extraordinarily, that chattering cacophony is soon outdone by the sound of a big gun firing, a . . . Turkish one. Of course! For the resourceful Kiwis have captured a Turkish gun, so why not use it? All you have to do is swing the big bugger round, and, to the amazement of the Turkish snipers in their houses, they can see the gun that defended their city an hour ago now turned round for a close-up attack.

But they won't be able to aim it precisely, surely? It's not set in position? The En Zeds have that worked out too. On the reckoning that there is no problem so great that enough elbow grease and fencing wire can't fix it in the short term, an obliging corporal swings open the breech lock, sticks his head in the massive barrel and looks down it. He'll yell for them to stop when he sees the snipers' house. So the gun is now pushed slowly round and STOP! He sees it! Out pops his head, in pops a shell. The Kiwis muck about with the mechanism and BANG! CRASH! The gun discharges its shell and leaps into the air! The men firing it are flung on the corpses of the Turkish soldiers who must have manned it when they were breathing; they are stunned but look up and see with delight that the shell has gone straight through the snipers' house! And now out come the snipers, 1, 2, 3, 4 . . . 28! Twenty-eight men were hiding in that one bloody house! (Maybe it wasn't a machine gun, maybe they were all firing rifles together.)

The Australians roar with laughter and relief.

The battle continues, there is a trench just 200 yards away blazing at them; but they are in the town and even as the sun is setting a yell is heard, and passed on with a shout:

'THE TOMMIES HAVE TAKEN ALI MUNTAR! HURRAH HURRAH!'[58]

It is not a rumour, it is a fact, even though there is more to it than that shout. The Canterbury Regiment has linked up with the British soldiers of the 53rd Infantry Division and finally have control of Ali Muntar, even while those trenches to the south of Gaza have been fully taken over, also by the soldiers of the 53rd Division.

In the town proper, the Kiwis of the Wellington Regiment of the New Zealand Mounted Rifles Brigade and the Troopers of Australia's 2nd Light Horse Brigade have been able to link up, and are now taking control of the northern section of the ancient city. Some of the New Zealanders are stunned to see some local markets have instantly sprung back to life, sensing new customers and new currency.

From his HQ inside the most robust part of Gaza, the frantic German commander, Major Ernst Tiller – even while fearing a knock on the door from the enemy – gets a desperate message through to General Kress von Kressenstein, reporting that the British forces had entered Gaza, by 'N. and E., and situation very bad'.[59]

•

Chauvel, meanwhile, is preparing to move his HQ into the town proper to begin preparing it for a likely Turkish counter-attack, as they will surely try in short order.

And yet, now the stunning development as Chauvel is advised that General Dobell is at the other end of the hastily placed field phone line.

Yes, General Dobell?

Withdraw. Get your men out of Gaza.

'But we *have* Gaza!'[60] protests Chauvel.

'Yes, but the Turkish are all over you,'[61] Dobell replies, insisting that just before 5 pm there had been reports of 3000 Turkish infantry and two squadrons of cavalry moving south-west towards Gaza from Huj, while another 7000 have been reported on the march coming from Hareira. So there are 10,000 Turks, coming for you right now!

No, they aren't. We can see these 'reinforcements', regiments hovering in the far distance conspicuously *not* moving towards us; the only thing they reinforce is the impression that the British commanders do not know what the hell they are talking about. Why, a cloud of dust previously seen on the Tel el Sheria road which had caused alarm had proved to be a small convoy of wagons *fleeing* Gaza!

Perhaps Dobell and Murray know something that Chauvel does not, but on the facts as they are presented the order is insane.

Nevertheless, orders they are, and must be followed – even when coming from an absurd distance away by a general who has no real idea of what the situation on the ground is.

With disgust, Chauvel passes the order down the line to his own men.

' . . . Owing to the lateness of the hour and the strength and position of the enemy forces pressing in from the north and east and the difficulty of continuing the attack in the dark in the town of Gaza, the G.O.C. Desert Column has decided to withdraw the Mounted Troops.'[62]

They must get out of Gaza and immediately head back to their starting point of that morning, at Deir el Belah . . .

The news is not well received.

For, inside Gaza, at around twenty past six, as the shadows are rapidly lengthening – and ever more Turks are being dispatched to the world of eternal darkness – a messenger arrives with the extraordinary order.

AS SOON AS IT IS DARK BREAK OFF THE ACTION AND RETIRE.[63]

Both Brigadier General Granville Ryrie and his Kiwi counterpart, Major General Edward Chaytor, commanding the NZ Mounted Rifles Brigade, are stunned.

How could General Dobell possibly want them to give up what has been so hard won?

Gaza is ours!

We have taken just about no casualties, are about to strike a dagger into the heart of an enemy who is wilting before ours, and you want us to pull back? We have stormed his citadel! We have him at our mercy, Jacko is about to surrender, and General Dobell wants us to . . . what?

WITHDRAW YOUR BRIGADE AT ONCE . . . CONCENTRATE AT PRESENT DHQ.[64]

In the name of GOD for what reason, bar treason? How can such an order be given out of the blue, with no previous warnings of even that possibility being on the horizon? The only explanation can be that the order has come from those too far removed from the action to know what is going on. Well, it is not good enough.

For the moment Major General Edward Chaytor refuses to follow the order, until it comes in writing.

Brigadier General Granville Ryrie refuses to follow any order, even written, at least until all of his wounded men have been gathered up and evacuated.

'Not a man,' he orders grimly, 'is to be left behind.'[65]

As it happens, it is while word of the withdrawal is spreading that the news of the greatest breakthrough of all gets through: it has been confirmed that Ali Muntar has finally fallen, to the joint attacks of the 53rd Division and the Kiwis of the New Zealand Mounted Rifles!

Unbeknown to Dallas and Chetwode, the day has now been won at the end of the day. Chauvel's men of the 2nd Light Horse Brigade and the New Zealand Brigade are flooding into Gaza from the north and the east, even while the 53rd has subdued all of the trenches to the south and south-west. With the confirmed fall of Ali Muntar, it can only be a matter of time before the remaining Turkish garrison in Gaza also falls – likely by dawn at the latest.

The order is not changed.

Withdraw. Retire. Get out of Gaza.

For his part, Ion Idriess is standing in the streets of Gaza with hundreds of other troops. Their state? It is 'utter amazement'.[66]

'Confirm the order!' yells officer after officer to the signallers; so stunned they are nearly sure it must be 'the work of spies'.[67]

It *can't* be true?

But the voice of each signaller rings out in turn: 'RETIRE!' 'RETIRE!' 'RETIRE!'[68]

That order is soon repeated to all and sundry among those besieging Gaza, 'from brigade to regiment, and on to the distant squadrons and troops'.[69] We are out. Withdraw.

And so withdraw they do, completely gutted that right within the jaws of victory, defeat had been *imposed* upon them. Bastards.

The worst of it is, they are not remotely ready to retreat. The New Zealanders rustle up some spare horses, and the men ride back in scattered separation, searching for regiments that had already relaxed into victory and now yell for each other as the evening falls, a quarter moon providing the light for a full retreat. Idriess finds himself in the middle of an impromptu meeting of the En Zeds and the officers of Macarthur-Onslow's 7th Regiment, whose horses are five miles away, to the north: 'Everyone was mad.'

No, make that furious. An oath is sworn by the officers: 'If we can't find the horses, we shall collect together and march straight back into town with the bayonet!'[70]

They could bloody do it, too! But the horses are found, and the mutinous oath disappears into discretion and other oaths surface about the bloody officers. 'We just could not understand what the "Big Heads" were doing.' [71] Making a Big Mistake, all are agreed on that.

Brigadier General Granville Ryrie will dwell on the outrage for many moons to come.

'When we got the order to pull out,' he will say, 'the town was undoubtedly ours. The New Zealanders held ground from which they dominated the whole position, and my men were actually in Gaza.'[72]

The claim of 10,000 reinforcements being on their way is ridiculous. Where? The Turkish prisoners inside Gaza clearly do not think they are about to be liberated, indeed, in a black irony, some attempt to escape from Gaza and are shot running across a graveyard, falling among the tombstones in what will prove to be convenient to gravediggers.

Yes, late in the day, certain planes and patrols had indeed reported some enemy movement towards the town, including cavalry and columns of soldiers. But if they were going to abandon the town at the first sign of such movement, why attempt to take the town in the first place?

The lions slink out, thanks to a command by donkeys.

They have no choice. They are ropable with fury as they make their ridiculous retreat.

'The march back of the mounted brigades from Gaza,' Henry Gullett will chronicle, 'was one of the sorriest movements undertaken by Australians and New Zealanders during the war.'[73]

And not just them.

The British soldiers, too, are incandescent with rage, none more than those who must descend from Ali Muntar, carefully wending their way through the bloody corpses of comrades who have given their lives to take it. Collectively, they have suffered almost 4000 casualties, advancing into the teeth of the storm, and, just as their forward elements had finally entered the Gaza plaza proper, they had been pulled out!

Among Chauvel's men, the mood collective is a curious cross between rage and sheer exhaustion – most of them are in their third night without sleep – and so ludicrous do they still regard the order to withdraw that no precautions are taken against a Turkish counter-attack. The Troopers smoke pipes and cigarettes, talk lightly and swear even as many keep a gimlet eye on dead mates, carefully carried on limbers – two-wheeled carts – now being pulled along by their riderless horses, a rough equivalent of knights being carried back on their shields. In the distance they can hear the unearthly 'blood-curdling screams'[74] coming from hyenas who have slunk in from the hills to feed on what is no doubt a rich feast of fresh cadavers. At least it helps keep some of them awake.

'As we groped our way back,' said one of the squadron leaders, 'all ranks were almost comatose from exhaustion.'[75]

Not to mention, disgust. For, make no mistake . . .

'There was not a single private in the British infantry, or a trooper in the mounted brigades, who did not believe the failure was due to staff bungling and nothing else.'[76]

In fact, there is at least some resentment from those being forced to retreat that the Welsh and English infantry had not been up to the mark. 'General opinion,' one Light Horse Trooper will write in his diary, 'if a division of Scotties had attacked with the Australians, Gaza would have fallen.'[77]

Mostly, however, the rage is aimed at those who have given the order. After all, if they are withdrawing because of the imminent arrival of Turkish reinforcement, where are the brutes? The Imperial Mounted Division have been assigned the task of providing a rear-guard to allow the others to get away, but barely fire a shot in anger.

With Hellfire Jack Royston's 3rd Brigade acting as rear-guard, the Light Horse move back to Deir el Belah, 'neath 'stars . . . like chilled steel'[78], where dozens of Turkish prisoners have been taken, most of them straggling bedraggled to their fate – but not all. Some, of course, take advantage of the darkness to slip away in the night. This is frustrating to Trooper James Tattam of the 7th Australian Light Horse Regiment, but as an Australian drover of the Old School, he finds a solution. Given that he is responsible for 30 Turks, and two of the brutes have scarpered, he knows there is only one way to make up his 'mob' and prevent a court martial. There! Two passing Bedouins are obliged at gunpoint to join the Turkish prisoners. It can be sorted out later, but the main thing is he will be handing over a full tally.

At Eastern Force HQ, late on the night, even General Dobell realises his error, as two communications from the enemy are intercepted. One is from Kress von Kressenstein to his fellow German officer Major Tiller, sent hours before, and looking for a way of saving Gaza:

HAVING REGARD TO THE DISPOSITION OF TURKISH TROOPS AND
LEADERS, CAN [A RELIEVING COUNTER-ATTACK] BE SUCCESSFUL
AT EARLY DAWN? I BEG YOU TO DO YOUR UTMOST TO HOLD OUT
SO LONG.

Clearly, the German is aware that the Turks are completely on their last legs, and that much is confirmed shortly afterwards with the reply of Major Tiller:

YOUR TELEGRAM RECEIVED. PLEASE ATTACK, AT ALL COSTS, AT
2 O'CLOCK TO-NIGHT. [79]

Major Tiller had also reported the loss of Ali Muntar:

POSITION LOST AT 7.45 [P.M.][80]

These are not the communications of a force about to trap the forces of the British Empire – they are of a beaten force, desperately trying to find a way to survive the night, only for, extraordinarily, those attacking forces to leave of their own accord!

Things had got so bad that 'the G.H.Q.s at Gaza and Sheria had actually exchanged farewell messages, and arrangements were made to destroy all papers, and blow up the Headquarters'.[81]

And so who is that man, in the hours before dawn, firing off orders with a fervour only to be equalled by the glumness with which he is soon reading reports back from the front lines?

It is, of course, General Dobell, desperately trying to undo his egregious error, by commanding General Dallas to send his infantry forward once more. But it is too late. Not only have the Turks fully taken back Gaza overnight – and Ali Muntar! – but the British soldiers are exhausted, with their munitions dangerously depleted. They can barely defend themselves if the Turks counter-attack, let alone go again. (And anyway, what is the *point*, when even if they take Gaza at huge cost of life, there is just as likely to be an order coming to withdraw once more?)

The full failure and folly dawns with the dawn. When Major Tiller realises – shortly after he has burned all his papers and prepared to surrender – how the British have simply abandoned the field even while victory was theirs he positively . . . roars with laughter.

Chauvel's men are shattered with exhaustion. A Trooper, fast asleep, will lose his position in the column, falling back or going forward as he sways uncertainly, only for one of his mates to reach out and jerk him awake, before all is silent once more, bar the soft whinnying and occasional grunts of the horses.

'I think it is one of the longest nights I ever put in,' Granville Ryrie records, 'and it was hard to keep awake as it was the second night without sleep. I wish I could draw the funny things I used to keep seeing . . . The men looked to be riding huge buffaloes as big as elephants with enormous tails.'[82]

Everywhere he looks as dawn breaks, there is equal exhaustion.

'Our eyes were like burnt holes in a blanket.'[83]

Having suffered 220 casualties, with 70 good men killed *for nothing*, they arrive back at Deir el Belah at half past eight in the morning and tumble into their tents. Somewhere, somehow, there must be an explanation for this, and someone held accountable.

•

Dobell and Chetwode write hasty reports which reach the same delusion. The outraged troops had been told to get out of Gaza because of the threat of 'impending reinforcements'. But now, incredibly, the true culprit is revealed; it was the water.

'At 6.10 pm,' writes Chetwode, 'the majority of my mounted troops having been unable to water their horses during the day, I, with the approval of the General Officer Commanding Eastern Force, instructed General Chauvel to break off the engagement and retire his divisions west of the Wadi Ghuzze.'[84]

Dobell says very nearly the exact same thing: 'Very few of the horses had been watered during the day and it was necessary to withdraw the mounted divisions for this reason.'[85]

This is news indeed to General Chauvel, who declares a plentiful supply of water. Why, half of the horses in the 2nd Light Horse Brigade were watered during the day!

One of his Troopers, Jeff Holmes, had documented the same: 'We found several water holes and feed was in abundance.'[86]

A debacle?

Not a bit of it!

'This action,' Dobell writes in his official report to General Murray, 'has had the result of bringing the enemy to battle, and he will now undoubtedly stand with all his available force, in order to fight us when we are prepared to attack. It has also given our troops an opportunity of displaying the splendid fighting qualities they possess. So far as all ranks of the troops engaged were concerned, it was a brilliant victory . . .'[87]

Murray adds his official voice, noting in his report to Whitehall that, apart from the defeat, it actually was a morale-boosting triumph:

'It was a most successful operation, the fog and the waterless nature of the country just saving the enemy from complete disaster. It has filled our troops with enthusiasm, and proved conclusively that the enemy has no chance against our troops in the open.'[88]

The whole thing is a masterpiece of minuting a mess into a respectable retro-spectacle.

As to what to do now, Murray essentially takes General Dobell at his word. They will attack again, with a larger force, and this time crack the nut. Chetwode and Chauvel are far from sure, realising that the Turks – no fools – will improve their defences, reinforce their lines, and not allow themselves to be taken by surprise again.

Chauvel, particularly, is a God-fearing man, who begins and ends every day in prayer. With this plan of attack it looks like they will need God on their side, less in the moral sense, than giving themselves even a chance.

Nevertheless, Dobell's assurance of the easy victory to come is gratefully accepted by Murray and effectively returned in kind.

The Troopers themselves do not feel that way.

Captain Stanley Parkes, of the 3rd Light Horse Field Ambulance, has talked to many men wounded and furious and he writes a very different private report for his journal: 'A great opportunity has been lost and the Turks are in great strength now . . . it is quite evident there has been [a] lot of bungling . . . everybody is disgusted with the display.'[89]

The Troopers of the Light Horse have simply lost all faith in the high brass.

'Have just heard that General Murray directed operations on Gaza – from Shepherd's Hotel in Cairo,' one writes in his diary. 'Some General, I don't think.'[90]

And they are equally dismissive of the crowing of the local press, starting with the *Egyptian Gazette* running with the page one headline 'DEFEAT OF 20,000 TURKS NEAR GAZA'.

'When we read such lies as this', Ion Idriess notes, 'how can we believe the news of our victories in France?'[91]

But in London, the War Cabinet under Prime Minister Lloyd George and the War Office under Sir William Robertson remain unaware of the colossal nature of Murray's error, and believe his sunny account that the sunny uplands of Gaza will soon be theirs. So does the British press, which glories in this near 'victory', something that does not pass unnoticed by the Turks and Germans.

For, only days after the battle, it is recorded an enemy aeroplane flies as low as it dares over the most forward mass of British forces to drop a message:

You beat us at communiqués, but we beat you at Gaza. [92]

In fact, the War Office is so confident that Gaza will fall on the next attack that, as Murray will recount, 'In a telegraphic communication dated March 30th, I was instructed, in view of the altered situation, to make my object the defeat of the Turks south of Jerusalem and the occupation of Jerusalem.'[93]

Yes, well. Gaza first. But this time, as Murray advises Whitehall, he will organise more water, closer to Gaza – enough for two divisions to be fully replenished at the Wadi Ghuzze. With that in mind, cisterns are built and arrangements made to pump the water forward.

And this time, he will throw in three infantry divisions and two cavalry divisions – some 60,000 men in all.

Both General Dobell and General Murray are very confident, sure that this second battle will result in an easy triumph. Murray writes Dobell to offer him encouragement that already sounds like congratulations: 'When your next move takes place, I have every confidence it will be most successful.'[94]

Dobell shares his certitude, penning his own musings to his commander about whether it will even be necessary to use gas-shells: 'Neither the enemy's numbers nor the strength of his positions are likely to force the necessity upon me, so far as I can judge.'[95]

And even if it does, they still have their secret weapon in reserve. Late in March, an Australian Flying Corps mechanic manages to get a close-up look at them as they move up to the front on a train.

'They resemble a small war vessel inside with the engines,' he records in his diary, 'the gun turrets, port holes etc.'[96]

But don't tell anyone anything.

'Great secrecy observed,' another records. 'All under cover.'[97]

•

Less secret is the heavy artillery – 18-pounders and the massive 60-pounders – being moved forward on the recently rushed railway construction pushing ever closer to Gaza, to be dragged into position from there by roaring, straining, tractors, positioned so they can 'blow Ali Muntar into the sea'.[98]

One of the veteran Australians is less convinced.

'That hill,' he comments, 'reminds me very much of Achi Baba at Gallipoli. I remember Achi Baba was to be blown into the sea many times, but it always seemed to bob up again.'[99]

CHAPTER SEVEN

THE SECOND BATTLE OF GAZA

*Chauvel was no hard-riding gambler against odds ... He fought
to win, but not at any price. He sought victory on his own terms.
He always retained, even in heated moments of battle, when
leaders are often careless of life, a very rare concern for the lives
of his men and his horses.*[1]

Official Historian Henry Gullett, *The Australian Imperial Force in Sinai
and Palestine 1914–1918*

Boor?

The boss will see you now.

On this misty morning in Wyton, Huntingdonshire, Alaric Boor
heads to the office of the Head of Flight Training, Royal Flying Corps,
knocks, enters upon invitation, and salutes.

You wanted to see me, Sir?

'Yes, Boor. You are officially gazetted as a Flying Officer in the
Royal Flying Corps as of today.'[2]

It is wonderful news.

And now his mind races to just how many hours he will have
to log to become a Flight Lieutenant, how many weeks that will
take if he pushes hard – though he knows no other way – and just
when he will be able to fly his own missions. As a young man, St
Augustine used to pray 'Oh Master, make me chaste and celibate,
but not yet.' Alaric now prays for the war to end, but not before he
gets *one* mission in.

•

Work harder!

Daha çok çalış!

The words are Turkish, but the yelled meaning is understood universally. *Hurry up, you lazy sods!* The Arab workers toiling this day are being barked at by Turkish soldiers, who are in turn sneered at by German officers. Formally, they are all under the orders of Djemal Pasha, but practically and particularly they jump to the desires of Colonel Kress von Kressenstein. And he wants them to strengthen the flanks here in Gaza so that it can no longer be so easily skirted as General Chauvel and his men had done in their most recent attack.

For well over a year the mounted forces of the British Empire have been revelling in fighting in the open country, so different from the Western Front, where men are still dying in their tens of thousands charging across no-man's-land at heavily armed bunkers. Very well then, General Kress von Kressenstein will deny the British such open country and build a maze of defences that would do the Western Front itself proud, a wall of redoubts, bunkers and trenches, with barbed wire in front built atop formidable natural defences and backed by machine guns and artillery against which the British may manoeuvre all they like – they will still be coming up against a bristling wall of whistling death.

Such moves do not escape Murray – as regular reconnaissance patrols report just what the Turks are doing.

'Not only were the Gaza defences being daily strengthened and wired,' he will recount, 'but a system of enemy trenches and works was being constructed south-east from Gaza to the Atawineh ridge, some 12,000 yards distant from the town. This put any encircling movement by our cavalry out of the question, unless the enemy's line in front of us could be pierced, and a passage made through which the mounted divisions could be pushed . . .'[3]

If there is to be no outflanking, Murray and his senior officers must come up with a new plan – a full-on frontal attack in two parts. Of course, to do the job, he requests more troops from Whitehall. Alas, as General Murray will recount, 'no additional troops were to be sent to me, since it was considered that, in view of the military situation of the enemy, my present force would suffice'.[4]

Look, why would they send more? Murray's current force had been enough to get into Gaza last time, so surely with better organisation they can do the same this time?

As the Troopers of the Australian Light Horse move *en masse* closer to Gaza as a prelude to the coming battle, they take occasional rest in the native villages that abound all around in the coastal areas, allowing them to observe close-up the ancient way of life.

Trooper Fred Tomlins of the 1st Light Horse Regiment is one who stops with his mates, to ask for water for their horses.

'They offered us an earthenware jar full but when we said we wanted enough for two horses it was a case of *mafish* there is none. One of the bints was busy crushing barley into flour with the aid of two stones. This was rather interesting so we spent some time watching the process and yarning to the old man. We gave him Backsheesh . . .'5

Such interactions can be fascinating.

'Even though the conditions under which we live are the worst ever,' one Trooper writes home. 'I love it. I love Egyptians and their ways and customs, their country is absolutely full of interest and their history is nothing less than the history of the world . . . I always feel terribly selfish travelling about seeing new and bonzer places and am thinking of you all the time and how you'd enjoy it. But there you are buried in dirty little North Sydney, which is about as interesting as a dead Turk.'6

Across the shimmering desert, the Australians can see the bristling Turkish fortifications all right, and note that every now and then a single shot rings out, followed by a plume of dust as the Turks 'register' their guns, working out the precise elevation for the distance required to put shells down at specific points where they reckon the most attackers will be massed. If there is not an identifiable feature to aim the guns at, they build cairns and the like in the night.

Christ Almighty.

The only bit of good news for the Troopers of the Australian Light Horse is their new guns, as each mounted squadron is issued four Hotchkiss light machine guns, to replace the single Lewis machine gun they have been making do with.

•

Those bloody Bedouin bastards. Yes, it is hard to get by in these parts without them being involved in some fashion. As locals who have prospered here for millennia, they have learnt the virtues of claiming neutrality between warring powers. But, in truth?

They are only 'neutral' the way a shark is neutral, when you are watching from the beach or the extreme shallows. Go out into deeper water and you'll find out soon enough just how neutral they are. This morning – this too bloody early, yawning, dawning morning – Ion Idriess is with 14 fellow Troopers of the 5th Light Horse Regiment guarding stacks of grain in an outpost when suddenly 200 bloody Bedouin attack from all sides! You take the dozen on the far right, I'll take the next dozen, Ion the next dozen and so on.

Amazingly, the Australians actually beat them back and are so elated they even pursue them into the desert, only to look behind and see, yes, 50 MORE bloody Bedouin taking the bloody grain! It is the oldest trick in the book, a trick the Bedouin had no doubt imbibed with their mother's milk: bait and switch.

Bastards. The British coddle the bloody Bedouin and chastise any Australian who attacks them, but the Troopers know them for what they are.

'These people cut the throats of our wounded,' Idriess records, 'they dig up our dead, they snipe us; they steal everything they can lay their hands on and they are the Turks' best spies; in fact German and Turkish officers dressed in filthy Bedouin's rags are often undetected as they wander freely throughout our big camps.'[7]

To add insult to injury, when they check the stacks of grain, they find that they are protecting an illusion. The bloody Bedouin have carefully slit the giant stacks from the bottom and have been stealing grain for who knows how long? As long as they can and as long as we let them. One day the Light Horse may be short of grain and what then? Well, we'll ask the Bedouin to lend us some I suppose.

•

On 15 April 1917, Murray moves his own Advanced General Headquarters forward to Khan Yunis, five miles from Rafa, and all is in readiness for the first stage of the attack to begin in two days' time.

It will not be easy. General Murray's Intelligence Department has it that there are now 8500 Turkish and German soldiers in Gaza, with another 4500 immediately to the east, and another 8000 spread along the fortified line on the Gaza–Beersheba axis.

It is double the number of soldiers they had defending Gaza in the first assault. Over 18,000 Turks alone are now ready to repel what is coming; for they know what is coming: the British and the Australians, riding into a new wall of defenders.

•

In the lead-up to the second attack on Gaza, it will be reported that General Murray first details his plans 'to a group of very silent, depressed generals'[8], while the troops themselves are becoming ever more aware that they are operating under 'wretched leadership'.[9]

All that General Dobell can do is set out the plans with more detail to his senior officers. This will indeed be a different kind of battle. If the Turks want a Western Front battle, we shall give them one – including artillery barrages, and for the first time in this theatre, poison gas, as well as our secret weapon . . .

After the first barrage of a day, the soldiers and artillery will move forward, consolidate their positions on the second day, and on the third day, after another barrage, storm the enemy trenches and take Gaza itself.

The verdict?

As before.

The Commander of Desert Column, General Philip Chetwode, and the Commander of the Anzac Mounted Division, General Chauvel, are just two of the senior officers who are far from convinced that the Dobell plan will succeed, and they are not alone. It will be reported that, on the eve of the attack, one British commander finishes his briefing to his senior officers by saying: 'That, gentlemen, is the plan, and I might say frankly that I don't think much of it.'[10]

The Australians think still less.

After the first battle of Gaza, Chauvel had written to Chetwode on the strength of his men.

'The harder the task I gave to the mounted troops of the Desert Column, the better they carry it out, and no man could wish to command finer troops.'[11]

It seems exceedingly odd that, despite their derring-do in the first attack on Gaza, out-manoeuvring the Turks with their speed and skill to storm the ramparts from an unexpected direction, for this attack they are essentially being asked to attack a defensive wall, where speed and manoeuvrability will count for little?

And yet, orders are orders.

Nearing midnight on this eve of battle, Lieutenant Guy Haydon and his comrades of the 12th Regiment move out as part of the newly reformed 4th Light Horse Brigade, making their way through ranks of the lightly cheering British troops, who wish them well on their mission to attack the redoubts further out on the Turkish fortified line.

Dawn, 17 April 1917, Gaza, belated tanks for the occasion

All is in readiness.

Before the ramparts of Gaza, no fewer than three infantry divisions, the 52nd, 53rd and 54th, crouch on the lee side of their sand dunes, knowing what is about to come.

Sure enough, right on 5.30 am, a staggering array of 16 heavy guns, 92 18-pounder field guns and 24 4.5-inch howitzers opens fire on the Turkish trenches defending Gaza. At the same time, in the waters just off Gaza, two Royal Navy monitors and the French coastal defence ship *Requin* join the cacophony of catastrophe.

And . . . *fire!*

Their artillery batteries erupt, and now pour salvo after salvo upon the foremost trenches of Gaza, the artillery batteries of Ali Muntar and other batteries in the city itself, the key railway depot and junction just north of Gaza at Beit Hanun, and the most crucial bridges that cross the wadis around it.

Observers with their field-glasses, one of them in a basket beneath a massive balloon launched for the occasion, are satisfied to see vast plumes of dust pouring skywards from their designated targets, even as tiny ant-like figures, Turkish soldiers, rush hither and thither. So here are some more shells for a chaser, which include firing 50 rounds directly on Ali Muntar.

Of course all of the shells are flying hundreds of yards over the heads of the British infantry, but they duck down reflexively anyway. Johnny Turk is no doubt also ducking, with the difference being that it won't help, as the shells will hopefully be landing *on* him. And even some that don't might kill him as, for the first time in this theatre of war, gas shells are being used.

What is clearly needed is an Artillery Barrage for the Ages, which goes for . . . ages. In fact, the first barrage goes for just a little over two hours. There will not be a second barrage of such might as this far from Britain's supply line of shells, it has not been possible to amass a huge amount of munitions, and they will simply have to make do.

Clearly, the Turks do not suffer the same lack of supply. For the counter-fire from their own batteries is more than munificent as shells rain upon the British forces.

Under the withering fire, at least for the moment, Dobell holds back the huge force he has assembled, which boasts 30,000 horses, thousands of camels, motor transports and, their secret weapon, which the Turks hopefully have no idea of . . . tanks.

Tanks? Yes, that new invention that has created such a stir in France is now in the desert with the Light Horse. Well, eight of them are anyway, each named like a ship, with perhaps a touch more casualness i.e. *Nutty* (named after the tank commander Major Nutt), *Tiger*, *War Baby*, *Pincher*, *Sir Archibald*, *Sir Reginald*, *Ole-Luk-Oie* and *Kia-Ora*. These murderous machines have a fame all their own.

Some of the tanks are 'males' with 6-pounder guns jutting out each side – each capable of delivering 6-pound shells a distance of 4000 yards – as well as three Lewis guns. The others are 'females', with no cannon but five Lewis guns protruding from every side. Both types weigh 29 tons, are powered by perpetually roaring and strained Daimler Foster engines and are 26 foot long for 13 foot wide, with steel sides.

If they can just get among the Turks, and up close to the redoubts, it will be carnage. But, can they?

General Dobell holds them in reserve for now, hopeful that the infantry attack can make serious advances without them. Anxiously, those who can keep their eyes fixed on Turkish positions hope for some sign that the gas shells now exploding on them will have some effect. No movement is observed, but does that mean the gas has worked or failed? No-one knows. The only certain thing is they will have to wait until the damn gas disperses before they go in.

After one last burst of ten minutes from Dobell's 18-pounders, the soldiers of the 52nd, 53rd and 54th Divisions leave their sheltered positions and move forward, leaping, running forward, ducking and zig-zagging – the most modern of attacks now followed by the most ancient – hoping the defenders of Gaza have been substantially wiped out.

Alas, General Dobell's judgements on the weakness of the enemy line have been greatly exaggerated, based on the recent past and not the reinforced, bristling present. For the Turks had wasted no time in previous weeks preparing every defence and digging trenches so deep they risked turning into tunnels. The barrage has affected them very little and they now present in force, bringing withering fire on their attackers. The attacking infantry are mown down like wheat before whirling scythes – by carefully placed machine guns spewing death towards them. The only hope the attackers have is for their secret weapon to be unleashed, their own previously unseen Ace of Spades.

And now here it comes. It is one tank, *Sir Archibald* – the first time a tank has been engaged in this theatre – accompanying a brigade of the 54th Division out on the far right, only for shells to start landing all around.

Far from protecting the soldiers as was planned, the tank seems to be a shell magnet, and many soldiers are wounded and killed by association with the thing, which is soon enough left as a smouldering ruin after a direct hit.

Still, the British soldiers are so numerous that 20 of the survivors do reach their goal, the Sheik Abbas Ridge, and start to dig in with an intensity expected in the midst of falling shells. At least they have taken most of the Turkish outposts lying to the south of Ali Muntar, and have secured their start lines for the main assault, due in two days' time.

•

Before Gaza, the British troops remain dug in, surviving the best they can as the day belongs mostly to the artillery batteries of both sides exchanging salutations.

Positioned some miles out on the right flank with the 12th Australian Light Horse of the 4th Light Horse Brigade, Lieutenant Guy Haydon does his best to settle Midnight down, just as all the other Troopers are doing with their own mounts. This far into the war all the horses know that the sound of artillery, rifle and machine-gun fire signals they will likely be in action soon, and right now there is more of that sound in the near-distance than ever before.

18 April 1917, Gaza, the readiness is all

Both opposing forces are aware that yesterday was merely the opening stanza of this bloody saga, the softening up part, and the most important thing today for the attackers is to first dig in, while also sending out careful patrols to look for any weaknesses in the enemy line. For the Turks the day is spent bringing men and munitions forward and getting ready for what they know is to come.

Lieutenant Guy Haydon and the 12th Regiment are sent up along the Wadi Ghuzze in a fruitless search for water, returning in the heat of the day, thirstier than ever.

In the night, they carefully move out to bivouac at El Mendur, on the right flank of the Gaza Line. Dawn of 19 April finds them threading their way through artillery being moved forward, just as most of the Anzac Mounted Division is doing the same, ready with the rest of the Desert Mounted Column to attack the Gaza Line. Though the dismounted Troopers of the Anzac Mounted Division assigned to attack the Atawineh Redoubt eight miles east of Gaza have little hope of actually capturing it, they will have fulfilled their task if they can but pin down the Turks so Jacko can't reinforce the main attack on Gaza.

5.30 am, 19 April 1917, Gaza, Dobell tolls for thee

It is time to do or die.

Just as on the first two days of the battle, Dobell's artillery unleashes at dawn, raining shells – or at least sprinkling them liberally – on the Turks defending Gaza. This time the principal target is the achingly familiar Ali Muntar.

This time the barrage includes gas shells.

Across most of the Gaza–Beersheba axis, the troops of the Desert Column listen keenly to the sounds of the artillery . . . and are mostly pessimistic.

'We know Gaza should have fallen on the second day of this our second attack,' Ion Idriess writes. 'It hasn't! . . . We are rather quiet. Sleepless, of course, but we wonder about our grand army. It is very sad – instinctively we know that it has been smashed. There has been bitter fighting all the way to Gaza but we don't know the actual result. We have ceased to wonder what has happened to the two great surprises we had for the Turks. Each must have been a dud else our men would have taken Gaza days ago.'[12]

One of those surprises is the gas shells, and it has – surprisingly – indeed been a dud, doing little damage either to the Turks in the trenches, or on the heavily fortified peak of Ali Muntar. This is not the murky Western Front; the gas disperses quickly in the dry heat and the desert breeze. Perhaps if they had more shells it might have made a difference, but like everything else around here, they are in short supply. And so with a whimper not a bang the gas shells cease.

But the second surprise, the tanks? The one tank used on the first day has made no impression, and been destroyed. Hopefully, their day will come and that day is today!

In the meantime, under orders from General Dobell, from dawn the troops of Desert Column range against the fortified Turkish line that stretches out from Gaza, charging forward into the storm of bullets, and shrapnel. Their job, is to 'demonstrate' against the Ottoman positions, making sure that they can't move troops from there back to defend Gaza itself.

Positioned some way behind a low ridge, for Lieutenant Guy Haydon and the rest of the 12th Australian Light Horse, it is time to launch their own attack. With just two hours sleep the night before, then having to trek to this position – much of it right by artillery batteries preparing to unleash, with their horses' reins twisted around one foot as they lie in the sand – they are as exhausted as they are . . . resolute.

Suddenly their world is just one shattering roar, even as the earth trembles and enormous geysers of sand and dust – and no doubt human limbs – are hurled skywards all around the Turkish redoubts.

With that amount of shelling it is unlikely that the Turks are going to be able to bring much fire on them, and with their fellow 4th Brigade Troopers of the 11th Light Horse Regiment by their side, the Troopers of the 12th Light Horse now leave the safety of the wadis and, still on their horses, make their way a mile forward to, as one of Haydon's Troopers will recount, 'a low ridge, through open sloping country clothed with the most beautiful blood red poppies which made a gorgeous natural carpet, thrown into strong relief by the yellow and white daisies, dandelions and a profusion of delicately tinted flowers'.[13]

It is from here, with their heads just above the ridge-line, that they can clearly see the most perfect panorama of the shocking challenge they face. For there before them in the distance to the left are two more high ridges intersecting, both lined with bristling and barking Turkish guns – on the left a fortification that will be known as Tank Redoubt, and out to the right on another ridge is the equally formidable Atawineh Redoubt.

Both redoubts dominate the bare terrain of the Valley of Death that lies before them, upon which, out to their left even now, British soldiers of the 54th Division and two dismounted Australian battalions of the Imperial Camel Corps are doing their best to attack Tank Redoubt – only to be torn apart by Turkish artillery and bullets.

And that fire is now coming their way!

But wait!

Out to the left, a sole British tank, *Nutty*, is shuddering forward, puffs of smoke bursting forth from its turret, which immediately draws Turkish fire away from the 12th. The Turkish batteries are in part guided by the Taubes overhead, which are not only dropping bombs, but helping to direct the artillery batteries.

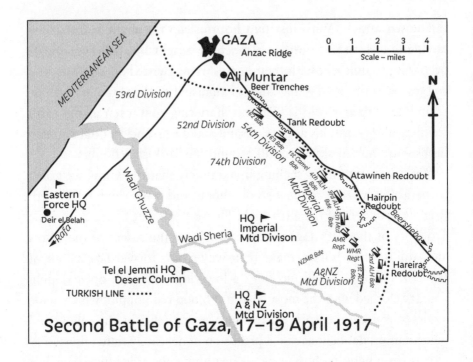

Second Battle of Gaza, 17–19 April 1917

'High explosive shells were literally rained down on the tank,' Haydon documents, 'which concentrated fire accounted for hundreds of casualties amongst the British storming troops.'[14]

Good God Almighty.

'It was like shooting at sitting ducks,' one of Haydon's fellow Troopers of the 12th, Chook Fowler, records. 'Yes, it was just murder.'[15]

Are they really to continue heading into this hell themselves?

They are.

'Advance!'

Leaving *Nutty* to its fate, Guy Haydon and the soldiers of the 12th abandon the cover of the lee side of their ridge and, after galloping 1000 yards until the fire becomes too fierce – and their horses too easy as targets – they dismount and, less the Trooper in each section assigned to take the horses, advance on foot from there.

'I wondered,' Fowler will chronicle, 'how anyone could walk through the machine-gun bullets and shrapnel that seemed to fill the air all the time as we advanced towards the Turkish line.'[16]

The strangest thing? Looking to his left and right, he sees that his mates don't look frightened. But he is not fooled, all but certain that they 'felt as scared as I was . . .'[17]

They are but men, up against an *industrial*-level killing capacity.

As they start to march forward, they can see the 11th Light Horse by their side being torn apart by exploding shells, and machine-gun and rifle fire. Within minutes, Haydon and the 12th are to know *exactly* what that is like, as the shells start to land among them, and men sink to the ground – sometimes without a sound, already dead, sometimes screaming, sometimes with a whimper, sometimes with a bang.

Forward!

At least they have a little support from the Inverness and Ayrshire batteries from behind, bringing fire down upon the Turkish defenders. And yet, alas, that artillery fire seems to be having little effect on the devastating fire sweeping them, just as it is on their fellow Troopers of the 3rd Brigade on their right.

'The enemy artillery fire was the heaviest we had experienced,' one of the 3rd will note, 'with shrapnel and high explosive. It was reported that the Turks had more than 250 big guns in action. Our troop, by short sharp rushes, got to within striking distance, but the heavy casualties made it impossible to go any further.'[18]

The worst for the 12th Light Horse Regiment comes as they pass a strange mound of earth, 'with a pole sticking out on top'.

What on earth is that?

They are not long in finding out as shells explode all around and dozens of them are wounded or killed at once. 'As we came close we soon knew it to be a "key" range for the Turkish guns, as immediately eight guns opened up with shrapnel.'[19]

Down! And dig in. The best they can, the men of the 12th use their bayonets and scrabble small pits in the hard clay soil they can lie in to gain some respite from the blizzard of bullets. This is going to be a long day for some, and an eternal night for no few.

Across the fortified line, it is the same.

The troops and Troopers of the British Empire push forward; the Turks, bolstered by German and Austrian artillery, more than hold their own. And the closer the attackers get, the more vicious the fire upon them is, and the more appalling the conditions they are trying to fight in are.

'The fire was terrible, rifle, machine-gun and shrapnel swept the ground and it was so dusty that at times one could only see about twenty yards,' Haydon will write home. 'There we lay with our noses glued to the ground and the shrapnel ripping all amongst us, then we got the order to move forward again . . . how the devil any of us got out alive the Lord only knows. This was the hottest fight of the lot . . .'[20]

It seems only by the grace of God, or *inshallah*, that the men of the 12th Regiment are able to take some cover in a small wadi tributary, which gives them shelter from the worst of the fire. To their right, the 3rd Australian Light Horse Brigade makes three charges on Atawineh Redoubt, only to suffer devastating losses each time and be pushed back.

•

In desperation for a breakthrough, General Dobell now throws in the tanks, and all of *Tiger*, *War Baby*, *Pincher*, *Sir Reginald*, *Kia-Ora* and *Ole-Luk-Oie* are soon clanking their way across the sand ridges and towards the Turkish redoubts.

They sound like nothing anybody has ever heard, because nobody ever has; it is an extraordinary sound of roaring engines mixed with the eternally circular flap-flap-flap of the tracks, previously described by one Digger as being 'like the padding of gigantic webbed feet'.[21] As the tanks flap-flap their way over the sands, their noses and tails rise and dip with a sway that is positively unearthly, like they are some alien monsters come to devour them all, 'so repulsive, so inhuman, so full of menace'.[22]

In the belly of their roaring beasts, their backs against the engine cover, the drivers of these spitting, grinding, roaring metal monsters do their best to guide them. Unlike on the Western Front, where they have had previous experience, the sand of this desert sticks and slides particle by particle in a way that a clod of dirt will not. From grease turned to grit, to sandy sprockets that suddenly throw the tracks of the tanks out of alignment; it is clear from the first that the tanks are struggling just to get across the sand, let alone engage the enemy.

Did someone say target practice?

For the Turkish artillery, it is like lining up sick elephants waddling towards them, and through laying their artillery and firing over open sight they are quickly able to blow the first two tanks apart.

Out on the far left, however – closely watched by Guy Haydon and the men of the 2nd Brigade – against all odds, *Nutty* is still going! Or is it?

It's hit!

'Suddenly the tank began to wobble in circles,' Ion Idriess chronicles, 'like an antediluvian monster shot through the stomach.'[23]

But now look.

Against all odds . . .

'The tank righted itself, and under a tornado of shells again clanked straight for the redoubt.'[24]

The amazed Troopers behind can see through gaps in the billowing clouds of smoke and dust that the tank is able to trample the barbed wire in its way and bring sustained fire on the enemy trenches just a quarter mile ahead, as they rush forward.

Alas, a high explosive shell lands right under *Nutty*, the blast finally finishing the tank, as the crew 'come out of it burning'.[25]

Still the surviving Troopers don't stop, as the forward survivors of the 1st Anzac Battalion of the Camel Brigade fix bayonets and charge.

'Only thirty Australians reached the redoubt and twenty British infantry,' Ion Idriess chronicles. 'They were mad-men – the Turks lost their nerve at the blazing tank groaning upon them, at the glint of steel as maniacs burst from the smoke. They fled, six hundred of them! Under Germans and Austrians.'[26]

For the next two hours the Australian and British Troopers manage to hold on to what has been so hard-won, but the fire they take is overwhelming as a Turkish counter-attack builds.

Despite it all, Lieutenant Archie Campbell, one of the cameleers, is able to direct his six machine-gunners to make the most of it; mowing down Turks in masses.

One of those gunners, Trooper William Barry, has his right arm shattered by shrapnel, and is told by Lieutenant Campbell to save his life and retreat, get out the best you can.

'What about my gun, sir?'[27]

Leave it.

'I think I can carry it,'[28] Trooper Barry counters, and heads off, the gun over his left shoulder, the stump of his right arm trailing blood.

As for Lieutenant Campbell himself, the young Queenslander seems invincible on this day. He has been shot several times but still stands. Seeing the tide has not just turned but is becoming a tidal wave against them; he gathers the Turkish prisoners they have taken and orders them to run at once, for the British line! They do exactly that, but Campbell remains, still firing for a few moments more before placing his revolver back in his holster and running back from the redoubt to find . . . a German officer standing straight in his path, stock still and covering *him* with a revolver.

Both officers recognise the moment.

It is man on man.

The German has chivalry, even giving Campbell the chance to surrender. Should Campbell bow to such chivalry, or go for his gun? Deciding on the latter, he whips his right hand down and even manages to get his revolver out of his holster before . . . he is blown backwards, completely knocked from his feet.

A shell has exploded right in front of him. When the dust clears, the chivalrous German officer is no more than scattered human remains spread on the ground before him. Such is war. A stroke of good fortune for one combatant is devastating bad luck for another, and Campbell will live to fight another day.

Alas, he is in a tragic minority. Campbell had led 102 men into battle on this day, only 10 of whom make it back to where they began at dawn. It has been a disaster by any definition.

Elsewhere along the line, the Turkish fire is unrelenting on any troop movement, and all the remaining tanks are quickly destroyed.

Lieutenant John Davidson of the 3rd Australian Camel Battalion is in no doubt about the value of the metal beast: 'Curse the tanks!' Thanks to them, 'We got it in the neck.'[29]

'It is the heaviest scrapping we have had,' Guy Haydon will recount, 'worse than the landing on Gallipoli and even worse than in France.'[30]

Out to the east, Ion Idriess and the men of the 2nd Brigade have had a similarly grim experience. Assigned the task of preventing the garrisons at Beersheba and Chereiff from moving to the west to support Gaza they, too, must 'demonstrate' against the assembled Turkish forces, and keep them busy.

At least they are not alone.

'Here were congregated brigades of Australians, Yeomanry, Camelry, and by Jove, some of the engineers with a ton of gun-cotton to blow up some railway bridges. There came the *buzz-zzzz wheeze-zzz crash* and down hurtled three bombs killing six men and wounding fifteen, and killing thirty horses. If a bomb had dropped on that gun-cotton then the whole brigade would have gone too.

'We moved out across the plain towards the hills of Chereiff. The sun grew blazing hot, clouds of stifling dust arose. Again came the Taubes; they roared as they swerved viciously down. We dismounted and blazed hatefully while their machine-gun spat down as they roared and rocked above.'[31]

In the end it becomes clear that further advance is impossible and they are ordered to stay in their wadi until they can withdraw. It is much the same situation along the line.

When their artillery support stops completely, the fire upon them becomes devastating and, as the Desert Column is torn apart, the heroic work of the stretcher-bearers is counted on more than ever. In a manner that would make both Simpson *and* his donkey weep with admiration, all through the battle these stunningly brave men go back and forth into the front lines, carrying back the wounded. They never stop, and the Official Historian will later record that 'Captain W. Evans, of the 3rd Light Horse Brigade Field Ambulance, worked all day under the fire of the guns, and, assisted only by four men, handled no less than 240 wounded.'[32]

One of these is already well known and beloved throughout the entire AIF.

'Cotter, the international fast bowler,' Gullett chronicles, 'was prominent all day among the stretcher-bearers . . . [33] He behaved in action as a man without fear.'[34]

Trooper Tibby Cotter and his comrades never stop.

With bullets flying, and shrapnel hissing by, with men dying all around, they simply go about their task, gathering up the wounded and getting them back to relative safety where they can get treatment. As the battle goes on, inevitably, they are a dark hue below the waist as the fresh blood all over them dries, and even starts to flake off their pants. Cotter – who has been attached to the 12th Light Horse Regiment since February 1916 – simply keeps going.

As shocking as it is to take a bayonet to the guts, it is at least something to meet Tibby Cotter.

Tibby!

One method of evacuation tried on the day is to put the wounded on sleds and pull them back behind horses at full gallop, which works well bar for the fact that, all too frequently, the sleds wipe out the field-telephone wires between the front lines and Brigade Headquarters, which . . .

Hello . . . ?

Hello . . . ?

Despite such communication problems, by the time the sun is high in the sky on this day, General Dobell is under no illusion. The net gain for his forces both at Gaza and along the fortified line is . . . not much. The Turkish artillery, machine guns and rifles have stopped them at nearly every point, and the enemy's fortified positions remain practically untouched. For their trouble, the attackers have been completely decimated and the battlefield is strewn with their blood, their limbs and their corpses.

They have been annihilated.

At one point when Kiwi and Yeomanry reinforcements arrive, Hellfire Jack Royston puts them with some of the survivors of his 3rd Light Horse Brigade to mount a bayonet charge . . . only to call it off at the last minute. The 10th Light Horse Regiment, which had been nearly wiped out at the Nek, is more relieved than most, with just 35 men left standing this time, from over 200 who had gone forward.

Back from the front lines, frustrated beyond measure at being kept in reserve for the entire day, and without a chance to prove themselves, are the men of the 4th Light Horse Regiment.

Adding insult to injuries too bloody and devastating to bear, by mid-afternoon a message from Gaza to the German HQ at Tel el Sheria is intercepted, telling Kress von Kressenstein not to worry, as they were in no need of reinforcements. Yes, there had been a spot of bother here and there, but the British would need to throw more than 40,000 soldiers at them to properly bother them.

At the end of this brutal day, in his HQ at Deir el Belah, General Dobell looks over the devastating reports coming back from all his separate units, and starts tabulating. So far, in the course of his battle, they have had nearly 5000 casualties, of whom 1500 have been killed.

It is, not to put too fine a point on it, a . . . disaster, heading towards catastrophe.

Should they continue, by bringing in the major reserve force – the 74th Yeomanry Division – and suffer more casualties for an uncertain result? Or bow to the obvious – they have lost this battle.

As night falls the Australians fall back.

Guy Haydon and the 12th Light Horse Regiment had started the day 220-strong. They are now missing no fewer than 70 of their number to the casualty list.

The Turkish guns are still blazing at 9 pm; angry and red on distant hills. They are still blazing at 11 pm too, but there are few soldiers left awake to watch them. The men fall to rest where they can, any dirt will do. The tension of battle is stolen by slumber, all care gone, as Ion Idriess notes, for 'a few hours of the most blessed sleep we have ever had, which is saying a damned lot – in fact, words fail'.[35]

One Trooper at least tries, however.

> *Dear Mother and Father,*
>
> *Our endeavours were unsuccessful and we retired leaving a large number of dead on the field. It was the worst cutting up since Gallipoli this brigade has had.*
>
> *Stephen*[36]

•

For the second time in a month, the Australians of the Light Horse find themselves retreating from Gaza, carrying their dead and wounded, while cursing the Generals who have brought them to this insanity. The only upside right now is some rest at last.

'Our horses didn't have their saddles off for seven days and nights,' Guy Haydon will report to Bon. 'They had a rough time but we didn't lose one, and the old black mare is still going strong.'[37]

Appalled by the results of the battle, the good men who have been lost, Ion Idriess is one of many who feels he knows that the root cause of this whole devastating debacle has been 'all because some English general wanted the honour of taking Gaza by infantry. Infantry cannot fight any faster than they can march.'[38]

Seriously! In the first battle, the Generals had let the Light Horse have their head and by rapid movement they had actually stormed the high citadel. This time they had sent the infantry up against the fortress to beat them all, Gaza, while the Light Horse had gone up against a solid wall of guns where the ability to manoeuvre was a little beside the point. Idriess has, consequently, no respect at all for these Generals whose idea of a good battle is to set up a camp completely remote from the action, and risk, and every day or so report on the 'progress' you have made as more men die for the next scrap of land. It is insane. And he and another 12,000 men of the Australian Light Horse have a better idea if anyone would care to listen:

'We can't understand why they don't let us gallop in as mounted troops and get the thing over. It will have to be done at the finish – after the Turks have fortified all Palestine.'[39]

The worst of it is the first of it: they have been here before; they *were* there! 'Gaza should have fallen on the first day, at a cost to us of only a few hundred lives. Thousands [of lives] have twice now been thrown away in two attacks . . .'[40]

Bloody Hell. That is what they have seen these past few days and that's what the future will hold unless something changes. A General or two might be a good place to start.

The whole exercise has been a catastrophe and, on hearing the news, Lawrence of Arabia is another figure who is furious, convinced that Murray's ineptitude has placed the entire Arab Revolt at risk.

For his part, General Murray is in no doubt where the fault lies and is quick to sack Lieutenant General Dobell, the commander of Eastern Force, even if he publicly spreads a little seasoning on his reasoning.

'It became apparent to me,' he will recount, 'that General Dobell, who had suffered some weeks previously from a severe touch of the sun, was no longer in a fit state of health to bear the strain of further operations in the coming heat of summer. To my great regret, therefore, I felt it my duty to relieve him of his command, and to place the command of Eastern Force in the hands of Lieutenant-General Sir Philip Chetwode.'[41]

Now, who can replace Chetwode's position in his previous command of the Desert Column?

Well, there can only be one choice. General Harry Chauvel, who has done so well with his Anzac Mounted Division. In a solemn ceremony, Sir Philip hands over the lance and standard of the Desert Column to Chauvel, the engraved band around records the name of each battle fought – many still are to come – and it is done.

Chauvel is in charge; promoted to the rank of Lieutenant General, to boot – the first time an Australian has reached that rank. The capable New Zealander, Major General Edward Chaytor, will take over Chauvel's previous command of the Anzac Mounted Division.

The two failed attacks on Gaza have left a bitter taste in the mouths of the Desert Column survivors. Generals with clever words can claim what they like, but the truth is all too bloody obvious to every man left: 'We have lost eighteen thousand men, and gained nothing.'[42]

What makes it worse is the lack of understanding from so many, including much of the Australian public. A small example that comes at this very time is when one of Ion Idriess's mates in the 5th Light Horse Regiment receives a care parcel from Australia, addressed to 'a lonely soldier'. Which is charming. Less so is the note inside from an anonymous Australian woman, as recounted by Idriess, 'expressing the pious wish that a brave soldier in France should get the parcel and not a cold footed squib in Egypt'.[43]

Outraged, the Trooper gets some photos of the graves of mates who'd been killed at Gaza, and sends them to the woman, 'with compliments from a cold footed squib in Egypt'.[44]

•

There is an old Turkish saying.

Damlaya damlaya göl olur.

Drop by drop becomes a lake.

It is a warning as well as an instruction. One hour can turn a battle, one battle can turn a war.

What have they and their German colleagues learnt in the last two attacks on Gaza? Firstly, that they can take on the perfidious British and their allies in a head-to-head battle and *win*.

With this in mind, Kress von Kressenstein and his Commanding Officer, Djemal Pasha, are more determined than ever to hold the fort, and not only reinforce Gaza but also stop the British ever breaching the Gaza to Beersheba line.

The elated Kress von Kressenstein, thus, gives the orders: that 30-mile line, stretching out into the desert, across the only precious wells in the area, must be further fortified. As ever, his purpose is as singular as his monocle, and he will see that order become reality immediately or know the reason why.

The Turks and Arabs must, for the moment, give preference to their shovels over their rifles to dig trenches, build redoubts, construct defences and anticipate the inevitable attack, defeating it with preparation before it has even begun.

There are to be no more British patrols roving north of this line. More than a line in the sand across which no-one can cross, it is to be an armed, fortified connected series of entrenchments. And from here, the Turks can launch their own patrols to the south to attack the British.

And what can the British and their allies do in response?

It is precisely as it had been in France when the Germans had dug in.

There is only one thing you can do. To prevent a Turkish counter-attack, and defend your own line, you must dig in yourself.

So it is, that in the high summer of 1917, two roughly parallel trenches snake across the desert, anywhere from a few miles to many miles apart.

In terms of offensive actions against the Turks at the moment, there is only one bit of good news for the British. That strange chap,

T. E. Lawrence, with his strange ideas about activating the Arab tribes against the Ottoman Empire, is actually achieving wonders.

Time and again, he and his Arab warriors are launching ambushes on Turkish trains in the Hejaz, that desert region – boasting Damascus itself – that lies by the Red Sea. Negotiating with different Arab tribes as he goes, Lawrence is gathering strength and, from being merely a thorn in the side of the Turks, he is turning into an open wound as they must bleed resources to try to thwart those ambushes and pursue Lawrence and his raiders, all to no avail.

Time and again, Lawrence of Arabia manages to disappear into the sand dunes whence he came with his men, only to appear a week or two later, at a seemingly impossible distance, to strike again from a completely unexpected angle, whereupon he and his men disappear once more!

Worse still, for the Turks, Lawrence's forces are growing, the initial raiders spawning new bands.

June 1917, Cairo, pass the port

Riots again.

This time the troops are gathering outside of a particular establishment, and for very good reason.

'Generals out of a job to the number of ninety or so,' Banjo Paterson himself would recount, 'had accumulated in Shepheard's Hotel where they either just existed beautifully or they made themselves busy about such jobs as reporting upon the waste of jam tins. Others became town commandants, or examiners of an army diet. So many were they that there was little room for junior officers in the hotel and no room at all for noncoms or the rank and file. These latter riff-raff were forbidden to enter the hotel, even to buy a drink or to meet a friend, lest they should come between the wind and the nobility of the staff officers. This created a very unpleasant feeling and the troops rioted outside Shepheard's by way of voicing their protest.'[45]

Hundreds of them!

Hurling abuse! Throwing beer bottles! And even burning a car!

It will take several hours for the Military Police to restore order, but the message of the soldiers remains long after they have been dispersed: they have lost confidence in their military leadership, who send them out to battle, while they stay here, swanning about and doing fuck-all!

As it happens, Whitehall is starting to feel much the same, at least when it comes to General Archibald Murray. His explanations for the failure to take Gaza in this latest battle have never been satisfactory.

Broadly, as he will later explain, his forces had been outgunned.

'The enemy force in front of me was then five divisions,' General Murray will recount, 'with considerably increased numbers of Austrian and German gunners and machine-gunners, and it was abundantly clear that, owing to the relaxation of pressure further east, the Turks had been able to reinforce their units heavily from depots in the north of Palestine.'[46]

When questioned as to just what he needed to get the job done, Murray would request a further 'Two complete divisions and enough field artillery to complete all divisions to a normal scale. With the troops which I had at the time I could hope for no more than a local success.'[47]

For Whitehall, such excuses and demands are underwhelming. And history itself, or at least the Official Historian, Henry Gullett, will take a dim view.

'Sir Archibald,' he will write, 'failed mainly because Dobell, who was leading his Palestine army, was equipped neither by experience nor by temperament for an important command against a European force. There is something fine about Dobell's boundless confidence in his capacity to crush his foe at all hours and on any ground. But battles against Europeans are not won by the mere exercise of boundless confidence. Dobell was not the only British leader who, having achieved success against native troops in petty wars, had made such mistakes.'[48]

The bottom line for Whitehall is that the failure of Murray's troops to take Gaza at the second go – all while suffering over 6000 casualties, of whom over 500 had been killed outright – is simply not good enough. And all this while he has barely left Cairo?

Murray himself is not good enough.

But who can replace him?

Prime Minister Lloyd George is so eager to move on he has already offered the job to the legendary South African, General Jan Smuts – famed for his brilliant mounted commando campaigns *against* the British in the Boer War, and for his shrewd grace in concluding that war in personal negotiation with the steely Lord Kitchener – but the great man has declined on the grounds that (*sniff*) Palestine is no more than a side-show.

Who else then?

There is one, currently on duty at the Western Front, in charge of the Third Army, holding the line around the Arras sector. A vastly experienced professional soldier and officer, he had been one of the first into France as commander of the Cavalry Division and even though there had been only very limited opportunities for cavalry in that deadly arena, his charges had still fought brilliantly on foot, most particularly at Messines during the First Battle of Ypres.

Let us sound Allenby out . . .

•

Another night at Third Army HQ, some miles back from the Western Front. With the darkness comes the endless gloomy flashes to the east, reflected off the low cloudbank, followed a few seconds later by booms of dirty thunder even as the very ground itself shakes.

The whole eastern horizon is a pulsating menace, despite the distance. General Sir Edmund Allenby wonders at just how appalling it must be for those soldiers on both sides who are under such a barrage, day and night. As ever, his thoughts go to one English soldier in particular.

As he does every evening, the General heads down the corridor of his HQ in this old chalet and pushes the door open to the office where the casualty reports come in, heads off to the window which faces the pulsating light to the east and asks with his back to the officer-in-charge, 'Have you any news of my little boy today?'[49]

As ever, the officer-in-charge – knowing General Allenby is referring to his and Lady Allenby's only child, Lieutenant Michael Allenby, who at the age of 19 is on the front lines with the Royal Horse Artillery – replies, 'No news, sir.'[50]

As a father, he seeks no privileges for his son, no special care be taken. He asks only the indulgence that he know that his son is safe so far, so he can sleep that night.

(Far from being sheltered, Michael is constantly in the thick of the action and, only a few months earlier, had been awarded the Military Cross for his bravery, rescuing a wounded man under heavy fire – something that is the pride of Sir Edmund and Lady Allenby's life.)

Ah, but there is other news for you tonight, General Allenby.

A cable.

From London.

It is requested you journey to the capital immediately to discuss a possible transfer of command.

Really?

Despite his recent run-ins with his Commander-in-Chief Sir Douglas Haig on the subject of the Battle of Arras, which had finished just weeks before, Allenby is reluctant to change posts. For the job is not done!

Following his brilliant plan, his Third Army had cracked the German line wide open near the French city of Arras on the Western Front and had advanced further in less time – four miles in just one day! – than any Army since the beginning of trench warfare in October 1914.

And yes, the Germans had then regrouped and managed to stop them, which had seen both Allenby's Third Army and General Sir Henry Horne's First Army suffer over 160,000 casualties. But, after regrouping, receiving reinforcements from Britain, Allenby is confident that they could see it through.

And this is General Allenby all over – the only thing about him that has ever retreated is his hair, he stands at six foot four inches, sturdy (and perhaps a touch burly) English oak, and the idea of leaving France is anathema to him.

As would later be documented by the historian and fellow iconic officer, Field Marshal Sir Archibald Percival Wavell, 'He believed he was being removed from France and relegated to an unimportant command because of the limited success of the Arras battles.'[51]

(His biographer will later come to the view that Allenby was removed because he had 'jettisoned his philosophy of cheerful obedience'[52] to Haig, making the latter want to see the last of him.)

Prime Minister Lloyd George, the Welsh wizard, is both beguiling and frank in their meeting at 10 Downing Street.

The East *needs* him, he is the *only* man for the job! He will *have carte blanche!*

'You can ask us for such reinforcements and supplies as you find necessary, and we will do our best to provide them. If you do not ask it will be your fault. If you do ask and do not get what you need it will be ours.'[53]

But, make no mistake.

'[I want Jerusalem] as a Christmas present for the British nation.'[54]

Jerusalem? Back in Western, Christian hands for the first time since the Crusades. It really would be a Christmas present to beat them all for the British Empire. For the Prime Minister's goal, as he had openly stated to the War Cabinet a short time earlier, is not just military, but political and moral. The British public is tiring quickly of the endless stalemate on the Western Front, the devastatingly long casualty lists being published in the papers, *every day*. But an advance in the Middle East? A chance to take back the lands of Christ – Bethlehem, Jerusalem, Nazareth, Damascus – from the perfidious Turk who has ruled it for the last 400 years? It would lift the English-speaking peoples, starting with the people of the British Empire!

Lloyd George had already directed his Director of Propaganda to begin a campaign with the slogan, 'The Turk Must Go', and Allenby's delivery of Jerusalem would be an enormous part of that.

Yes, difficult, but doable. And once Jerusalem is secured, the seat of Ottoman power in the Middle East, Damascus itself, could be next! The fall of an empire and a front of the war is a dream within reach, if the right soldier reaches for the glittering prize. Why, if everything falls into place, the British Cabinet is already discussing – almost as an afterthought – the possibility of declaring Palestine as a new Jewish homeland. Lord Balfour, the Foreign Secretary, is particularly keen on it.

General Allenby agrees to go.

When asked by the Prime Minister himself, what can a General do but cede to the request? As Allenby takes his leave of Downing Street, Lloyd George reaches into his bookcase and gives the General a copy of George Adam Smith's *Historical Geography of the Holy Land*, telling him it will be, 'a better guide to a military leader whose task [is] to reach Jerusalem than any survey to be found in the pigeon-holes of the War Office'.[55]

•

Attennnnnn-shun!

General Harry Chauvel, the newly appointed Commanding Officer of the Desert Column, has arrived to inspect some of his Australian troops.

Trooper Maurie Evans surveys him with a gimlet eye, not sure what to expect. All of them have prepared as well as they can, polishing their buttons, shining their brass, and putting their slouch hats with emu feathers poking out from the khaki puggaree on their left-hand side at just the right rakish angle.

Now, they are in parade formation, in lines, each Trooper standing beside his mount, with all his saddlery laid out on a blanket before him. And here comes General Chauvel, trailed by his aides, and the 1st Light Horse Field Ambulance regiment's own officers. Evans himself is pointed out to Chauvel as one of the regiment's veterans, who had come over with the first contingent.

Chauvel stops before him, and looks him up and down.

'Oh, er, you came over with the first contingent?'

'Yes.'

Pause. Sir Harry has not *quite* mastered the art of a quick word on full parade just yet.

'Did you get on the peninsula?'

'Yes.'

Another pause.

'Were you there with Colonel Sutherland?'

'Yes, sir.'

'And, er, did your health stick with you all right?'

'I was off sick from dysentery on the peninsula.'

There is a much longer awkward pause.

'Ah well, er, you got a bit of a spell that way.'[56]

It is on the tip of Evans's tongue to offer a smart remark along the lines of he can think of better ways of getting a spell, but he thinks better of it. Chauvel moves on; and good luck to the next man he tries to 'chat' with. Chauvel is not one for small talk, but he is one for big battles, and he is one of ours! To be an Australian commanded by an Australian is a novelty that the diggers and Troopers of the East delight in.

An amused Evans records his conversation with Chauvel in his journal, and, as the shocking heat of the desert dies away, he records beauty, too, with the glory of sundown.

'In the twinkling of an eye the glow fades, the stars rush out,' he notes in his diary, 'and the darkness of an eastern night descends on land, sky and sea.'[57]

Hopefully the tide will turn on this war, and they can all go home. *Inshallah.*

CHAPTER EIGHT

ENTER ALLENBY

Such then was the state of things prior to the advent of Allenby –
troops rioting, officers disregarding orders, and generals wearing
wrongly coloured socks. Then came Allenby. And everything was
altered in the twinkling of an eye.[1]

Banjo Paterson, *Happy Dispatches*

28 June 1917, Cairo, cometh the hour, cometh the man

Formally, General Allenby is only to take command of the Egyptian
Expeditionary Force as the twelfth bell of midnight tolls on this day.
But he does not bother waiting that long and his polished boots of black
leather are barely on the platform of Cairo Railway Station before he
is on his way to the Egyptian Expeditionary Force GHQ. Situated at
the great colonial chateau of the Grand Continental Hotel on Opera
Square – overlooking from its sweeping balconies the trees, lawn and
lake of Ezbekiyya Gardens, while on the far horizon are the Pyramids –
the newly arrived General goes briskly and unannounced from room
to room to introduce himself to each officer, work out precisely what
it is they do and where they fit into what they are pleased to call the
'scheme of things'.

If only an actual scheme existed.

As near as Allenby can work out for the moment, there appears
to be very little in train to, how should one put this . . . win the war.
The most senior officers are 'monitoring the situation' the best they
can from this far back, but there is no urgency, no straining forth,
no whip to even crack. It all puts him in an ill humour when a rather
nervous Major General arrives with a folder several inches thick under

his arm, 'dealing with details of dress, discipline, the administration of martial law, and such matters'.[2]

Allenby looks through the first three pages with rising colour – each document more petty than the last.

He cannot contain himself.

'Is the rest of this of a similar nature?'[3]

An affirmative nod is all he needs.

Without another word, the newly arrived General takes the whole folder and throws it across the room, which sees a hundred pages loosely flutter to the floor. The cavalry is not only in General Allenby's background, it is in his very blood, and he knows that battles are not won by bureaucracy.

'Never again waste my time,' he thunders, 'on minor details that could be answered by a junior officer.'[4]

Let the word go forth.

They don't call this six foot four inch behemoth 'Bull' Allenby for nothing! He is descended from the Lord Protector Oliver Cromwell himself – whose most famous blast of thunder was, 'I beseech you, in the bowels of Christ, think it possible you may be mistaken!'[5] – and communicating with a certain vigour is something of a family tradition.

At least for Allenby there is one familiar face who can give him orthodox counsel on the whole situation. After the debacle of the attacks on Gaza, Chetwode has replaced Dobell as Commander of the Eastern Force. Edmund Allenby and Philip Chetwode are old friends and brothers-in-arms, with Chetwode having a year earlier been a Brigade Commander in Allenby's Third Army on the Western Front, and, in fact, they go back as far as the Siege of Ladysmith in the Boer War.

As soon as Sir Edmund had set foot on the docks at Alexandria, General Chetwode had been there to greet him, and handed him his proposal on how the Turkish nut could be cracked. The answer is Beersheba. Chetwode's Chief of Staff, Brigadier General Guy Dawnay, has come up with a novel plan to take it, and it is well worth looking at, General.

The starting point is that it's now obvious that the Turks are digging in and are intent on holding the Gaza–Beersheba line, a formidable obstacle given that they have built trenches and redoubts on high ground lying right on wadis, with the approaches from the south being vast waterless plains without cover. And just to be extra sure, they have endless rolls of barbed wire to further slow down any forces that dare to try to overcome all the other defences.

With all that in mind . . .

'It would be fatal, in my opinion,' General Chetwode ventures, 'to make a half-bite at the cherry and to attempt an offensive with forces which might permit us to attack and occupy the enemy's present line, but which would be insufficient to inflict on him a really severe blow and to follow up that blow with fresh troops pressing closely on his heels.'[6]

What General Allenby must understand is that the Gaza line goes from the sea for some 30 miles along the Gaza–Beersheba road, and is defended – as near as our intelligence can work it out – by at least 50 battalions, over 33,000 men with another 1400 cavalry and 260 guns manned by 5500 artillery crew. The only weakness comes where the fortifications are much thinner between Hareira and Beersheba itself – that part of the line where the reckoning of the Turks is that there is not enough water out there to support a big attack.

The key to attacking this line will be both speed of movement and making the enemy *think* the attack will be coming from elsewhere right up until the moment they strike. We *have* been hitting Gaza, the Turks expect us to *keep* hitting Gaza, so what if we pretend we are going to do just that, with traditional British Bulldog stubbornness when it comes to changing tactics or targets? If we make the Turks think we are going to hit Gaza, the bulk of their forces will be congregated there, just as we hit the thinner defences in between Hareira and Beersheba instead, and drive through!

Beersheba. Allenby is struck by the counter-intuitive notion, the very improbability of the target. Why Gaza is bad enough, the only approaches are over a bare plain with no cover. But a surprise attack *further* inland still, over such difficult territory, the Turks will never be expecting it!

Chetwode, too, is a cavalry man, and is speaking a language that Allenby appreciates, focusing on the virtues of men on horseback moving fast and attacking from an unexpected angle.

Go on, General Chetwode . . .

If we can move fast enough and attack with overwhelming force, ideally creating havoc behind the enemy lines, our cavalry forces will be concentrated on our right flank, with a sure water supply, and be able to roll up the fortified line from there, attacking from three sides: in front, behind, and on the flank! It can be done in a day!

Allenby studies the plan closely.

The sheer madness of it is genius.

Yes, the difficulties of moving a mass of men and *materiel* that far into the desert while escaping detection would be many. But equally, an outrageous victory could be possible.

How many men will we need?

Two big infantry corps and one smaller mounted corps, about 100,000 men in all. One British infantry corps will attack the enemy's left flank around Beersheba, while another infantry corps will pin the enemy down at Gaza.

•

One hundred thousand men are under his command, but General Allenby is not quite sure what to make of this one, the Australian chap in charge of the Desert Column. There is no doubt that the military record of General Harry Chauvel is outstanding, and it had been Chauvel's men, after all, who had actually *got inside* Gaza and established temporary dominion, before being pulled back for what, in Allenby's view, was an absurdity. (If possession is nine points of the law in civil life, it is close to ten points in military situations. Allenby was never a man to voluntarily give up hard-won positions in difficult terrain, and for the life of him can't understand why Murray did.)

But standing here now in front of Allenby, there is about the rather exhausted if still neat-looking Australian a certain – what is it? – *diffidence*, a certain stand-offishness?

Allenby is Chauvel's Commanding Officer and there is no doubt that the Australian is properly respectful of that. But there is certainly no *more* than that coming from him. It is almost as if Chauvel is assessing Allenby, waiting, listening, keeping his own counsel and working out just what the new chap might be bringing, what his intentions are.

One reason for Chauvel's slight remoteness is that he wants it exactly that way. Time and again in this war to date, he has had to push back against the British assumption that the Australians must automatically do exactly what the British Government asks of them. He does not. Australia is no longer a colony.

So it is that when Allenby moves to have Chauvel and his men come under Allenby's administrative control, Chauvel declines.

As has been agreed between the Australian and the Imperial Government, he is answerable first to General Birdwood, the Englishman who the Australian Government has appointed as Commander-in-Chief of the Australian forces, and secondly to Australia itself. And so when Allenby now insists he wishes to make a direct approach to Australia's Prime Minister Billy Hughes to ask for more men to be sent from Australia, General Chauvel is clear.

No, General Allenby.

(Chauvel will take the precaution of writing to both Birdwood and Hughes, reporting Allenby's intent.)

The Australian's projection of a sense of independence is further emphasised when the English General expresses his dissatisfaction with the fact that, instead of being born and bred to the cavalry, Chauvel's Chief of Staff has a background as a field gunner, while his Quartermaster is a Royal Marine. Thank you, General Allenby, but General Chauvel is quite happy with both officers.

The towering Allenby tries insistence.

Chauvel is persistence itself, and is not for changing. He is his own man, with a very strong record of success. Yes, General Allenby can remove him with the stroke of a pen, but it would be at his peril. Infantry are useful in this war, but far more important are the fast-moving mounted troops and Chauvel's demonstrated capacity to command them with deadly efficiency is a key asset.

And so Allenby leaves it, for the moment, but in Allenby's first letter to Sir William Robertson, Chief of the Imperial General Staff, however, the Australian general is the first item on the agenda.

'Chauvel is not a trained cavalry leader,' he writes, 'and, though he has capacity for command, and fighting instincts, he would be improved by having a trained and experienced cavalryman as his [Chief of Staff].

Such a one I have not available. FitzGerald, who commands the 5th Mounted Brigade, could do it; but the Australians, including Chauvel, cannot bear the sight of him.'[7]

•

The word spreads.

The arrival of Allenby has already seen many senior officers dismissed, and the question is, who might be next!

By now, Major Banjo Paterson's Remount Depot has moved from within the sight of the Pyramids to much closer to the front, up at Moascar,[8] and the poet is suddenly privy to many hushed conversations concerning 'the imminent issue of a tin hat to some general whose headgear had been mostly brass'.

Oh yes.

'This expression "tin hat" arose from the tin extinguisher that was used in the old days to put out a candle. When Allenby issued a tin hat to a man that man was forthwith extinguished.'[9]

One contender whose name frequently arises is General Chauvel. Yes, he is currently in charge of the Desert Column – clearly the most important command of the entire campaign, as it is always the spearhead of the attack – but will General Allenby leave him there?

Banjo has heard a whisper that Chauvel might be due some new brass, charge of a whole corps? 'They'll never give it to Chauvel,' one brass-bound Brigadier says to Paterson. 'Fancy giving the command of the biggest mounted force in the world's history to an Australian. Chauvel's sound, but he's such a sticky old frog.'[10]

And that officer is not the only that thinks so.

'There's an extra big tin hat being got ready,' Banjo is told of Chauvel's likely fate. It feels well informed enough that the poet fears for the fate of his old friend.

•

One who is particularly impressed with the whole Allenby approach is Major Richard Meinertzhagen of the Intelligence section based at Deir el Belah, who, after meeting the General in his first days there, records in his diary:

'My word, he is a different man to Murray. His face is strong and almost boyish. His manner is brusque almost to the point of rudeness, but I prefer [it] to the oil and butter of the society soldier. Allenby breathes success and the greatest pessimist cannot fail to have confidence in him. The Egyptian Expeditionary Force is already awakening from its lethargic sleep under Murray, and I'm happy to say that GHQ will shortly move into Palestine and be near troops instead of wallowing in the flesh pots of Cairo.'[11]

Good God! Comfortable paper warriors hear chilling reports that Allenby is wandering the corridors of Cairo's Savoy hotel, collaring every lurking officer he can find and barking, 'Get ready to go to the front!'[12]

And it is hardly as if Allenby is hiding his intent.

'We're a bit far from our work up here,' he observes acidly to his officers. 'I'd like to get up closer where I can have a look at the enemy occasionally.'[13]

Meinertzhagen heartily approves the idea of moving GHQ to the front.

'This move will stamp out the so-called East Force with its iniquitous independent attitude, and the Chetwode policy of much bluster and no action. Chetwode is an excellent soldier but must be driven. If he acts by himself his every action is bluff and he is a very nervous officer, attributing to the Turks all sorts of wondrous strategy and tactics. Apart from this he is a soldier with sound ideas; when he lacks the initiative and courage to carry them out as planned that is just where Allenby will find a very useful and talented servant.'[14]

Indeed.

Open parenthesis.

There is an obvious connection between Allenby and Meinertzhagen in that both are passionate ornithologists and both have a classic education resulting in a great facility to translate ancient Greek. Where they differ is that Allenby plays by the rules, and Meinertzhagen plays by his own. There is an unworldly ruthlessness to the Intelligence operative, and in the colonial wars in Africa at the turn of the century there was no doubt as to his proclivities.

'Richard Meinertzhagen was a killer,' it has been noted by Elspeth Huxley. 'Animals he killed for sport and tribesmen he killed for duty.'[15]

Even the concept of murder is hardly shocking to him, as he will himself write, 'I have no belief in the sanctity of human life or in the dignity of the human race.'[16]

Close parenthesis.

•

They will say many things about Lawrence of Arabia. They will never say he lacks audacity, and today is a case in point.

On this day, Captain T. E. Lawrence – dressed in Arab robes and indistinguishable in dress from his companions, while his skin is now deeply tanned – is riding at the head of his posse of camel-borne Arab guerrillas towards the Ottoman stronghold port of Aqaba, on the southern extremes of the Hejaz desert and the northern tip of the Red Sea. Yes, the port is heavily fortified and defended with many guns, but those guns are pointed towards the sea on the reckoning that no-one would be mad enough to attack from across the 600 miles of all but waterless desert to its north.

They had not reckoned on Lawrence. Over the last two months he and his men have paused only to replenish water supplies at the highly scattered wells that only some of the Arabs know, to blow up Turkish railroad tracks, and to use much of the 22,000 gold sovereigns that Lawrence carries courtesy of the largesse of the British Government to recruit more Arab fighters from tribes they pass along the way. He and his band are now 500 strong, closing in on their quarry.

And there they are!

Just to the north of Aqaba is a small Turkish outpost. Mounting their camels once more to use their humps and heads for shields, the Arab guerrillas charge down the sandhills with nearly as much speed as their English leader. They go straight at the Turks and quickly over-whelm them, showing no mercy for the fact that, just the day before, an exhausted horseman had ridden into their camp with news of a Turkish slaughter of Arab women and children. They are, consequently, now without mercy.

Aqaba itself falls just four days later. It is a major blow to Ottoman prestige, and a demonstration that Lawrence's ideas work! The only problem is that Aqaba is so isolated that the British, as yet, have no way of knowing about what is less a mere victory against the Turks in their most isolated stronghold and more a triumph of all Lawrence's ideas. Well, Lawrence will tell them, and soon sets off on his camel, in the company of eight tribesmen, to ride for 150 miles across the Sinai Desert to tell his superiors. His only guides are the stars, and a map from the Royal Geographical Society archives.

•

That stately figure, bumping along the roads that lead from Cairo, to Kantara, to parts east? Why it is none other than General Allenby himself, as his biographer will recall, getting around 'in a particularly disreputable Ford truck . . . He sat perched up on the front seat alongside the driver, an Australian, who was clad only in a sleeveless vest and very attenuated shorts. The picture of these two, with one of the personal staff bumping painfully in the body of the truck behind, remained long in the memory of those who witnessed it.'[17]

Just a bare five days after arriving in Egypt, and now eager to gain familiarity with the terrain that his forces will be fighting in, he insists on visiting these front lines some 300 miles to the north-east. One of the first things that takes his interest as he arrives among the foremost troops is the rare sight of a man at least his age and likely more. Who on earth is that ancient officer standing in a trench and what is he doing fighting in this century? A quick conversation reveals him to be one Captain Hubert Berkeley who – while really too old to be upright in a trench – is a man of no little proven ability.

Would he like to be in charge of desert transport?

He would.

Allenby promotes him on the spot, and moves on, issuing a similar blizzard of promotions, demotions, commotions – all done with no emotion, just tightly clipped orders.

'[Allenby] went through the hot, dusty camps of his army like a strong, fresh, reviving wind,' the Australian Official History will recount. 'He would dash up in his car to a Light Horse regiment, shake hands with a few officers, inspect hurriedly, but with a sure eye to good and bad points, the horses of, perhaps, a single squadron, and be gone in a few minutes, leaving a great trail of dust behind him.' And no wonder the trail is so great, Allenby is a towering figure in more ways than one: 'His tall and massive, but restlessly active figure, his keen eyes and prominent hooked nose, his terse and forcible speech, and his imperious bearing, radiated an impression of tremendous resolution, quick decision and steely discipline.'

Here is a leader at last! And he is actually here, with the likes of us! 'At last they had a commander who would live among them and lead them. Within a week of his arrival Allenby had stamped his personality on the mind of every trooper of the horse and every infantryman of the line.'[18]

(And the Arabs, too, are impressed, not least because as Allenby writes to his wife, 'Many of the Egyptians look at my name and believe it will bring good luck. I am called Allanebi, that is "Allah" and "Nebi". Allah means God and Nebi the prophet.'[19] And it certainly helps that local Arabs have been raised on the legend that one day just such a prophet would arise, to lead them victorious through the gates of Jerusalem!)

Beyond meeting and assessing the troops, Allenby is surveying the local ground and avenues of attack with particular care. Just inland from the Mediterranean coast, the country is mostly like an ocean of sand with a heavy swell, represented by the unending series of sand dunes. Once away from the main track, getting carts with supplies and the guns on limbers over those dunes would be nothing less than a nightmare – if it was possible at all. Twenty miles inland the terrain proves to be harder and drier, but still so sandy the wheels would inevitably require endless digging out.

And on the early approaches to Beersheba?

When Allenby consults the book given to him by Prime Minister Lloyd George, *Historical Geography of the Holy Land*, he reads:

'Of all names in Palestine there are hardly any better known than Beersheba. Nothing could more aptly illustrate the defencelessness of these southern slopes of Judah than that this site which marked the frontier of the land was neither a fortress nor a gateway, but a cluster of wells on the open desert.'[20]

His eyes remain peeled for enemy movements, fortifications and planes . . . but being a very keen ornithologist, his eyes are drawn inevitably to something in the sky other than Taubes, and he is also delighted to send his dear wife, Adelaide, a report of just how wondrous the desert is on that front, most particularly around the coastal strip.

'Of birds, there are larks, wheatears, shrikes, bee-eaters, hawks, vultures. Flamingos frequent the mouths of the wadis . . . In the oases, and near the villages, are date-palms, and great quantities of fig-trees, apricots and almond-trees.'[21]

Inland, in the area still closer to Beersheba, the growth is of course so much more sparse but, my dear, here is the extraordinary thing.

'The people all look like Biblical characters. Face, dress, and everything like pictures from the Bible. Keen, handsome faces; picturesque Arab dress; ornaments of beads, coins and enamel, much as one sees in the Egyptian museums.'[22]

Most importantly, he comes to the conclusion that Chetwode's plan really might work. Gaza, from the look of it, is practically impregnable. But the far end of their line, around Beersheba?

Here, with mounted troops and armoured cars providing close protection, he ventures as close as he dares, to find it really looks promising.

Most of the heavy Turkish fortifications and the troubling ridge finish at the tiny settlement of Hareira, which is four miles to the west of Beersheba. The most important thing is that to the east of Beersheba, at the far end of the line, there seems to be nothing at all in the way of Turkish presence, providing an open flank which his forces can close with a push and a shove.

Beersheba itself, baking on the banks of the Wadi Saba, hardly looks imposing at his first gaze through his powerful looking glass and seems to be little more than a scattering of old and mostly mud-brick buildings and new barracks, some gnarled trees, a desultory railway station and a white mosque shimmering in the sun, all with a lugubrious air common to all people and things who are just hanging on but have been mostly forgotten. In the words of one close observer, Trooper Richard Dunk of the 3rd Light Horse, 'Beersheba . . . lies in a shallow saucer at the foot of the Judean Hills which rise abruptly from its outskirts to the north . . . It promised no prize in comfortable quarters of foodstuffs. But it contained that which was still more essential and coveted, for the village was rich in springs of good water. Perhaps never since the far off days of Abraham had the water in the old wells been needed by parched men riding in from the desert.'[23]

It is equally no mini-Gaza in terms of defensive infrastructure.

Rather, it is well out in the open and, rather than being on high ground, it has in various spots around it several bits of high ground that tower over it. Inevitably, thus, to defend it, the Turks – likely on the advice of German engineers – have built the principal defensive fortifications on that high ground, allowing the defenders to instantly see whatever attacks might be coming at them, and to fire on any that come within range with all of their artillery, machine guns and rifles. They are the kings of the castle, and any dirty rascals who try to scale the cliffs will be propelled fatally back to the sand.

On the eastern side, the most formidable fortified defence point that must be overcome is Tel el Saba, situated at three miles from the outskirts of the town. Between Tel el Saba and Beersheba, the natural defence is the Wadi Saba, which is traversed by a bridge.

The summit of Tel el Saba, 1000 feet above the plain around it, is a plateau measuring the equivalent of about a dozen football fields, defended by steep sides all around as it stands at the meeting of the Wadi Saba and the Wadi Khalil.

Most importantly for the purposes of the defenders, Tel el Saba still has many of the original structures built upon it over the centuries, some even by the Crusaders. These have now been dragged into the twentieth century with trenches and stone huts bristling with machine guns, and artillery batteries – and no proper attack on Beersheba's east side could be made until the battalion of Turkish soldiers atop Tel el Saba, with its artillery crews, is quelled. It would still take some doing, to destroy the heavily fortified stone huts, together with the men inside, but Allenby is convinced it can be done.

Meanwhile, the defences to the south and west of Beersheba are equally problematic. Around the south-western approaches to the town are a series of well-constructed semi-circular trenches protected by wire. Heavy earthworks have been constructed to bolster the defences of those trenches and the only way the infantry will be able to storm them will be over open ground, vulnerable to all the defenders' machine-gun positions.

It will be difficult but, with enough men supported by heavy artillery, it can be done.

Beersheba it will be.

Writing to his wife on paper headed by the script for the Egyptian State Railways and Telegraphs, Allenby reports on 9 July: 'My Mabel ... I have gazed upon Gaza, at a few miles distance and I have been within 8 miles of Beersheba, but we have got neither place yet ...'

Yes, here he is 'in the land of the Philistines', replete with the kind of life form that is his great passion. 'Of birds there are larks, shrikes, hawks, vultures and flamingos ...'

Meanwhile, 'All the men and animals are looking well and in good spirits. The men are burnt as black as Arabs. One sees them sitting in the blazing sun, often with practically nothing on, and with the appearance of enjoying it. The Australians especially enjoy being grilled.'[24]

Returning to Cairo on 12 July, Allenby cables to London the genesis of the emerging plan, and asks for additional troops to not only replace the 10,000 casualties lost to the first two attacks on Gaza, but even more to give added heft to the coming attack. Shall we say another two Infantry Divisions? It is also agreed that each division will be provided with three 18-pounder batteries, and four 60-pounder batteries. (The latter are *enormous* – at five tons it takes 12 horses to haul the guns forward, and the 60-pound shells need at least two men to manhandle them into the breech, dear friends, once more.)

And he will need more planes – Bristols, Martinsydes and RE 8s – to keep the skies clear of the Taubes that are harassing and observing the dispositions of his own troops, and planes to observe exactly what the Turks are doing. The War Cabinet smiles upon the request, Lloyd George fulfils his promise, Allenby asks and he shall receive.

Allenby's force will be boosted from six to ten Divisions, while field artillery will also be boosted significantly, and three additional squadrons of aircraft will be sent.

•

Who the *hell* does this blighter think he is? On this train bound from the Suez Canal to Cairo, it is not just that there is a stranger sitting in a private compartment reserved for officers. It is that he is an Arab! Have a look at him. Reading his book, completely unconcerned by their glares, he is all white silk robes, a curved dagger at his side, a rope of gold around his head and – the *piece de resistance* of his ignominy – bare feet! The only thing that gives the British officers pause is his blond hair. It has to be said that very few Arabs boast that. And the fact he appears to be reading Homer in the original Greek makes him a rarer Arab, still. Still, Arab or not, is this cove an *officer*?

A British Sergeant is commissioned to ask the question.

'Excuse me, sir, what army?'

'The Meccan Army.'

'Never heard of it!' says the Sergeant.

'Well,' drawls the man in perfect Oxbridge English, 'would you recognise the uniform of a Montenegrin Dragoon?'[25]

Not actually, no. The sergeant retreats in confusion, the Arab grins in delight.

It will take some sorting out, and that only after the badly outgunned Sergeant withdraws and the train slows. In short order the carriage empties of British officers in uniforms conventional and Montenegrin as they must change trains to catch the Port Said–Cairo Express and they are all on the platform when it happens. Admiral Rosslyn Wemyss, the Naval Commander-in-Chief, happens to be among those on the platform with his entourage when one of his officers recognises, why, none other than . . . Lawrence of Arabia!

The sun has burnt his skin so dark and what little shows of him through his Arab dress – no, really – is so sand-blown and weathered that he really does look like a native of these parts, but Lawrence brings extraordinary news to his fellow British officers.

He and his Arabs have successfully attacked the Turks at Aqaba, from the desert side, and it has fallen!

And they, in turn, have news for him. While he has been away, a new force has hit the British forces. General Sir Edmund Allenby is here.

'Allenby! What's he doing here?'

'Oh, he's in command now.'

'And Murray?'

'Gone home.'[26]

Lawrence is perturbed. Murray had had his flaws, but had, after tutoring, understood what Lawrence was doing with the Arab Revolt. Will Allenby be the same?

'I climbed back [onto the train],' he will recount, 'and fell to wondering if this heavy, rubicund man was like ordinary generals, and if we should have trouble for six months teaching him [as I had Murray]?'[27]

•

Lawrence does not have to wonder long, a meeting is arranged in Allenby's suite at the Savoy Hotel, even though it has been substantially packed up in readiness for the move to the front. It does not begin well, Allenby gazing down from a height of six foot four inches to lecture the slight five feet five inches figure staring up at him curiously.

'He was full of Western ideas of gun powder and weight – the worst training for our war – but, as a cavalryman, was already half persuaded to throw up the new school, in this different world of Asia, and accompany Dawnay and Chetwode along the worn road of manoeuvre and movement.'

Lawrence avidly puts his case, that he and the Arabs can tie up as much as a third of the Ottoman Army in the greatest game of cat and mouse the world has seen, leaving the way clearer for Allenby's own forces to push along the Mediterranean coast through Palestine and Syria!

Lawrence keeps talking, and is at least gratified that Allenby is listening. 'He was hardly prepared for anything so odd as myself – a little bare-footed silk-skirted man offering to hobble the enemy by his preaching if given stores and arms and a fund of two hundred thousand sovereigns to convince and control his converts. Allenby could not make out how much was genuine performer and how much charlatan.'[28]

Lawrence does not help him out. The main thing is, that by the end of their meeting, Allenby is clearly not *against* what the Intelligence officer is doing. To Lawrence's proposal that he and his rising band of Arabs be given enough gold to bribe more Arab leaders, and enough guns to really attack the Turkish Army along the Hejaz Railway, General Allenby even says, 'Well, I will do for you what I can.'[29]

The two take their leave, with Lawrence broadly satisfied.

Allenby will continue to support him, which is what counts. But the General will also go on with his own manoeuvres and the plans of Chetwode and Dawnay. One thing Lawrence can hope that Allenby has gleaned from the success at Aqaba is that attacking the Turk from the unexpected direction really can work wonders.

•

Allenby continues to move with typical speed. One of his first orders is that the settlement of Kantara on the Suez Canal be transformed into a massive inland port, with more ships, looking from a distance like so many 'squatting ducks'[30] starting to congregate there as they disgorge ever more supplies ready for the coming big push. With that, comes this:

'In this huge mushroom settlement,' Henry Gullett will note, 'thirty miles of metalled roads were laid down on the heavy sand; various bases, which had hitherto been scattered over northern Egypt, were concentrated there, and a marked improvement made in the handling and dispatch of supplies to the advanced army. Simultaneously swarms of happy, singing, hard-working Egyptian labourers, spurred on by enthusiastic engineers, in the heat of the summer months duplicated the desert railway from Kantara as far as Maadan, 80 miles from the Canal – a work which had an immediate and substantial effect in the speeding up of supplies.'[31]

On this particular day Major Richard Meinertzhagen is with General Allenby and explaining the latest intelligence from spies, Lawrence's Arabs and deserters from the Turkish Army – when they are interrupted by Allenby's Military Secretary, Lord Dalmeny, looking very grave. He hands the General a telegram, bearing the news.

IT IS MY PAINFUL DUTY TO INFORM YOU LIEUTENANT HORACE
ALLENBY, ROYAL HORSE ARTILLERY, IS OFFICIALLY REPORTED
KILLED IN ACTION 29TH JULY 1917. THE ARMY COUNCIL EXPRESS
THEIR SYMPATHY.

General Allenby finishes reading it, brings his hand to cover his eyes for a moment and whispers 'My son . . .' before composing himself, and turning back to Major Meinertzhagen.

'Go on . . .' he says.

Meinertzhagen is impressed.

'I thought it a great example of self-discipline.'[32]

Meinertzhagen finishes the briefing as quickly as he decently can, before leaving Allenby to weep in private, and then complete a letter he had been engaged in writing to his wife about birdlife.

'I have just got your wire. My darling sweetheart I wish I could be with you but I know how brave you are; and you will be strong and bear this awful blow. You and Michael fill up my thoughts and I feel very near to you both . . . He was always the same, keen in his work, thoughtful beyond his years, cheerful and brave . . . He always kissed me when we met and when we parted, just as he did when a child . . .'[33]

August 1917, Moascar, Egypt, a horse for a kingdom

Mercifully, given the numbers of Walers killed, there has been a surge in their supply, but still demand exceeds it.

'Hardly had we got our first shipment of Australian horses,' Major Paterson will recount, 'very wild characters some of them, than brigadier generals began to drop in. Every one of them wanted horses, and each general wanted the best horse; any other general could go and eat coke so far as he was concerned, for every man has to fight for his own hand in the Army. Highly placed staff-officers looked in to pass their latest remarks on the war and incidentally to grab a good horse or two for themselves, their friends, or their subordinates.'

But now, everything has changed with the arrival of General Allenby. Just as he has done with everything else, Allenby is insisting on a complete change in priorities.

'Allenby's orders were very strict. No officer, not even a staff popinjay or a brigadier, should be allowed to select a horse for himself. We had to issue the horses. The best had to go to the fighting men; the next best to the staff; and the culls and rejects to the men on lines of communication, camp-commandants, doctors, water-supply officers, and such-like cattle.'[34]

A possible exception to the orders not to favour senior officers in preference to fighting men is when the most senior officer is *also* a fighting man, and there is no better example than Hellfire Jack Royston. These days, the Commanding Officer of the 12th Light Horse Regiment is still in temporary command of the 3rd Brigade, which has come to resemble him: constantly on the move, *looking* for action.

Hellfire Jack is very fond of horses, far fonder than they are of him when he is in his rhythm. They reckon Hellfire goes through nags like other blokes go through cigarettes – and he had even set the Light Horse record, by going through 20 in a day! Banjo Paterson, thus, is understandably cautious when this Geebung Polo Club level rider approaches him in much the same manner 'as Chinese junks make for port at the first smell of a typhoon . . .'[35]

For on this day, Royston rides up unannounced and casually tells Paterson he just happened to be passing.

'I just dropped in to pick out a few horses for my brigade,' he says.

'That is forbidden,'[36] Banjo replies.

'Well, at any rate I'll pick out a horse for myself. You must do the best you can to keep him for me.'

Looking around the compound Royston points to one magnificent black horse.

'My horses get a lot of work,' the Brigadier General allows carefully, 'and that fellow will just suit me.'

All right, sir. Just this one, just this once. But, just like Mr Toad in *The Wind in the Willows*, one new black beauty is never enough and even as he trots away, Banjo all but sets his watch for what he knows will happen next.

Sure enough, cometh the dawn, cometh the Royston, his eyes flickering back and forth at the fresh mob of horses that has arrived in the night!

Yes . . . General?

'There's no harm in my *looking* at 'em,' he tells Banjo. 'I'm always up early so I thought I'd ride round to have a look at 'em.'

Of course, sir. Quite normal, and expected, to come on successive days. But this time you'll be leaving without a new one.

For once, Royston is not too upset.

After they both gaze for a few moments upon the vision splendid, on the sunlit plain extended, Royston gallops off. On his old horse.

•

More bloody training? Does the bloke know we've already been at war for some time out here? The bloke does, but at Allenby's behest a new training regime is instituted, designed so that his troops and their horses will be at peak condition for what he intends is to come.

Now many Squadron, Regiment and Brigade exercises are undertaken, together with dozens of tighter reconnaissance patrols: with a hidden aim, to get the Turks used to seeing the troops of the British Empire moving around in front of them – sometimes 'reconnaissances in force' with large bodies of mounted Troopers – without automatically assuming that there is a major attack coming their way.

For both mounted and unmounted forces, the principal terrain they cover is in the 10-mile-wide swathe of land that lies before the Turkish line, so that the attackers can be thoroughly familiar with the landscape and its challenges, while the defenders won't panic when they see forces moving about there.

All good? Right, now Allenby orders them to do all of the above at night. You must be so familiar with the territory you will be moving through that you can do it blindfolded – which will be essentially the case when we actually get to the nights before Z-Day – as the day of attack is known in military parlance.

As time goes by, and both the Troopers and the Walers get tougher and more resilient, the test becomes to see if they can do it all with progressively less water. Yesterday you had the normal allotment of two gallons to survive. Today we are cutting that by 75 per cent and you can do it on four pints. Similarly, a horse needs ten gallons. Can they still operate on just three gallons?

Both the Troopers and their steeds must be toughened to continue operating, even when half-mad with thirst. It is hard, and no mistake.

'The sun,' one of Guy Haydon's Sergeants records in his diary, 'took its toll, burning its way like white hot iron into every pore of the skin, seemingly scorching the backbone until that member felt as if it was being charred by a slow fire.'[37]

There seems to be only one living thing not bothered by the searing heat.

'The flies, which in the east are never reckoned in less than billions, fought viciously for a landing place on man and beast. The one redeeming point of these patrols was the skirmishes with enemy cavalry, the surprise attacks against their outposts and the more extensive reconnaissances into enemy territory to ascertain their strength and to secure topographical surveys for the coming decisive assault . . .'[38]

Inevitably there are skirmishes with patrols of Turkish cavalry, and sometimes prisoners are taken. Some of the enemy's steeds are impressive, but not all.

'In a party of 20 Turkish cavalry captured by a Light Horse patrol,' one officer will note, 'their horses were so miserably thin one of our men hung his hat on one's rump, thereby greatly annoying the owner.'[39]

Meanwhile, General Allenby works to ensure that the troops are getting all possible support from the air. For he is equally insistent that the Royal Air Force must have more planes, more pilots and begin to establish air supremacy against the *Deutsche Luftstreitkräfte*, German Flying Corps, with their Albatrosses and Rumplers continually spying on, dropping bombs on and harassing the troops of the British Empire. Urgent cables are sent to Whitehall, and promises extracted.

'Our own pilots,' Lieutenant Colonel Richard Preston, the Commander Royal Artillery of the Australian Mounted Division, would recount of the time before Allenby, 'starved alike of aeroplanes and of materials for repairs, gingerly manoeuvring their antiquated and rickety machines, fought gallantly but hopelessly against the fast Taubes and Fokkers of the German airmen, and day by day the pitiful list of casualties that might have been so easily avoided grew longer.'[40]

Those days must stop!

Key appointments?

Allenby moves quickly.

While a little put out initially by Chauvel's diffidence and independent spirit, there is no way around the fact that this column, with its ability to get Troopers *en masse* to attack the enemy from positions they never expected, is not only the most powerful force Allenby has, but the Australian General is far and away the best performed of his officers, with a record of success unmatched by anyone else.

And so Allenby confirms Chauvel as General Officer Commanding the newly named and restructured Desert Mounted Corps; and today he becomes the first Australian in history to command a corps – which is, by the by, historically, the largest force of mounted men ever assembled. The 20th Corps will be commanded by General Chetwode, while the 21st Corps will be under General Sir Edward Bulfin. All three Corps will be under the direct control of Allenby himself.

For this battle, it will be Chetwode's 20th Corps and Chauvel's Desert Mounted Corps who will be tasked with attacking Beersheba, while it will be the job of the 21st Corps to make the enemy *think* that the real attack is coming on Gaza once more, by positioning themselves just to the south and proceeding as if they are about to launch. Each Corps will have a squadron of 15 or so RFC planes at their disposal, as will GHQ, and those squadrons are in the process of being established.

Chetwode is gracious enough to drop Chauvel a formal note, on his confirmation as Commander of the Desert Mounted Corps:

'You and I have worked together in the greatest harmony. We have together helped to write a small page of history . . . I shall always be proud of having such a fine body of men under my command as your Anzac mounted troops and grateful to you for the able way in which you have led them. I cannot say how much I envy you the command of the largest body of mounted men ever under one hand – it is my own trade – but Fate has willed it otherwise.'[41]

As for fate, Allenby is still dealing with its cruelty, penning another mournful letter to his wife, both in private torment that is observed in public:

My Sweetheart,

I had a message from the Sherif of Mecca, King of the Hejaz, in Arabia, to express his sorrow and sympathy on the death of my son . . . The Sherif of Mecca is in revolt against the Turks and is our ally. His followers are harrying the Turks on the Aleppo–Medina railway and are causing them a whole lot of trouble . . .

Bye Dear Love
Edward[42]

•

Flying Officer Lieutenant Alaric Boor is as pleased as he has ever been in his life. It is not just that he now has his 'wings', but, much more excitingly, he has been officially posted to his unit, the Royal Flying Corps Squadron No. 113, which had been formed on 1 August in Ismailia, to counter the Turks in the Sinai. He is one of the first pilots to be posted to the Squadron, whose primary role will be observation of the enemy.

After journeying through France and Italy on trains, Flight Lieutenant Boor – he still can't quite believe he has his 'pilot's wings', the badge he proudly wears on his left breast – is even now boarding the HMT *Aragon* in Taranto on the underside of Italy's 'boot', together with his Commanding Officer, Major Horace Haycock, and they will soon be on their way to Alexandria. The few days of shipboard life will give him the thing he most lacks, precious time to write to family and friends, and, more particularly, his dear fiancée waiting for him in Perth, Ida Rawlings, who has been so shattered by the death of her brother Frank at the Battle of the Nek and worries about Alaric incessantly.

Please, dear God, let Alaric be spared.

A part of Boor's excitement is the exotic nature of the land they are travelling to. As one who had won the Ancient History Prize at the University of Melbourne he knows better than most just how extraordinary the contours of conflict are in this land.

But none of the ancient conquerors could even have *dreamed* of the wonder of having the world flow beneath them in flight; what once was Greek myth is now Egyptian reality, as Alaric will soon be soaring beneath the sun, wary not of wax melting but of flak flying from Turks, Arabs or Germans so far below.

•

It is not as if there is not some time for a little fun, as various units of the Light Horse are rotated back from the front, just safely south of Gaza.

The thing about this particular settlement is that it has enough water to sustain large numbers of both British and Australian troops at once.

They are curious coves, these English, most of them with plums in their mouths and an unseemly obsession with keeping their uniforms clean and their salutes sharp. Some of them, however, are not bad bastards and they suggest an excellent way to pass the time.

Why not a 'Test Match' between us? The best cricket players of Imperial Yeomanry against the best players of the Australian Light Horse?

Yes, why bloody not?

(What these colonials don't know is that the reason the English have a curious confidence about them is that they have a secret weapon in their ranks, none other than J. W. H. T. Douglas, who had, before the war, been the captain of the English cricket team that won the 1911–1912 Ashes series.) Douglas is a notable batsman in his own right, with an amazing 26 first-class centuries to his credit – a fact completely ignored by the Australian crowds, who have always delighted in referring to him, in honour of his initials, as Johnny Won't Hit Today. In fact, the pugnacious if proper and dapper Johnny *can* hit, in at least two senses – having also won a gold in boxing at the 1908 Olympics! Douglas is now revealed to be playing and, as you might expect, the coming 'Test Match' causes huge interest and excitement among both the English and Australian Troopers. On the day of the big match, all those who are not on guard duty are in the crowd to cheer their teams on.

'The wicket,' the account of a padre there on the day will go, 'was formed of sandy soil and tibbin – grainless chaff – and was as well watered as any Adelaide wicket, and rolled with a full water drum.'[43]

The Australian team enters the field dressed in their khaki breeches with their regulation sky-blue shirts, singlets and canvas shoes, while those born and raised beneath the Southern Cross gasp to see the English side emerge in perfect whites, with creases on the bloody seams! In the bloody desert? What are they going to produce next, ice cream? The explanation is that by pure happenstance all the best players of the selected English side also prove to be among the echelon of the most senior officers, meaning they all have orderlies to help procure the said clothing, and put creases in them!

And so let us play.

After winning the toss, Australia bats first.

Is it their fault that they are bowled out for just 57 runs?

It is not.

They have given it their all.

It is like that poem from your famous poet, Banjo Paterson, 'Saltbush Bill', about the stoush between the English new chum, and the Australian drover . . .

> So the new chum rode to the homestead straight, and told
> them a story grand
> Of the desperate fight that he fought that day with the King of
> the Overland;
> And the tale went home to the Public Schools of the pluck of
> the English swell –
> How the drover fought for his very life, but blood in the end
> must tell.

I mean, just 57 runs! It surely must be very embarrassing to you Australians. Why, with J. W. H. T. Douglas in our ranks, we should be able to knock that out in a few overs!

Yes, you're probably right, but you might as well pad up anyway, yes?

And, in short order, the man himself strides out to the crease, in the manner of one who has seen a few pitches in his time, single-handedly beaten many teams from all over the world and will be happy to do the honours again today. And yes, of course the Diggers from the cheap seats are crying out, 'Johnny Won't Hit Today!' but Johnny himself is clearly convinced he certainly will hit today.

Well, we'll see about that. Douglas is accompanied to the crease by George Kekewich, an Old Etonian like they don't make them anymore and now noted batsman for the famed City of London Yeomanry unit, known as 'The Rough Riders'.

Now who is this rather athletic figure standing at the northern end of the field on this stinking hot day, waiting for the Australian captain to throw him the ball to begin the opening over? Whoever he is, he did not bat. But now, as J. W. H. T. Douglas takes strike for the opening ball of the innings – gazing confidently around the field settings to decide where he will hit his first boundary – the bowler runs in with a distinctive, long, loping run.

His first ball makes a *ssssst* hissing sound as it strikes the pitch, and careers past the Englishman's bat in a tenth of a flash!

J. W. H. T. Douglas straightens up. There is only one man he has faced in his career able to put a ball down with that kind of speed. And he looks closer at the fast bowler who has just delivered it. It is one and the same. TIBBY COTTER!

(In fact, he is known as 'Terror Cotter' to the English Test side and English cricket fans.) The Australians in the crowd roar at the joke and the English jokingly boo. Now this will be *something*.

And for the next ball, at least, Douglas knows what he is dealing with, and this time takes strike with intent and fierce concentration. Again Cotter unleashes. Again there is a *ssssst*, and a small puff of dust where the searing ball strikes the pitch. This time there is the crack of ball on wood. Alas for Johnny Didn't Hit Today, it is his middle stump!

Gone for a duck.

Worse still for the Yeomanry, the rest of the English team do little better, with Tibby steaming in from the Pyramid end of the ground, and the entire English line-up is gone for . . . 4! Bloody Moses Almighty! Just four runs, one of them a bye! Tibby – who has finished with the figures of 9/2 – is chaired from the field by the cheering Australians, and even the English players roar their regard.

It will be something they can tell their grandchildren, a boast in bars for years to come – they were once skittled by that typhoon of terror, that gazelle of grace known as Tibby! For just a few precious hours, the war has stopped and the curious game of cricket has once again united the men of one empire, safe on a foreign field, before they collectively fight another empire altogether.

•

General Allenby, as is his wont, is everywhere at once, so omnipresent and so rumbling and grumbling, so long and strong and damaging to those who displease him that a short-hand develops between the senior officers of the units under his command: 'BBA', short for 'Bloody Bull's About'.[44]

He is coming your way like a cyclone of change so batten down the hatches and save what you can!

From camps to HQs to hospitals, from workshops to depots to rest camps and back again, his first action upon his return from his reconnaissance is to confirm and organise the move of General HQ to the front at Palestine, a little north of Rafa, at a camp set up at Umm el Kelab.

Early August 1917, Hellfire Jack not flash

It is 'Hellfire' Jack all over, and all up, and none are surprised.

Not for him a plebeian finish by bullet or shrapnel. Of course, for him, it has to be something *unheard* of, something you can barely believe.

For you see, the General has heard a lot of talk about poison gas – consisting of chlorine and phosgene – and what a threat it might be to his men. What can he do to protect them?

Well, he reasons, surely the most important thing is to be able to recognise the smell of it, by having just a little sniff himself? Alarmed, his senior staff officers try to talk him out of it. But Royston insists.

It seems like a good idea at the time.

Alas, while the aphorism might still hold that *it is an ill-wind that blows no-one any good*, this particularly ill-wind – bearing chlorine and phosgene gas – makes Hellfire wheeze, cough, nearly suffocate and suddenly blue.

'The result,' Banjo Paterson will recount, 'was that I found him in a hospital, a badly shaken man, passing green urine, and ordered away for long leave ... Thus one of the most picturesque personalities in the British army dropped out of active service.'[45]

Still, at least the enlisted men now know *not* to sniff poison gas on purpose.

To fill the vacancy as Commanding Officer of 3rd Brigade, General Chauvel offers the position to Colonel William Grant, the 47-year-old Queenslander – warmly known to his men as 'Old Bill' – who had been commanding the 11th Light Horse Regiment with great effect. Often impulsive, Grant is one of those officers who is always spoiling for a battle, who wants to fight, wants to get into 'em. (Just quietly? He is like a sane version of Hellfire Jack.) Chauvel regards him as a thruster, just the kind of officer you need at the front. And Grant is also regarded as a notable bushman, particularly for his capacity to steer by the stars on long night marches.

Grant accepts the offer to be the permanent Brigadier General of the 4th Light Horse Brigade.

•

Allenby receives countless missives, but rarely with such glorious term of address as this one:

> Heroic Leader and Dispenser of Victory - General Allenby,
> May God keep him.

Ah, it must be from Prince Feisal, never one for beginning with, 'Dear Sir'. Allenby reads on:

> I have received your honoured letter dated 14th Oct with
> great respect . . . God has made victory the ally of the
> armies of Right.

(Feisal tactfully does not clarify to which God he refers to . . .)

> We were much gratified by your statement that you were
> using every endeavour to supply the deficiencies of our
> army . . . I have informed Major Lawrence of some of our
> necessities the lack of which is still the cause of the
> arrest of our movement.
>
> General of the Northern Armies.

There is no signature, simply the seal of Feisal. Well, the Heroic Leader Allenby can ensure necessities will be delivered to you, victories however you will have to supply on your own.[46]

•

While direct reconnaissance of Beersheba is difficult, it is at least possible.

Bit by bit, based on such recces, mixed with aerial observation, intelligence from the prisoners they occasionally capture, together with some careful bribes to Bedouins who have encampments nearby, a clear portrait of Beersheba emerges, with – brush by brush, stroke by stroke – each piece of information lending colour, light and shade to give a good picture of what awaits.

Lying at the foot of the Judean Hills to the east, the town bakes on the northern bank of Wadi Saba, which, when the rain comes, flows into Wadi Ghuzze.

The town boasts an army barracks, several warehouses, a small hospital, water tower, railway station – with a road leading to Gaza on the Turkish side of their defensive span – a square of houses and even a German beer garden for the handful of German officers and soldiers based there. The buildings are sturdy, made of stone with red-tiled roofs, and would be able to withstand bullets if it came down to a last stand. The local population beyond the troops are mostly Arabs, with a sprinkling of Christian and Jewish colonists. The most beautiful ancient-looking building in Beersheba is one of the newest, the Great Mosque, built in 1900 and placed deliberately between Gaza and Hebron, a holy way-station between the two important towns. As with a hospital, houses of worship are off limits to either attack or tactics; but they are noted nonetheless.

All up, intelligence reports conclude that Beersheba is defended by about 4000 soldiers manning two concentric fortified rings: an outer series of well-constructed trenches – six feet deep, and four feet wide – and barbed wire which traces, as one report will describe it, 'a semicircle along the high ground north-west, west, and south-west of the town . . . at an average distance of 7000 yards from the town.

On the north-east, east, and south-east the outer defences are not continuous, but consisted of a series of strong posts.'[47]

The inner defensive line runs around the actual perimeter of the town, with the only real break in the north, which the Turks control in any case. But the rest consists mostly of redoubts with intersecting zones of fire from commanding positions, glorified fortified rubble and low stacks of sandbags. Should the outer ring be breached, this line will be the Turks' fall-back position. As near as can be determined, the line to the east of the town does not have rolls of barbed wire, on the grounds that no-one would be crazy enough to attack from that direction – there is no cover, and Tel el Saba stands as a scything sentinel, ready to cut down all who approach.

The Turks have half-a-dozen machine guns and no artillery actually on the hill.

Very well then.

Chetwode's 20th Corps will start the attack from the west after the artillery barrage has softened the most outer of the Turks' defensive lines. Once the infantry has secured that outer line, the artillery can be brought forward.

It is further decided that the 20th Corps needn't sacrifice lives unnecessarily by forcing the inner perimeter too. No, simply by getting close enough to direct fire on that line, and *threatening* to break it, they will be able to pin the bulk of the Beersheba garrison down, allowing Chauvel's Desert Mounted Corps to attack from the east and north-east against what will hopefully be a much thinner line of defenders. (And this well help to keep the 20th Corps fresh for the fighting that will take place in ensuing days, after Beersheba is taken.)

Tel el Saba shall be subdued by the New Zealanders and the 1st Australian Light Horse Brigade.

Thereafter . . .

'The Desert Mounted Corps . . . will complete the defeat of the enemy's left flank and threaten his left rear and the line of retreat of his army.'[48]

In the meantime, water remains the problem.

This is a key part of the reconnaissance, for unless the attackers can find sufficient wells in the area for the men, *and* their horses, it will be impossible to move them into position and sustain them for the length of time necessary to pull the action off. Allenby himself personally questions local Arabs on this point, favouring the older ones: What wells (known by the locals as the 'tears of Allah'[49]) were once used when you were young? Where were they? For through British engineering dry wells can be made fluid again. Old memories are tapped, and new markings made on old maps. Preliminary reconnaissance shows the only sure supply found so far is at Bir el Siani, otherwise known as Esani, some miles (too many miles) south-west of Beersheba, and which therefore is too far away to use as a launching point for the major attack – though it may still serve as a staging post.

Allenby pores over the maps, together with information provided by Adam Smith's *Historical Geography of the Holy Land*, ignoring the footnotes about who begat who and which smiting took place where. Instead he focuses on finding the remnants of ancient towns to the south and south-west of Beersheba – many of them with 'Bir' in their name, the Arabic word for 'well' – which means the people of Biblical times *must* have lived off wells which should still have water today.

General Allenby is eager that the timing of the attack be made as soon as September. That should give them the time to resolve remaining problems and if they can just crack the line by then, that will still give them several weeks before the rains of November come – cloudbursts which will make the suddenly flooding wadis and low-lying flats impassable – thus, this likely dry progress might be just enough to follow up on the breakthrough and fight the 65 miles to get all the way to Jerusalem.

(As it happens, Allenby has an even more ancient book which already tells him something of the winter rains in the Biblical lands, starting with Deuteronomy 11:14, 'then I will give you the rain for your land in its season, the early rain and the latter rain, that you may gather in your grain, your new wine, and your oil'.)

The danger in delay is that, with every week that passes, the Turks will be continuing to strengthen their line. Right now it has been estimated that the two armies the Ottomans have in the Gaza–Beersheba line, the Seventh and Eighth Armies, have around 40,000 rifles, 260 artillery pieces and 200 machine guns at their disposal. What will it be if the attackers wait another six weeks or so?

And yet, as some of his staff point out to General Allenby, making such an advance so long before the rains would inevitably mean the logistics of supplying water to their army in the bad lands, the dry lands north of Gaza, would be more than problematic – they might well be insuperable.

Well, so be it. Risks must be run if they are to be in the running to win. The most important thing of all is to make sure that Beersheba does fall before they roll up the line to Gaza, and then they can worry about the dash to Jerusalem.

So, what date *will* we make Z-Day?

There is much to-ing and fro-ing, but soon enough a circle is placed around the last week of October, with the exact date to be decided once they know more on movement of men and munitions.

No matter the date, however, Z-Hour will be the crack of dawn.

CHAPTER NINE

POSITIONS, EVERYONE

But Chauvel could have no misgivings about the capacity of his troops. In the sheer quality of their grand young manhood, in their brigade and regimental leadership, in their experience gained over eighteen months' hard fighting in all sorts of rough conditions, the men of the 1st and 2nd Light Horse Brigades and the New Zealand Brigade were then without peer among mounted troops engaged anywhere in the war.[1]

Official Historian Henry Gullett, *The Australian Imperial Force in Sinai and Palestine 1914–1918*

10 September 1917, Hejaz, passing strange

Another day, another attack.

And this'un is a big one for Lawrence of Arabia and his growing band of Arabs, some 80 of them for this attack . . . plus two ring-ins who have recently joined, two army instructors who had been sent Lawrence's way by the British Army to help train the Arabs in Lewis guns and the Stokes mortar.

The Lewis gun instructor is Sergeant Charles Reginald Yells, from Kapunda in South Australia, described by Lawrence as 'an Australian, long, thin and sinuous, his supple body lounging in unmilitary curves. His hard face, arched eyebrows, and predatory nose set off the peculiarly Australian air of reckless willingness and capacity to do something very soon.'[2]

After giving a month's instruction, Yells and the English instructor, Sergeant Walter Brooke, had asked if they could stay on with Lawrence, who had readily agreed, only pointing out that life would be tough on camels, frequently without water, often under attack and living cheek by jowl by towel with the Arabs, and that as they did not speak the language, 'If anything goes wrong with me, you will be in a tender position.'[3]

'I am looking for just this strangeness of life,'[4] Yells had replied, and Sergeant Brooke had expressed a similar sentiment.

Are you two sure? This life is not for everyone.

'For years we lived anyhow with one another in the naked desert,' Lawrence will write of their existence, 'under the indifferent heaven. By day the hot sun fermented us; and we were dizzied by the beating wind. At night we were stained by dew, and shamed into pettiness by the innumerable silences of stars.'[5] And that is the good part. The hard part is taking on an Empire determined to kill them.

Yes, they are sure.

Which is why both men are beside him now, with Lewis gun and Stokes mortar in hand, as yonder train comes into view, two locomotives hauling 10 carriages packed with Turkish soldiers – their rifles bristling from the windows, their machine guns from sandbag nests on the roof – approaching the very bridge they have wired with explosive.

Lawrence waits until the second engine is above the explosive and drops his arm as the signal to the Arab to press the plunger.

'There followed a terrific roar, and the line vanished from sight behind a spouting column of black dust and smoke a hundred feet high and wide. Out of the [black smoke] came shattering crashes and long, loud metallic clangings of ripped steel, with many lumps of iron and plate; while one entire wheel of a locomotive whirled up suddenly black out of the cloud against the sky, and sailed musically over our heads to fall slowly and heavily into the desert behind. Except for the flight of these, there succeeded a deathly silence, with no cry of men or rifle-shot, as the now grey mist of the explosion drifted from the line towards us, and over our ridge until it was lost in the hills.'[6]

But now the chattering of heavy rifle and machine-gun fire comes and as the smoke clears, it reveals that the locomotives have left the tracks and the carriages and the Turks are being completely riddled with fire.

Sergeant Yells is firing his Lewis with the best of them – they are, after all, his pupils – with devastating effect, while Sergeant Brooke is lobbing his mortar bombs right among the devastated Turks. As the survivors try to flee from the killing zone, Yells is without mercy.

'The sergeant grimly traversed with drum after drum, till the open sand was littered with bodies. Mushagraf, the Sherari boy behind the second gun, saw the battle over, threw aside his weapon with a yell, and dashed down at speed with his rifle to join the others who were beginning, like wild beasts, to tear open the carriages and fall to plunder. It had taken nearly ten minutes.'⁷

It is nothing less than a catastrophe for the Turks, as the wound in their side represented by Lawrence's activities in the Hejaz Desert now sheds blood as never before. They will have to put ever more men there to try and bring the situation under control, which, alas, must inevitably leave them more exposed elsewhere.

Lawrence's experience with the Australians, meanwhile, deepens and, whatever else he will say about them, it will never be that they lack confidence or aggression. In his celebrated book *Seven Pillars of Wisdom*, Lawrence will fondly recall an episode a week after blowing up the bridge in the Hejaz Desert, having breakfast with the South Australian pilot Lieutenant Ross Smith and some of his comrades when a German plane comes over.

Smith looks up, looks back down at his plate of sausages, and reluctantly but carefully puts them aside. He jumps into his Bristol Fighter in the company of his observer and, as Lawrence will describe it, 'climbed like a cat up into the sky', closely followed by another Australian pilot and his observer. It is at this point that a third Australian pilot, whose own observer is not handy, looks to Lawrence of Arabia in the manner of, 'Well, are you going to come, too?'

The Englishman leaves him in no doubt.

'No, I was not going to air-fight,' Lawrence will write, 'no matter what caste I lost with the pilot. He was an Australian, of a race delighting in additional risks, not an Arab to whose gallery I must play.'⁸

Never mind.

Captain Ross Smith's Vickers gun begins to chatter and he brings the German plane down in flames, whereupon he lands, walks back to his spot and, after taking up his sausages, happily reports to Lawrence that they are still hot. For Smith it appears to be the only thing worth remarking on and he finishes his breakfast with nary a word, washing it down with coffee . . . until half an hour later, well, I'll be damned, another enemy plane comes over, the German pilot likely looking for his lost companion. Off the two Australian pilots go again with their observers, and this time it is the other pilot who does the honours, before they return once more.

September 1917, east of Gaza, water, water, here and there

Hush.

Snatches of singing.

Coming this way.

. . . long way to go . . .

. . .

. . . the sweetest girl I know!

. . .

Closer still, and it all comes clear. It is some men of the 12th Australian Light Horse Regiment in the early stages of a patrol, singing together – as out to the far east purple shadows thrown by the Judean Hills are slowly topped by 'needles of molten flame'[9], as the sun rises.

> *It's a long way to Tipperary*
> *It's a long way to go.*
> *It's a long way to Tipperary*
> *To the sweetest girl I know!*
> *Goodbye, Piccadilly*
> *Farewell, Leicester Square!*
> *It's a long long way to Tipperary*
> *But my heart's right there.*

QUIET! All quiet now. Getting too close to Turkish lines, it's time to get to the business at hand. In the first instance, Lieutenant Guy Haydon and his patrol are looking for Turkish patrols, and are hungry for action. Far more importantly, they are here to look for wells in the area between Esani and Khalasa that can be resuscitated, the places in the desert able to provide enough water to sustain an entire army as it moves through the desert to attack Beersheba. It is gruelling work, going from ancient place to ancient place, but at least they are not starting from scratch.

In fact, Haydon is working from a map first provided by the Palestine Exploration Fund, a quaint British society dating back to 1865 devoted to the study of the Biblical Lands. The foundation of this map had been drawn by three intrepid British officers – including one hard-rising Lieutenant of the time, H. H. Kitchener, the former British Secretary of State for War! (As if that is not enough pedigree, the map had been improved upon, by one T. E. Lawrence, back in the time before the war when he was making his way as an academic in the field of archaeology.)

It is comprehensive, and includes everything from towns to stone buildings, forts, ruins, passable roads, rivers, large wadi beds and . . . wells. And the Palestine Exploration Fund insists that Khalasa once had wells enough to sustain a population of 60,000 so they must be substantial! The key is to locate those wells now, and determine just how usable they are or might be.

Haydon himself takes down highly detailed notes on each site they get to.

> *Bir el Esani – Fresh, 196,000 gal per day. Well, water hole and*
> *springs.*
> *El Ausegi – Dry, 3 cisterns, 44,000 capacity.*
> *Bir Asluj – 80,000 g.daily, 3 wells, 1 blocked up.*[10]

Etc. Etc.

On sites particularly close to the Turkish lines, they leave their horses behind and move in the moonlight on foot, trying to get a better feel for the lie of the land in the semi-darkness and just where the enemy might have sentries posted.

Upon their return, if not for her white coronet, Midnight at midnight would be practically invisible, but Guy Haydon sees her now, returning to his beloved horse and settling for the night. In the heat of the morning they go again, moving through this infernal country of sun-blasted and blistered desert, criss-crossed by wadis, peppered with rocks and rocky outcrops – and indeed a long, long way from Tipperary, or anywhere else, for that matter. Hereabouts, temperatures would get to 115 degrees in the shade – on a moderate day. As it is, the only shade provided comes from that which you bring with you in the form of your horses, and all the Troopers can do to gain some respite is position their horses between them and the sun, as they take their scanty day-time meals.

Other patrols head out on similar water-finding excursions, and the New Zealand Field Troop is particularly successful, finding the old wells at both Khalasa and Asluj, both of them within coo-ee of Beersheba – no more than 15 miles ride away. Yes, the Turks have blown the wells up, but in a strange kind of way wells are a little like cockroaches – they can't really be definitively destroyed, only damaged.

The most extraordinary thing? When they look at the 100-foot deep wells closely, all the top stones have profound grooves in them – some of them inches deep – from nigh on 20 *centuries* of first the Romans' and then the Bedouins' camel-and-goat-hair ropes rubbing into the stone as they lower their buckets!

The army engineers estimate that those wells can be repaired, as it is mostly a matter of digging them out, and securing their walls so they don't fall in.

Intelligence also now reveals that Beersheba likely has about 5000 soldiers of – get this – the Ottoman Empire's III Corps, comprising the 27th Infantry Division and the 3rd Cavalry Division, defending it.

The same ones many of the Light Horse fought at Gallipoli? The ones who had gunned down the Light Horse at countless battles and filled the graveyards with 9000 Australian dead?

Yes, one and the same.

It is something right there, to summon the blood and stiffen the sinew of the Australian Light Horse. The chance to take on *those* Turks once more is not beyond their wildest dreams, but smack centre of them.

The III Corps at Beersheba is armed with rifles, together with about 60 machine guns and a couple of dozen field guns, most of which are dug in west, south and east of the town. Along the entire Turkish front from there to Gaza is another 40,000 rifles, and the key will be to ensure that the enemy cannot flood Beersheba with support, for fear of a breakthrough elsewhere.

The Corps commander is Colonel Ismet, a seasoned officer whose fine aquiline nose, slight build and pleasant presence belies a powerful military mind. He served as Chief of Staff of Turkey's Second Army at Gallipoli. It had been on that blood-drenched peninsula he had first come to an appreciation of how hard and hardy are the Australians and New Zealanders, but he is confident that, if it ever came to it, as reinforcements to Gaza most likely, he and his men shall beat them once more.

•

Another day, and another detailed deception is planned. The officers meeting today have subterfuge as second nature; their schemes are occasionally indulged by orthodox command but mostly rebuffed with a roll of the eyes. But this gathering – led by Major Richard Meinertzhagen of Intelligence – is particularly important. It is to refine ways in which they can make the Turks believe that they are intent on attacking anywhere *bar* Beersheba. Ideally, they must make the enemy believe they will be attacking Gaza for the third time, requiring the Ottoman Empire's strongest forces to be positioned there.

But how?

Colour and movement. Artillery and aggression. Ideas are put forth, rejected or grasped – and if the latter, then they are refined. Slowly, a comprehensive plan is formed, whereby the Turk will be made to think that Gaza will shortly be under siege – even beyond the fact that the 21st Corps will be in position just to the south of Gaza, as if they are about to launch – all while tens of thousands of Troopers are to be whisked away to attack Beersheba. And yes, it will clearly not be possible to move that many men towards Beersheba without at least some of them being spotted from the air and by scouts on the ground, but the Turks must be convinced that *those* troops are the feint.

The best thing? None of the artillery attacks on Gaza will be wasted – as they will simply weaken the ancient city for the time when, a few days after Beersheba hopefully falls, it will genuinely be under attack once more, but from *all* directions.

In such meetings, General Chauvel is consulted on all matters concerning him, and Allenby's confidence in him grows when it comes to mastering detail, offering fresh ideas and being clearly in command of the situation.

Very quietly, though?

'Walking on pretty thin ice with all these people . . .' Chauvel writes to his wife after one particularly high-powered meeting with other corps commanders and their chiefs of staff. 'When I look around the room and realise I am absolutely the only one who is not in the British regular army and cannot put PSC after my name (That's Passed Staff College, a qualification anyone who aspires to high command in the Brit army should have), I do get a bit of funk on lest I should be caught out in a want of knowledge on some technical point.'[11]

So far, so good.

•

In the Levant – these Biblical lands – one may be awoken by a wail of prayer, but today you can hear the moan of an Australian as the cursed sound of reveille rings out over the desert camp just outside the village of Abasan el Kebir, some five miles south-east of Khan Yunis.

As ever, the sound brings instant activity as the men of the 12th Light Horse rise, stretch, curse, scratch, smoke, feed their horses and get ready for a quick breakfast before heading out for training, and of course the grooming of the horses. (The fact that the horses are twice as well groomed as their Australian riders, and probably have better table manners, is a tribute to the care and priorities of their keepers.)

But this morning proves to be one of . . . those mornings. The whistle blows, and they gather around the Regimental Sergeant Major, who again bellows the traditional greeting.

'*Shun!*'

Standing at 'shun in the sun, they are told that orders have come from Divisional Headquarters. We are moving out, as soon as everyone is ready. And you better be ready before the RSM is, which will be in less than two shakes past 15 minutes from NOW! Scramble!

And scramble they do.

It is all part of the extra training that General Allenby is insisting on. Each unit must become ever more accomplished at reacting quickly to surprise orders, operations with no notice, and meeting up with other units at a specific rendezvous in the desert, far away, where inspections will take place. As the time has gone on, these distances have become ever further away as the ability of them and their steeds to travel far on little water is also tested – and lifted.

Go!

Haydon and his comrades become a blur of movement – every pack whacked on the back of their steeds all but instantly. No instructions needed, no distraction permitted. Each piece of kit is hastily gathered and grasped, each man treating the drill as though it is battle joined, the rattle of each rifle checked, loaded and locked before a nod is given. One order YELLED and they are soon on their way, as staff officers measure on their watches just how long it takes for them to turn out. The 12th Regiment is good, but there is not a unit in the British forces as good as one of the Horse Artillery batteries, which turned out 'complete in full marching order, with all its ammunition, rations, and stores correct, in eleven minutes from the receipt of the order'.[12]

Why are they doing all this?

That, of course, is not explained. But overall the sense builds that they are working their way towards another big stunt, some way of cracking the Turkish nut, and Jacko's melon in the process. When they start doing all of the above at night, some clue is provided as to what is in store.

•

General Allenby is relieved and pleased in equal measure.

The War Cabinet has approved his scheme to pursue the Chetwode plan to attack the enemy around Beersheba.

From London, Prime Minister Lloyd George sends a cable:

STRIKE THE TURK AS HARD AS POSSIBLE, IN THE COMING AUTUMN OR WINTER.[13]

Yes, Prime Minister.

Allenby reads it at his new HQ, at Umm el Kelab, a little to the north of Rafa and just 18 miles from Gaza. It is a flimsy HQ, made of quickly fabricated wooden huts and tents – ready to move forward at short notice, as soon as an advance is made. Of course, the heat, dust storms and flies make things dashed uncomfortable, but Allenby doesn't care. The first principle of leadership is to understand the lie of the land you are fighting in and the condition of your men and the enemy, and make decisions accordingly.

How on earth could that be done from Cairo?

No, here is best, not that Allenby himself spends too much time in the camp. The General can't stand still, he is everywhere always and the arrival of Allenby just ahead of the large cloud of dust caused by his 'Tin Lizzie' rattling along the sandy tracks, inevitably lifts morale among the front-line troops and confirms there is a real change in the wind.

'I could not count the times I have shaken hands with Allenby,' a Light Horse Brigade Major said a few months after the new leader's arrival. 'Between the canal and Gaza I never set eyes on Murray.'[14]

The Troopers agree, with one of them noting of the banishment of the brass from the Savoy, 'It was impossible that they could apply to the campaign that intimate knowledge and fierce energy which are as essential to victory as sagacity and valour in the field. The army applauded the move.'[15]

'The new CinC breakfasted with us today,' one officer notes on 10 July. 'He is a smart looking man, and looks as if he would stand no nonsense.'[16]

General Chauvel continues the run of good impressions.

'He gets out among the troops, looks in at hospitals, has a cheery word for the wounded.'

Best of all?

'[He] does not have a fit if he's not saluted . . . which appeals to the Australians.'[17]

For his part, Allenby himself is uplifted by what he sees.

There is a lot about the Australian character – the lack of fuss, the desire to *bloody well get on with it* – that appeals to the English General and, just as he has been impressed by them on the Western Front, so is he impressed by what he sees here. Put simply, the Australian Light Horse are the best Troopers he has, and he intends to throw them in the cauldron where they will be the most use. And for his part, Allenby makes a good impression on the Australians, just for the fact that he is here, up front, with them and not sending orders from 200 miles away.

This is not to say he is a good bastard. But at the very least he seems to be that rarest of all things, a Pommy bastard who is not a bad bastard. And Allenby's HQ? It is portable, humble and has an excellent view of the sand. It is a far cry from Cairo and within coo-ee of all he commands. Allenby describes the detachable digs to his wife in a letter home on this day in August:

'My camp is on a ridge, four miles from the sea . . . Between me and the sea are 2–3 miles of sand dunes. The site is clean and healthy, breezy, and comparatively cool. I am in a big wooden hut with a bedroom, sitting room and bathroom . . . The windows are covered with netting . . . I am in sandy soil, 300 feet above sea level. There are very few flies and, I think, no mosquitoes.'[18]

Even the mosquitoes think twice before attacking Allenby.

Remarkably, Allenby is increasingly open to fresh ideas, anything that can heighten the chances of success, especially when it comes to subterfuge. Which is why he has summoned one brilliant officer on his General Staff, Lieutenant Colonel John Belgrave.[19] Belgrave is one of the hush-hush boys, from that newly established unit of Military Intelligence, MI-7.

Allenby wishes this bright young fellow to expand on an interesting memorandum he has authored.

Well, Belgrave, let's have it.

Belgrave, an ascetic, no-nonsense kind of man, who prefers facts to flourish, sets out this outrageous but tempting idea once more.

It's all about confusing the enemy.

We need to contrive a way whereby one of our officers will drop a haversack filled with false plans and 'proof' that the real target is Gaza.

Belgrave is reinforced in the notion by, who else, Major Richard Meinertzhagen. As Belgrave and Meinertzhagen both know, to win a war in this part of the world you need ruses, subterfuges and cunning, not just more men better manoeuvred. In this field, Meinertzhagen is in his element, with no less than Lawrence of Arabia noting of him that the mercurial Major, 'took as blithe a pleasure in deceiving his enemy (or friend) by some unscrupulous jest'.[20]

But can this haversack 'jest' be pulled off convincingly? Allenby is not sure, but he is sure these two wily men can pull it off if anyone can. Permission granted. Tell no-one.

To support the ruse, a series of false radio messages will go out after the haversack is dropped on a network known to be monitored by the Turks, ordering troops to move towards Gaza. Small boats will be massed on the shore south of Gaza, just as if that amphibious assault is soon to take place. And to complete the facade, on the morning of the actual attack on Beersheba, the Royal Navy will open a massive fusillade on Gaza, just as if it was the prelude to an attack. It is unorthodox, it is unpredictable, but it is also bloody exciting.

September 1917, Ismailia, Egypt, Boors have wings

For Alaric Boor, life is good. After completing his training in England, he arrived at his posting – No. 113 Squadron, a unit based in Ismailia on the Egypt–Sinai border, and formed only months before. The No. 113 Squadron is devoted to reconnaissance – working out the enemy's trench placements, artillery battery positions and troop dispositions – as well as transport, co-operating with the Army to provide their aerial needs, and sometimes offensive action, otherwise known as dropping hand-held bombs on the enemy. Occasionally, they use their .303 forward-firing Vickers gun and .303 Lewis gun from the rear cockpit if they are engaged in dog-fights with German Taubes.

Boor is flying the Royal Aircraft Factory RE 8 – Reconnaissance Experimental 8 – a British two-seat biplane with a 140-horsepower V12 engine, designed for reconnaissance and as a bomber. True, the RE 8 can be a bit on the tricky side of things: a rather lumbering bother to fly, notoriously giving no warning before they stall, not to mention having such a propensity to burn on crashing that some pilots insist on flying with an empty reserve tank, but . . .

But Boor does not complain. He is simply thrilled to 'have my wings', as he explains to his parents, and is eager to do whatever is necessary to help the war effort – not least because the sooner they can win this war, the sooner he can get home to his Ida and marry her.

September 1917, Umm el Kelab, Z marks the plot

Syria.

Intelligence tells Allenby that the Ottoman Empire has a formidable five divisions placed there in a strategic reserve, which could relatively easily be deployed to Gaza if it comes under attack. How to keep them there?

More subterfuge must be worth a try. Perhaps a phantom invasion? Can we not make it appear that an amphibious force is being prepared to launch? Camps and tents will be erected on Cyprus, and many 'bogus wireless messages'[21] sent, to collectively give 'the enemy the impression that troops are to be landed in his rear north of Gaza'.[22]

As with the haversack proposal, it is Lieutenant Colonel John Belgrave of Intelligence who takes the lead, sending a memorandum to General Allenby to this effect.

Allenby endorses Belgrave's plan and duly informs the Senior Naval Officer Egypt, Rear Admiral Thomas Jackson, that, 'In connection with my projected operations I am making arrangements to induce the enemy to fear an operation in the bay of Alexandretta,'[23] on the Syrian coast west of Aleppo.

Forenoon, 20 September 1917, Remount Depot, Moascar, Egypt

Snap to!

Here at the 'Remount service' at Moascar near Ismailia – a vast complex of horse corrals and stables, featuring 700 horses, 300 mules and six officers who also resemble mules in behaviour and disposition – the soldier-handlers are not much given to standing to attention or snapping off salutes. The whole place is casual by nature and a man is judged by his ability to break in brumbies, not by shiny boots or strict observations of military protocol.

But this is different.

It is the Commanding Officer of the entire Egyptian Expeditionary Force, General Edmund Allenby himself, who has swung by on a quick visit.

Major Banjo Paterson had come to know General Allenby a couple of decades back in the Boer War, in fact he had been present one dark night when Allenby had arrived in the wee hours to break up a drinking session of officers and take command of a cavalry squadron of NSW Lancers.

'Daylight revealed him as a sinewy well-set-up man,' Paterson's account recorded 'at least six feet high, and broad and strong as a London policeman. In facial contour he bore a distinct resemblance to Kitchener, but he smiled often and his expression was free from the secret sorrow that always seemed to harry Kitchener's soul. He set about the reorganization of the squadron with the enthusiasm of a scientist experimenting with a new sort of beetle.'[24]

And ever and always, he had a particular style about him.

'He neither bounced nor bullied anybody, but explained things as carefully as a school-teacher dealing with a lot of children. He got hold of the blacksmiths, and told them that he would give them a certain time to get all the horses properly shod and that then he would come round to see that they had done it. He stirred up the cooks, and if he found any dirty utensils on an inspection, the man responsible was "for it". He made the young officers take a pride in their troops; if a man was slovenly dressed, or a horse not properly cleaned, trouble always followed.'

In sum?

'Soldiering is a trade and Allenby had learnt it. The work was just a routine to him, and he betrayed no more worry or irritability than a mechanic repairing a motor car. Of course the men growled at his strictness . . . but before long the new major began to get things into shape.'[25]

The fact that Allenby had gone on to accomplish great things with those NSW Lancers had seen him continue to rise in his soldiering trade. Paterson had roughly followed his fortunes since, and been pleased to hear he had taken over the Egyptian Expeditionary Force, and thrilled that he has now – with typical attention to overseeing every moving part of the force he commands – come to visit them at the Remount Depot.

But can that be him?

It is not just that General Allenby is of course a lot older . . . it is that he is so much slimmer . . . and grimmer.

The loss of weight has come from the privations of the war in France, together with the Egyptian heat, which can melt the flesh off a big man in a matter of weeks, if not days.

His grimness comes from the devastating actions he has been involved in on the Western Front, and their consequences; the grief he has known. In one of his first actions there, when the Germans had attacked with all its forces at Mons in Belgium, Allenby, 'had dismounted his cavalry and thrown them into the fighting line in a vain effort to stop the German rush'.[26]

Many of his own men had been killed for no result, just as his own son, Banjo knows, had been recently killed.

And so Paterson looks his old friend up and down.

'Where he had been granite before he was steel now . . . a great lonely figure of a man, riding silently in front of an obviously terrified staff. He seemed quite glad to recognize a friend in me.' The great soldier is delighted to see the great poet and they talk of old times like the young men they once were. Banjo teases Allenby that he has all his staff properly terrified. Allenby is amused but remarks:

'I am afraid I am becoming very hard to get on with. I want to get this war over and if anything goes wrong I lose my temper and cut loose on them. I haven't got down to finding fault with the Remount service yet, but it seems to me that your Australian horses are a common hairy-legged lot, compared to the horses that your Lancers brought to South Africa.'[27]

These two Boer War survivors finish their conversation a little awkwardly with a salute, one of them now a commander-in-chief, the other a jumped-up horse-handler, but two chums still.

Carry on, General Allenby. As you were.

General Allenby will do just that, pausing first to drop into the cookhouse to go to the most significant source of both good and bad morale in any army, the Chief Cook!

Noting this particular cook, an old fellow, also bears the ribbons of the Boer War, General Allenby asks first about his service, before inquiring about his family, and now gets to it.

What sort of food are you serving up?

'They gets stoo, sir, and plum puddin',' the old fellow says, 'and any amount of tinned fruit. The chow in this war, sir, is Guv'ment 'Ouse compared to what we got in South Africa.'

An amused Allenby nods approvingly.

'Very good,' replies Allenby. 'Very good. I'm glad to hear it. Carry on.'

Again, a small pause.

'Now,' the General says, hauling out his notebook, 'I want to go to the 10th Division.'

This proves to be something of a problem as someone has misplaced the division and it is not quite apparent to anyone where exactly it is right now, which sees a brave staff officer step forward and say, 'If you please, sir . . .' only for Allenby to cut him short.

'I don't want to hear you talk,' he says icily. 'I've enough men following me about to staff the whole British Army and you can't find me a division.'

Another, even braver staff officer steps forward.

'Just at present, sir –'

'I don't want to hear YOU talk, either. I want to get ON with this inspection. Where's this division?'

Finally – they know it must be around here *somewhere* – the missing division is located, and Allenby indeed heads off, leaving Banjo behind, along with a very good impression, none more so than on the Chief Cook.

'That's the sort of general for me,' says he. 'A bloke that knows his own mind. My word, he did roar up them staff officers a treat. Do 'em good. Take some of the flashness out of 'em.'[28]

As Banjo chronicles it, the word spreads, powered by one question and one answer:

'What's this new bloke like?'

'He's the sort of bloke that when he tells you to do a thing you know you'd better get up and do it. He's the boss, this cove.'[29]

And the boss is pleased with how things are shaping up.

'I was out yesterday to about six miles south of Beersheba,' Allenby will write to his wife after his next reconnaissance sortie. 'We were covered by a cavalry reconnaissance, but the Turks were very quiet.

A few of them were to be seen, in their entrenched line, but they were not shooting.'[30]

No, they are waiting, for Allenby's next move.

Mid-September 1917, Cyprus, new buoy in town

Having put in place the essence of his plan for the haversack ruse, Lieutenant Colonel John Belgrave has been appointed by General Allenby as General Staff Officer in Cyprus – the highest-ranking British officer there – and intends to move quickly. Right, men, the first thing we need to do is make some dummies.

What?

26 September 1917, Gaza–Beersheba Line, a German thunderbolt

Djemal Pasha seethes.

On this day, Enver Pasha orders the dissolution of the Ottoman Fourth Army, which Djemal has commanded in Syria and Palestine since the end of 1914. Broken into parts, the troops will be redistributed.

Enver Pasha hands over military command of Syria and Iraq to the newly formed 'Yildirim Group' – a Turkish name meaning 'Thunderbolt' – under the command of . . . a foreigner. Djemal Pasha will now be answering to the ex-Chief of Staff of the German Army, General Falkenhayn.

The Yildirim Group is a German-led initiative, with an HQ staff consisting of 65 German officers and just nine Turkish officers.

For Djemal Pasha, it is not just the dishonour of his military command being handed over to a German who has never laid a foot in the region, it is the disaster he foresees in General Falkenhayn's plan to switch the Ottoman forces on the Gaza–Beersheba Line from a defensive to an offensive footing – to launch an attack that will supposedly push the British out of the desert and into the sea for good.

Djemal Pasha had fought the proposition, penning strongly worded protests to Enver Pasha in Constantinople:

'I would like to clarify that I cannot consent to Falkenhayn, who drove a nail into the Germans in Verdun, driving [another] nail into us in Sinai. I regard it as the strongest *vatansizlik*, treason, to tolerate an action that would be a disaster for the salvation of the fatherland.'[31]

But for Enver Pasha, the promise of German military assistance to the depleted Ottoman forces is too strong, and Falkenhayn is given free rein.

General Mustafa Kemal, whose III Corps troops from his Seventh Army are that day marching into their positions on the left flank of the Ottoman line, headquartered in the desert town of Beersheba, also protests: 'If a German commander is in a position to order Turks to die by the thousands, it is obvious that the interests of the State are not being watched . . .'[32]

Himself underwhelmed at such presumption and subordination, Enver Pasha orders Mustafa Kemal to return to Constantinople forthwith for a stern word, leaving his men in Palestine.

General Kress von Kressenstein, newly promoted and installed in the HQ of the Ottoman Eighth Army in the Palestinian village of Huj, 10 miles north-east of Gaza, has no objections to the recent shake-up. In fact, the monocled-one is decidedly pleased, not to mention that his own request to the Ottoman Government for reinforcements has just been granted. To go with the three divisions he currently commands in the Eighth Army, another two divisions will soon be sent his way. With their arrival, he will be able to hold the Gaza–Beersheba line with two corps, with another corps in reserve north of Gaza, some 40,000 men in all.

And yet the ranking officers of the Yildirim Group are worried.

What are the British up to?

Turkish intelligence tells them there has been an enormous amount of radio traffic from Cyprus lately, and a lot of it seems to be about the arrival of new forces.

Could it be that they are about to launch an amphibious landing at Iskenderun on the Turkish coast, or on the Syrian coast? Several things point to it. Local informers are telling them that the Royal Navy has laid out many buoys in a Cypriot harbour, as if a large flotilla is about to arrive, even as large troop camps are being constructed in various locations on the island. Local contractors report that the

British have put in orders for enormous amounts of provisions, and intercepted radio messages indicate that a large force will soon arrive. The Turks had even got a leaked cable from GHQ in Cairo to Cyprus to confirm that everything was underway to accommodate the large force about to arrive.

Can it be?

Are the British about to launch?

To get more information, a Turkish plane is dispatched to fly over Cyprus and it is true that there is no obvious signs either of a massive build-up of troops, or the assembly of a fleet. But can the Turkish command be sure?

It cannot.

Whatever else, it is obvious that, until things can be more certain, it would be unwise for the Turks to move any of their five divisions in Syria anywhere, let alone down to Gaza as some have pushed for. After much discussion, the Turkish High Command sends just two divisions to base themselves north of Gaza, ready to move if it comes under attack, and one brigade to bolster Beersheba on the off-chance that the British try to make an attack from the fundamentally water-less wasteland that abuts it.

10 October 1917, Tel el Fara, ruse-coloured spectacle

It is a strange thing to be preparing for battle in the shade of a structure built eight centuries before, but such is the case for the Australians who are now conducting their patrols in the occasional blessed shade cast by Tel el Fara – referred to by the men as 'El Favo' – which, as one Trooper describes it, is a 'man-made mountain . . . a relic of Crusader days'.[33]

At the time that the English zealots were seeking to re-take the Holy Land, the fort was constructed at one of the key crossing points of the Wadi Ghuzze, on the southern side, and it still roughly stands as a monumental reminder to those seeking to do the same now – the locals have been through this before, and many times at that.

The tents at this Australian camp are laid out on the desert floor in neat rows, with many areas set aside for where the horses can be tethered, watered and fed. Between the tents, Troopers of the Australian Light Horse are making their way back and forth on business unknown, occasionally stepping aside for open-top armoured cars bearing officers, who they even occasionally – very occasionally – salute. On the edge of the encampment, some squadrons are doing training drills in the heat.

It is a singularly hot and dusty afternoon, but no-one comments on it for a very simple reason – it would be like saying the Nullarbor looks dry, or the Pacific looks wet. *Every* afternoon hereabouts is hot and dusty in some manner, so there is just no point.

And now look.

At one of the horse staging areas, a group of Australian Light Horse Troopers are saddling their horses, clearly going out on patrol. First, over the horse's back goes the blanket they will be using tonight when they bivouac out there. Now comes the military saddle, specially designed to give the horse maximum comfort for the great weight to be borne, as the saddle also has many hooks and scabbards from which will hang the rider's rations, ammunition, rifle, greatcoat, ground sheet, mess tin and canvas water bucket, plus a nosebag with the horse's grain ration for the day and all the rest, including spare horseshoes with nails and hammer.

Once the saddle is on, and the horse has an extra bandolier of ammunition hung around its neck – and everyone is ready – now, and only now, do they all mount to head out from their tent-camp at Khan Yunis to keep tabs on Jacko. Nominally, they are working out where he is and just what might be the best way to knock his block off. On this day, as it happens, a stranger has joined them, a tall and dapper sort of fellow, nudging 40, with eyes that look straight through you and lips that you'd reckon were *born* sealed. He is clearly not disposed to have a chat, and they are under strict orders not to ask.

He's from Intelligence. So, in the meantime . . .

Do not ask questions.

Allow him to accompany you until you get close to Turkish lines.

He will do the rest.

And, sure enough . . .

Just as the first signs of the Turk become apparent, the lone rider gives them a dismissive wave, and heads off on his own. A bit queer, how the bloke rides, yes? He is a good rider, but he does it in the classic manner they have already noted of Englishmen who have been raised chasing foxes and playing polo – always leaning forward, never relaxed – but there ya go. And there he goes.

See ya, sport.

In the searing sunlight, the sole rider – it is Major Richard Meinertzhagen – keeps moving further out into no-man's-land, that narrow band of desert that lies between the two roughly positioned armies, to where Turkish patrols have been most recently sighted, up around the Turkish outpost of El Girheir.

Every nerve in Meinertzhagen is a'jangle, his eyes squinting through the shimmering haze for some sign of the Turks, his ears straining for the clink of horses' trappings against the light rustling of the desert wind. One attempt has already been made to do this a month before by Meinertzhagen's colleague, Captain Arthur Neate, but it seems likely he simply hadn't got close enough to the Turks.

This time, there can be no room for . . . room. He must get close.

Occasionally, he pauses to have a swig from his canteen.

At last, *at last*, he hears it! It is the distant crack of rifle shots and, sure enough, small spurts of sand arise around him. Exactly as he had hoped for, he is under fire! Wheeling his horse about in the direction whence he has come, he gallops away, with the Turks in full pursuit.

But even the Turks must be careful, for they have been caught this way before. The closer the horseman gets to his own British lines, the more likely the pursuers will be ambushed by a patrol.

And yet, once they stop the pursuit after a mile or so, the strangest thing . . .

For now the horseman stops also, removes his Lee-Enfield rifle from his horse's saddle scabbard and fires off a shot at them from a distance of some 600 yards.

Enraged – this is not meant to be the way these things go – the Turks wheel their horses back in his direction and fire back.

'Now was my chance,' Meinertzhagen will recount, 'and in my effort to mount I loosened my haversack, field glasses, water bottle, dropped my rifle – previously stained with some fresh blood from my horse – and, in fact, did everything to make them believe I was hit and that my flight was disorderly. They had now approached close enough, and I made off, dropping the haversack . . .'[34]

Slumped in his saddle even while galloping away, the horseman still manages a quick look behind him and is satisfied to see the Turkish patrol has stopped, and is retrieving what he has dropped.

'I now went like the wind for home and soon gave them the slip, well satisfied with what I had done and that my deception had been successful.'[35] *Inshallah!*

Even once returned safely to GHQ, back in British lines, however, the ruse goes on, and a message is quickly dispatched to other HQs in the area.

> URGENT. While on reconnaissance patrol in No Mans Land
> this afternoon, about x 21 d4. 3, a Staff officer lost
> a haversack. If found, the haversack is to be returned
> forthwith to General Headquarters without being opened or
> its contents examined in any way.[36]

Patrols are sent out with orders to attempt to retrieve the haversack, and, effectively, the Turks are so advised when a wireless message is transmitted in a code which it is known the enemy has broken: 'Determined efforts are to be made to-night by troops in the sector involved to recover the lost haversack mentioned in G.R.O. No. 102.'[37]

'Oh, Lord!' Captain Ferdinand Tuohy will chronicle his own remarks when Meinertzhagen returns to Corps GHQ that evening at Rafa.

'Here's one of these GHQ wallahs! Nice business this afternoon! Can't go out on patrol without giving the whole show away to the Turks! Found your blessed haversack yet? I should say not! Not likely to, either! The old Turk's fairly gloating over it by now. Contained the whole plan of the push, I suppose. The fellow who dropped it ought to be strung up! Prancing about up to the Turk with operation orders in his pocket!'[38]

The Desert Mounted Corps brass, apparently, feels the same, and – in a cipher they know the Turks have – are quick to cable General Allenby bitterly complaining about 'the staff officer's stupidity and negligence'.[39]

Meinertzhagen is delighted to be so stupid!

•

The Australian Troopers call them 'furphies' – wild rumours that can usually be traced back to any two Diggers at 'Furphy's Farm Water Carts' – originally manufactured at Shepparton, Victoria, and now in service at Gallipoli – where, between guzzling gulps, blokes would tell each other the most outrageous things and the tales would take on such a life of their own they soon became Gospel.

But is this a furphy, or dinkum? There's talk, mate, we are going to attack Beersheba, way out in the desert!

Trooper Maurie Evans is one who documents the talk, most particularly after a large supply dump is moved to the east, out in the broad direction of the remote Turkish outpost.

'It is I think an attempt to take Beersheba . . . We shall probably go round the back somewhere while the infantry make a frontal attack.'[40]

Further indication that something is stirring is the increased air support, with No. 113 Squadron newly arrived to join the other three Royal Flying Corps of the Palestine Brigade.

12 October 1917, Huj, near Tel el Sheria, fool me thrice

In his large tent at Ottoman Eighth Army HQ at Huj, north of the Gaza–Beersheba line, General Kress von Kressenstein now closely examines the contents of the haversack, which have made their way to him.

At first glance through his monocle they appear to be an amazing treasure trove of important papers, some of which are stamped 'Secret', and including one which maintains there will be no attack on Turkish lines for at least three months, and maybe longer – and even then it will be framed against Gaza. Kress von Kressenstein had been among those who suspected that perhaps Beersheba might have been the next target. However, according to this document, a landing will be made on the coast nearby, with a landing on the coast north of Gaza being launched at the same time as the French land on the Syrian coast to fight Ottoman forces there. Most wonderfully, there is the rudiments of a cipher code, which will allow the Turks and Germans to decode more of the British communications they are intercepting.[41]

And there is still more.

As recorded by a Turkish officer, Colonel Hüsnü, a precis of the contents includes:

> The attack on the SINAI front has been delayed and will
> commence during the season of the heaviest rains (the
> beginning of the year) . . .
>   . . . The main attack will be made on the western part
> of the GAZA front. Points of debouchment will be prepared
> close to the right flank of the GAZA position before the
> attack. Night attacks and the employment of tanks are being
> considered. [42]

All very well, but is it genuine? Not all the senior Turkish officers are so convinced. As to the senior German officer?

'Though Kress thought the papers may have been intentionally dropped,' Colonel Hüsnü will record, 'he was inclined to believe in their genuineness.'

For one thing, 'von Kressenstein always believed in an attack on GAZA, and this confirmed his opinion. In addition he considered it probable that the British would not send us wrong information in this way.'[43]

So they must prepare accordingly, with the bulk of their forces to be positioned to defend Gaza.

(Just quietly though? Despite Kress von Kressenstein's decision, there remains consternation in senior Turkish ranks, Hüsnü recording, '[von Kress] was suspicious and astonished. He was most anxious to believe that the papers were genuine, and was continually asking other people's opinion.')[44]

Are they, perhaps, falling into a trap?

The German intelligence officers are having the same debate. An officer by the name of Schiller is particularly suspicious. With Teutonic thoroughness, he examines each item in the haversack meticulously: a map, an electric torch, a flask, a map, sandwiches and the key item: a wallet and a notebook combined. Schiller pores over the scribbled pages of scrawled pencil; stops and laughs. It is so elaborately casual, so temptingly real . . . It's a forgery! A clever one, an impudent one; but to him, a clear fake.

It's a con. But just as they relax, a breathless signals officer appears: 'The English have just sent out a wireless message saying that every effort is to be made tonight to recover a haversack that was lost this afternoon in no-man's-land.'

'What's that?' says Schiller, wanting there to be no mistake. The message is repeated, and a copy of the message placed before him. Now, as far as anyone knows, the British have no clue that the Germans have broken their code. Schiller paces the room, trying to work out how things actually lie.

'It can't be! It can't be!' he mutters. 'If these notes are genuine, all our reckoning has been wrong; that they're going to attack Gaza first, not at Beersheba?'[45]

Sir, it seems that way.

'I'm certain they're faked,'[46] Schiller still declares, albeit this time with a hint of uncertainty. The information in the notebook goes directly contrary to both the movements and the intelligence gained from prisoners taken only yesterday, and *also* against wireless transmissions that have been intercepted. But perhaps *those* transmissions had been intended to be intercepted? Just which ones are bluffs, and which ones are true? And what if the prisoners captured have been unwitting decoys? The notes 'captured' today clearly state that Allenby will be in Cairo until the 4th of November – which means there could be no major attack before that time, as it is unthinkable that a leader like Allenby would not be present for the attack.

Returning to the notebook, Schiller finds a letter wrapped around a photo. It is from the man's wife dated from many months before, and has been unfolded, read, refolded and tucked away so many times that the paper at the folds is fraying. To fake intelligence, to fake briefings, that is something any officer in this room can do. But to fake emotion; to show sentiment tipping over into sentimentality, well that is the hardest thing of all.

And as he reads the letter – with its short, clipped British emotions giving way to joy as the woman writes of the tiny hands and feet of her little baby – he finds himself moved. It ends with that embarrassed mix of politeness and love that only the British possess:

Good-bye, my darling! Nurse says I must not tire myself by writing too much, so no more now but I will write again soon and then it will be a longer letter than this. Take care of your precious self! All my love and many kisses. Your loving wife, Mary. Baby sends a kiss to Daddy.[47]

The last sentence is jammed against the side of the paper, a final thought crammed into the tiny space left. It seems very real. And if this letter is real, well, that haversack has just saved an empire for the Turks. Now the other documents found are re-read, including one that bears a complaint from a British commander noting the impossibility of maintaining a large force anywhere near Beersheba, because of the water shortage; a map with arrows pointed at the intended artillery targets at Gaza – and details of a minor operation by mounted troops on Beersheba, intended to fool the Turks into thinking the major attack will go in there, instead of Gaza.

So, it is to be Gaza.

CHAPTER TEN

WELL MET BY MOONLIGHT

Nine-tenths of tactics are certain, and taught in books: but the irrational tenth is like the kingfisher flashing across the pool, and that is the test of generals.[1]

T. E. Lawrence, *Seven Pillars of Wisdom*

The fierce individualism with which he fought Turks, Arabs and English staff officers lay close to the heart of the Australian light horseman. He lived under few restraints, and was equally careless of man, God, and nature. Yet he stood by his own standards firmly, remaining brave in battle, loyal to his mates, generous to the Turks, and pledged to his King and country . . . Probably his kind will not be seen again, for the conditions of war and peace and romance that produced him have almost entirely disappeared.[2]

Bill Gammage, *The Broken Years*

15 October 1917, Beersheba, ripe for the sack

It is not quite that Kress von Kressenstein is a man on a mission, but he has certainly come with great purpose. There has been talk of abandoning Beersheba, of shortening the defensive line. The German officer will not have it, and needs the Turkish leadership in place to understand the importance of holding on to the town at all costs.

His instructions to the newly appointed commander of the III Corps on site, Colonel Ismet, are clear: 'Beersheba can be subjected to an attack of one or two infantry brigades and cavalry from the west and from the south of the Wadi Saba. It is impossible that large mounted forces will operate from east of Beersheba.'[3]

But be ready to move at a moment's notice to wherever the attack *does* come!

'If Beersheba is not attacked and heavy fighting occurs on other points of the line it is probable that the Beersheba Group will receive orders to advance in the general direction of Abu Galyon . . .'[4]

Yes, General.

For all that, Colonel Ismet does not quite share the German's confidence, and will actually give orders that all the wells and key buildings in Beersheba be wired with dynamite, with one central switchboard, so that if the worst does come to the worst and the British overwhelm them, they can at least blow the whole town up, and deny them water.

•

Norris . . .

Here, sir.

Nyle . . .

Here, sir.

O'Leary . . .

. . .

O'Leary?

Christ. Thomas O'Leary, *again*. Ever and always for the officers of the 4th Australian Light Horse Regiment, there is a problem with this Queensland jackaroo. Yes, he is a superb horseman and fine soldier, and yes, when the heat is on he never lets you down, but when the drink is on he always gulps it down. There are wells in this land that currently contain far less liquid than O'Leary. And with a skinful he's always a problem, usually resulting in charges like 'Insubordination', being 'Absent Without Leave', and more, particularly 'Drunkenness'. Even in these parts, O'Leary can sniff out alcohol at a distance of 20 miles in the middle of a *khamsin*.

And so it proves on this day. For, sure enough, when O'Leary is found by the Military Police, he is as drunk as *three* lords, and promptly arrested. Look, under any other circumstance O'Leary would assume the usual position – back in the stockade. On this occasion, however, it is decided to merely fine him 10 shillings. The Queenslander remains a good Trooper when he is sober, or least not that drunk, and the way things feel right now, it seems likely that the Army will need every good soldier they can get into their saddles.

•

Fellow Australians!

Over the course of this war to date, Flight Lieutenant Alaric Boor has occasionally come across his countrymen, but not often. And even then, when on the Western Front, there had been little time to talk, while at Salonika the only other Australians had been nurses, and they were *always* too frantic to converse at length.

But now?

Well, now, he and his fellow pilots of 113 Squadron – based at an aerodrome at Weli Sheikh Nuran, between Rafa and Shellal and 10 miles due south of Gaza – are flying side-by-side with the No. 1 Australian Squadron. And there is, at last, some time in the mess to compare notes. A particular joy, apart from catching up on the news from home – where the second conscription referendum put up by Prime Minister Billy Hughes will take place just before Christmas – is talking to men like Lieutenant Ross Smith who, just like Alaric, has also spent a lot of time in the trenches, only to now find his true metier, *flying!*

In the meantime, the orders for all of them, and all units of the Royal Flying Corps and Australian Flying Corps east of the Suez, known as the Palestine Brigade, are clear. The skies must be kept clear of German planes along the entire line from Gaza to Beersheba – or at least the Germans must be kept so high that they won't see much. Under no circumstances can they be allowed to fly over the spots where our troops are secreted in wadis and settlements and report back to their commanders that a huge movement of men and munitions is afoot.

Equally, and this is more particularly a task for Boor in his RE 8 and their key role as observers – they must themselves be on the lookout for enemy troop dispositions in one area in particular: Beersheba. The key is to try and look without being seen to do so, rather like getting an eyeful of a beautiful woman on a Melbourne tram. And speaking of women . . . inevitably in the officers' mess stories emerge of romantic escapades back home and while training in England. Alaric listens with interest and a grin, but does not join in. He is serious about Ida Rawlings, which makes her his only romantic pursuit in years. She is not an escapade, so he has no stories to trade.

18 October 1917, Moascar near Ismailia, horse and carriage

Certainly there is movement at the station – men and *materiel* being piled on to trains leaving Kantara and heading for the front that currently rests near Rafa, each carriage stuffed with corps and cargo. But Major Banjo Paterson has a better idea. With nearly 200 horses due to be delivered to Rafa, and 50 riders to take them, why not *ride* them there?

Yes, that's it!

It will help give the horses condition. And for Banjo Paterson personally, it will be a pleasure to get away from the depot, see some more of the country, and get close to the front lines once more, see some old friends and get more meat for verse, or some anecdotal artillery for articles. At the very least, the trip will provide fodder for his letters, for it is, Paterson writes to his wife, 'a godsend to get away as we have had two years real solid depot work seeing nothing and hearing a lot of what other people were doing and I think one gets very, very sick of it. We started for the first day to Kantara on the canal and thence by very easy stages up through the desert to Palestine the same road that Napoleon and Moses . . . went in the olden days.'[5]

Little council maintenance seems to have been done on the road since that time; but the ride is enjoyable nonetheless, some feeling a strange kinship with soldiers dead for 3500 years! The Australians travel as those ancients of days gone by once did, and the hold of history cannot but be felt.

Day after day, they push towards the front, with the traffic on rail and track getting ever thicker the nearer they get, and all of Kantara, Romani, Bir el Abd and Bir el Arish providing the water and feed they need – before heading off at the crack of dawn each day – as they get closer to Rafa and the Holy Land.[6]

So it's shift, boys, shift,
For there isn't the slightest doubt
That we've got to make a shift
To the stations further out

With the packhorse runnin' after
For he follows like a dog,
We must strike across the country
At the old jig-jog[7]

Beyond everything else, it is a chance to see how the war is progressing, the way it is working, the nitty-gritty of the rough-and-tumble, and this includes seeing up-close the famed Ismailia flying depot, where the Royal Flying Corps seems busy as never before, with endless planes heavily laden with bombs taking off and heading towards the Turkish lines.

Banjo and his troop happen to be passing when a squadron of eight planes take off in quick succession, only for one of them to return a short time later with mechanical difficulties. The pilot has only just brought his aircraft to a halt before he jumps out, and rushes towards Major Paterson, the closest officer to his own rank of Lieutenant.

'Come on, let us have a drink,' he exhorts the Australian poet. 'I want a drink badly.'

'It seems to me a bit early to have a drink,' Paterson replies, evenly.

'When a man has just landed a machine,' he says, 'with a dozen perfectly good live bombs under it, believe me, he wants a drink.'[8]

Fair point. While his men struggle to find the water they need for their 150 horses – Clancy of the Overflow would not be feeling at home in these dry and dusty parts – Paterson heads off to the base's wet canteen to have a drink with the shaken pilot. When he has settled a little, the poet even dares ask him . . .

'What might have happened if you had landed the machine roughly and started those bombs off?'

The answer is indescribable catastrophe, as of course all 12 bombs would have exploded, and it wouldn't just have been him and his observer killed. 'These flying boys are being tested,' Paterson will note, 'and they are coming through it in great shape.'[9]

Yes, they might need a stiff drink to maintain that shape now and again; but none blames them, they only join the toast.

22 October 1917, Tel el Fara, where there's a well, there's a way

Something is up. No-one in Ion Idriess's 5th Light Horse Regiment is quite sure what it is, only that they have to ride through the night to the small settlement of Esani – about 16 miles south-west of Beersheba, and eight miles from their starting point of Tel el Fara – and then set to on an important task.

They must both mount a guard on those fixing the wells previously blown in by German engineers, and help them, before moving on to Khalasa and Asluj, where they must do the same thing. How, exactly, are the sweating Troopers to fix the blown-in wells?

Well, mate, it starts with a pick and shovel, and they don't call them 'Diggers' for nuttin'. In short order, all of Idriess's 5th Light Horse Regiment are split into working parties, and set to in following the orders of the Australian and New Zealand Field Engineers, who are directing the works.

Under the hot sun, the Australians of the 2nd Light Horse Brigade are digging ever deeper, removing the sand and the ancient stones, endeavouring to restore the old walls as they go. It entails the filling of a lot of buckets attached to ropes, which are then hauled up – and the engineers are to build a rough support to hold up those walls as they go – but at least there are many willing workers and they can do it in intense shifts. The reward, by which time they are no less than 100 feet deep, is first moist soil and, as they dig deeper . . . *water at last!*

With that accomplished, the engineers provide the finishing touches, installing engine-driven pumps, pipes and rows of canvas horse troughs. Clearly, there needs to be enough water to sate an army, because that is what will be coming through.

For now word spreads, first as whispers, then as rumours, and soon confirmed.

'We know the whole plan of fight, Chetwode's, we believe. The Turkish left flank must be turned by the Desert Mounted Corps and the Anzacs must take Beersheba on the first day.'[10]

There can be only one day; for after that there will be no water. Oh those boys on the Western Front can sit in a trench for yonks and play football at Christmas, but out in the East you get a day. Dash in a flash, and bash, are the tactics.

Understood.

Oh, and after we smash through Beersheba, we'll continue right through to behind Gaza. In short: 'there will be merry hell to pay'.[11]

Ion Idriess is not alone in thinking, 'I wonder if my luck will pull me through?'[12]

For it is luck; there's no doubt of that. It might be easier to fight this war as the Arabs do, not just believing in fate, but knowing it is unchangeable. Why worry about whether you die? It has already been decided. Back to digging the wells.

Esani, of course, looks just as it did when they started, an ancient sea of dusty dwellings; part faded fortress, part reminder of the antiquity that will remain long after you are dust. It is still a cross between a place that looks as though it is about to be excavated or has just been blown up.

But at least it now has water.

'We are on duty day and night here,' Idriess faithfully reports to his diary. 'We do not mind, we realise this water digging as the most critical part of operations, [and] . . .'

And, wait!

The word comes through.

'BBA.'

The Bull is about? No, the Bull is *here*!

General Allenby is indeed still doing what he does remarkably well, storming about making sure that everyone is being as energetic as himself in the pursuit of victory.

'We thought quite a lot of him coming out all this distance and seeing with his own eyes what is being done,'[13] Idriess records. Carry on! And they do before moving with Allenby himself to Asluj, a small settlement featuring, 'a picturesque mosque which, with the other snow-white buildings, looked very striking in the brilliant full moonlight'.[14]

The difference between the hell of the day and the beauty of the night in this desert continues to fascinate.

•

It has been a long haul through dust and heat, but at last Major Banjo Paterson and his 50 rouseabouts are able to deliver their fresh horses to their intended destination just back from the front, at Rafa.

The recording official at Rafa notes with astonishment that: 'The distance and heavy nature of the route really did no harm whatsoever to them, rather the reverse as the animals actually improved.'[15]

Extraordinary fellow, Paterson. I doubt he'd suit the office, but damn fine in the desert.

As to Banjo and his men, with their mission accomplished they find it hard not to suddenly feel like stage-hands – behind the scenes in a play of great moment. Everywhere they look all is hustle and bustle, prep and priming, a hive of great activity, a sense of grand and momentous things afoot. An expedition is to begin, an Allenby expedition, that has been in the works for four months or so, and is about to play out.

One man who does make time for the great poet is Lieutenant Colonel George Macarthur-Onslow, the Commander of the 7th Light Horse Regiment, and he is almost giddy with enthusiasm as he speaks to Banjo. He can't be specific you understand, but it is the General who has inspired him: Allenby.

'It's all or nothing with us,' he tells Banjo. 'We have to smash right through the Turks and come out on the other side. I think Julius Caesar would have funked trying it.'

I came, I saw, I funked? What gamble is being taken here?

A big one.

'If we get held up,' says Macarthur-Onslow, 'we'll be out of provisions and horse-feed in a couple of days, and then you can write to me at Constantinople. But don't worry, we'll get through all right.'

Macarthur-Onslow is clear about what, precisely, will get them through.

'We're more frightened of Allenby behind us than we are of the Turks in front!' he laughs, full of infectious confidence. 'We'll go through Palestine looking over our shoulders, and the first thing you'll know we'll be in Damascus.'[16]

Damascus? It is the first that Banjo has heard of such an ambition. And yet the fact that the Ottoman Empire will likely still have something to say about that comes just moments later as, from out of the clear blue sky, comes a swooping German plane, diving low to drop bombs ... and being greeted by roaring British anti-aircraft guns for his trouble, combining to send up a wall of flak to fly through if he dares. Banjo is more than a little concerned – did you know bombs are falling within 100 yards of us? – while Macarthur-Onslow barely blinks.

Welcome to the front. It is a lot different from handing out horses in the backblocks.

Either way, there is little time to tarry and both men must away.

26 October 1917, Gaza, crafty Brits, fleet afoot

What are the British up to now?

For in his Command Headquarters at Gaza, German commander Major Ernst Tiller receives a singularly troubling report.

A fleet of small boats has been spotted just off Deir el Belah, five miles south-west of Gaza. Taking his field-glasses in hand, Major Tiller can now see them himself. The crafts are departing and, as they do so, the British naval guns begin from afar, attacking the mouth of the Hesi. In short order, a large column of British troops – surely just dropped by the small craft – are spotted marching on the beach in the general direction of Gaza!

Something is afoot, apart from those troops. Another attack on Gaza?

It seems more than likely and Major Tiller is quick to place all of his troops on high alert.

•

Back in the day, the Biblical day, *manna from heaven* was the food sent from God that rained on the starving Israelites as they made their Exodus from Egypt and headed for the Promised Land. So, having sustenance fall from the sky around here is not unprecedented, just ... unusual. So what is dropping today? Smokes!

Yes, it is tobacco, now falling on the Turkish soldiers at Beersheba, and indeed all along their fortified line to Gaza! It makes manna look like muck, fags falling from the Father above! For those who have long ago run out of tobacco, it is a sign from God to renew the habit, smoke 'em if you got 'em and wonder about where they came from as you puff. Some troops have seen precisely where, it had been the most extraordinary thing. No sooner had a British plane gone overhead in the early evening and they had all ducked for cover – fearing their bombs – pouches of tobacco had suddenly dropped from the skies to land all around their trenches and redoubts. Clearly, a supply drop for British troops gone blessedly wrong and the booty is theirs!

Cautiously at first, but now with some enthusiasm, the more nicotine-starved of them are soon puffing away. The flavour, true, seems a bit different, maybe a *lot* different, but maybe this is just the way of English tobacco? The main thing is, it is tobacco and does offer some relief.

Back at headquarters not long afterwards, Major Meinertzhagen receives his report. The mission has been accomplished, and the pouches of tobacco, lightly blended with opium, have been successfully dropped on the Turkish soldiers. Ideally, they will develop a taste for them, and smoke them continually, becoming ever more . . . befuddled.

It is true that General Allenby had initially been against the plan, likening it to poisoning the enemy, which is simply not done, but Meinertzhagen manages to circumvent the edict, firmly believing the ends would justify the means. If you look at it the right way, it's giving aid, comfort and a lovely sense of well-being to the enemy. If it saves just one British soldier, as a glassy-eyed Turk misses his mark, it will have been worth it. And there is every chance of that, as he will later observe, after sampling the opium-laden cigarettes, that, 'they were indeed strong. The effect was sublime, complete abandonment, all energy gone, lovely dreams and complete inability to act or think.'[17]

26 October 1917, Tel el Fara, Hodgson's choice

Something is up.

The commanding officer of the Australian Mounted Division, Major General Henry Hodgson, has sent out an order to all troops.

'The Divisional Commander directs that steps be taken at once to have the points of all bayonets sharpened by the Armourers.'[18]

No-one is quite sure what it bodes, but it seems fairly certain the General is not having them do it so they can better cut potatoes. And there is more.

> It is to be noticed that the country is built for mounted action, whereas any dismounted attack is handicapped for want of cover. The Divisional Commander hopes that all Brigades will endeavour to profit by their knowledge of this fact.[19]

The whispers become louder and soon have an exultant ring.

The stunt? It's Beersheba!

Privately, despite his careful order, General Hodgson clearly thinks there might be the opportunity to mount a charge, something he has long advocated. In fact, after a few small successful charges by the Light Horse in the Levant, Hodgson had recently requested his men be issued with swords, a request which had been denied, hence his push for them having at least sharpened bayonets.

Now, his directive insists, when it comes to mounted men holding their bayonet in the air, it is important to bear in mind that, 'it has the same moral effect as a sword, as it glitters in the sun and the difference could not be detected by the enemy'.[20]

27 October 1917, Gaza, boom crash opera

As dawn breaks it is so still you could light a match in the gentle fog and it would not even flicker or flutter, let alone blow out. Which is handy, for this fog covers hollows that conceal the mass of artillery batteries that have been moved forward in the night.

The Germans call such conditions *windstill*, and up from those hollows in the morning butterflies are prancing, birds are singing, and the Bedouins in their camps are rising to tend their camels. Clearly, another demonic day in the searing sun beckons.

But now it happens.

Precisely as planned, at dawn, some 218 guns of the 21st Corps, which have been moved forward in the night to do the honours, roar in thunderous unison: Gaza is under attack! The guns belch, the artillery crews move in a blur of highly choreographed catastrophe, and the shells land all over Gaza, Ali Muntar and surrounds – in what, with the 15,000 rounds of heavy shells alone to come over the next four days, the Official History will record as the 'heaviest [shelling] carried out in the course of the war outside the European theatres'.[21]

The observers of the British Army have the satisfaction of seeing plumes of dust arise from, first, the ramparts of Gaza and soon artillery batteries in the town, followed by the railway siding just to the north, and then the ammunition dumps.

This barrage over the next four days will surely confirm the Turkish view that they have been right to concentrate their troops at Gaza.

In weary Gaza itself – which has been under siege from one empire or another for 3000 years or so – all is dust, destruction and a little death, as residents get to their basements, soldiers to their bunkers and artillery crews to their guns, as counter-battery fire must quickly get underway. It is alarming, but not surprising. Just as Allenby had hoped. Colonel Kress von Kressenstein is quickly apprised of the news and can at last relax. The British have returned to Gaza for another beating.

2 pm, 28 October 1917, Tel el Fara, dogleg and doggerel

Men, bring it in tight.

Colonel Murray Bourchier wants a word.

As one, the Troopers of the 4th Light Horse Regiment – now including Trooper Thomas O'Leary, who has recently returned to the regiment from his drunken escapades at the rest camp at Port Said – gather around this respected young officer from a distinguished farming family in Victoria as he gives his orders.

Saddle up and pack light. Beyond your weaponry and ammunition, you may take with you no more than one blanket, one ground sheet, and a greatcoat. We are travelling fast, by the light of this full moon. We have a big ride ahead of us to Beersheba. We will be moving out at dusk, and heading 30 miles to the south-east to get to Esani, and doing another 30 miles tomorrow night to get to Khalasa.

(Though Beersheba is just 20 miles as the crow flies from Tel el Fara, so circuitous and duplicitous is our route that we will cover 70 miles to get there.)

There is joy among the Troopers, and none more so than in the 12th Light Horse Regiment, as witness the words of one of Guy Haydon's mates, Trooper Thomas Hoskisson:

'The "cold-footed" Light Horse who have been marking time in Palestine according to stay-at-home critics, have at last come into their kingdom.

'After many dreary, sweating months in the desert, choked by sand and tantalised to the verge of madness by flies, exposed to the burning rays of the sun by day and drenched by night dews on patrol, keeping in touch with the enemy and occasionally handing him out a surprise packet of no mean order, we passed under the shadow of Tel-el-Fara on the evening of October 28.'[22]

Two of the Troopers heading out, Arthur Bennett and Reginald Browne, amuse and distract themselves by working on a Banjo-esque poem to describe their task:

> There was movement at El Favo, For word had gone around
> That 'Old Bill' had ordered, 'Saddle up', with three days
>   rations found.
> Soon all was in readiness to go we knew not where,
> As we mounted on our chargers, our hearts as light as air;
> They knew something was doing – their dumb instinct seemed
>   to tell,
> And before that march was ended they had done their
>   duty well.[23]

Unbeknownst to them, Banjo Paterson himself is only a few miles away, and closing fast.

•

In this camp, just five miles from Gaza, William Grant's 4th Brigade of the Australian Light Horse begin a long pull to the east – in staggered starts, with each regiment given a precise time to head off – on what they already know will be a gruelling journey.

All of the mounted Troopers have been on long journeys before.

This time though, as they take their leave, things are different.

Instead of the usual way – moving at dawn after packing up and striking their tents – they are moving at dusk, and leave those tents standing, with lit lanterns inside. Later, a skeleton crew will go to each tent and light a lot of cooking campfires in front of each pod of tents, before extinguishing the lanterns at the usual time – about 9 pm. Tomorrow and each day until the battle for Beersheba begins not only will they do the same, but also new 'dummy' camps of tents will be set up to make it look like a large force is assembling in front of Gaza!

Just as they had done in Gallipoli, everything is being done to convince the enemy that they are still here in force, and offer no clue that, in fact, they are moving *en masse* many miles away.

To any Turkish or German eyes that spy from on high, to any Bedouin in the pay of the same, all the tents will be there – even as small squads of horsemen go back and forth on the banks of Wadi Ghuzze around Tel el Fara with the specific purpose of raising large clouds of dust. During the day, intense air patrols from the Royal Flying Corps and the Royal Naval Air Service have been proceeding back and forth along the entire fortified line to keep the Taubes from getting close enough to observe *too* closely. From distant hilltops at night, the lights in the tents and the fires outside will give an equal impression of the British being about to besiege Gaza.

On this evening, in the middle of the throng travelling in column of route, four abreast, Lieutenant Guy Haydon is astride Midnight as his 12th Regiment keeps pace with their fellow units of the 4th Brigade, and the 11th and 4th Regiments. All of them bear three days' rations of bully beef and biscuits for themselves, and two nosebags of 19 pounds of grain for their horses, hanging from each side of their saddles. Another day's worth of grain for each horse will be carried in Brigade wagons which will come along behind.

Through the dusk, across the desert ramble, and into the night, they keep moving.

On both sides, and in front, a screen of Troopers – who occasionally give their position when the iron horseshoes of their mounts strike sparks from stones – keep pace. If there proves to be any different kinds of Turkish delights hidden in any of the wadis the broad mass of troops is skirting, it will be the screen that takes the immediate hit, not the mass of men now moving through the night.

For the moment, mercifully, there is nothing. Under orders, there is no smoking and no talking above a muffled whisper, but the night is filled with the sounds of thousands of horsemen on the move. Behind them comes a supply convoy that extends six miles and includes some 300 four-wheeled vehicles, most pulled by camels, mules and packhorses.

For those in the middle of it, it seems extraordinary to think that the Turks in their posts just 10 miles to the north can't be aware of it, but at least the route soon takes them well away from the fortified line as they embark on their circuitous long haul, and in any case a key part of Allenby's plans has been to habituate the Turks to just such noises in the night over previous weeks . . .

Back in the day all roads did indeed lead to Rome, but tonight, and for the next few nights, they all lead to Beersheba.

(Mercifully, the rain has held off, and as Allenby has just dropped a note to his wife, 'Good weather now, for fighting.'[24])

Nearing midnight, Grant's 4th Brigade of the Light Horse make camp in a wadi a mile from Esani, to settle down for the rest of the night. No fires.

Dawn finds men in place around Esani, a quarter of the way on their journey with the job ahead of remaining hidden in wadis through the day – with most sections taking shelter either in the shade of their horses, or beneath blankets strung between four rifles stuck into the desert by their bayonets – and not letting the Turks understand just how many are heading their way.

•

On this fine morning of 29 October, Banjo Paterson, experiencing his first dawn at Rafa, awakes to the sound of shells bursting on Gaza.

'There were six or eight warships working off the land,' he will record, 'their huge guns (14 inches they say) used to make [the] ground shake and there was one continuous roll of firing like beating a big drum very quickly.'

Poking his head out from the tent, he can actually 'see the shells bursting all along the Turkish position and it did seem impossible to believe that any human beings could stand such a fusillade for a moment. Great clouds of earth used to fly up and it seemed as if nothing could live a moment in such an inferno but the Turks stuck it out gamely enough . . .'[25]

Which is true enough. Though it is not to say they are unconcerned. For it is not just the pounding their forward defences are taking. It is also that the British camps have been closely observed in recent days, and there is no doubt that they have *six* infantry divisions still right here in the Gaza sector, with another over to the east.

All signs point to a third battle being about to begin. And yes, there has been increased movement around Beersheba, but at Huj, the commander of the Eighth Army, General Kress von Kressenstein, is not concerned, sending Colonel Ismet in Beersheba a cable.

> The enemy has concentrated one infantry and one cavalry
> division and the camel corps against Beersheba. Beersheba
> has been reinforced by two regiments . . . The forces in
> Beersheba opposed to the above enemy concentration are
> sufficient and no further reinforcement will be sent. [26]

•

At much the same time, British Intelligence is able to secure an enemy communication, which is promising, and a sign that the Haversack Ruse has worked!

> An outflanking attack on Beersheba with about one infantry
> and one cavalry division is indicated, but the main attack,
> as before, must be expected on the Gaza front. [27]

•

For Banjo Paterson and his men, there is no time to tarry. At Rafa, he and his rouseabouts have now been given orders to deliver 186 horses to the forces which will soon be besieging Beersheba, and they must start right away.

To the east, those two Troopers paying homage to his style of poetry are continuing to live the experience that will give them the lines.

> *Next day we lay in idleness till the sun went down, once more.*
> *Then another four hours march we did, as we had done before;*
> *Our horses neighed for water, but none for them was found,*
> *And our water bottles empty ere another sun went down.*[28]

•

For the men of Brigadier General William Grant's 4th Brigade, it is coming time to move once more. Their entire day at Esani has been spent looking after the horses – including getting them what water they can from the canvas troughs – and waiting to move again. And now, just gone 6 o'clock, they depart. Yes, another moonlit night, but now so dusty – for it gets drier the further east they go – you would hardly know.

Amidst swirling plumes of grit that blanket them all, the 4th Brigade's 800 men are again part of a massive movement in the moonlight, an eerie cavalcade of dusty phantoms, plodding along in an ancient land on paths previously trodden by at least a dozen ancient armies with much the same task. And yet each soldier of the 4th Australian Light Horse Brigade is their equal tonight; for they ride on the track of Alexander, they drink from the well of Moses, they feel the breath of history in the darkness.

Are the great ghosts marching with us?

And will we be joining them in the hereafter come the battle that awaits?

The horses whinny, the stirrups lightly clank, the saddles squeak, but there remains no talking, no smoking, just . . . moving. The beaming moonlight shows it all, however.

In General Chauvel's Desert Mounted Corps, they are 10 brigades strong now, all on the move.

True, they only have to travel 10 miles tonight, but this is rough, twisted country to travel through, filled with wadis that must be crossed, sandhills that must be struggled over, and possible patrols which simply must be avoided. It is only 10 miles as the crow flies, but they are not riding crows and so must make their own arrangements.

As they continue to the north-east the moonlight feels brighter still, reflected as it is by the massive white chalk and sandstone cliffs which form the wadi walls that lie between Esani and Khalasa.

The mood is tense, but upbeat.

After two rounds of defeat at Gaza, followed by months of clashes with the Turks in endless skirmishes, and a little trench warfare, this stunt feels like they will soon be getting to grips, properly, once more.

Arriving at Khalasa – which proves to be little more than the scattered ruins of an old village – there is again no chance of a warm meal for the simple reason that there can be no fires, and all they can eat is their cold rations. Far more troubling, however, is the lack of water. The first arrivals had had their share, but by the time the first of Brigadier General William Grant's 4th Light Horse Brigade arrives at 10 pm, it is all but gone. There is just enough to wet their whistle, but not nearly enough to sate their thirst. With their horses, they settle down the best they can for a troubled night.

9.45 am, 30 October 1917, between Esani and Khalasa, Hun on the run

With the rest of the 12th Light Horse and still sweltering in the camp at Esani, as they wait to move off again in the cool and cloak of the early evening, Lieutenant Guy Haydon is among the first to see it. At first, it is no more than a speck in the air coming from the north. But it emerges in all its horror soon enough.

It's a German plane, a Rumpler CII!

Somehow – likely threading his way through patches of cloud – it has got through the screen of Bristol fighters that had been patrolling to the north of the moving troops to prevent precisely this, and the German pilot has clearly spotted the troops on the ground! For now he roars back and forth, just above rifle range, his observer no doubt taking photos of the columns of mounted Troopers, the infantry, the guns, the supply wagons, the trucks.

It is nothing less than a disaster. Within 30 minutes, once the Rumpler is back behind its own lines, the jig will be up and all their efforts to confuse the Turks about their true intentions will have come to naught. Unless . . .

Unless the Royal Flying Corps can come to their rescue.

For now a Bristol F.2b Fighter from the aerodrome at Deir el Belah suddenly appears.

Captain Arthur Hicks Peck and his observer, Captain John Lloyd-Williams, have indeed seen the Taube and come at it from on high. As the troops watch from below, enthralled, a game of aerial cat and mouse is pursued. The Taube twists and turns, soars and dips, tries to disappear into the same clouds whence it came. But all the while, Peck stays with it, waiting for the right moment . . .

Now!

Holding down the trigger of his forward-firing Vickers machine gun, a stream of .303 bullets, at the rate of eight rounds a second, bursts forth, and starts to tear into the flimsy fabric fuselage of the Taube. In short order smoke starts coming from its engine, even as it loses altitude and the troops below cheer themselves hoarse.

Though the Taube is mortally wounded, the two Germans on board are still capable of fleeing, and no sooner has their plane crash-landed than they are out and heading north, carrying satchels. Mercifully, *die beiden deutschen Piloten* are quickly captured and the satchels are found to contain, 'photographic plates, marked maps, and notes'.[29]

For the moment the Empire is saved.

30 October 1917, Asluj, night moves

With the enemy so close, it does not do to travel with too much ceremony, for fear of snipers taking shots at the man in the middle. But the Australian Troopers already on site at Asluj, preparing for the mass who are about to swarm in, recognise the new arrival soon enough anyway. It is General Chauvel, with his Desert Mounted Corps HQ of General Staff Officers, come forward to keep a close eye on proceedings.

(If he is looking tired, it is for very good reason, as he has been working as hard and as long as he ever has in his life. 'General Chauvel . . . is a wonderful man,' one of the officers on his personal staff will write at this time, 'as wiry as half a dozen ordinary men. He works from early morning until very late at night . . . The old general is a great favourite among all with whom he comes into contact.'[30])

Whatever else is to happen, there will be no repeat of the first attack on Gaza, where someone far removed from the battle gives an insane order to snatch defeat from the jaws of victory. Certainly not on Chauvel's watch.

Chauvel quickly convenes a meeting of his senior officers to make sure all is put in place. The brigade will move out in the wee hours of the morning, at around 1 am, to cover the final 25 miles to their launch position at Iswaiwin, some four miles to the east of Beersheba. The six brigades in play must arrive at their position before dawn so that no passing Taube will see such a force being moved into position.

Afternoon, 30 October 1917, Asluj, wild about Harry

Look alive now, and let the dog see the rabbit . . . !

Yes, there is enduring resentment among the Australians at the idea of saluting British officers, but there is nothing of the kind for General Chauvel. He is right up the front with them. (Visits by top brass have happened before, and are referred to by the troops as 'Royal parties'. They generally arrive in high ceremony, do a few inspections, grumble a little or a lot, and leave in a cloud of dust. But this is different. Chauvel is one of his men, and at one. They are all in this together and he is not going anywhere but to the front with them.)

Z-Day is tomorrow.

For now, General Chauvel, his slight, light form moving through, beetle brows lifted in greeting, a smile accompanying each salute, continues his quiet inspection, asking questions, receiving reports, giving orders about the precise placements of the Anzac Mounted Division who will be leaving from here at Asluj, and the Australian

Mounted Division leaving from Khalasa, which is eight miles and three hours back.

Yes, there is tension. But Chauvel is comforted by two things. He has the strong feeling that he and his men could have done no more than they have, in preparation. And at least for the moment there is no sign that the Turkish garrison in Beersheba is aware of the threat it faces.

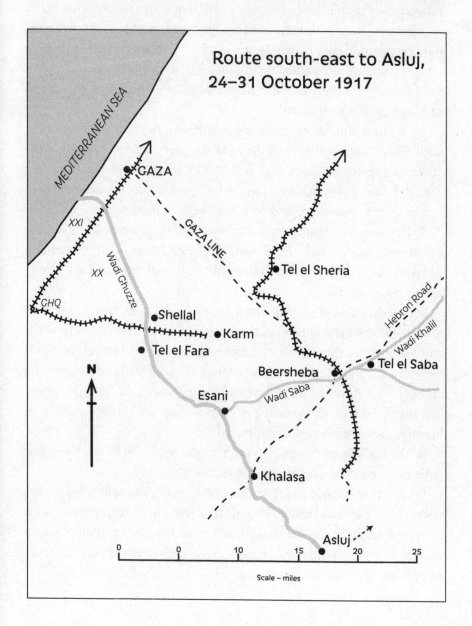

Route south-east to Asluj, 24–31 October 1917

30 October 1917, Karm, before the storm

At Karm, four miles from El Buggar, Banjo Paterson is stunned to find himself in the midst of heavy preparation as a large mass of men of the 20th Corps prepares to get underway.

Having left at dawn with his men and horses – and orders to get the horses to Beersheba – Paterson and his group have arrived here to find themselves in the midst of a throng so large that it very nearly defies belief.

'I found countless thousands of troops, tents, camels, motor wagons, traction engines, supply depots, yeomanry . . . infantry, in fact a whole army. Countless thousands of mule wagons, motor wagons and camels were loading up with supplies from this place (which was the end of the railway) for Beersheba.'[31]

At the first hint of the descending darkness, the first infantry of the 20th Corps are on their way in their staggered starts, beginning the 10-hour approach march that will ideally see them in position long enough before dawn that they can get some rest before the action begins.

The 60th Division are to attack Beersheba from the south, while the 74th Division will launch from the south-west. It seems like even the moon has disappeared as the dust generated by so many horses and Army boots blots everything out, and the horses and soldiers simply follow those in front.

Behind the last of the infantry come the 242 guns being pulled by hundreds of weary horses, plus thousands of camels carrying shells and supplies; a caravan of catastrophe-to-come that stretches an extraordinary six miles: wagons, trucks and animals all heading into the night. All up it means the desert stillness is now filled with the ceaseless tramp of feet, the snorting of horses, and the throaty rumble of heavily loaded trucks edging forward.

In the middle of the throng once more is Major Banjo Paterson, with his remaining horses and rouseabouts.

'I . . . never expect to see such a sight again,' he will write to his wife. 'The road ran over rolling downs like the Cunningham Plains country and the huge stream of traffic had spread out until it was a mile wide and this multitude surged along in dust unspeakable. Never have I seen or dreamt of such dust.'[32]

It will billow upwards, outwards, and into the night.

At El Buggar, nine miles to the east, General Chetwode is doing much the same with his own troops of the 20th Corps, and he opens his HQ there at 5 o'clock. Around and about this outpost, he has over 40,000 soldiers, including artillery crews. It is from here, tomorrow, that he and General Allenby – who is due to shortly arrive – will run the show. For now, Chetwode has his last meetings with his senior officers, going over the maps of Beersheba and its surrounds and designating precisely where he wants them and at what time.

Yes, sir.

•

Saddle up, and we go again.

It is 6 o'clock and nearly fully dark in Khalasa when Lieutenant Guy Haydon and his men of the 12th Australian Light Horse are told that they must head out towards Asluj. The plan is to have a brief rest there, before setting off again in the wee hours to arrive at a point on the Turks' flank so as to be able to attack Beersheba from the east.

With the 1st Light Horse Brigade, the now Lance Corporal Maurie Evans, who describes Asluj as 'a queer little place, ringed in with hills', is told the same.

'We move out of here tonight and attack Beersheba from the east in the morning, having to circle the place to do it.'[33]

The night is hot, heavy and dusty, the route is the longest of all their night moves – with the Anzac Mounted having 25 miles to cover, and the Australian Mounted a further 10 miles on top of that – and extremely dark.

'We are ordered to hang on to what water and food we have,' one Trooper records in his diary. 'The next we get we are to capture from the Turks.'[34]

Though the rule of no smoking still applies, in the 4th Light Horse Regiment Lieutenant Colonel Neil Smith manages to get around it by lighting his pipe and puffing away on it under the cover of his great-coat, to 'keep it smothered, but the poor cigarette smoker had no hope. We moved steadily.'[35]

At 9 pm, the last of the Desert Mounted Corps men are arriving at Asluj. Immediately, there is a problem. Alas, as their intelligence summary will record,

No water available to water horses. [36]

Simply put: last in, worst served. There are so many other mounted Troopers who have already passed through that the wells at Asluj simply had not been able to keep up and have now run all but dry. Such little water as is available must go to replenish the water bottles of the men themselves, and only then can the Walers and camels receive a drop.

Will the horses be able to cope with another journey to Beersheba, starting in just a few hours, without water?

There is no choice. They will simply have to.

•

It is a low-lying cloud of dust in the desert moonlight. From on high it would look benign. In the middle of this, the 20th Corps is on the move, more than 40,000 men and 214 guns – of which three-quarters are 18-pounders, while the rest are 4.5-inch howitzers and 60-pounders – converging on its designated spots, secreted in wadis to the south and south-west of Beersheba, while the Desert Mounted Corps is to go to similar wadis to the east and south-east.

True, for the mounted Troopers it is not ideal to be facing a battle at the end of a 30-mile night march, but that can't be helped.

Onwards.

The dust is clinging, choking, oppressive and you cannot see further than 20 yards in any direction. Just follow the man in front of you, and trust that our scouts out the front know what they are doing.

The Troopers and infantry of the 11th Light Horse Regiment keep moving, trying to take their minds off just what they'd give to be able to take vast swigs of water right now. But they can't, and neither can their horses.

Aware of their discomfort their Commanding Officer, Colonel John Parsons, tries to help.

'You fellows should copy my example,' he says blithely to a few Troopers he approaches. 'For the past ten miles, I have carried a small pebble in my mouth, and I haven't felt the need for a drink.'[37]

The Troopers left in his wake look at each other. Gawd help us all, he's serious!

One Trooper simply can't help himself.

'If the Colonel travels ten miles without a drink on a small pebble, how far will he go on a brick?'[38]

As Parsons is still within earshot he is – mercifully for the Trooper – able to join in the muffled laughter of all.

Onwards, in the dusty moonlight.

As dawn breaks, and the men of the 4th Australian Light Horse Brigade can see each other for the first time since dusk of the previous evening, all they know is two things: They are approaching their desti-nation, a position just beyond a ridge a little to the east of Beersheba. And each and every one of them is completely covered in dust, as are their horses.

'We looked a strange sight,' Lieutenant Smith will recount, 'every face was thickly covered with grey dust, making each man look like the next. I addressed Padre Weir, the Brigade Chaplain, as Bill, taking him for a trooper under all the dust.'[39]

•

Quiet conversations take place in the quiet watch of the night. The 4th Light Horse Regiment's Regimental Sergeant Major Alex Wilson tells Sergeant Jim French – for no good reason that he cares to expand on – 'I am sure there is a bullet waiting for me at Beersheba.'[40]

Maybe, Sergeant Major. There will no doubt be bullets for all of us. The trick is to duck them or shoot the Turk who's about to fire at you, first.

Wee hours, 31 October 1917, Asluj, bowled over

As ever, Tibby Cotter and his mate 'Bluey' stick tightly together. After watering their horses in the wee hours at the canvas troughs by the newly constituted wells, they prepare to move off with the rest of the 4th Brigade.

But, first things first.

Beyond everything else, Cotter – who, after his heroics in the second battle of Gaza had been promoted to Lance Corporal, only to decide he preferred to be a simple Trooper and so reverted to the lower rank – has developed a reputation as 'one of the best foragers in the AIF'. 'He would come to light with a bottle of champagne in the middle of the desert,' his mate Bluey would say, 'and the lads in the section all looked to him to turn up with something unusual.'

And on this momentous occasion, Tibby lives up to his reputation, telling Bluey that he has secured 'a yard of ling', a kind of long, round fish, and that once they get to their destination, he will 'treat the boys to a Stammell fish supper in Beersheba, and be damned to the consequences'.[41]

The boys in question, Troopers Jack Beasley and Rex Coley, grin at the thought.

Stammell's is the most famous fish restaurant in Sydney, which comes complete with a wine licence, an elevator for the ladies, private dining rooms and the swishest fare in the whole country. Only Tibby could claim that they only had to take Beersheba and he will whip them up a fish supper and be half-believed!

(Unbeknownst to them, at this very moment people all over Australia are reading a letter about Tibby's exploits, published in the leading sports paper, *Referee*, reassuring everyone from Palm Beach to Perth, from Darwin to the Derwent, that Tibby is doing well and might soon be decorated.

'I note your remarks in issue of *Referee*, of 17th ist., re Albert Cotter,' a W. Cameron writes. 'My cousin, Donald Cameron, who is at present commanding the 12th L.H., has written me, remarking on the splendid work Cotter has been doing, and stating that he had been recommended for decoration. Knowing that I should be much interested in Tibby's welfare, and the freemasonry that exists amongst cricketers generally, he wrote me on the matter; and it gives me much pleasure to enclose the par in your paper.'[42])

But half a world away the splendid Cotter seems uncharacteristically nervous in the serious moonlight, as they saddle up their horses, before wrapping cloth around every moving thing hanging off those saddles, to prevent making any unnecessary noise. (Most tightly tied down are the billy cans, which long ago replaced the British 'Tommy Cookers' to boil tea. The Australians love them, but they can reverberate like a drum if allowed to move about.)

For now, just as they tighten the straps, and prepare to trek onwards, Tibby picks up a clod of earth and, in that oh-so-familiar action, swings his arm over, hurtling the clod off into the far darkness in the direction of a dry wadi where no-one is camped. Three or four seconds later they hear the thud of it landing.

'That's my last bowl, Blue!' the great Australian fast bowler says to his mate. 'Something is going to happen.'[43]

Well, something is *already* happening, Tibby. So saddle up, son, and let's get going.

In short order, the Anzac Mounted Division are on the move from Asluj, set to travel 17 miles to their designated gathering point, six miles east of Beersheba.

'The horses, despite their great loads,' one Trooper will note, 'were touched with excitement as they always were when marching in large bodies.'[44]

And despite their exhaustion, the horsemen feel the same.

This, the Troopers know, is the last long haul before they get to their positions near Beersheba, and as they proceed in the light of the remarkably bright full moon, many feel a curious mix of exhaustion and exhilaration. It is hard to sleep when you know it may be your last, and come the dawn there are many friends they will surely see for the final time. Battle is near, fate beckons, but so does slumber and finally the weary have rest.

CHAPTER ELEVEN

BEERSHEBA BESIEGED

From camp to camp through the foul womb of night
The hum of either army stilly sounds.

Shakespeare, Henry V, Act IV, prologue

Since the early April fiasco the new G.O.C. (General Sir Edmund
Allenby) had drawn the wand of a magician over the desert.
His stupendous task was now complete, and the time ripe for
a general advance. The infantry were long since snug in their
trenches before Gaza, and for months shadows were moving up
through the darkest nights to our front lines.[1]

Trooper J. C. Ryan, 4th Australian Light Horse Regiment, in a letter to his
brother, recounting the lead-up to the Battle of Beersheba

These Australian countrymen had never in all their riding at home
ridden a race like this . . . all rode for victory, and for Australia.[2]

Official Historian Henry Gullett, The Australian Imperial Force in Sinai
and Palestine 1914–1918

5.30 am, 31 October 1917, Beersheba, by the dawn's early fight
Trooper Ion Idriess is with his comrades of the 5th Light Horse
Regiment of the 2nd Light Horse Brigade, still moving forward after
a hard night's riding – and they are just enjoying the first rays of the
sun warming them after the freezing darkness.

'Away went the longing for sleep,' Idriess will recount. 'Out came
pipes and cigarettes along the column. Mates looked at one another
with a half-smile, musingly. The valley grew wider and wider, Bedouin
cultivation made its appearance in ever-increasing plots. Then, five

miles away between the hills, we caught sight of the white mosque and houses of Beersheba.'³

If all goes well, it will soon be theirs, complete with its wells!

And now, with pipes and cigarettes popping into every mouth and puffed on – they hear it.

The sounds of battle. They are faint and far off, but soon to be loud and near. As exhausted as they are, their horses also prick up their ears and whinny, becoming restless. From deep experience they know that what often comes with that sound is action and there is every chance they will soon be right in the thick of it.

Far, far to the west, the soldiers before Beersheba can see a light's throbbing glow on the horizon, accompanied by a low rumbling. Clearly, on this morning, Gaza is under attack, and Jacko must think he has his hands full with the attentions of the 21st Corps.

But he has no idea.

For now, with the 20th Corps and the Desert Mounted Corps massed around Beersheba, the real battle is about to begin.

The first gleams of dawn mean the flashes to the west start to ebb as the sun grows, but it occasions furious activity around the 200 or so 18-pounder, 4.5-inch howitzer and 60-pounder guns that have been moved into position before Beersheba overnight, each of them with around 200 rounds to fire.

For while it had been one thing to get those guns and howitzers of General Chetwode's 20th Corps into position – the last had arrived at 3.15 am – they have always needed light to aim them properly and such is the case now, as the artillery crews get their bearings.

Some of the guns are primed with high explosive and shrapnel and aimed at the Turks' forward trenches, while the others are to bring heavy fire on Jacko's artillery batteries in the hope that they can be knocked out before the infantry of the 20th Corps – the soldiers of the 60th and 74th Divisions – launch. The shells coloured black are the air-burst ones, loaded with shrapnel to kill Jacko, while those that are red are pure high explosive and are designed to wreck Jacko's guns if they can just land among them.

By 5.45 am all is ready.

The crews are in their places, the shells are stock-piled beside them.

At precisely 5.55 am, as planned, the orders are given to the artillery crews.

Using a loud-hailer, the battery commander shouts the settings for range and direction.

Range 2150 yards, angle 24 degrees, 2 minutes.

The guns are trained accordingly, with the gun layer turning one handle for the right elevation, and another for the correct traverse.

After the Sergeant of each crew checks the settings, it is on to the next step.

Another crew member now opens the breech, while a second puts a shell in, and the first closes the breech.

'No. 1 gun ready!'

'No. 2 gun ready!'

'No. 3 gun ready!' the Sergeants call, one by one to their crews.

Everyone turns away and blocks their ears, as the man who closed the breech prepares to pull the lanyard that fires it.

And . . .

'Fire!'

The battery commander watches closely to see where the shells land, yelling fresh orders instantly to alter the gun's elevation and traverse accordingly, so that the fire will become ever more deadly in its accuracy.

•

In Beersheba, for the populace not in uniform – some 500 residents – this morning starts out just as any morning. From first light there is movement on the dusty streets even as the muezzin make the call from the minarets of the mosque, for the faithful to attend morning prayers.

Those ethereal voices mix and mingle in the ancient pathways of the town, just as they have for centuries past, a sombre tune of faith to Allah.

Allahu Akbar, Allah is Most Great.

Hayya 'ala-s-Salah, Come to prayer . . .

Suddenly, from the near distance for the first time, comes the sound of either rolling thunder or . . . an artillery attack?

Smoke starts to rise from the trenches that defend the perimeter on the southern and western sides of Beersheba.

We are under attack!

Colonel Ismet is instantly apprised, and does the obvious, giving orders for some of his reserve troops to move to those trenches.

For the moment, the Colonel is not overly worried. Beersheba is well defended by nearly 5000 soldiers, 28 artillery pieces, numerous machine guns and two planes. In this war the heavy advantage is always with the defenders with a sure supply of water, and it is out of the question that the British could mass much of a force in this desert.

•

The five-man battery crews of the British are now going at it like navvies, all of them spaced in batteries of six or four, each some ten yards apart. And load! And . . . fire! And ignore the puff of acrid smoke that blows into the gunners' faces every time a breech is opened to eject the shell casing and insert another shell.

At this 'rapid fire' rate of six shells per minute it is exhausting work, but the gunners never waver. Their focus now is 'Hill 1070' a mid-sized hill that forms part of the outer Turkish defences, atop which the Turks have an artillery observation post, a dugout with a steel roof and trapdoor. Nearby are heavily entrenched artillery batteries, and soldiers with machine guns behind rolls of barbed wire that will help protect them against any sudden rushes.

The collective roar of the cannon is shaking the dusty dawn to a pulp, echoing and re-echoing in the Judean Hills, and turning those hills into dust and dirty air; a topography toppled in sheer seconds.

With 1200 shells falling every minute from the 200 guns, the dust plumes are enormous as there is not a single breath of wind to disperse them, and they simply get thicker and higher.

In the middle of that smoke, the British artillery crews know, flying shrapnel will be cutting the Turks to bloody pieces – and hopefully also cutting some of the rolls of barbed wire in front of them. On the edges they can already see furious activity, with Turkish soldiers and guns on limbers and in carts being rushed forward. But even that vision does not last long.

For so big are the guns, so powerful the 60-pound shells, that before long those plumes of smoky dust have becoming billowing clouds drifting all over Beersheba, and it is no longer possible to see just what effect the barrage is having on the town's defences.

Positioned well in front of the artillery crews, the infantry soldiers of the 20th Corps, having crawled as far forward as they can while still retaining at least a little cover – as their ears ring with the crack of bullets and the shrapnel shells bursting all around, together with the soft moans or outright screams of comrades who have already been hit – prepare themselves to launch. One in 10 of them has a shiny biscuit tin lid strapped to his back, so that as they lie prone ready to attack, the rising sun will flash off their backs and allow the observers in aircraft to always know and report back their precise position.

Their hearts in their mouths, their rifles in their hands, their stomachs holding something a lot stronger than mere butterflies, they grip their rifles, pray, hold tightly to their bags of bombs and make ready to rush the Turks. Beneath their pounding hearts, Mother Earth continues to tremble and shake with the sheer trauma of the outrages being done to her – or maybe it is just their own uncontrollable shaking – as massive shells from both sides explode all around. For the moment, all they can do is use their bayonets to gouge out small shallows to press their bodies into, to try to escape the Turkish bullets flying overhead, while some place their rifle butts before their heads as further protection.

Many of them do not escape, with whole pods of British troops being wiped out as the Turkish artillery takes its toll; and beyond the dozens of dead, many more are wounded. The survivors hold their position, knowing they must wait until their own artillery has weakened the enemy and destroyed the rolls of barbed wire that lie between them and the Turkish trenches.

•

For his part, Lieutenant Guy Haydon and his men of the 12th Regiment have arrived at their designated destination, in the dry and dusty Iswaiwin area, six miles east of Beersheba. They, too, are close enough to *feel* the battle's roar, but a ridge between them and the town means they can see none of it. For now they must get the saddles off their horses, feed and water them the best they can – with what very little they have left – and secrete themselves in the scattered wadis, far enough apart that a single bomb from a Taube will only take out one of them, not several. (It is on the same principle that the other regiments of Lieutenant Colonel William Grant's 4th Brigade are scattered in wadis and gullies, over a wide area.)

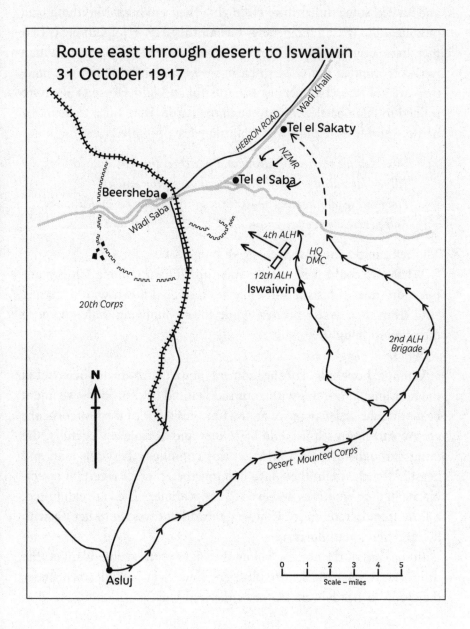

**Route east through desert to Iswaiwin
31 October 1917**

They are told, to their disgust, that while all of the 1st, 2nd and 3rd Brigades are on standby and will likely soon be thrown into action, they are being kept in reserve.

For Christ's sake!

It is like being locked in the cellar next to a house having a riotous New Year's Eve party and told there's some chance you might be let out and invited some time before midnight. They can hear everything, and only imagine what's happening, but all they know for certain is that they have been left out. True, under the circumstances, many a'man would be content not to be in harm's way. But they are not just men, they are soldiers, Troopers of the Australian Light Horse. They have trained to be in battle, want to be in the battle, were born to be in the battle – and it is just not right that they are not part of it.

Next day we started off again and marched the whole night long,
Till we landed in a wady at the breaking of the dawn;
Then our leader handed round his fags to smoke he said we may,
And peacefully we lay about till four o'clock that day.

All they can do for now is . . . have breakfast.

What else could it be for the men of William Grant's 4th Brigade but a dry mix of biscuit and bully beef, swilled down with a sparing swig from their water bottles, while their whinnying Walers look at them questioningly.

Where is ours?

Coming, hopefully. For the moment all we can spare as you stand in the morning light – still with your saddles and bridles on, as we might be getting the order to move at any time – is some of the few corncobs we are carrying with us. And so soldier and horse chew ruefully, the latter through their bits. Strange, this complicity between man and beast. After the night they have had together, there is a certain resemblance in their emotions and even . . . appearance. They are exhausted, a little trepidatious as to what lies ahead but anxious to get on with it – and very, very dusty.

In the case of the horses, 'below the edges of the saddle-blankets the dried sweat was caked, a reddish-grey; and wet hair gleamed under the cloths as heads went down to the feed-bags'.[4]

In the distance, the sound of the battle rolls on, and as they gaze to their west, they can see 'black clouds of smoke and thick dust marked the bursting of high explosive shells'.[5]

The fight. They are missing it. The best they can, they try to get at least a little sleep.

At least most do.

'We had visions of a cup of tea,' Captain Cyril Smith of the 4th Light Horse will recount. 'With a few pieces of deal (we always carried wood if we could get it) I managed to get the quart pot boiling and was one of the few who tasted tea that day.'[6]

Who knows what lies ahead? But a cuppa tea can't hurt.

6.50 am, 31 October 1917, Royal Flying Corps aerodrome, Weli Sheikh Nuran, air mail

Quickly now. Before getting the briefing out on today's mission – crucial reconnaissance on the key German and Turkish positions at Beersheba – Flight Lieutenant Alaric Boor just has time to write his parents a quick note, telling them a little of the task before him, providing air support for the troops below.

> *. . . I do hope everything goes alright for me and my observer, and I hope the other troops get on as well . . .*
>
> *Cheerio!*
>
> *Don't worry; I'll be alright, I feel very confident this morning.*
>
> *Your Loving son,*
>
> *Alaric.*[7]

A quick cup of tea, and now it is time for his briefing from his friend and Commanding Officer, Major Horace Haycock, in his tent just back from the actual dusty airstrip of No. 113 Squadron's base at Weli Sheikh Nuran, just east of Rafa.

```
Your mission is to fly over Beersheba and look for signs of
new defensive forces having been moved in, together with
freshly dug trenches or newly established barbed wire. Get
photos and make a report. Also make sure that you can spy
```

no new Turkish or German forces on their way from the north
coming down the Hebron Road.

The young Australian salutes, and is on his way, gathering his observer, 2nd Lieutenant John Muller from Yorkshire, who has made his way to the RFC from the Middlesex Regiment. The two have been flying together for the last six weeks and there is an easy rapport between them; but today both feel nerves and excitement. Z-Day! And they are part of it!

•

Cease fire!

At 7 am, the order is given, in order for the dust covering Beersheba to drift off with the tiny breeze and allow determinations to be made as to just what effect the barrage had had.

It takes a good while, but at least from what can be determined in the still swirling filth, much of the barbed wire is still intact!

What to do?

Launch the infantry anyway as planned, or bring down the hammers of hell from the artillery for another hour?

In the end, General Chetwode decides to do both, and gives orders for his forces to unleash one more ten-minute burst of artillery at 8.20 am, after which the mass of soldiers is to advance.

•

After arriving at their plane, an RE 8, Lieutenants Boor and Muller quickly climb aboard and do their pre-flight checks . . .

Fuel? Full.

Fuel cocks? On.

Controls? Full, free and correct.

Harnesses? Fastened.

All is in order for Lieutenant Boor to give an order of his own.

'*Contact!*'

The mechanic swings the four-bladed wooden propeller, and the engine roars to life.

In less than a minute, they are airborne, and heading for Beersheba, their direction set by heading towards the vast plumes of dust rising in the desert ahead, while always keeping an eye out for the enemy. It is an extraordinary thing to be engaged in, a deadly activity right in the middle of beauty unimagined.

'I have seen many sunrises at whose beauty I marveled,' another Australian pilot will describe it, 'but never before had I witnessed anything that could come within coo-ee of the riotous blaze of colour . . . covering the Holy Land, as it were, with a cloth of gold. It seemed impossible to realise, while nature was all aglow, that war was being waged with all its relentless cruelty, that we, who had been privileged to witness the glory of God's handiwork, were scanning the heavens for something in the way of Hun airmen to kill.'[8]

Onwards Boor and Muller fly towards Beersheba and the clouds of angry dust billowing from it.

Whatever is happening down there, it is vigorous, for neither Boor nor Muller have ever seen plumes like it. The artillery fire must be intense! The engine roaring, the plane buffeted as the desert air heats up and the wind rises, they gaze down, earnestly looking for any change from the previous days, any Turkish guns being moved, any significant scrap of intelligence that might make all the difference and allow the Gods of War to smile on the attackers on this day. Their eyes can win this battle, and the duo are as concentrated as condensed milk as their craft comes closer to the fray . . .

8.20 am, 31 October 1917, outskirts of Beersheba, plying pliers for wires

Fire!

Again the shattering roar breaks out, even as the ground shakes and the air fills with choking dust. Under the cover of the dust, the British scouts of the 20th Corps crawl forward, with goggles on their eyes, and scarves around their noses and mouths. For all that, it is their ears that are now most at risk as they crawl ever closer to the concussive blasts just up ahead. In their pockets . . . pliers. They keep crawling forward at speed and yet it still feels like an eternity before they indeed get to the remaining rolls of barbed wire. In only a short time – and despite the fact that trenches just 50 yards in front of them are being pounded, throwing out flame, stones and even body parts – those rolls of wire are soon mere slivers on the ground.

It cannot come soon enough for their comrades behind, who are themselves taking shells from the Turkish artillery, causing a constant stream of grievous wounds as the shrapnel scythes through them. Here, an ear. There a jaw. Over there still, a man gives a light whimper and simply lays his head down, dead, *part of a foreign field that is forever England* . . . or close.

But now their own artillery stops and, at last, they can charge. As one the infantry of the 60th Division rise, and with a low roar charge into the billowing maelstrom of the dusty dead, dead ahead, their bayonets to the fore, eager to finish the Turks who have survived in the trenches. It does not take long, as they slash, thrust and kill, all with a primal passion that comes from a place perhaps long ago. This battle is at close quarters, ugly and ancient, each man fighting for his life and for the other's death. One British soldier, Corporal John Collins, covers himself in glory in the wider assault by constantly going out under fire and rescuing wounded soldiers, before taking up the bayonet and taking down 15 Turks.

Just 15 minutes after the barrage had stopped, Hill 1070 has been taken by the 60th Division – as have 90 bloodied, shocked, Turkish prisoners. Most importantly, the hill will make an excellent artillery observation post to allow the men of the 20th to ever better direct the fire of the batteries now being dragged forward over the broken ground by straining, heaving horses and set up. By firing from the lee side of that hill – which is just over three miles from the outskirts of Beersheba – they soon start to smash the inner Turkish defensive line, even as their soldiers edge towards the next line of trenches. Yes, the closer they get, the more intense the machine-gun fire upon them is, but still their progress is inexorable.

•

It has been a difficult morning for Colonel Ismet, and no doubt about it.

With the artillery barrage to the west being followed up with infantry attacks, it is clear that Beersheba is in for a tough time. From his position on a high hill west of the town but within his own defensive rings, he is still not overly concerned. As near as he and his men can discern, Beersheba is only under attack by one division.

And yet, it had to happen and now it does.

Turning back to face Beersheba, he looks well beyond it to the plains on the far side, and what does he see?

Cavalry? The whole plain appears to be swarming with it, each speck becoming a dot, each dot becoming a horse with rider atop!

Surely, they are not intending to attack *en masse*? No, it must be yet another diversion, a mere demonstration to confuse and distract him. Their aim must be for him to move his own troops from the spot where the British are now attacking, to where they merely *might* attack. A staff officer is sent to try to divine whether the arriving cavalry is there for purpose or for pomp.

When that officer does not return, Colonel Ismet reluctantly gives the orders for a battalion of infantry and a machine-gun company to bolster the defences at Tel el Saba; a second battalion to move to the trenches to the south-east of the town, while also sending a division of cavalry – 1100 strong – to defend an outer defensive position by the name of Tel el Sakaty, and the Hebron Road that runs by it. They must make sure that Beersheba cannot be encircled.

9 am, 31 October 1917, above Beersheba, through the glass darkly

There it is!

Having skirted the plumes on the south-western side of Beersheba, Lieutenant Alaric Boor carefully guides his RE 8 on a steady path, flying back and forth. He is sure not to overly concentrate on the eastern and south-eastern perimeter of Beersheba – so as not to forewarn the enemy of the intended attack – but those parts are indeed his focus. Watching closely from on high, looking out for any Taubes or Fokkers, is his fellow Australian, Lieutenant Ross Smith in his Martinsyde plane.

Thus with confidence that Smith has his back, Boor now brings his RE 8 over the besieged town. He and his observer Lieutenant Muller note one large mob of Ottoman cavalry with artillery moving north from Beersheba along the Hebron Road towards the hills around Tel el Sakaty, and it is equally obvious that the trenches defending the approaches to Beersheba to the south of those Tels have also been strengthened.

After taking precious aerial photographs, Muller carefully marks down on specially designed paper every variation from what has been seen on previous days – where the enemy strength is now, where there appear to be gaps, each fleeting observation now permanently recorded.

The most crucial thing is that there is no sign of rolls of barbed wire on the eastern approaches to the town. If any fresh rolls had been put there overnight it could change everything, as when such rolls remain intact they are impassable for horse and man alike. But, it's all clear!

Nor is there any sign of any recently dug horse pits – trenches so wide that no horse could jump them. With a final waggle of the wings to the Australian troops below, who they can see are massing just to the east of the town, Alaric nudges the joy-stick, and their plane completes a graceful turn, heading back towards General Chetwode's 20th Corps HQ at El Buggar.

•

Send them in.

The order comes from Chauvel, at 9 am, to Major General Chaytor of the Anzac Mounted Division. It is time to commence the attacks on Tel el Saba and Tel el Sakaty.

Subduing Tel el Saba will be particularly difficult, as much of the ground approaching it is 'swept by the fire of numerous machine-guns and field guns concealed in the town . . . [and] on the strongly entrenched hill'.[9]

How to advance against such withering fire?

Carefully.

As ever, the view of the Desert Mounted Corps is that their job is not to die for their country, but to make the Turks die for theirs. With the support of fire from the Royal Horse Artillery coming from 3000 yards back, the New Zealand Mounted Rifles Brigade endeavours to attack Tel el Saba from the north. The Canterburys go in on the right, the Aucklanders on the left, only to be placed under such ferocious fire that it is only the Aucklanders who manage to make much headway, storming to within 1800 yards and taking immediate cover in the Wadi Saba. (It is at least a place to regroup, and to position their Vickers machine guns to lay down some suppressive fire as they make their next advance – without their horses, because riding a horse into that storm of fire would simply be to kill it, and then themselves in turn.)

•

From high in the sky at last Alaric sees it. *There it is, Johnny!*

It is with no little relief that Flight Lieutenant Alaric Boor and Flight Lieutenant Johnny Muller fly over the newly acquired position at El Buggar Ridge, now Chetwode's HQ. It is not that they are low on petrol, but in a desert where discernible features are no more plentiful than landing spots, the sight of British-held territory is always welcome.

The Western Australian pushes the joy-stick forward, pulls back on the throttle, and brings the RE 8 down low over the Desert Mounted Corps HQ, so they can drop the report – all of it wrapped in cloth, with a spanner for ballast, and a streamer for visibility – to those officers who eagerly await the news below.

Once their precious cargo is dropped, Flight Lieutenant Boor pulls back the joy-stick to gain altitude for the flight back to the No. 113 Squadron's current base at Weli Sheikh Nuran, to the south-west, only to take pause . . . and some alarm. The plane is not reacting to the controls?

He tries again.

Still no reaction, at least not to him.

For now, as if by an unseen hand, the plane, while at an altitude of 300 feet and just half a mile from the El Buggar airfield, is starting to spin out of control.

They are losing altitude!

There is no time for panic, training and instinct now act as one for Alaric. Furiously he hauls on the joy-stick, and stamps on the rudders, trying to bring the nose up and back on an even keel. But nothing works. The engine shrieks like a banshee, the ground spins and comes closer, both men roar as the air rushes past them, each wildly searching for the notion that will free them from this fall and . . .

Blackness.

It is just before 9.30 am and many of the soldiers defending the El Buggar HQ have been watching, appalled, as the plane simply spirals out of the sky. It has landed with a shattering crash just beyond yonder ridge, and smoke is already rising from it. Christ! The RE 8s – those damn finicky planes are notorious, and when something goes wrong, they drop from the sky like a shot duck. It is a nightmare the men have seen before, but only action may wake them from it. With a quick shout for 'Stretcher-bearers!' they race towards the point of impact, praying that the pilot and observer might still be alive. A crash in the desert may be survived, has been survived, it all depends on the luck of forced landing.

Running up one sand dune, they gasp in horror. For now they see what awaits them on the next.

The plane has hit the only thing it could hit in these parts – a sand dune – and come to rest, burning ferociously, with its tail in the air. Beating back the flames the best they can, they manage to get both men out of the wreck. The observer is dead, but the pilot is alive! He's very badly injured and unconscious, and they know the odds of survival from here, but at least there is still a *chance*. Alaric is put on the stretcher and raced back to the HQ, in the hope of saving his life. Quickly now!

The stretcher-bearers taking the body of Muller may take their sombre time. His maps and notations are searched for now; intelligence from a dead man that may yet save hundreds of Australians, Kiwis and British today.

In the meantime, the least that can be said is that the Frenchwoman who had told Alaric two years before that, '*Vous aurez de la chance!*'[10] – he will have good luck, merely for having seen the Virgin Mary tilting atop the Cathedral at Albert – has been proved definitively wrong, though the fact he is still just alive is something.

•

It is a strange case of slow and methodical meeting wild and woolly. The progress of the Aucklanders in attacking Tel el Saba is planned and painstaking – the method is mad bursts of 25 yards at a time, while the machine-gunners send swarms of angry bullets at the Turkish defenders. It is daring and literally dashing, finding whatever cover they can behind rocky outcrops. By 10 am, they are within 700 yards of Tel el Saba. To support them, at 10 am Chaytor sends in the 2nd and 3rd Light Horse Regiments to attack the enemy stronghold from the south so that the defenders will be getting fire from two flanks at once – while also ordering the Inverness Battery to bring its own fire on them. Progress towards Tel el Saba will be made by flinging the kitchen sink at it, military style. As ever, among the Australians of the Light Horse as they move forward there is disgruntlement in every section over the same issue.

'On this day I was put in charge of our section's horses which rather peeved me,' Trooper Humphrey Kempe will recount. 'Although one was always scared to some degree or other in the front line, particularly with machine guns, as they drew fire from all arms and were cheerfully known as suicide sections, it usually seemed better to be out in front in action rather than to suffer the boredom and inaction of comparative safety.'[11]

At least on this day it looks like there will be plenty of action for everyone. Attacks on the Turks are coming from all quarters, and they will surely crack this nut. But there remains a need for speed. Sunset will call an end to all battle and they must take Beersheba before the darkness falls.

•

General Chauvel has established Desert Mounted Corps HQ on the highest hill in the area – Khashim Zanna, positioned some five miles south-east of Beersheba and three miles south of Tel el Saba.

Passing by at this time, one Trooper from the 3rd Australian Light Horse, who has the wind up with all the shooting, takes comfort to see Chauvel and his entourage there.

'I recall about this time seeing just off the side of the road General Sir Harry Chauvel with one or two of his staff at breakfast, and quite a calming effect on the mind it was to see this quiet, domestic, homely occasion. They had a trestle table which in the circumstances was an unusual sight and the scene looked most engaging not to say inviting.'[12]

The breakfast does not last long, as Chauvel and his officers are afforded 'a dress circle view of the show'.[13]

And what a show it is!

From the moment Chauvel and his most senior officers – including Major General Hodgson of the Australian Mounted Division – arrive atop the hill at mid-morning and bring their field-glasses to bear, they are relieved to see Chetwode's soldiers of the 20th Corps already advancing. Having taken Hill 1070, they are now closing in on enemy trenches 500 yards ahead.

It is with even more satisfaction that Chauvel sees the artillery batteries of the 20th Corps being dragged forward to their new positions just below the crest of the ridge, and soon furiously firing on the defences that lie on the town's perimeter.

Close by, General Chaytor is keeping his own glasses tightly trained on his men of the Anzac Mounted Brigade, and is satisfied to see one particular group is making rapid headway.

With one look he can see that Brigadier General Granville Ryrie's men of the 2nd Brigade are already moving at all speed on Tel el Sakaty!

•

And a good thing, too.

As Ryrie himself had spotted a convoy of ten wagons leaving Beersheba and heading out on the Hebron Road, he has been quick to send his best officer, Lieutenant Colonel George Macarthur-Onslow, to cut the road before they can escape.

At a brisk trot for the moment, Macarthur-Onslow is leading his men in artillery formation – which quickly proves wise, as shells start to land among them. With the signal to gallop – the extended arm going round three or four times, as in the action of a bowler – Macarthur-Onslow does precisely that and now two regiments of Australians are charging forth as the Turkish artillery crews in the high ground, north of the Hebron Road, try to get a bead on them. Amazingly, though the shells continue to fall, they are all short, long or wide and they do not cause a single casualty among his men. Not necessarily the same can be said for the large camp of Bedouins the 7th Light Horse Regiment now charges through, as chooks, sheep, donkeys, camels and angry Bedouins scatter, to be left in their angry wake.

'Men were shouting, women wailing, kids howling, shells bursting,'[14] Ryrie records of the situation in the Bedouin settlement when he passes through just a minute later.

It is not until the 7th Regiment skirts Tel el Sakaty to reach the Hebron Road that Macarthur-Onslow calls a halt, and they are just in time to capture the convoy – pulled by eight horses and two mules – on their way out of Beersheba.

They have barely had a chance to look up, but when they do, they are surprised to see a battery of Turks with machine guns and rifles equally surprised above them on the heights. The Australians have moved so fast that the Turks, who were supposed to be lying in wait, have to scramble for their weapons, giving the Australians just enough time to follow that most general of orders: SCATTER, you bastards!

Cutting the Hebron Road has been the Australians' first objective, and getting the convoy and that many prisoners is a real bonus.

Taking the high ground right by the road will be more problematic, as the 7th Light Horse Regiment now come under heavy fire from the Turkish troops dug into the hills just to the north of Tel el Sakaty, as well as the latest arrivals upon it.

Macarthur-Onslow orders his men to take cover in the wadis and gullies that mercifully abound. It's here that one of Macarthur-Onslow's best men, Corporal Eddie Picton, leads three Troopers in an action to capture 39 Turkish soldiers. The 7th will be able to keep the Hebron Road covered but, once reinforcements arrive, Macarthur-Onslow will have to work out how to subdue the enemy in the hills above Tel el Sakaty.

At least those reinforcements are on the way, as Ion Idriess's 5th Light Horse Regiment has just received its own orders – Advance on Sakaty at once[15] – to support the 7th Light Horse Regiment. At last!

Cantering forth, 'the battlefield unfolded like a panorama – a four-mile wide open plain, the low hills fronting Beersheba, and running away to our right the white Beersheba–Hebron road between frowning hills'.[16]

For the most part Beersheba is still buried in billowing clouds of dust that have steadfastly refused to obey orders to stand down, though from the base of those clouds the Australians can at least see motor lorries with massed troops on the back racing forth to outlying fortifications, clearly including Tel el Sakaty.

On their own side, Idriess notes that 'as far as the eye could see were our own troops pouring from the hills on to the plain until they were moving regiment after regiment, brigade after brigade, in dust cloud after dust cloud – all moving steadily [forwards] . . .'

Again, Idriess is thrilled, as he is sure all of them are, 'with the terrible intoxication of war when the movement is rapid'.[17] Yes, he is scared, too, most particularly when the first shells start landing among them, but that fear is countered by something that comes from deep within, something savage that arises in armed men galloping towards their quarry.

And now, they see ahead the 7th Light Horse Regiment hunkering down in their wadi – 'bullets splattering the dust up merrily all up around'[18] – and bringing fire on Tel el Sakaty. Idriess and the 5th Light Horse Regiment are quick to join their fellows.

'Rifle and machine-gun fire grew into a steady roar, the air was one continuous whistling hissing as if thick with vicious serpents, the ground spurted dust and flying pebbles and splintered bullets.'[19]

Amid the shattering cacophony of chattering guns and endless explosions, more than a few of the thirsty Australians can't help but think of . . . water.

Beersheba has plenty. They now have next to none.

Come to think of it, the Bible's famous Psalm 22 was probably written in these very parts: 'My strength is dried up like a potsherd; and my tongue cleaveth to my jaws; and thou has brought me into the dust of death.'

(And the British infantry are in exactly the same position. 'We were suffering very badly,' one of the soldiers will recount. 'Most of us had swollen tongues and lips and were hardly able to speak, but the company humourist, a Cockney, was able to mutter, "Don't it make you mad to fink of the times you left the barf tap running?"'[20])

Sparingly, they sip on their canteens, while their horses whinny plaintively.

'The morning rolled on bringing its heat, its hot rifle bolts, its thirst, longingly we thought of the cool wells at Beersheba, and by Jove I experienced a choking feeling of the senses on remembering that we *must* take these wells,'[21] Idriess notes.

Amid all the firing, the small advances made, when they secure a small high point, Idriess is able to get a bo-peep to the south, and sees something that thrills him. It is the 1st Light Horse Brigade of Brigadier General 'Fighting Charlie' Cox, now charging across the plain to attack Tel el Saba from the south, in support of the awesome Aucklanders. Followed by the artillery!

'The Somerset Battery came galloping with the sun shining upon their spinning wheels. They wheeled in splendid order and almost instantly the guns were flaming through the clouds of dust actually within close rifle-range of the Turkish Redoubts.'[22]

The battlefield is ablaze, Beersheba beckons; and all the Australians now are in the fire.

•

In the makeshift hospital Casualty Clearing Station at El Imara – a large tent with a Red Cross upon it – Alaric Boor is fighting for life. The blood from his body is diluted by the sweat of the doctors joining him in the fray.

So young.

So much promise.

So much life left to live.

There is a pulse still, but it is weakening. The military medical men work faster now, doing everything they can to turn the spark of life still left in him into at least an ember that they can work with.

Alas, alas, even as the sun goes higher so does his mortal light fade, one last weak sigh is the last breath that Boor takes, and now all is still.

He has, as his Commanding Officer will write to his parents, 'entered the great silence'.[23]

What has caused this dreadful accident?

It will never be certain.

'Whether his controls jammed or not it is impossible to say,' Major Haycock writes, 'but knowing his ability as a pilot I cannot help believing something went wrong with the machine, but whether it was that or a slight error of judgement we shall never know. He had flown the same machine all the time he had been out here and he spoke warmly of her – both of the machine's rigging and engine.'[24]

It is fate, and Alaric is a fatality. He will be buried when there is time and where there is peace – neither of which are present on this day. Beersheba beckons and must be taken. For Alaric and for all those who gambled their lives on this day, and lost, we must win before darkness falls.

•

The news is good for the 20th Corps. The ongoing artillery barrage appears to have reduced the barbed wire before the inner Turkish trenches to smithereens, while also destroying several redoubts.

And now is the hour for General Philip Chetwode.

Just after midday, he gives his orders. Or rather, one order.

Attack.

With superb discipline, the three brigades of the 60th Division charge forth.

•

'I was in the front of the first assaulting wave as platoon runner,' one British soldier, Private Blunt of the London Regiment, will recount. 'We were in a little wadi behind a ridge. It was necessary to get over the ridge, and off the skyline as quickly as possible. Once over the ridge it was a rush down the valley and a charge up the opposite ridge where the Turkish trenches were at the top . . . When we got to the Turkish trenches we jumped straight in and shot or bayoneted or took prisoner all that were there. We advanced about 300 yards beyond the trenches where we worked "like hell" with our entrenching tools digging ourselves in.'[25]

Just 30 minutes later, the last of the Turkish inner ring defences west of Beersheba also fall to the swarming infantry of Chetwode's

20th Corps, meaning that again the artillery batteries can be brought forward.

Both defensive rings around Beersheba, on their south-western side, are now in the possession of the 20th Corps, and in the process they have captured 419 prisoners, six enemy artillery pieces and many machine guns, at a cost to themselves of over a hundred men killed and a thousand more wounded. But these battles will be for naught unless Beersheba itself falls before the sun does.

•

Atop Khashim Zanna, Major General Chauvel, together with the Commanding Officers of the Anzac and Australian Mounted Divisions, is pleased with the news – though the fact that Tel el Saba is still holding out is a real worry, particularly for Major General Chaytor, whose responsibility it is.

Napoleon once observed that an army marches on its stomach, but so too must army commanders eat while merely contemplating. For now Chauvel, Hodgson and Chaytor, with their senior staff officers, settle down for a quick lunch behind a long trestle table, as, with regular pauses for using their field-glasses and pens, they mark off the newly captured positions on the maps, together with the positions of their most advanced forces and where the reserves lie. (The last does not take long, as there are now precious few reserves left – little more than the 4th Light Horse Brigade, and the 5th Yeomanry.)

And yet there is a problem, first determined by the most senior gunnery officers of the two divisions. For just as they have their field-glasses on the enemy batteries still firing furiously from the north bank of the Wadi Saba, and Tel el Saba itself, they suddenly realise that so too do the Turkish and German officers by the enemy batteries have their field-glasses on this hill; that the guns are swivelling towards them, and that can only mean . . .

Take coverrrr!

A sudden whistling – accompanied by their own sudden intake of breath – presages the inevitable, and while everyone from Chauvel himself to the lowest ranking orderlies dives for cover, high-velocity shells land all over the hill, 'scattering maps, field-glasses, and staff officers like chaff before the wind!'[26]

It is a miracle no-one is badly hurt, but as good an indication as any that Beersheba still has a lot of fight left in it. Oh – and that the enemy's artillery capabilities seem to be stronger than first thought. Ion Idriess can see that Chauvel and co. have another problem:

'Taubes were roaring all over the fortifications, the plain, the wadi and the ridges, their heavy bombs exploding in series of smashing roars. Through the glasses, we watched them bombing Chauvel's and Chaytor's headquarters four miles away where the generals directed the battle. I wondered what their thoughts were, for all the operations, apart from the dust, were spread plain before them.'[27]

•

One thing that is plain enough, despite the dust, with the aid of the directed artillery, the New Zealand Mounted Rifles have now fought their way to within 400 yards of Tel el Saba. Which is one thing. It is quite another thing entirely to work out how to close that last gap, as the only path is not only swept by fire from the stronghold they are seeking to subdue, but also taking heavy punishment from the Turkish flanks. The hill ahead is steep and rugged, and overlooks the bed of the wadi for some 400 yards to the east, where it makes a sharp bend. What now? And how?

The first answer, at least, is for General Chaytor to order increased artillery fire from the Anzac Mounted Division on the Turkish defenders, while Brigadier General 'Fighting Charlie' Cox dispatches the 3rd Australian Light Horse Regiment to attack Tel el Saba from the south, which is soon followed by the 1st Australian Light Horse Regiment with orders to attack on their left.

A progress report is sent to the ever more worried General Allenby, who is now at the 20th Corps HQ at El Buggar: 'Attack on Tel el Saba still held up. Will be attacked again with reinforcements.'[28]

At 2 o'clock, the breakthrough comes at last.

As the 2nd Australian Light Horse Regiment has fought its way to get close enough to bring heavy fire on Tel el Saba from its southern flanks, it means the fire coming from Tel el Saba in turn is both distracted and diminished – allowing the New Zealanders the slackening they need to round the bend, charge along the wadi floor and up the lower reaches of the hill on which Tel el Saba is perched. Hand-to-hand fighting through the rocks and ruins proceeds forthwith.

•

Among the men of the 4th Australian Light Horse Brigade, positioned out beyond Iswaiwin, frustration grows as the temperature rises.

And they are not the only ones.

Equally annoyed at being left in reserve are the soldiers of Brigadier General Percy FitzGerald's 5th Mounted Brigade, positioned just a mile to the east. The battle of their lives is going on just over yonder ridge and their only involvement so far is to be left on the bench, in reserve, dodging bombs dropped from planes on high?

It is unconscionable!

All around, it is clear that a Battle for the Ages is underway.

In the intense heat, the rolling thunder of the artillery shells and endless chatter of the machine guns coming from Tel el Saba and surrounds is an indication that the ferocity of the battle is only intensifying.

And now look!

The men of the 4th Brigade gasp at the sheer audacity of it.

One of the brigades is ignoring the furious fire coming from Tel el Saba, and galloping straight for its base.

'The guns were on them as they swept along,' one Trooper will recount, 'squadron by squadron. Behind them riderless horses and horseless men ran around with seeming aimlessness. One wondered why those who lay still did not get up.'[29]

Still the red dust cloud rolls on, getting closer.

'The pattering of hooves spread far into the distance and came back, soft and continuous, like the sound of running water.'[30]

It is a panorama of action that no eye can turn from.

'Gun teams passed at a laboured gallop between hill and hill – little gun teams dragging toy guns and ridden by little men, crouched with arms as they plied the flaying whips. Little ammunition limbers followed them nimbly, rolling and bounding, with shells bursting in their path.'[31]

(In the midst of the throng, things are grim and getting grimmer. 'With machine guns and artillery the Turks were depleting our ranks,' one soldier will recount, 'so that less than half of us were still marching on at 500 yards range.'

But now one of the soldiers, a Cockney, starts lustily singing the refrain from a song they'd all loved at their last concert party: 'I've never heard of anybody dying from kissing, have you?'

As one, they all take it up, bellowing it out. 'I'VE NEVER HEARD OF ANYBODY DYING FROM KISSING, HAVE YOU?'

They march on.

'Men were killed singing that song.'[32]

They march on!)

And now, below the crests of the ridges, the Australians can see the guns being worked into action, even as the horses that dragged the guns forward are themselves dragged back.

'From the muzzles of the guns, tongues of flame, half seen in the bright sunshine shot out and back. Little men toiled beside the breech blocks.'[33]

It is not, however, as if the Turks are visibly wilting, as they are clearly giving as much as they are taking, as both the attacking gun crews and Troopers are now engulfed in artillery fire, with the resultant plumes of dust only moving forward sparingly if at all and, making matters worse, Taubes are swooping in just a little higher than rifle range to drop bombs on them.

This is extraordinary!

'The little men lay down among the rocks and bushes . . . Beneath them the earth was being thrashed by a shrill hail of iron. All the hilltops were spouting earth and flame as the shells found their billets.'[34]

•

Against all odds, and overwhelming force, the brave Turkish defenders of Tel el Saba are indeed holding on, and all the attackers can do is slog their way forward by a series of desperate rushes on foot that lose both time and men – time used by the Turks to shepherd their reserves into open trenches to the east.

A trench captured is like a moat crossed, only for the attackers to see a sea of Turks waiting; and it is waiting that is their most potent weapon. All know that if night falls with Beersheba held, the British, Australians and Kiwis will have to retreat for water. It is not enough to dominate a skirmish, the whole game of chess must be won before the sun is gone. The 1st Light Horse Brigade has dismounted now near Tel el Saba, but they wait feverishly to ride once more.

•

With enormous courage, the New Zealand Mounted Rifles Brigade are continuing to attack Tel el Saba, despite the intense fire coming from its blazing bunkers on the hill.

To get close enough to bring their own heavy fire, there is mercifully a meandering wadi which gives a good measure of cover, and provides the added bonus of having several deep pools of water, which allow the men and their horses to have their fill.

Just 800 yards from the enemy, the horses of the 11th are 'retired', and the key tactic from now on is for the men of the three squadrons to run like scalded hares bitten by a snake, zig-zagging and hoping not to get shot.

It is time-consuming, a tri-part attack that starts and finishes in startled fits, and it is deadly, as each man must hold his nerve and keep up his pace, fire and faith whatever happens. Your comrades may fall, but the plan is working, progress is steady. But, as they all know, the time is coming when steady progress will no longer do.

•

And now the commander of the most forward regiment, the Auckland Mounted Rifles[35] – Lieutenant Colonel James McCarroll – tries something never before done in the history of warfare. After confirming that his signaller is in direct contact with the commander of the Somerset Battery, positioned slightly south-east of Tel el Saba at a range of 3000 yards, he starts focusing on where the shells are landing and gives orders accordingly.

'Up 50.'

Behind him comes the sound of the signaller furiously working his flags. The directions are acknowledged as having been received by the Somerset Battery signaller.

And sure enough, the next shells move forward roughly 50 yards! And yet they are still a little off-target.

'Right, 20 . . .'

Another flag-flurry in a hurry is the result, the dust lightly swirling and eddying at the signaller's feet as he does so.

And now the shrapnel shells start exploding even closer to the designated Turkish machine-gun nests atop Tel el Saba, destroying one of them!

'That's the stuff to give, 'em,'[36] Lieutenant Colonel McCarroll exults.

No sooner has he said it than the signaller faithfully sends back those precise words to the Somerset Battery.

(Later, the commander of that battery will be asked what he made of said message. 'I could not find it in my book of signals,' he replied graciously, 'but I would like to say that we understood it perfectly, don't you know. It was – eh – rather novel for the service . . . It is to be preserved in the record of the battery as a memory of you fellows.'[37])

Onto the next target.

'Up 20, right 20 . . .'

McCarroll, meanwhile, makes his way forward as far as he can, investigating the best route.

'To go up out of the wadi was difficult open ground and the banks were about twenty feet high. It looked to me, by keeping close to the north bank the men could get up in single file, then the bend in the wadi gave us some cover.'[38]

At 11 am the Inverness Battery is also brought into play and while they keep heavy fire upon Tel el Saba, the Somerset Battery is able to close up to within 1300 yards, at which point its own fire starts to become even more accurate. There remains a lot of work to do, but, little by little, the fire on the Turkish stronghold becomes ever stronger and the New Zealanders are able to work closer still.

To give them even more help, Major General Chaytor orders Brigadier General Cox to have his 1st Light Horse Brigade attack from the south, to protect the left flank of the Kiwis. Their progress comes at a brutal cost, but at least they are eventually able to bring their Hotchkiss machine-gun and rifle fire to bear on the enemy's trenches and machine-gun positions on Tel el Saba, to set things up for a final rush.

•

Just after noon, a breathless runner appears, come to Colonel Ismet from Essad Bey, commanding the 3rd Cavalry Division, begging to report that there are 'two to three cavalry divisions to east and south'.[39]

The Turkish commander is shocked.

From the *east*?

In all their deliberations, it had never occurred to any of them that the enemy would be so mad as to advance across open ground where there was nothing to protect them from chattering machine guns and volleys of artillery; ground overseen by heavily fortified trenches and redoubts. And yet it had been because of that very lack of anticipation that they now have very few guns pointed in that general direction. Colonel Ismet sends more reserves and artillery crew to the east, before sending a cable to General Kress von Kressenstein, at Huleikat, north of Huj:

> On the South Front an infantry division has penetrated the Front of the 67th Regiment. On the East at least two cavalry divisions are pressing forward. In reserve are two companies which are insufficient to reestablish the Southern Front. What are your orders?[40]

Kress von Kressenstein trusts his own intelligence over the intelligence of the Turks on site, and expects reality to conform to it accordingly, replying thus:

> No, they are only two cavalry brigades. [41]

Colonel Ismet considers, with this many troops attacking them, if it might be wiser to get out now, so they can, you know, *survive*, and keep their forces intact?

But Kress von Kressenstein will not hear of it, telegraphing in reply:

Beersheba will be held. The battle will be continued. [42]

They agree on the latter point.

For his part, Kress von Kressenstein remains confident of the outcome. After all, the situation in the First Battle of Gaza had been much worse than this, only for the British to suddenly abandon the whole fight! Regardless of where they attack, the trenches and guns of Beersheba will hold the British out 'til their water is out. His monocle glints with optimism and the full faith of having Gott on his side. The day will be theirs by nightfall.

Fight on!

•

Good news at last.

At 1 pm, Chauvel receives word from Chetwode. Though suffering over 1000 casualties, the 20th Corps have taken and held the two rings of defences on the south-west of the town, and the enemy has retired into the town.

The first part of Allenby's plan is now complete, and – just as had always been planned – the 20th pause their attack, their task accomplished. (Even if they did keep going it would be too slow – as the 20th are still two miles from Beersheba, the enemy would have time to blow up the wells.)

Can the Desert Mounted Corps execute the second part of the plan, and finish the job by successfully attacking Beersheba from the east, with such a rush the wells will be preserved?

Well, as Chauvel well knows, that cannot even be contemplated until one key obstacle is overcome – Tel el Saba must fall.

•

Meanwhile the 4th Light Horse Brigade are . . . doing nothing.

'Feelings,' one Trooper will record, 'were tense. For there is nothing worse than inaction when alongside the foe.'[43]

With the sun now blazing, the ground is radiating heat, and the stones that poke their heads through the desert floor are hot to the touch. The sun beats down, and they pass the pebbles, as they take shelter in the shade of the horses above, who whinny mournfully.

Few are more frustrated than Guy Haydon. They have been here *all day*, did he mention? With little food left for themselves and their horses, and just about no water in the blazing heat – aware that a *battle royale* is going on without them – the hours have crawled by. They have a thirst that ten pebbles could not sate, a desire for action that is overwhelming, and all that will soon be left them will be a long night-march back to Asluj in pursuit of mere *survival*.

The only thing that lifts them up?

'Our Brigade was in reserve,' Haydon will recount, 'and we knew that if any hot job happened along, we would get it.'[44]

Others are less confident, with one, Private Walter Keddie, also of the 12th Light Horse Regiment, recording that, 'We began to talk among ourselves saying Beersheba will be taken and us not doing anything . . .'[45]

All they can do for the moment is wait, and hope.

•

Tel el Saba refuses to be broken.

Yes, Chauvel could throw in the last of his reserves, but his finely honed instinct tells him to hold back for the moment.

'If there was one lesson more than another I had learned at Magdhaba and Rafa,' Chauvel will recount, 'it was patience, and not to expect things to happen too quickly. At Beersheba, although progress was slow, there was never that deadly pause which is so disconcerting to a commander.'[46]

Still, amid the endless roar of Taubes overhead, the stuttering staccato of their own guns firing back at the planes, the regular explosions of bombs landing all around, General Chauvel can't help but alternate between looking through his field-glasses at the battle all before him, and looking down at his watch, even as he goes through the relevant chronology of this battle to date.

36 Hours. That's how long many of the horses of Desert Mounted Corps have been without water, after they had run out at Asluj the night before.

12 hours. That's how long a ride it will be to the next possibility of water.

24 hours. How long before they can be *certain* of getting water.

1 hour and a bit. How much daylight is left before Beersheba enters darkness, at which point it would be impossible? The sun is due to set at ten to five. The Turks would be firing from protected positions on to their own unprotected flashes in the deep twilight, and it would be a turkey shoot, with the Turks as the Turks, and the Australians as the turkeys.

Things are coming to a head, one way or another, and Chauvel is not the only one who thinks so. For now, Chauvel is unsurprised to receive an inquiry from General Allenby at Chetwode's 20th Corps HQ at El Buggar – asking if he believes the panting horses may be watered in Wadi Malah. Allenby is sceptical they will take Beersheba by nightfall. Chauvel replies via telegram:

> WATER SITUATION . . . IS NOT HOPEFUL, AND IF COMMANDER-IN-
> CHIEF APPROVES, IT IS PROPOSED TO SEND BACK ALL TROOPS
> WHICH HAVE NOT WATERED . . . IF BEERSHEBA IS NOT IN OUR
> POSSESSION BY NIGHTFALL[47]

•

Watching through his glasses from atop a hill near to the wadi where the 5th Australian Light Horse Regiment is stalled, Ion Idriess leans forward.

What he can see now is worrying.

Planes roaring overhead, roaring German machine guns from atop the redoubt, firing right on the Kiwis from well-entrenched positions, as they keep chattering all the same.

How can the Kiwis *possibly* make headway against that? For five full hours they have attacked and been held off! Tel el Saba stands. And if Tel el Saba doesn't fall, there is no way that Beersheba can fall.

What must it be like in the middle of that?

•

The bullets whizz and bite, the shrapnel shrieks and slices. They say the eye of the hurricane is the calmest part; well, that does not apply to this bloody battle. When will it end? Now. For the men of the New Zealand Mounted Rifles RUSH that bloody enemy outpost that has been tormenting them just 400 yards to the east of Tel el Saba. With a yell louder than any shell, the En Zeds storm its ramparts with shocking speed and race for the summit. Sixty Turks throw up their arms in surrender. The Auckland Mounted Rifles grab the Turks' four machine guns intact, and turn them on Tel el Saba in an instant.

Onwards! The machine gun pauses only to let the New Zealanders race *en masse* to Tel el Saba.

The Turks atop it must make their own calculation quickly; they can see the wave of death is about to break over them. The choice: sacrifice their lives, or fall back to Beersheba and fight anew?

The latter course seems more sensible, but do they still have any choice? For now, with one last frantic rush, under the cover of fire from the Australians of the 1st Brigade, the Auckland Mounted Rifles Regiment make their move. Racing across the remaining ground so quickly that the rocky hill seems to rise before them, their speed and pluck combines with luck to let them capture the last yards in a flowing motion that is literally irresistible. In moments the En Zeds are atop the plateau to capture 130 stunned Turkish troops, who are now instantly transformed into prisoners with raised hands!

Tel el Saba is ours! It's ours! Beersheba awaits!

Another Turkish machine gun is captured as well and quickly turned to fire on those soldiers fleeing back to Beersheba. Sporting? Well, this is a war, not a game. Guns don't surrender, they kill people; and the Turks have the indignity of knowing that the rattle of fire bursting behind them is . . . theirs!

Through his field-glasses a delighted Chauvel can see more and more En Zeds and the Australians of the Anzac Mounted Division now swarming all over the summit, and every Turk has his hands in the air.

Tel el Saba is theirs. It has just gone 3 pm, and the blazing sun of the middle hours of the day is well gone.

It is time.

Gather the commanders.

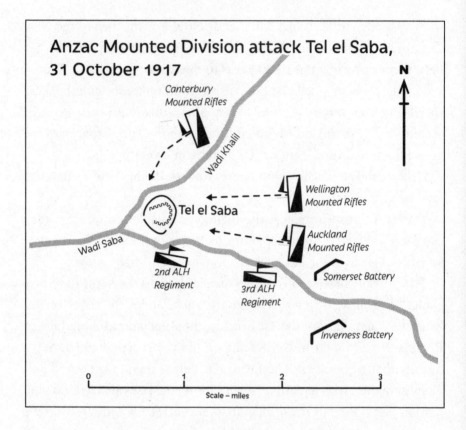

Anzac Mounted Division attack Tel el Saba, 31 October 1917

At Beersheba, the fall of Tel el Saba is a bitter blow, and yet still there is no wild alarm. It is not as if there will be any further attack from the east.

'We did not believe,' one German officer said, 'that the charge would be pushed home. That seemed an impossible intention. [But] I have heard a great deal of the fighting qualities of the Australian soldiers. They are not soldiers at all; they are madmen.'[48]

•

You summoned us, General Chauvel?

Yes, he has – to tell them what they already know. A choice is to be made. Between the two commanding officers of the only forces he has kept in reserve, the 4th Brigade of the Australian Light Horse, and the 5th Yeomanry Brigade.

General Sir Edmund Allenby.
(Wikimedia Commons)

An Australian Light Horse unit digging to locate a water supply outlet at Asluj.
(AWM H03769)

View of Beersheba (from the ground), 1917. (AWM B02371)

Aerial view of Beersheba from an aircraft of No. 1 Squadron, Australian Flying Corps, 1917. (AWM B02020)

Charge of the Light Horse at Beersheba. There is dispute as to whether this photo is of the actual charge or taken from a re-enactment staged the following year near Gaza for the purposes of the official war photographer, Frank Hurley. Regardless, this photo certainly gives an accurate representation of the charge. (AWM A02684)

Brigadier General William Grant, who led the charge at Beersheba. (AWM H00020)

Pilot Ross Smith (left) with his observer and Bristol Fighter F.2b of No. 1 Squadron, Australian Flying Corps. (AWM B01633)

Australian soldiers celebrating the capture of Beersheba, with captured Turkish artillery. (AWM H01373)

A team of the 2nd Australian Light Horse Field Ambulance. The ambulance wagon was designed to be light and able to move swiftly to support cavalry and horse artillery. (AWM B00450)

Troopers of the 1st Australian Light Horse Brigade water their horses at Esdud, Palestine, January 1918. (AWM B01507)

Ryrie at the head of the 2nd Light Horse, Esdud, January 1918. (AWM B01556)

The Light Horse on the move, through Bethlehem. (AWM B01619)

The advance on Damascus. (AWM B00256)

Chauvel, at the head of the Light Horse, officially entering Damascus. (AWM H10659)

Brigadier General William Grant or Percy FitzGerald must win or lose the day from here. We are going to have to throw one of your brigades into the fray, to take Beersheba from the east.

Even as Chauvel continues to speak, Grant's mind starts to race.

Maybe his men of the 4th Brigade should do exactly that?

Race. Charge! Yes, a full cavalry charge.

Instead of the horses delivering them to the battle and fighting their way forward from there, why not just keep going – *straight at the Turks?*

It would be a shock tactic, a tactic from the tenth century unleashed on the 20th! But if it worked, why, it would give them the best chance of getting into the town so fast the Turks would not have time to blow up the wells, as they surely would with a conventional fight; by the time the Australians arrived on foot, those wells would be exploding into uselessness.

The most important factor of all is the fading light. It is going to take at least 30 minutes to get the men gathered and formed up in three waves to move. By that time, there will be no time at all to attack in the 'traditional' manner.

The only option left is the extraordinary. Grant is *certain* it is the best course of action – a full cavalry charge, straight across open ground, *damn the guns, leap the trenches*, 'neck or nothing'.

And so it is Brigadier General Grant now speaks freely.

'The 4th Brigade,' he says, 'can take it if it is left to me to have a free hand.'

'How do you propose to do it?' Chauvel asks.

'Let us act as cavalry and not mounted infantry.'[49]

And Grant outlines his reasoning, trying to remain calm and sell the incredible.

Chauvel muses as Grant's words race. It would be bold, fast, and . . . it would be unexpected, to say the least! In the face of the oncoming charge, the Turks would expect the Australians to dismount a thousand yards away and work their way forward, just as is their usual practice. *But not this time.*

It might just work!

But can any cavalry charge 'work' facing artillery, machine guns and rifles, with planes dropping bombs overhead – a scenario not faced before by the Light Horse in this war? *Opinions, gentlemen?* Chauvel will be getting no argument from Hodgson, who has been a strong advocate for these kind of charges in this kind of country. Grant pointedly follows up with the observation that his brigade is positioned nearby and could be assembled within the hour!

Brigadier General FitzGerald – in the rather pompous manner that has always grated on Chauvel since he first met him 20 years earlier – demurs.

If anyone is going to do this it should be us. We are assembled much closer to this HQ and can get going much more quickly. Plus, as a British unit, we have actual swords which are going to be of much use when we get to grips with the Turks than mere bayonets. And, for God's sake, General, we are TRAINED cavalry! These men know how to cut, thrust and parry!

Grant cannot bear it.

But, General, my men have both rifles and bayonets and, as General Hodgson has pointed out, bayonets held above our heads, while not as good as swords, can still do the trick. We are the obvious choice for this, and we can get the job done. And though the 5th Yeomanry are positioned closer to this HQ, my Brigade is positioned closer to Beersheba, and can be in position more quickly.

Both Brigadiers make excellent cases, the tension rising a little with their reasoning. Chauvel, as impassive and cool as ever, almost remote, weighs each word.

On such decisions do men live and die, entire family trees suddenly have whole branches lopped off. The time is ticking away, but so important is the decision Chauvel wants one last look before making it – and asks for the precious aerial photographs to be brought to him once more – while Grant and FitzGerald leave him momentarily to ponder.

Gazing ever more closely at the photographs, with just Hodgson by his side, Chauvel is more convinced that this is the *only* way. While the defences around most of the town are obvious – from barbed wire entanglements to deep pits impossible for a horse to get through or over, the approach from the south-east does appear to be relatively clear. It is not to say that there aren't defences that are not obvious from the air, but they will have to take that chance!

A decision must be made, and Chauvel is the man to make it.

This has to be done, and it has to be done now. The fact that he does not like FitzGerald and never has since the days he commanded the local military force in Victoria, is neither here nor there. Much.

He follows his instinct, guided by military logic.

Mostly.

Putting his finger at the spot on the aerial photograph which he thinks is viable, Chauvel gives the order to Hodgson to be passed on.

'Put Grant straight at it!'[50] Chauvel says.

Hodgson, delighted – finally, a major charge – tarries nowt, and immediately leaves the tent to give Chauvel's decision to Grant and FitzGerald.

'Go right in,' Hodgson tells Grant, 'and take the town before dark.'[51]

FitzGerald blanches, but – *where did he go?* – Grant is already on the move and, only moments later, there is the sound of thundering hooves receding in the distance as the Brigadier, accompanied by his senior officers, rushes back to his own HQ.

'If I did ever favour the Light Horse,' Chauvel will later acknowledge, 'it was at Beersheba, when, in giving the lead to Grant, I was perhaps influenced by a desire to give a chance to the 4th and 12th regiments, which up to then had seen very little serious fighting.'[52]

The Australian has picked the Australians to charge; and there is nothing the British can do about it.

It is an extraordinary outcome, and thrilling, though as Charles Bean will comment, 'Australians had never ridden any race like this.'[53]

•

With the fall of Tel el Saba, Colonel Ismet has seen enough.

Beersheba may fall. Whatever General Kress von Kressenstein's orders of over an hour ago, Ismet has no interest in spending the rest of the war as a prisoner of the British Empire, or worse, killed. Thus he gathers his two most senior officers and, with a strongly armed escort of 20 infantrymen, prepares to leave on foot to the north, heading for the HQ of the 143rd Regiment, which he knows to be six miles away.

Before departure, he orders that the remaining reserves be rushed forth to defend the eastern perimeter. His final order is that all the wells in Beersheba which have been wired with dynamite – and are connected to one central control panel – be blown up if the enemy breaches the perimeter. (As fate has it, the German engineer assigned to do the wiring has been away on leave in Jerusalem, but his offsiders are instructed to finish the job immediately!)

Remaining troops must equally ensure, before evacuating, that all the trip-wires with booby-traps are activated. We must deny the British any succour whatsoever from taking over the town.

•

With things now in train, Chauvel again takes up his field-glasses, only to suddenly receive another cable, bearing an official order from Allenby:

THE CHIEF ORDERS YOU TO CAPTURE BEERSHEBA TO-DAY, IN ORDER TO SECURE WATER AND TAKE PRISONERS[54]

Well, yes! What on earth does Allenby think they are doing? It seems that the Chief has misunderstood the telegram from Chauvel advising on what will happen waterwise *if* Beersheba does not fall!

By return cable, General Allenby is assured things are already well in hand, and his troops are now preparing to take Beersheba. By cavalry charge. What will the Chief make of that? Chauvel will carefully avoid receiving telegrams for the next while . . .

•

'If they don't capture the town soon,' one of the more wizened Troopers says mournfully to the youngest among them, Harry 'Wickham', all of 16 years old, 'we're well and truly stuffed.'[55]

It would seem so.

In fact Harry Bell, for that is his real name, has come a long way from Walpeup, from joining up at Mildura just six months ago, training at the Seymour Camp, and arriving here in the Sinai, as one of the 'reinstoushments' just six weeks ago. Much of it had been exciting and new. A lot of it had been hideously hot and uncomfortable. But nothing has been quite as terrifying as this. Around him, other Troopers are desperate to get into the action. Harry is not so sure. Yes, it has been a very slow day. But still everything is happening so fast.

And now what?

A rider, a sergeant with a message from HQ, is trotting their way.

'All pack horses, excepting Hotchkiss rifle packs,' the sergeant calls out with that habitual volume that helps make up for lack of serious rank, 'fall out and remain behind!'[56]

What? What is going on?

'We're gunna charge Beersheba, mate!'[57]

Bloody Hell.

And just as the word quickly spreads among the Troopers – it's on, and we're going to charge, cobber – so too, does it seem like the Walers sense that there is action afoot, as snorting and whinnying breaks out across the lines. Saddles are thrown on, straps are tightened, Troopers swing up and on. Some of these horses have not had water for as long as 30 hours, and are all in. But the best reckoning is they likely have one last charge left in them, most particularly if there is water at the other end of it – and there is!

For his part, Lieutenant Guy Haydon is beyond thrilled with the order that comes through to his own wadi.

After a hot, frustrating day spent impotently listening to the sounds of battle in the distance, some Troopers of 12th Regiment had more or less given up, one saying, 'It's getting too late now to do anything.'[58]

But first comes a barked command, 'Stand by your horses.'[59]

And now the glorious specifics:

'The 12th and 4th Light Horse Regiments will charge Beersheba on horseback, the town is to be taken at all costs.'[60]

We are going to attack!

CHAPTER TWELVE

STRAIGHT AT 'EM

When can their glory fade?
O the wild charge they made!
All the world wondered.
Honour the charge they made!

Alfred Lord Tennyson, 'The Charge of the Light Brigade'

The Light Horsemen knew well that the fate of the battle – and
probably the campaign depended on this charge at Beersheba;
they also realized that, for the first time, Australian cavalry were
actually to charge! For this time the Light Horse were to act purely
as cavalry, although with only their bayonets as shock weapons.[1]

Charles Bean, Anzac to Amiens

It was a great day; 30 years' life was crammed into it.[2]

Trooper C. S. Roxburgh, 12th Australian Light Horse Regiment

31 October 1917, four miles east of Beersheba, Sound trumpets!
Let our bloody colours wave!

The word spreads.

A full cavalry charge. No dismounting half a mile out and fighting
our way forward in short rushes. We charge *to* the trenches and then
dismount and get into them.

Yet more shouts break out across the line, with the squadron leaders
of the 4th and 12th Regiments barking orders.

'A Squadron mount!'

'B Squadron mount!'

'All pack horses to the rear. Remainder, prepare for action. See that all equipment is secured tightly to your saddles.'[3]

'C Squadron mount!'

And in a moment, the regiments are now mounted squadrons, their lines extended, all at the ready; and the readiness is all.

> *'Stand to' then came the order with nerves all highly strung,*
> *Once again into the saddle our weary legs we slung.*[4]

Most of the Troopers are delighted. Not only is it *action*, which is always welcome, but it is action which – if successful – will get them what they prize most of all right now, water. The alternative would be a slow and dogged march back through the whole night ahead to get to the water at Asluj.

Among some, there is exultation.

In the 12th Light Horse, Trooper Colin Bull, a bookmaker's clerk from Sydney, offers a bet to a Corporal that, 'I will beat you in the gallop for Beersheba.'[5]

Beside him, one of the most popular Troopers in the 12th Light Horse, Ernie Craggs, is equally exuberant, 'laughing and joking as usual and full of spirit',[6] just as he always is, but this time barely able to contain himself for the joy of being about to make a *charge*!

•

Walking with purpose, Brigadier General Grant now takes the commanding officers of the 4th and 12th Regiments – Lieutenant Colonel Bourchier and Lieutenant Colonel Donald Cameron – together with their 2ICs, and walks them up to the crest of the ridge so they can all get a good look at both their destination and the ground they must cover to get to it.

There it is, gentlemen.

For a few seconds no-one speaks, as they take it all in, the distant, ancient town, now glowing in the light of the late afternoon. It is just half an hour before dusk, and the town lies on the other side of what is first a long and gentle slope, followed by another rise, all of it about three and a half miles away, the minaret of the town's mosque providing a central aiming point.

Those of vast military experience like Grant, Bourchier and Cameron recognise just how useful it will be that whatever defenders they meet will be silhouetted against that light, while we Australians will be coming from a much darker backdrop of our billowing dust.

As pleasing to the eye as that golden shimmer is, however, their eyes are soon drawn to the ground that lies between this ridge and the outskirts of the town, looking for obstacles, wire, horse pits, wadis.

Bourchier – a straight-speaking grazier from Victoria's Murray Valley – asks three quick questions of Brigadier Grant.

Has there been any close reconnaissance of just where the enemy is situated?

No.

Is anything known of the approaches?

Very little.

Are there any barbed wire entanglements in front of the Turks?

Not positive, but we don't think so.

And there is no time to find out anything further, men. There is only one course of action open to us. We charge, and let the devil take the hindmost.

(Taking the foremost will be Lieutenant Colonel Donald Cameron, Commanding Officer of the 12th Australian Light Horse Regiment. Cameron is usually a smiling nugget of a man. Right now, however, his face is as hard and taut as a diamond, gleaming with sheer intensity of purpose.)

Now, see there?

The track between Iswaiwin and Beersheba – W track – which descends from the ridge line right to the town will serve as a useful axis for both of your regiments. The 12th will keep to the left of it, the 4th to its right. And now look more closely through your field-glasses. You will note that such trenches as we can see of the Turks – about half a mile out from the town – seem to lie in the way of the 4th Regiment, while the 12th should have a clearer go of it.

Speaking quickly, because there is so little time, Grant gives tight orders. Once formed up, we will slowly ride our horses to the top of the ridge, and the first wave will keep going at that walking pace until all three lines are over. Now, be aware: as soon as we are visible, *en masse*, on their side of this crest, we will likely come under artillery fire.

The first of the targeted machine-gun fire will get to us at 2000 yards, and the rifle fire at 1000 yards – unless there are hidden nests out in front of what we can see. The scouts out front should be able to help us spot them if that is the case.

And bear in mind . . .

'Once they smell it, your horses will be so keen to get to the water in the wells of Beersheba they will gallop faster than ever.'[7]

It is inevitable that we are going to suffer casualties and possibly even severe casualties, but we cannot alter our course. The key is going to be sustainable speed, to cover the ground as quickly as possible, while making sure that the horses can cover the final burst at full gallop to maximise their chances of not being hit and getting there in sufficient numbers that they can overwhelm Johnny Turk.

So it doesn't matter how many men we lose, the important thing is to *keep going*, because they can't possibly get all of us, and the more resolute we are, the more likely it is that the defenders will break and run.

One last thing. It is not realistic to think our blokes will be able to accurately fire their rifles, while at full gallop. This will be hand-to-hand stuff in the trenches. So, have them sling their rifles around their backs, while holding their bayonets up. Once they arrive, they can jump off and get stuck in.

Grant now clarifies the formation he wants: the first two lines are to be A Squadron followed by B Squadron, charging in 'line formation', spread out in a single line abreast. The third line, C squadron, are to be in column formation, with Troops lined behind each other, with the usual distance of between 300 and 500 yards between following lines. Each regiment must have a scout out front by 50 yards.

The meeting is quickly over. But Shakespeare is in the wind.

'*Hark! the shrill trumpet sounds, to horse, away, My soul's in arms, and eager for the fray.*'[8]

While the squadron leaders now race off to brief and bring forward their men, Grant and his senior officers work out in which wadi to assemble them, and the exact lines each regiment will take.

Meantime, at Desert Mounted Corps HQ atop Khashim Zanna, Chauvel's staff advises the Notts Battery – which is attached to the Australian Mounted Division – what is afoot, and what will be required of them to support the charge. In response, the battery[9] of four horse-drawn 13-pounder guns moves as far forward as it can – right behind where the 12th and 4th Regiments are forming up – and keep observation on Turkish defences, ready to bring fire on all artillery batteries and machine-gun nests that are bringing fire on them.

•

With the specifics of Grant's orders barked on down the line, the cry goes up from the officers of both regiments.

'Form squadron column from line!'

'Imagine a line of hills broken by gullies in which we were hiding,' a Corporal of the 4th Light Horse will write to his sister, explaining the situation, 'and then a grassy flat of about two miles to a town . . . Well, we filed down out of the gullies and formed a long thin line with about four yards between horsemen.'[10]

All up, it takes nearly 20 minutes for all squadrons of both regiments to be in position on the lee side of the crest, and it is 4.25 pm before all 800 Troopers are astride their mounts, turning their attention to their Commanding Officers out the front.

In this last minute, there is just time for a few . . . last minute orders. The Commanding Officer of the 4th Regiment's A Squadron, Major James Lawson, a portly Victorian hotelier before the war, tells his two scouts – none other than Tom O'Leary and Alfred Healey – just what to do. It can be easily summed up: Go like the clappers!

O'Leary up front, Healey just behind. Signal whatever you can, when you can. You two will set the pace, and our lead elements will be 70 yards behind you.

(It is unspoken, but all three know, that like a dog getting from one side of the minefield to another without being blown up, the scouts and their path – as long as they survive – will make clear what is clear of wadis, unseen culverts, hidden machine-gun nests and horse pits). They are not canaries in a coalmine, that is a bloody easy job, they are two men, just two, who are going to charge the Turks!

If you were a betting man and asked to gamble who among us 800 is most likely to be dead 10 minutes from now, most of the money would go down on these two, but both accept the task cheerfully enough. Death or glory? No, more likely both.

Gotcha, sir.

Damn the odds, Tom O'Leary, whose passion for drinking and fighting is only narrowly outdone by his passion for gambling, is happy to back himself. His penny to your pound says he can outrace death, even if hungover. This day O'Leary – fined and admonished only days ago, for being absent at parade while drunk – will be very present indeed and lead right at the pointy end of the spear. God speed, Tom.

To the rear, the 11th Light Horse Regiment is also forming up, followed by the Troopers from the far-from-gruntled 5th Mounted Brigade and their commander, Brigadier General Percy FitzGerald, together with the 5th and 7th mechanised Battalions, who will be hauling the artillery forward, the packhorses carrying the Hotchkisses and rounds of .303 ammunition, and the stretcher-bearer units bringing up the rear.

Among those grim angels, Tibby Cotter is doing some hard thinking. He has been in battle against England at Lords, against the Turks at Gallipoli and now he is . . . merely carrying a stretcher for this, the biggest battle of the year, or perhaps on guard-duty with a truck? We are about to make a cavalry charge on the Turks, steaming in from the Paddington end, and *I* am not going to be a part of it? It is not right. It is against nature. Why not make a swap, get one of the blokes looking a bit nervous to take his turn at stretcher-bearing, while I take part in the charge? They can court-martial me later, I'm going to fight today!

It not only makes sense to Cotter, but also to the bloke he approaches to make the swap, and in short order Tibby takes his place astride a snorting steed, right in the heart of the 4th Brigade, 12th Regiment, with his mate Bluey, and right beside two other close mates, Troopers Jack Beasley and Rex Coley.

We're not quite the Four Horsemen of the Apocalypse, but we'll do.

We ride together. We guard each other's flanks, and back. Any bastard that tries to get us, gets it back. A charge! A *real* charge!

Over to Tibby's far right, among the hard men of the 4th Light Horse Regiment, a boy stirs restlessly. For Trooper Harry Wickham, this is a long way from Mildura. Yes, it is what he has signed up for, and yes, it was always going to be dangerous. But still he has the wind up more than a little. Just four years ago, he was at Walpeup Public Primary School, trying to memorise his times table – seven eights are fifty-six – and now here he is, about to charge straight at Turkish guns!

Wickham's horse picks up on his nervousness, whinnies and stamps her feet. Harry, as he has ever done, leans down and strokes her to calm her. Whatever the task, whatever the risks, it must be done, they have to get in formation.

Around and about him Troopers are steadying their own horses, shaking hands, sneaking quick glances at small photos in lockets and wallets of family and sweethearts. The mood is grim, but purposeful. This is what they want. To have at the Turks, straight on. No more feints, moves, insane retreats. Straight at 'em!

From their west, north and south comes the chattering of machine guns, and the endless shattering roar of the shells.

Up front, O'Leary trots forward to just beneath the crest of the slope, while the forward elements of both regiments now look to Brigadier General Grant, positioned high on the slope himself, between the two regiments.

To Grant's right, Lieutenant Colonel Bourchier is at the head of the 4th Light Horse Regiment, while to his left, Lieutenant Colonel Cameron is equally to the fore of the men of the 12th Light Horse Regiment.

Grant pauses.

Now is the moment.

All the King's horses, and all the King's men, 800 strong, are in formation in their three lines towards the crest of the ridge, waiting only on his command.

It is just after half-past four.

'Men,' Grant calls out, 'you are fighting for water. The only water in this desert is at Beersheba. Use your bayonets as swords. I wish you the best of luck.'[11]

Grant raises his right arm, as all falls silent, bar the impatient whinnying of so many horses. The arm drops, pointing now straight ahead over the crest of the hill, even as Grant gives the cry.

'Walk, march' was then shouted till the wady crest we reached;
'Unsling rifles,' came the cry, *'the cover's off the breech.'*[12]

Within seconds, these two mighty regiments of the Australian Light Horse, 800 strong, are Beersheba-bound. They push up to the crest at walking pace.

Their destination glimmers in the golden rays of the fading sun.

'Hiding in a depression behind the hills, was Beersheba, the white dome and minaret of the great mosque and the railway station, barracks and numerous buildings, growing plainer to us.'[13]

This is the way the farmer rides, a-plod, a-plod, a-plod. And for the first mile it really is a plod, a gentle move forward across the line. No need to rush just yet. Quite the opposite, they must get as close as they can *without* causing a massive dust cloud to alert the Turks to their approach and even more importantly, preserve the formation as long as possible.

Down the other side, however, things are immediately a little more frisky, even without the Troopers giving their charges a giddy-up. For one thing the slope is downwards. For another, it just might be that the horses can smell water. Either way, across the line, as soon as bullets start whizzing by, they break into a trot.

•

In Beersheba, Turkish and German officers scanning the horizons with their binoculars, looking for where the next attack is coming from immediately take pause.

What's that?

What?

That! *There!*

And now they can all see it. Just on the ridge line over the way, they can see horsemen appear, and coming down the other side. And now more. And more still! And look at their uniforms, their hats, their . . .

Emu plumes.

Australians?

Yes, Australians. A dark shadow passes over their hearts. In all of the battles to date, the Australians have been notable for their speed, their vigour, their ability to cover vast distances to attack from unexpected quarters . . . and their ruthlessness. Clearly, they are forming up to attack.

Orders are barked out.

Cephane, ileri! Ammunition forward!

Silahlar, hazır! Guns, ready!

Nişancılar, hazır! Gunners, ready!

•

And now it happens.

There are puffs of smoke in the distance, and within seconds there is the roaring sound like an approaching train . . . and now explosions. The Australians are being shelled!

To Guy Haydon's right, one of his mates goes down, together with his suddenly bloodied horse. To his left, the sight is much the same. Right in front, geysers of dust go up where more shells have hit, and it is all any of them can do to keep moving, as shrapnel whizzes past. All of them do as they have been trained, and lean far forward on their steeds, bringing their head down as close as they can to one side of the horse's head, for further protection.

Most of the shells and bullets, however, miss. How on earth? Still, theirs is not to reason why . . .

And if there are echoes of another cavalry charge long gone right now, then so be it.

> *Cannon to right of them,*
> *Cannon to left of them,*
> *Cannon in front of them*
>   *Volley'd and thunder'd;*
> *Storm'd at with shot and shell,*
> *Boldly they rode and well,*
> *Into the jaws of Death,*
> *Into the mouth of Hell*
>   *Rode the six hundred*

•

Standing in his saddle, Captain Jack Davies, who is commanding one of the troops of B Squadron of the 12th Regiment, turns to his 30 Troopers and roars:

'Come on, boys, Beersheba first stop!'[14]

'You'll do us, Jack!'[15] the Troopers cry back, knowing all such informality will be forgiven under the circumstances.

As one now, they trot down the ridge, the hooves of their horses immediately sending small eddies of dust swirling with every stride. Both regiments keep their eyes on their Commanding Officers, a little out in front, and to the left. Trooper Chook Fowler of the 12th happens to be right by the Regiment's Commanding Officer, Lieutenant Colonel Donald Cameron, when the Colonel spies something that concerns him.

'Pass the word on to [B squadron commander] Major Fetherstonhaugh to look out for the little hill on the left.'[16]

It is a small bluff, perfectly positioned to have a Turkish machine gun installed on its lee side, firing upon all those who would attack, from their left flank. The message comes back from Major Fetherstonhaugh soon enough that he sees it too – Hill 1180, on their maps – but there is no diminution of pace for all that. It is too late. They are launched, cantering now, and all they will be able to do is let their horses have their head.

In the distance, suddenly, they see puffs of artillery coming from the batteries near Beersheba, and just seconds later the chilling whine building to the blast of incoming shells. In anticipation of what is to come, many of the Troopers drive their spurs in a little more and increase their pace.

Steady now . . . Steady. The moment must come.

Sure enough, Bourchier drops his arm straight out from his shoulder and bellows 'Chaaarge!'[17]

> Then from our leader's lips came the cry we longed to hear,
> As he gave the order for to charge we raised a ringing cheer;
> With heads bent low on horses' necks, our bayonets gripping tight,
> We charged across 500 yards, all eager for the fight.[18]

And now more than 800 Australian Troopers of the Australian Light Horse are at full gallop, leaving clouds of billowing dust in their wonderful wake. The tremor of thundering hooves travels all the way to Chauvel atop Khashim Zanna hill, and undoubtedly to the Turks defending Beersheba.

'The good Australian nag,' one Trooper will recount to his brother, 'was [now] fired with the determination of his rider.'[19]

Raaaaacing now!

Like jockeys rounding the final turn at the Melbourne Cup – except that, waiting for them at the finishing line is no garland of roses, but Turks manning machine guns – the Australians lift their haunches, lean into their horses' necks, and drive their spurs into their flanks. Their steeds respond in kind, as bullets whizz and shells explode so close that many of the Troopers can feel the concussive blast on their faces and backs.

> *The Turkish rifle cracking and shrapnel flying high,*
> *There was no man amongst us who knew not how to die;*

Off to the north, as they thunder forth, they can hear the regular roar from their guns of the Notts Battery, firing from right beside General Chauvel's hill. It is strange how such violence can be somehow comforting, but there it is – a sense that Johnny Turk, too, is copping it right now, and won't be free to just line them up and knock them over.

As they charge and get closer, the rifles slung over their backs bouncing a little in the thundering charge, Guy Haydon and his comrades in the second wave can clearly see where the enemy trenches are situated by where the flashes are coming from their many rifle and machine-gun muzzles. Just behind and above them are the larger and brighter flashes of their artillery, which glow a little longer. And even brighter and bigger still?

They are the shells from their own artillery, specifically timed to explode just above the enemy to spread air-burst shrapnel over a wide zone, and now appearing, in this sudden twilight of dusk, 'like a row of red stars over the Turkish positions'.[20]

•

Ion Idriess is with the 5th Light Horse Regiment a mile to the north and has just climbed a hill by the Hebron Road when someone shouts, pointing through the sunset at the staggering vision before them.

'There, at the steady trot,' he will recount, 'was regiment after regiment, squadron after squadron, coming, coming, coming! It was just half-light, they were distinct yet indistinct. The Turkish guns blazed at those hazy horsemen but they came steadily on.'[21]

Idriess, of course, is not the only one gazing in wonder.

One British officer, staring open-mouthed, is heard to mutter, 'There goes those mad Australians again, they will all be shot.'[22]

Some of them indeed are as, just as Lieutenant Colonel Cameron had feared, a machine-gun nest on Hill 1180 starts strafing the 12th Regiment.

Out on the right of the first wave, Trooper Harry Wickham is one of the first to be hit, strafed by a distant machine gun which leaves angry red splotches all over the right leg of his breeches. With a throaty gurgle, he falls from his horse and hits the ground, as the succeeding waves of horsemen roll over the top of him. Stunned, he lies there with a shattered femur, his life-blood pouring from him. His only chance is that one of the coming stretcher-bearers of the 4th Light Horse Field Ambulance will see him, and save him.

To Wickham's left, in the heart of the 12th Regiment, another burst of machine-gun bullets swarm like angry bees and hit amidships the two Troopers riding beside Tibby Cotter – Jack Beasley and Rex Coley – and they fall together, badly wounded. Tibby Cotter and their mate Bluey are untouched, and must ride on, vowing to return as soon as this business is done.

And what of Trooper Colin Bull, who only 30 minutes earlier had bet his Corporal that, 'I will beat you in the gallop for Beersheba'?[23]

It is not to be, as he is cut down and killed in an instant.

At Desert Mounted Corps HQ, General Chauvel and his staff officers are watching the Turkish positions closely, as are the observers of the Notts Battery.

There! And there! And there!

The Officer Commanding the Notts Battery, Major Cecil Harrison, stabs his finger on the map at Hill 1180. Alas, it is now too dark to use the range finder so the hill's distance and direction from their current position will have to be approximate. Still, it is soon done, and after Harrison barks co-ordinates and orders, the four Notts crews are soon working feverishly to lay their four 13-pounder guns accordingly. Within 30 seconds, their guns are loaded and aimed at the hill.

And fire!

The guns belch smoke, the barrels recoiling on their cradles.

When the smoke clears, it is clear that there will be no more fire coming from those particular machine guns, as a cheer goes up from the battery crew.

And yet still the fire from the front is fearsome.

'The bullets got thicker . . . three or four horses came down, others with no riders on kept going, the saddles splashed with blood, here and there a man running toward a dead horse for cover,' Trooper Dengate will recount. 'I could see the Turks' heads over the edge of the trenches squinting along their rifles.'[24]

•

In the Turkish trenches in front of Beersheba, soldiers are indeed doing exactly that, down the sights of their Mauser rifles and Maxim machine guns, as they try to stop this human tide coming straight at them, even as they become aware that the ground is beginning to shake with that unmistakable terrifying tremor of massed thundering hooves. Of course, they have faced such tremors before. But not like this, *never* like this, never so many, and never coming at such speed. It is like a mini-earthquake, so strong that the very sights they are looking down begin to jump about.

More shouts ring out down the line.

Silahlar hazır! Guns, ready!

Askerler, hazır! Soldiers, ready!

All of them keep an eye on their squadron commanders, whose arms are raised. Disciplined soldiers, they know their fire must be co-ordinated, not haphazard. They are *not* to fire until the galloping Troopers are close, and even then only on the orders of their commanders.

Bekle! Bekle! Bekle! Hold! Hold! Hold!

Keep coming . . . keep coming . . . keep coming.

Turkish fingers tighten on their triggers, waiting for the moment.

Veeeee . . . şimdi! And . . . now!

And the officers drop their arms.

'*Ateş!* Fire!'

Even as the Turks ready their Mauser rifles, waiting as their water-cooled state-of-the-art Maxims now pour a furious fusillade at the oncoming Troopers, that cacophony of fire is soon joined by the welcome sound of their own artillery joining in!

Not that it seems to have much effect.

For one thing, the attackers are moving so fast it is very difficult to get the range, and while it is possible to bring down a certain curtain of fire that they must get through, again they are moving so fast that they are through the curtain in a split second.

•

Closer and closer, faster and faster . . .

'Their thousand hooves were stuttering thunder, coming at a rate that frightened a man – they were an awe-inspiring sight, galloping through the red haze – knee to knee and horse to horse – the dying sun glinting on bayonet points. Machine gun and rifle fire just roared but the 4th Brigade galloped on. We heard shouts among the thundering hooves – horse after horse crashed, but the massed squadrons thundered on. We laughed in delight when the shells began bursting behind them telling that the gunners could not keep their range, then suddenly the men ceased to fall and we knew instinctively that the Turkish infantry, wild with excitement and fear, had forgotten to lower their rifle sights and the bullets were flying overhead.'[25]

For those in the third line, the dust is so overwhelming they can barely see behind their horses' ears. It is shockingly difficult and some of their horses stumble and come down when they hit horses that have been shot in front, but at least any rifleman or machine-gunner at Beersheba will be only hitting them by fluke, because there is no way they'd be visible from 10 yards away, let alone from Beersheba.

•

Allahım yarabbim! Good God Almighty.

In all their born days, none of the Turks, and none of the German officers with them, have seen anything like it. The most terrifying thing? It is the small flashes that can be seen from just over the top of

364 • THE LAST CHARGE OF THE AUSTRALIAN LIGHT HORSE

the leading horsemen, against the backdrop of the billowing clouds of dust. It takes a moment before they realise what those flashes are.

Allahım yarabbim!

It is bayonets. Many of the attackers are holding above their heads the bayonets they shortly intend to plunge into Turkish bellies.

The shock among the defenders is palpable.

Who charges straight at guns, in this war? It is unheard of! But it is real, and they are now closer still.

Feverishly, the Turks work their guns. The only thing that gives them comfort is that these mounted Troopers always stop before they get to the actual guns, and charge on foot from there, so at least they have some time.

•

There is no order given, for in the midst of this thundering maelstrom, this man-made *khamsin*, no-one could have heard or seen an order in any case. No, what happens now, occurs spontaneously albeit with origins from *millennia* past, down to the well-springs of their soul.

It starts with Captain Jack Davies, right by Lieutenant Guy Haydon in the middle of the 12th Regiment, and spreads from there.

A yell?

A cry?

At the very least . . . his shout.

For with the 12th and the 4th Regiments still at full gallop, and some of the detail of the Turkish defences of Beersheba coming into view for the first time, the rampaging Australians follow Davies' lead and start to yell such battle-cries, such epithets, such primal ROARS that the sound of the guns is now the second most frightening sound that can be heard.

'You never heard such awful war yells as our boys let out,' Guy Haydon will recount, 'they never hesitated or faulted for a moment, it was grand.' (True, some of the cries are mere 'Coo-ees!' of sheer exuberance, but under the circumstances they can pass as war yells.)

Trooper Ernie Craggs is so exuberant with it all that he actually stands in his stirrups at full gallop and cheers . . . just before two bullets hit him, one in the head and one in the chest. Another man who is hit manages to get to him behind the shelter of his fallen horse, and holds his hand while he dies.

'He . . . did not have any pain, thank God.'[26]

Not far away, young Harry Wickham, bleeding badly, is gathered in by the blessed stretcher-bearers of the 4th Light Horse Field Ambulance, and rushed to the temporary dressing station at Khashim Zanna, where the Army doctors await.

The rest of the charge sweeps on. And now the bullets from the Turks come in ever thicker swarms – hornets now.

'Every now and again a rider would roll off or a horse fall shot but the line swept on. As we neared their trenches, our men were falling thicker and thicker and the pace became faster.'[27]

But there is no time to swerve, to duck, to dive. In all of this murderous madness, there is only one thing to keep doing. *They must keep going, keep charging.*

And no-one is doing it more furiously, or with more speed, than Tom O'Leary, who has extended his lead, for all the world like he is astride Kingsburgh coming down the final straight at Flemington to win the 1914 Melbourne Cup!

'The last half-mile,' Idriess, still observing closely, will recount, 'was a berserk gallop.'[28]

•

Allahım yarabbim, they are getting close.

But still the order holds.

'Wait until they dismount, then open fire!'[29]

The Turks can now see individual features of the marauders, including one particular madman well out in front of the others. There is little point in firing at him, because he is going so fast, and the much better option is to fire into the mass of horsemen behind him . . .

. . .

. . .

Among the Turks, there is a sudden burst of panic.

They're *what?*

They're *not* stopping to dismount. They're *still* coming!

Surely, they're not going to keep charging straight onto our guns?

They are! THEY ARE!

Ateş! Fire!

Ateş! Fire!

Ateş! Fire!

Frantically, the Turkish artillery crews load and fire, even as the machine-gunners and riflemen fire as if their lives depend on it – because they do – but things are so urgent there is no time to do much changing of the sights, to adjust the range. All they can do is make approximations and fire, fire, fire! The same applies to the machine-gunners and those with rifles. Just keep firing!

•

Among the thundering horsemen, all eyes remain on the scouts O'Leary and Healey who are, amazingly, still alive and charging forward. For the moment there are no signals from them of hidden pits or wire entanglements, and by keeping to the path they set all know that the route is at least possible.

Just half a mile to go!

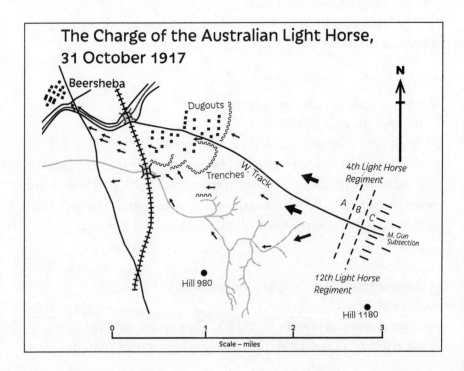

The Charge of the Australian Light Horse, 31 October 1917

Now, with every stride, even as the Troopers get low, the bullets whine past, the shells explode all around them, and the shrapnel hisses. The spirit of the charge has gripped their mighty steeds and they are now charging faster as a pack than they ever could have done individually, with a mass of momentum all their own.

And now a horse goes down, a Trooper falls off, hit badly. Sometimes the rider is killed outright but stays on, which sees the horse – somehow sensing that all the urgency has gone – immediately drop out of the race. And yet, through it all, the red dusty khaki tide of Troopers keeps sweeping forward, simply unstoppable in its ferocity. Even when they are just 400 yards off and the desperate Turkish gunners seem to be aiming for the horses alone, *still* the tide sweeps on.

Closer, closer, faster, faster.

•

And now, there they are!

It is not quite that the Australians can see the whites of the eyes of the Turks, but as they charge the last yards towards them, they can certainly see the distinctive khaki caps, and colourful tabs on their shoulders indicating which regiment they belong to.

Ion Idriess is still watching closely through his field-glasses.

For now it's about to happen!

After galloping like racehorses the Walers now must transform into steeple-chase racers . . . and so they do!

> *Our horses cleared the trenches, they took them in their*
> *stride—*
> *My word, it was glorious to see those horsemen ride.*[30]

At the fore, Thomas O'Leary and his horse are over the first trench in a flash, and keep going over the second and third line of trenches – another 30 and 60 yards back, almost before the Turks are aware what's hit them. Having spied the bridge that leads across the Wadi Saba, and the road into the town from there, O'Leary simply keeps going, crossing the bridge and turning at an angle of 45 degrees to go straight into Beersheba, and disappearing in a blaze of dust – a lone horseman, with his nearest support a good hundred yards back.

For his part, O'Leary's fellow scout, Trooper Alfred Healey, immediately dismounts after getting over the first trench and takes his rifle in hand running straight at the Turks, soon joined by Major Lawson and the 4th Regiment's A Squadron.

To the eyes of Lieutenant Colonel Richard Preston, Chauvel's Commander Royal Artillery of the Australian Mounted Division, 'amid the deafening noise all around, [the Australians] seemed to move silently, like some splendid, swift machine. Over the Turks they went ... and, dismounting on the farther side, flung themselves into the trenches with the bayonet.'[31]

From afar, Idriess sees it from a different perspective.

'A heart-throbbing sight as they plunged up the slope, the horses leaping the redoubt trenches – my glasses showed me the Turkish bayonets thrusting up for the bellies of the horses – one regiment flung themselves from the saddle – we heard the mad shouts as the men jumped down into the trenches.'[32]

Indeed, after leaping the first small trench and coming to a halt before the second some 30 yards back, the men with Major James Lawson follow his orders: *'Action front. Dismount!'*

The reason to dismount is purely practical, if on an extremely bloody level.

'If we had been armed with swords,' Corporal Carter will tell his sister, 'we would have sliced the old Turks up a treat. A bayonet is absolutely useless on horseback against a dismounted enemy, especially when he is lying down shooting at you, and your horse is going at full gallop.'[33]

Following procedure, one Trooper in every section takes the reins of the horses while the others grip their bayonets ever more tightly and prepare to get to work. Following barked orders, they run to the two Turkish trenches on either side with their legs pumping, their hearts pounding and a wild blood-lust having gripped their very souls, with Major Lawson himself right in the thick of it.

This is for those of the 8th and 10th Regiments, gunned down at the Nek, for those killed at Romani, Rafa, Magdhaba, the first two battles for Gaza and ... today.

The Australians are met with rifle- and small-arms fire, followed by a flurry of stick-grenades, which indeed fells several men. But not enough, as the others surge forward with bayonets in hand and jump into the trenches, some also using their rifles as clubs to crack Turkish heads. Major Lawson uses his revolver in turn and all is murderous madness. Screams and shouts fill the air, together with gurgling death-rattles and occasional fountains of blood.

Dozens of Turks are killed on the spot, as the Australians take vicious vengeance, though the sons of the Southern Cross lose some of their own in turn, so valiantly do the defenders stake their lives on defending this vital town.

Shots ring out, bayonets thrust, heads bust, men scream, and fall to the ground – some bleeding in small fountains. Many of the Turks fight bravely, but against this number of Australians, with line after line that just keep coming, there is little they can do.

As soon as Lieutenant Ben Meredith is off his horse, he hands the reins over to Trooper Cyril Smith and points his .45 calibre Webley revolver at a trench full of Turks. In this case they instantly raise their hands in surrender, only for one of them – as soon as the Australian's back is turned – to roll a grenade at the Australian officer that 'blew him to bits'.[34] That Turk does not last long as, outraged at the killing of his troop leader, Trooper Phil Moon dispatches the 'prisoner' with his bayonet.

The thundering of hooves behind signals the arrival of the second wave, B Squadron of the 4th Regiment, and as the first two trenches of Turks are finished off, now the two squadrons advance in rushes on the third and most heavily defended trench of all. Grenades help the Australians particularly, as cricket skills help them lob the explosives right over the stumps and into the nine-feet-deep trench, where they cause devastation.

Out on the far right, Staff Sergeant Jack Cox of the 4th Regiment is galloping at full tilt towards the trenches when he suddenly sees a pod of five Turkish soldiers – coming from some of the huts and tents just off to the side – running forth beside a mule with a heavy machine gun strapped to its back. They are under the command of an officer who is clearly yelling at them to go faster still.

Their intent is clear.

Within seconds they will be set up and raking the coming waves of Australians, which from such close range will be catastrophic. Acting more in the realms of urgent instinct than conscious thought, Cox drives in his spurs and charges his horse straight at the crew, yelling obscenities. The Turkish officer, spotting him, draws his revolver and fires at the Australian. Cox ducks, draws his own revolver and fires, hitting the Turk instantly.

It is time to try one of the few Turkish words, they have been taught.

'*Dur! Dur! Dur!*' Stop! Stop! Stop!

'*Teslim!*' Surrender.

'*Silahlarinizı birakin!*' Put down your weapons!

'*Dur! Dur! Dur!*'

Eager to live, the soldiers indeed *dur*, stop, and quickly *teslim*, surrender.

In the fighting for the main trench, the Australians have now jumped right into it and are moving along, their bayonets to the fore, slashing, stabbing, and scything a deadly harvest. Many of the Turks not immediately killed either throw their hands in the air – '*Teslim oluyorum!*', I surrender – or decide that discretion is the better part of valour, and flee.

In short order more than 60 Turks are killed in the third trench alone, with 100 prisoners taken, and, by the time the third wave of Troopers arrives, most of the Turkish resistance in the eastern trenches has fallen apart.

•

In the middle of Beersheba, a lone horseman gallops up the street. It is O'Leary, the only Australian among some 3000 remaining Turks, many of them rushing to new positions. O'Leary ignores them all, bar a six-man artillery crew he spies, pushing their gun to a new position. Overtaking them, he unslings his rifle, points it just above their heads, and pulls the trigger.

Hands up!

Their hands go up.

•

Out to the left of the 4th Regiment, the first wave of the 12th Regiment has also hit the first of the Turkish defenders. While the commander of the 12th Regiment A Squadron, Major Eric Hyman, and 30 of his Troopers dismount and are immediately charging towards the stunned Turkish soldiers, much of the rest of the first line are able to gallop on, towards Beersheba proper as shown by O'Leary, who has disappeared in a cloud of dust.

'Then came a whirlwind of movement from all over the field,' Ion Idriess will recount, 'galloping batteries – dense dust from mounting regiments – a rush as troops poured for the opening in the gathering dark – mad, mad excitement – terrific explosions from down in the town.'[35]

Major Hyman and his small band, meanwhile, are nothing if not busy – and none busier than Hyman himself, who leads the charge against the principal trench, with his revolver in hand, making every shot count. It is that .45 calibre Webley that allows him to pick off each Turk about to fire at him and his men, meaning they can all get close enough to jump into the trenches and bring their bayonets to bear, resulting in bloody carnage. No fewer than 60 Turks are killed in this one action, of which at least a dozen have been brought down by Hyman's revolver!

The succeeding waves of the Australian Light Horse just keep coming, an ocean of attack.

•

In the second wave of the 12th Regiment, the Commander of B Squadron, Major Cuthbert Fetherstonhaugh, is roaring forth with the best of them – and just 30 yards off the first trenches – when his beloved horse is shot and goes down, sending the officer flying. Pausing only to take his revolver and shoot the mare between the eyes to end her suffering, the Major is quickly running forward to the first trench, firing his revolver at Turkish defenders, only to be shot through both legs. Still the line sweeps on.

Above, two Taubes have appeared and come swooping low, dropping bombs, which start to explode among them. And still the thundering Australian horsemen keep coming.

And there is the first Turkish trench now!

In the same wave as Major Fetherstonhaugh, Lieutenant Guy Haydon atop Midnight sees the trenches now. Yelling to his men to jump down and take out every Turkish soldier they find, he keeps going and, galloping forth, gets ready to vault the first trench and attack the second.

Now, Haydon and Midnight have been vaulting over obstacles for all of 10 years, and won pennants, trophies, medals and accolades for their trouble.

At this point they are less a duo than a unit and Haydon need not even drive in his spurs for Midnight to leap. She knows what to do as well as he does and at the last instant surges up, her front legs flying forth as she launches over the trench, Haydon out of the saddle and using his own legs to cushion the impact of landing.

Unbeknownst to either, from below a Turkish soldier fires his Mauser straight up, sending a bullet first through Midnight's pelt and intestines before penetrating the saddle and finally . . . Guy Haydon. The bullet enters the Lieutenant's left buttock and finally stops, lodging right next to his spine. Midnight comes down just the other side of the trench, her fall allowing Haydon to tumble off onto the pile of dirt that had been thrown out to build the trench, before rolling himself into it. Feeling the wound with his right hand it is clear he has a hole in his buttocks you could stuff a pair of socks in, and lies there, shocked and bleeding as the battle rages all around.

And Midnight?

Though blood is pouring from her stomach, the steed now rises, and stands on the side of the pit the Light Horse is thundering from, meaning that those in the next waves will have to go around her, and not fall in upon him.

The battle rages on.

'Over trenches and through redoubts we went yelling like mad, with only bayonets in our hands. Horses and men dropped, but on we went faster and faster.'[36]

None other than Tibby Cotter charges at a field-gun that is being pulled into position and, quickly unslinging his rifle and bringing it to bear, is satisfied when the entire crew throw their hands in the air. Cotter lowers his rifle himself . . . only for one of the Turks to pull out a revolver and shoot him. Cotter immediately falls from his horse, bleeding badly.

'Several of our fellows who saw it,' one Trooper will recount, 'rushed over with revolvers, and the four Turkish drivers came down with no less than five bullets in each.'[37]

Guy Haydon, still at the bottom of his trench, sees none of it. Right now, trying to protect the heavily bleeding Midnight from staying in the open, he is throwing clods of earth at her in the hope of getting her away but she simply refuses to move.

'It is impossible to describe one's feelings,' Haydon will write home, 'but for myself although it is the heaviest fire I have been under, I never felt less afraid, and I was terribly disappointed in being shot before reaching the town.'[38]

For his part, Trooper Chook Fowler, who has been beside Haydon the whole way, is terribly surprised *not* to have been shot yet.

'The artillery fire was heavy for a time, but it soon passed over our heads, and then the machine-gun and rifle fire became intense. As we came closer to the trenches most of the fire went over our heads.'[39]

For this brief respite, Lord, let us give thanks.

But now Fowler also spies the trenches bristling with Turks and rifles and hand grenades ready to hurl and thinks better of trying to follow Lieutenant Haydon's lead.

'I doubt my horse could have jumped them with the load he was carrying and after galloping two miles.'[40]

Nor is he inclined to get off his horse and jump into the trenches with them.

'The Turks were big men, too big for me to tangle with so I kept going, the fire was now very heavy.'[41]

Things are willing all right, as first a bullet hits his haversack, and then two more make holes in his trousers, still without hitting him.

'Some horses and riders were now falling near me and all my five senses were working overtime and a sixth sense came into action – it is called the sense of survival. No horseman ever crouched closer to his mount than I did.'[42]

About 20 yards to his left, Fowler spots through the dust the path that others of the 12th Regiment have taken to get through to the bridge over the Wadi Saba that leads to the town, and soon wheels towards it. Yes, there is momentary alarm as he sees the Turks throwing hand grenades in his direction but, mercifully, he is moving so fast that they explode uselessly behind him and, praise the Lord, 'in a flash we were through with nothing between us and Beersheba . . . I counted five horsemen from the 12th in front of me and urged my horse on . . .'[43]

The Australian Troopers drive their spurs into their horses' flanks and press forward into the town, not knowing what to expect . . . but not this. For in passing, some are amazed to see, and even *smell*, some young gum trees pushing their way through the sandy soil. It is a little reminder of home at a time when they are doing all possible to secure a victory that will get them back there all the sooner.

Onwards!

Into the town proper Fowler sees two Turkish artillery batteries with six horses attached to each gun, clearly about to get away, but on the reckoning they will be dealt with by those coming behind, he gallops on, to find himself among the first Troopers into the town, as Turkish soldiers run every which way before them.

For now the sound of thundering hooves pounding on the hard-earth streets of Beersheba rings out as the Australians swarm in, the jingling of their spurs and bits the musical accompaniment to the battle's roar; the sight of their glinting bayonets – some already dripping with Turkish blood – striking terror into the hearts of those defenders who remain.

Back in the eastern trenches, as Henry Gullett will record, 'One of the troopers galloped on to a reserve trench, the Turks shot his horse as he jumped, and the animal fell into the trench. When the dazed Australian found his feet he was surrounded by five Turks with their hands up.'[44]

The remaining Turkish soldiers also soon bow to the inevitable and surrender, meaning the Australians can now charge for the town *en masse*.

'Where I was there was a clear track with trenches on the right and a redoubt on the left,' Trooper Ted Dengate will recount, 'some of the chaps jumped clear over the trenches in places, some fell into them, although about 150 men got through and raced for the town, they went up the street yelling like madmen.'[45]

Still well out in front, and now on the edge of Beersheba itself, Chook Fowler hears galloping and turns to see the 12th Regiment's own Captain Davies charging forth smiting every Turk he can reach as he passes – the only man in his regiment with a real sword.

Suddenly, up ahead, 'a terrific sustained roar broke out from more than one building . . . It turned out to be the Turkish ammunition dumps going up in smoke.'[46]

Fowler gallops, only to suddenly be confronted by a dozen Turks in a dugout who immediately jump to their feet and pull back the bolts of their rifles.

Many thoughts flash through Chook Fowler's mind, primarily, 'This is the finish', secondly, 'No good running away', and, finally, 'I'll do as much damage as I can before they get me.'[47]

Jumping from his horse and bringing his rifle and bayonet to bear he is . . . stunned, as the Turks throw down their weapons.

That's more like it!

The common expression on their faces is one of sheer shock, at how fast everything has happened.

Other Australians are noting the same thing.

'I've seen some surprised people,' Captain Jack Davies, still coming up behind, will note, 'but those Turks were certainly not expecting us, just then.'[48]

•

In the streets of Beersheba, all is soon combined chaos as the Australians run wild among fleeing Turks, even as many brave Turks still keep up the fight. Shots and shouts ring out with equal frequency, as explosions rend the air.

'Huge, mushroom-shaped columns of violet flame and smoke shot up here and there,' Lieutenant Colonel Richard Preston will recount, 'accompanied by sullen, heavy explosions. Shortly afterwards, the main store and some of the railway station buildings were set on fire, and the flames from these burning buildings lighted up the whole town.'⁴⁹

The Turks are blowing up ammunition dumps, buildings, railway engines and . . . wells! As the Australians nearby rush forward, the fires take hold, and trying to get them under control is beyond them. Most distressing is the potential destruction of all the wells, the very reason for taking Beersheba in the first place. Without water, the place will be next to useless.

For many Australian Troopers flooding forth now, the feeling is just like it was when they had fought their way to the outskirts of Gaza six months earlier.

'The sight of this blazing city . . . kindled an intense desire for possession. Once roused this inherent passion was demonstrated by lust for blood, and a frenzied desire for victory.'⁵⁰

Explosions are everywhere, as is fire and billowing black smoke.

Turkish soldiers are fleeing in greater numbers than ever, beams are falling from burning buildings, and shots continue to ring out as everything possible is done to gain control. Over there a sergeant has tackled a Turkish machine-gunner, taken his gun off him and is now threatening to blow all Turks within coo-ee – COOOO-EEE! – who will not surrender. Here an officer and his off-sider Trooper have run down Turks trying to spirit a howitzer out of town. On every corner, Troopers have their guns trained on a couple of dozen or so Turks who have surrendered.

Troopers Phil Moon and Bill Watkins are sent up to the minaret of the mosque to see if any snipers are up there.

Thank God there are not.

One of the Troopers with the 4th Light Horse Regiment, A Squadron, Sloan 'Scotty' Bolton – a train-driver from Geelong – is in the thick of it with the best of them, astride his beloved horse Monty, when he sees just up ahead a German officer supervising three mounted Turks pulling the gun on which he sits like Lord Muck to safety, with three other soldiers on the limber.

'Stop!' the Australian roars.

The German officer doesn't stop.

'Riding up to him,' Bolton will recount, 'I gave a fierce yell. My revolver misfired, so I struck him over the head with it. However he was wearing a steel helmet and I hurt my hand more than I hurt him. The blow knocked his helmet off though, and the next one was more successful, dazing him so that he offered no resistance.'[51]

As the German officer tumbles to the ground, the six Turks surrender, and Bolton turns them and the gun back towards the town centre, complete with a glowering German officer holding his bleeding head, clinging on to the limber.

As they near the town square, others take over and Bolton keeps going in the company of a mate, Trooper Ray Hudson. Still, explosions are going on all over, and it is obvious that the Turks and Germans are intent on reducing Beersheba to rubble, to deny the victors the spoils they are after.

Bolton sees a German officer outside one of the buildings focusing intently on a board with switches on it, and wires coming out the back!

'We rode over to him, gave a yell, upon which he immediately jumped to his feet, very much surprised that we were already in the town. We both pointed our revolvers at him with the order, "Hands up!"'[52]

The shocked German officer is given a wordless choice. You can flick the switch before you to blow up another well, or you can . . . live?

After a pause that seems like a lifetime – perhaps the one flashing before his eyes – the German officer raises his hands in surrender. There will be no more wells blown up in this town. Beersheba is theirs, the prize almost intact, the triumph total.

•

Trooper Thomas O'Leary is discovered down a side-street, with a gun he has captured, and six Turks of the artillery crew. No-one is going to get away on his watch, and no other regiment than his own will get the credit for the capture of the gun!

Around Beersheba the 'mopping up' operations continue, quelling the last of the resistance.

Stretcher-bearers are busy, bringing in the Australian Troopers who have fallen, many of them with grievous wounds. For the most part they are dropped to aid posts that have been set up at Chauvel's HQ, where the medics can work on them, before the stretcher-bearers go out again, sometimes having to gather their own fellow bearers who had taken a bullet or worse in the course of fulfilling their duties.

In the meantime, what is in effect a stocktake of those captured is taking place. 'I had just finished counting my little lot of prisoners,' Captain Davies will recount, 'and sent them away under escort (it was a beautiful moonlight night and I counted them like a lot of sheep with Marnie and Haft keeping tally. 647 and 38 officers was the number as well as I remember the odd figures . . . 4th Light Horse got 350 odd more . . .'[53]

By the time the darkness falls completely, all know at last it is over.

> The Turks completely routed, for shelter they did run;
> We knew Beersheba—it was ours at the setting of the sun.
> Once more in fancy I can see the noble charge they made,
> Across the land all swept by shell – the gallant Fourth Brigade;

Prisoners are now corralled by the railway yard, and between the 4th and 12th Regiments there prove to be no fewer than 700 of them – including 38 Turkish and German officers – while they have also captured nine precious big guns and three machine guns. The prisoners taken by the rest of Desert Mounted Corps will more than double the tally, while adding railway rolling stock and an entire aerodrome, including a couple of Taubes!

The priority now for the Australian Light Horse is to gather their wounded and water the horses.

One of the former is Tibby Cotter.

When his mate Bluey gets to him, back at the first trenches hit by the 4th Regiment, he is being cared for and is moaning softly, still breathing, but bleeding heavily from the bullet wound.

'Tibby!' Blue calls out, the cry strangled as it comes forth.

Recognising the voice, Cotter opens his eyes.

'Blue,' he gasps, 'you can have the fish supper on your own.'[54]

He gives out one last gasp, and is still. Tibby Cotter lies dead in the moonlight.

Further back, they make another discovery, an eerie one at that. For it is Regimental Sergeant Major Alex Wilson of the 4th Regiment who had told Sergeant Jim French just the night before that, 'I am sure there is a bullet waiting for me at Beersheba.'[55] Now, sure enough, here he is, dead with a bullet through his head, but, in a sight so strange none who see it will ever forget, he is sitting completely astride his dead horse in a pit.

•

Not far away is Lieutenant Guy Haydon, lying in his own pit, and still bleeding from the wound in his rear. Midnight is in the moonlight, just next to the pit.

'I lay in the hole for about 2 hours,' Haydon will recount, 'listening to poor devils groaning all round me.'[56]

At last, at around 9 o'clock, a medical orderly arrives with a lantern, accompanied by those indefatigable stretcher-bearers. Following the groans, they start to bring the wounded to the light of the lantern, where emergency dressings are applied to stem the bleeding. The worst of the wounded are put on the sand-carts and rushed into Beersheba for better medical care, but there are too many wounded and not enough sand-carts. A strange triage takes place whereby those most in danger of dying but still with a chance of survival are given priority in the carts, while those who will almost certainly die, and those who might live anyway, are left behind to take their chances for the moment.

Things are indeed grim.

'Four of the poor chaps died there within a yard or two of me,' Haydon will recount, 'but it did not worry me, I had got past worrying.'[57]

Now the sand-carts come back and start to take the next lot, and the next lot again.

It is his Commanding Officer of B Squadron 12th Regiment, Major Fetherstonhaugh – himself one of those gathered in for urgent medical care – who will write to Haydon's parents back at Bloomfield, explaining the thing that their son will not.

'Guy would not allow them to take him in that night as there were others he considered worse cases than him, so he stayed out all night. You will all be very proud of your gallant, self-sacrificing son . . . He deserves a decoration.'[58]

For now, things are grim and getting grimmer.

'At last there was only myself and one man left,' Haydon will write home, 'and we had to lie there all night. One of the boys got me a blanket off a dead horse but it was terribly cold . . .'[59]

In the distance, he can hear the regular cracks of rifles. Every shot in the dusk represents an oft weeping Trooper or officer sending their beloved horse, or the horse of a fallen comrade, to the great beyond.

And that is where the mighty Midnight is, dead, right beside Guy's trench.

Haydon weeps. And shakes with the cold.

•

Yes, there is still the odd angry shot ringing out around Beersheba and in the distance as the last of the Turkish resistance is quelled. But the primary sound now is that curious snorting, shuddering sound that thirsty horses make when at last getting water! All over the town, the engineers and Troopers have set up canvas troughs next to the working wells that have been captured, with the pumps going nineteen to the dozen and the frisky horses – maddened by just the smell of water, so close – are lined up to get their fill.

Around the campfires that have sprung up all over town on this night, the Troopers whose horses are already sated are eating – what is this again, Jacko? – Budapest tinned horse scraped over black Turkish bread toasted on the fire. Some of the luckier ones are eating the food prepared by Turkish cooks just hours before!

'The surprise was so well timed and complete,' one Trooper will recount, 'that we found the enemy coppers full of food for the evening meal, with ladles ready to serve same.'[60]

Don't mind, if they do!

'The Turkish flour is like pollard,' another appreciative Trooper will write to his family, 'and the bread is brown. Some of it was just out of the ovens, and it went down alright after army biscuits . . .'[61]

It is with similar joy that many of the Troopers are already wearing some of the booty they have just captured, including fresh German underwear and jackboots discovered in a warehouse, while they have also purloined things like revolvers and field-glasses. Tonight they'll sleep on brand spanking new bivy sheets and tomorrow ride on new saddles!

Around those fires as they talk softly in the night, with the glow thrown by the still burning buildings giving their faces an ethereal glow, some themes emerge.

There is grief for those who have fallen, never to rise again, and tragic news shared of just who has copped it, like Tibby, Wickham and Craggs.

There is awe for those among them who had done so well in the thick of battle. Did yers hear about what Cox, O'Leary and the likes of Scotty Bolton did?

As more troops march in from outside, including now much of the rest of Desert Corp and the 20th Corps, there is stunned pride at what, as a body of mounted Troopers, they have accomplished.

'Fancy only a bayonet, which is about 18in. long, to face a horde of well-armed and trenched devils!' Trooper Tom Latimer from the 12th Light Horse Regiment's signals section writes. 'They faced shell, shrapnel, machine-gun, rifle-fire, and bayonet, with only a weapon like a carving-knife. The charge, oh, Lord, dear people, it was glorious! Nothing could stop them. At the Jackos they went full gallop, cursing and yelling.'[62]

Even those who were in the thick of it can't quite believe it.

'The capture of Beersheba was complete – one of the most amazing bluffs ever known in warfare,' Sergeant David Harris of the 12th Regiment will write home. 'Our weapons, the rifle and bayonet, are useless when travelling at such terrific pace, yet we had successfully charged through continuous lines of well manned trenches which had prevented the advance of a whole mounted army corps.'

As deep as Harris's pride is, however, he is sure, like so many of his contemporaries, to give credit where it is due.

'But the victory belongs to the horses, the riders' feelings and intentions were of no account in that mad race . . . These Australian horses, after years of gruelling warfare from Sinai onwards, had, after days on reduced rations, carried an average of 18 stone over 40 miles of steep and rugged country, in one night. Then, following a burning day, after being without water for 27 hours, they carried off this brilliant charge – four miles through flying lead.'[63]

At least their hero horses are now eating into the massed supplies of Turkish barley that have been captured, while the water situation is perilous, but just manageable.

Yes, Scotty Bolton has saved the town and all its wells from being blown up. But, as recounted by Lieutenant Colonel Richard Preston, 'the whole place was a nest of explosive charges, "booby traps" and trip wires'.[64] And of course it is the surviving wells, which are most laden with charges, and so under the supervision of the engineers, everything must be done very . . . carefully.

Some of the first horses who had got to the troughs had drunk so quickly they had vomited, but with 4000 horses to be watered, it is soon obvious that some rationing will have to apply until the engineers can get some of the blown wells working again. It will be no small thing to get *all* the pumps going, and right now a lot of the hard yakka is done with ropes lowering buckets to the cool water 100 feet below, and hauling it out – a process that will go on all night long.

Some of the horses will have to be given just enough water to revive them before being sent further afield on the morrow. For, with the horses of the likes of the 11th Regiment, all the Wellingtonians, Aucklanders and Canterburys now coming into town, together with so many of the soldiers from the 20th Corps, it is clear that the demand for water from the new arrivals will outstrip even Beersheba's capacity.

In General Chauvel's Desert Mounted Corps HQ, now set up in one of Beersheba's few residences – the comfortable stone house where Colonel Ismet had his command post – arrangements are already being made for the Anzac Mounted Division to remain in Beersheba in coming days, while the Australian Mounted Division will be moved on to Karm, where there is enough water to sustain them.

Still, there is time for the beaming General to congratulate Brigadier General Grant on his incredible achievement.

As Chauvel characterises the feat, 'By this mounted action, Grant had done in a few minutes, with two regiments & fewer casualties, what it would probably have taken two Brigades, dismounted, a couple of hours to do. So far as I know, such a charge by mounted men against entrenched infantry is unique in the annals of cavalry.'[65]

He has already said much the same to some of the Troopers, describing the charge as 'the greatest mounted feat in modern warfare', while General Chaytor agrees, saying, 'It's magnificent, I have seen nothing better.'[66]

Meantime, inside the Beersheba Town Hall, all through the night, the doctors and orderlies of the Field Ambulance are endeavouring to save the lives of grievously wounded Troopers, many of the Australians now transferred here from the first-aid station at Khashim Zanna.

'Hardly started to unpack,' Sergeant Patrick Hamilton of the 4th Light Horse Field Ambulance will recount, 'when seven loads of wounded arrived . . . and first patient on the operating table in under 20 minutes.'[67]

Over there, the 4th Brigade's holy man, Padre Weir, is performing the last rites for five Troopers who are rapidly fading despite the best attempts by the medicos to stabilise them. One by one, they are wrapped in blankets and placed to the side, while the doctors concentrate on saving those they can. Nearby, wounded Troopers are talking, one saying, 'All I could do was ride my horse, wave my bayonet around my head and yell.'[68]

'Wouldn't have missed it for worlds,' a wounded mate agrees.

'The horses were magnificent,' says still another. 'We came in so fast at the end that the Turks lost their range and fired over our heads.'[69]

Still another is already composing an account for his parents of what he had seen on the day.

One of Hamilton's fellow ambulance men, Private Norm Challis, covered in blood, is exhausted but, 'in high spirits. He had been out with stretcher bearers and sand carts following close behind the galloping troops. They had applied field dressing and picked up the wounded spread over two miles, but mainly around the trenches.'

Norm offers a wan smile of satisfaction to Hamilton.

'It was the real thing,'[70] he says simply; what they had trained for.

Still out on the battlefield, as yet ungathered by the ambulance men, many grievously wounded Diggers and Turks are clinging to life, in terrible pain. Sometimes in the night, they can give succour to each other, sharing water bottles, their enmity gone in their common suffering.

Guy Haydon, however, is now completely on his own.

'I shivered all night long,' he will recount, 'and in the morning my wound was so stiff that I couldn't move.'[71]

At last, at dawn, they come for him. Frozen stiff, weak, he is taken to Beersheba Town Hall, where his wound is cleaned and dressed. Only a few beds along, alas, Trooper Harold Wickham, as pale as a sheet, is breathing with progressively more labour. A gasp, a shallow breath, a bigger gasp, a bigger breath, a small gasp, a tiny breath . . . a kind of rattle . . . and he lies perfectly still.

Dead.

He is just 16 years and seven months old, one of 55 Australians killed.

•

Taubes!

There are two of them, and they have no sooner arrived over Beersheba the morning after the charge than they start dropping bombs. Most fall ineffectually, but a couple of bombs hit the tents of the 4th Field Ambulance amidships.

'In the black dust and smoke the horses were rearing and neighing in terror,' Sergeant Patrick Hamilton will describe. 'Men were running and shrieking.'[72]

Hamilton, who had been in a nearby tent, grabs his medical haversack and runs just 20 yards before reaching his mate, William Brownjohn, whose left leg has been blown off, above the legging. Applying a tourniquet to stem the flow, Hamilton is soon off again, running past six horses that have been disembowelled by shrapnel, their blood forming massive puddles by their heaving sides.

And now someone mentions his best mate, Norm Challis, who had been so satisfied the night before with all the lives they had saved after the charge.

'Oh no, not Norm!'

'Yes,' comes the reply. 'Challis, Carney, Schmidt and Lake all killed instantly. Shockingly mutilated. We've wrapped their bodies in blankets and laid them over there.'[73]

Grieving will have to come later. For now, Corporal William Oates has had his right arm blown off, while Hay has had his left buttock cut clean away. And then there is Bill Taylor . . .

In Hamilton's view he proves to be 'one of the worst types of casualty, shell shock'. Standing between two horses at the time, one of the bombs had exploded just a few feet from him, and not a single bit of shrapnel had hit him. 'But we placed him on a stretcher, a pathetic, incoherent weeping wreck . . .'[74]

In the air, Lieutenant Ross Smith and others of the Australian Flying Corps' No. 1 Squadron chase the deadly threats away.

•

Now striding around Beersheba, taking it all in, is none other than Major Banjo Paterson, as delighted as he is incredulous at the news of the successful charge!

'The town was as full as London, [with] all sorts of staff officers rushing around . . .'[75]

Everywhere he looks there is activity, as Troopers feed and water their horses; engineers are at work fixing the wells; warehouses of supplies are opened up and goods distributed; and roll-calls are being conducted to work out just who is missing from each Regiment.

Looking around the town, Banjo is walking along the railway embankment to get a better look at a mob of Turkish prisoners and some newly captured guns when there is a sudden massive roar and he is clean knocked off his feet.

'A poor wretched Egyptian soldier,' he will recount, 'had tripped over a concealed wire and exploded a Turkish mine and was blown to pieces. It made me feel lucky I wasn't 20 yards further back I can tell you . . .'[76]

Only a short time later Banjo will be there when a mine is discovered under the steps of a house Troopers are billeted in.

Booby-traps are everywhere! While circling Beersheba looking for artillery positions Lieutenant Colonel Richard Preston sees a trip-wire. It is cut, and very carefully followed to its source, 'a detonator concealed in twenty cases of gelignite in the railway station – enough to have laid the whole town in ruins'.[77]

Catastrophe has been averted, but not for everyone.

'All together,' Banjo Paterson will recount, 'about 18 people were killed by these mines or bombs or whatever you like to call them.'[78]

But what's that now?

In the near distance, the poet sees a flurry of salutes, and even hears cheers, as a notable figure arrives in a Ford truck.

•

'BBA!'

'Bloody Bull's About.'[79]

This version of General Bull Allenby, however, is not an angry one. As he alights, it is not quite that the English General is beaming as much as his Australian driver – for that fellow in sleeveless vest and short shorts is like a *light-house* of sheer pride as he keeps looking around – but it is close.

Mostly, as the Bull walks around Beersheba, accompanied by Generals Chauvel, Hodgson, Chaytor and William Grant, among others, he is simply stupefied.

How on earth have the Australians done this? Mounted a charge, like the old days, and actually succeeded? How did the Troopers get over the trenches?

'We jumped the bloody things!'[80] Chauvel replies.

As for you, General Grant, *well done*.

While the Queenslander stands to attention, Allenby personally pins upon his lapel a bar for his principal existing decoration, the Distinguished Service Order, this one for showing, 'conspicuous dash and determination in the manner in which he handled his Brigade. Quickly appreciating the situation, he ordered his regiments to charge into the town of Beersheba, which they did, jumping the Turkish trenches which were being held at the time. It was owing to this Officer's promptness that the town was occupied in time to take a large number of prisoners.'[81]

In his personal remarks, Allenby does not prevaricate.

'Grant,' he tells him, 'this was the most marvellous charge in modern warfare! It changed the tide of the battle completely!'[82]

Cheers.

To the assembled gathering of beaming officers and dusty Troopers, Allenby is gracious in his remarks.

'You did something that teachers of military history say could not be done. You galloped over strongly defended positions and demoralised the enemy. He's finished. His cavalry will never face you again. You have put new life into my army and you rank with the finest cavalry the British Army has ever had.'[83]

Unlike General Murray after the Battle of Romani, Allenby will not mince words when it comes to paying credit to the Australians.

'The honour and the glory of securing the town,' he will write to Equerry of King George V, to be passed on to His Majesty, 'went to the 4th Australian Light Horse in a cavalry charge that in notoriety ranks with the Charge of the Light Brigade at Balaklava in 1854.'[84]

(This time, however, it had a happier ending.)

For now, it is time to get back to work, as Allenby gathers his senior officers to make orders for the next phase of operations, which, he decides, will launch on Gaza itself with an artillery barrage starting just before midnight on this very day, and a massed attack of infantry from the first hours of the following day. No rest for the wicked, or the English . . .

The job of the Desert Mounted Corps in coming days will be to attend to the watering needs of the horses and establish supply lines, and thereafter to lead the push into the Holy Land.

They know the drill. In time for Christmas would be nice . . .

●

It is time to bury our dead.

But first, all the dead out on the battlefield must be gathered in.

Troopers do not have to be sent out in a detail to collect the bodies and personal effects of the dead, for those who can are doing it from first light, looking for their mates, and hoping against hope they might still be alive.

It is a grisly business, made all the more horrifying when among the dead are men they have known well.

Like Tibby Cotter.

'We were surprised to find Cotter amongst our casualties,' one Trooper will recount, 'knowing he had been detailed for that day as a stretcher-bearer.'[85]

As will subsequently be sworn by one who was there, those fellows who 'picked up the lifeless body of Australia's great express swear that he lay as though bowling – with his right arm stretched out in the familiar action so well known to cricketers and the [SCG] Hill alike'.[86]

Tibby is carried back to a cemetery that has been established beneath a pod of gum trees on the edge of town, as are the likes of Troopers Jack Beasley and Rex Coley, Ernest Craggs, Lieutenant Ben Meredith, the four stretcher-bearers from the 4th Ambulance just killed, and . . . Trooper Harold Wickham, his corpse the easiest of the lot to carry as he died as no more than a boy. All up, while the 20th Corps has lost 116 KIA, the 4th Light Horse Brigade has had 35 killed and 39 wounded.

Presiding over the burials of those in the 12th and 4th Light Horse is Chaplain William J. Dunbar, now with the 11th, who had arrived in Egypt the previous year and had served with both the 12th and 4th Light Horse and had known most of these men personally.

He is devastated by the tragedy of it all, one that will soon be all the greater for he has himself just seven days to live; he will go out under fire to attempt to rescue a wounded man and not return. For now . . .

Let us pray . . .

Around the open graves, many a Trooper openly weeps as the shrouded figures are carefully lowered by ropes to their eternal resting place, and the first of the sods thrown upon them.

> *Once more in fancy I can see the noble charge they made,*
> *Across the land all swept by shell – the gallant Fourth Brigade;*
> *As heroes then they bravely rode, and where those heroes fell*
> *The wooden crosses standing the story sad can tell;*
> *No more upon their horses' backs those gallant men will ride—*
> *Their fight it was for freedom, and in freedom's cause they fell.*[87]

'We paid attention to the graves of our fallen comrades,' one Trooper will recount, 'with little crosses and white stones we made them look like Christian graves.'[88]

(Within a few months a group of Australian Troopers will make a special trip back to this cemetery with a loaded cart pulled by mules. In the cart, specially constructed sturdy white crosses with the names of the fallen painted upon them, by use of a 'paint brush' made from the mule's mane. Each name was painted on by Sergeant Jim French who rode in the charge himself.)

It is with rather less ceremony that the Troopers get to work burying the 500 Turkish corpses that are being gathered, and placed in a mass pit on the edge of town. Some of the Light Horse note the ill-preparedness of the Turks to counter their charge – one sign that they had never contemplated this tactic is that many of the dead Turks have their bombs actually *wired* to their belts. Also significant is that many of the rifles and guns captured have their sights set at 1600 yards and more – indicating these young Turks had indeed been so flustered they had no time, or had forgotten, to adjust their sights.

•

And yet such is the way of war. The badly wounded are evacuated, the dead are buried. The rest move on to the next battle.

Before leaving Beersheba, Lieutenant Colonel Murray Bourchier, the Commander of the 4th Light Horse Regiment, manages to dash off a note to his parents in Strathmerton, Victoria.

> *My dearest mother and father.*
> *Just a hurried line to say that I am safe and sound after our brilliant attack and capture of Beersheba. I led my regiment in a cavalry charge on the position and the troops behaved like angels. 'Australians will do me . . .'*[89]

THE AFTERMATH

*General Grant's action forms a notable landmark in the history
of cavalry, in that it initiated that spirit of dash which thereafter
dominated the whole campaign.*[1]

Lieutenant Colonel Richard Preston, *The Desert Mounted Corps*

It was like riding through the Bible.[2]

Trooper Ted Whitmore, 9th Australian Light Horse Regiment

Early November 1917, Palestine, nigh on Zion, Gaza stripped

The fall of Beersheba indeed proved to be the breakthrough that
Chetwode had promised and Allenby was banking on. With the
left flank of the Turks' fortified line now completely exposed, the
Australians, New Zealanders and British simply rolled up the Turkish
defensive line from there, able now to attack each outpost from *three*
sides.

Just a week after the charge – filled with fighting the badly shaken
enemy – an extraordinary thing happens. When Allenby's forces push
towards Gaza on the morning of 7 November it is to find not only no
resistance, but, once they enter the ancient citadel – there are no Turkish
soldiers there! Against all odds, the Turks have managed to . . . scarper
in the night, without Allenby's forces being remotely aware, leaving
the way clear for the British, Australians, Kiwis et al, to advance *en
masse* into Palestine proper.

In the meantime, an event of enormous significance had occurred
as a direct result of the victory at Beersheba on 31 October.

Just two days after the key Ottoman outpost had fallen – and it seemed clear that the victory would presage the capture of all of the Holy Land, and likely bring the Ottoman Empire to its knees at last – the British Foreign Secretary, Arthur Balfour, writes to Baron Rothschild, the famous banker who was also the head of the British branch of the Zionist Federation.

> Dear Lord Rothschild,
>
> I have much pleasure in conveying to you, on behalf of His Majesty's Government, the following declaration of sympathy with Jewish Zionist aspirations which has been submitted to, and approved by, the Cabinet.
>
> His Majesty's Government view with favour the establishment in Palestine of a national home for the Jewish people, and will use their best endeavours to facilitate the achievement of this object . . .
>
> Yours sincerely,
> Arthur James Balfour[3]

A key foundation stone for the future had just been laid.

•

There were, of course, many more battles to follow Beersheba and the fall of Gaza, in which the Australian Light Horse were front and centre, as they pushed north, fighting the Turks all the way.

It is only fitting in this Biblical land that on the march north the Australians must first take Bethlehem itself.

'Late in the afternoon the cars drove into Bethlehem,' Lieutenant Colonel Richard Preston will note of their arrival on 8 December, 'where our men were received with transports of joy by the inhabitants, nearly all of whom are Christians. The poor people crowded round their deliverers to kiss their hands, shouting and weeping, and pressing offerings of food on them, much to their embarrassment.'[4]

As for the enemy? They are collapsing into a retreating rabble; ever more disorganised.

'As our pursuit increased,' one Trooper will recount, 'and became more threatening, the Turks, Germans, Austrians [and] confreres in the air abandoned them, after which the retreat became a rout. They shot their mules and oxen in the limbers, and all along the line were shattered remnants of their convoy.'[5]

Onwards, they push across 'John the Baptist Wilderness', at which point Jerusalem is at their mercy.

In fact, the 'Christmas present for the British people' is perfectly timed, falling to the Desert Mounted Corps a neat fortnight before Christmas Day on 11 December 1917 when General Allenby himself walks through the Jaffa Gate, just as the Arab legend had long proclaimed, that one day the prophet Allanebi – 'Allah-Nebi' God's prophet – would do, liberating Jerusalem!

No matter, Allenby actually dismounts before the gates and walks through to show humility. Jerusalem is theirs. (As it happens, Jerusalem had almost fallen to an earlier conqueror of peculiar qualifications: a cook, one Private Murch from the English Midlands. Needs must, Murch had made in the early morning light a quick recce for fresh rations at the outer village of Lifta – specifically, looking for eggs. Inevitably, word spreads to nearby Jerusalem of a man in British uniform being about and next thing Murch knows he looks up to see a man on a white charger approaching, holding a white flag! It proves to be the Mayor of Jerusalem, offering to surrender. The horrified Murch will not have it. That is not what he has come for. With some force, thus, he yells out: 'I don't want yer city! I want some heggs for my hofficers!'[6] With which, he beats a hasty retreat, before another accidental capture could occur.)

Since the Charge at Beersheba six weeks before, they have taken over 12,000 Turkish prisoners and captured 1000 artillery pieces.

It is here in Jerusalem's famous Barracks Square that General Sir Harry Chauvel receives his greatest honours in recognition of his extraordinary efforts. For it is no less than the visiting Duke of Connaught who, on behalf of King George V – and in front of Chauvel's fellow senior officers – pins on to the Australian's left breast the gold and silver Knight Commander of the order of the Bath, a regal betterment of his previous knighthood.

Also pinned on this occasion was the blue and yellow Grand Officer of the Order of the Nile, bestowed by the Sultanate of Egypt for service to that country.

•

For the next year, the forces of Allenby, led by General Sir Harry Chauvel's Desert Mounted Corps, spearheaded by the Australian Light Horse, are front and centre of the drive north to bring the Ottoman Empire to its end.

One by one, the citadels fall.

'Their two main lines of railways fell into our hands,' one Trooper will write to his brother in Australia, 'and we are now utilising them. After sixteen days continuous travelling and fighting Jaffa and Ramleh were evacuated, and our portion of the Light Horse is now resting among the corn and wine, the olive and orange groves and vine-yards of Biblical fame . . .'[7]

Yes, there will now be months of consolidation, moving supplies and men forward, but finally all is in readiness for what will be known as the 'Great Ride', a massive movement of men on horseback pushing into the heart of the dying Ottoman Empire, across nigh on 500 miles of desert.

The push against the retreating Turks goes on; but the stakes will never be as high as that day of the charge, that instant legend that blazes the trail to victory after victory. For the moment there are no more charges *a la* Beersheba, but make no mistake . . .

'General Grant's action,' one of his officers will note, 'forms a notable landmark in the history of cavalry, in that it initiated that spirit of dash which thereafter dominated the whole campaign.'[8]

Henry Gullett himself, war correspondent and Official Historian, agrees.

'From then on to the end of the war the Turks never forgot "Beersheba" and the [German and Ottoman] infantry, when galloped, as after Beersheba they frequently were, invariably shot wildly and surrendered early in the conflict. The charge had dealt a heavy wound to the enemy morale, from the High Command down to the men in the ranks.'[9]

And now? Well, now the Light Horse approach what really might be their last battle, depending on how faithfully you read or follow your Bible. For they are near to what is now known as Megiddo, but was known as . . . Armageddon. Yes, that one!

For the Bible had prophesied that the battle to end not just all battles but humanity itself is to be fought at Armageddon. Mercifully, this particular battle is brief, as the enemy keeps falling back.

(Unbeknownst to the Australians, among those wounded at the Battle of Megiddo, aka Armageddon, is none other than the Commanding Officer of the Troops who had opposed them at Beersheba, Colonel Ismet. He has put every ounce of his being into stopping the Australians, starting from his service at Gallipoli, only to finally fall to them.)

Onwards to Nazareth, where the British Yeomanry do the honours, and approach so rapidly they are able to take the 3000-strong town while most of the inhabitants are still in their beds! The Australians are tightly behind, ready to leapfrog once more to the prow of the push.

'Through historic Nazareth in the moonlight, and on to Tiberias, and the Sea of Galilee, where some bloody hand-to-hand fighting took place. Our horses were unsaddled, watered, fed, and given a swim in the Sea of Galilee.'[10]

For many of the Troopers it feels like the very time of their lives. 'Like the flashing pictures in a giant kaleidoscope,' one Light Horse Trooper, Walter Teare, will recount, 'the Biblical scenery was passed in one big panorama. With Jerusalem and the hills of Judea over our right shoulders, we waded our brave old horses across the River Jordan, and, in the half-light of a shivery dawn, led them up a steep hill . . .'[11]

They are now no less than on the high road to Damascus.

'One night, to the noise of loud explosions we camped in the hills [outside Damascus], and at daybreak rode down a goat track into the bloody Barada Gorge – "The Gorge of Death." The carnage that we witnessed there still throngs memoryland. I will skip it. Suffice to say that, our horses "hurdle raced" over dead and dying. The writing was on the wall . . .'[12]

Damascus – the city which, on the Day of Judgement, had been prophesied to fall, *'Behold, Damascus is taken away from being a city, and shall be a ruinous heap.'* (Isaiah 17:1) – is just up ahead.

Well, we'll use our own judgement and see what happens.

They have traversed 450 miles of desert and mountains in just under a fortnight, hailed as the 'greatest exploit in the history of horsed cavalry'.[13] It's said to be the largest column of mounted horsemen since the time that Alexander the Great and his troops had forced their way across the same territory.

And they are not the Turks' only problem. While the forces of the British Empire are closing fast on Damascus from the south, so too have the British forces at Salonika in Northern Greece finally broken free to turn east towards Constantinople, with little resistance left between them and the Ottoman capital.

•

It is, of course, the nature of warfare to produce strange outcomes. But few are stranger than what occurs on 29 September 1918, as on that afternoon Lieutenant Colonel Donald Cameron, with two squadrons of his 5th Light Horse Regiment, approach a 5000-strong garrison of Turks dug in at the town of Ziza, Palestine.

The Turks, in turn, are surrounded by no fewer than 10,000 Arabs of the Beni Sakr tribe – Bedouins who want to kill them to a man.

All the fight has gone out of the Turks and they would be more than happy to surrender to the Australians. But herein lies the problem. Cameron and his men are only 200 strong, and under the circumstances, the Turkish commander – as he advises via an emissary – is afraid to surrender to them.

'He maintained,' Cameron will recount, 'that [my] small force was not strong enough to protect his men from the Bedouin if the garrison laid down its arms.'[14]

Sending an officer of the 5th Light Horse Regiment forward, Cameron soon has back from the Turkish commander a scrawled message.

> *To the O. C. British Forces, Colonel Cameron. I hereby surrender unconditionally all my force, guns, ammunition, stores etc. and in so doing claim your protection for the safety of my soldiers, wounded and sick.*
>
> *Signed at Ziza, 29th September, 1918*
> *Bey Wahaby, Commandant.*[15]

What to do?

The previously unthinkable.

Cameron sends back a note telling the Commandant to keep his men to their guns, while he sends a direct and forceful warning to the besieging Bedouins – any attack on the Turks would see the Australians attack *them!* Happily, the 7th Australian Light Horse Regiment now arrives in force, closely followed by the 2nd Brigade's commanding officer, Brigadier General Granville Ryrie, who takes the entire matter in hand.

At the head of his men, Ryrie takes the Australians forward and *into* the Turkish position. He now passes a further message to the besieging Bedouins, to make the general threat particular indeed: If any of you try to attack, the first of you who come within range of our guns will be shot on the spot.

With which, the Turks and Australians settle down for the night together, sitting around the same fires, exchanging rations – the Australians eating Turkish *chapatis* with delight, and the Turks trying cans of bully beef with grim distaste – 'and by many signs expressing reciprocal respect and admiration'.[16]

Occasionally from the perimeters will come the sounds of machine guns chattering and single rifle shots, as Turkish sentries fire, as warned, at any Arab who comes within range. In response the Australians – pass the chapatis – roar in appreciation: 'Go on, Jacko! Give it to the blighters!'[17]

Unthinkable.

An admittedly restless night is passed – with ears and rifles permanently cocked, and at least one eye on the perimeter for any sign of an attack – but when a brigade of Kiwis arrive with the dawn, the Turks are at last happy to lay down their arms and become the prisoners of the men they had been fighting beside the night before.

Onwards!

•

Now if the road to hell is paved with good intentions, the road to Damascus, for Lawrence of Arabia, is paved with Australians; everywhere he looks – up ahead, on his flanks – pushing, pushing, pushing, as his Arab forces and those of General Chauvel close in on the prized ancient citadel of Damascus.

The Englishman is wary of their speed, their pushiness. When Damascus finally falls after 400 years of Ottoman occupation, he wants it to fall to *him*, and his band of Arabs, but certainly not to the damn Australians. (Quietly, Allenby is entirely onboard. The Australians are all very well, in their place, but an Englishman should be in first place when Damascus falls.)

Consequently, relations between the two forces are not always warm, least of all when Lawrence's men form up tightly on the Australians' right flank, and the two must co-ordinate their advances.

'At one stage in the operations,' one of Brigadier General Granville Ryrie's Troopers will recount, 'an Arab dispatch rider, mounted on a flea-bitten mongrel pony, galloped up with a dispatch for Ryrie. Opening the missive, which was written in Arabic, the old General turned it upside down and gazed at it from various angles . . .'

There is a long pause.

'Can't you read it, General?' one of his senior staff officers asks.

'Read it be damned,' Ryrie replies acidly. 'If I had a cornet I might be able to play it!'[18]

Now, where were we before we were so rudely interrupted?

Pushing to Damascus.

'I have come, gentlemen,' Allenby tells a gathering of his senior officers, including Chauvel and Hodgson, on the morning of 17 September, 'to wish you good luck and to tell you that my impression is that you are on the eve of a great victory. Everything depends . . . on the secrecy, rapidity and accuracy of the cavalry movement.'[19]

Nearing noon on 30 September, the forces of the Desert Mounted Corps are very close, only to find the way blocked by what looks to be some 2000 Turkish soldiers on a ridge at a place called Kaukab – famous in the Bible as the place of the conversion of St Paul on . . . the road to Damascus.

What to do? The answer is to send in the best troops they have, known as 'Bourchier's Force'.

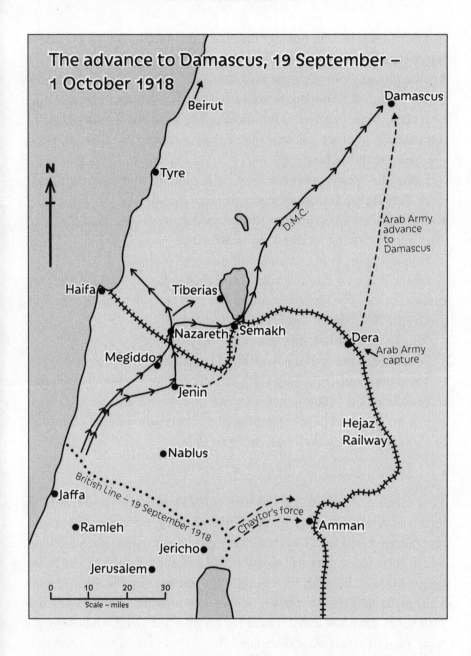

The advance to Damascus, 19 September – 1 October 1918

That would be the same 4th and 12th Light Horse Regiments who had charged the year before at Beersheba. (This time, however, courtesy of General Hodgson's successful agitation, they have *real* swords – 1908 pattern British cavalry swords, all of 42 inches long and issued just the month before, freeing them from the need to tightly grip mere bayonets. 'They taught us to turn your wrist over and lock your elbow for the charge,' one Trooper will chronicle. 'They reckoned that the thrust sword at arm's length could out-reach a lance . . . by a couple of inches. That cheered us up quite a bit, until we wondered what happened if your sword went more than a couple of inches through the bloke with the lance!'[20])

Lining his men up behind their own ridge in line formation, just as at Beersheba, Bourchier gives the signal and they move forward *en masse*, heading down into the valley that separates them from the Turks and readying to climb the other side.

Half a league, half a league, half a league onwards . . .

Major Norman Rae is leading, and they gallop towards a foe they cannot yet see. The tension is unbearable and one rider near Rae breaks and yells, 'Why don't you fire, you bastards?'[21]

Why indeed? When they get closer they can see the answer.

For the reputation of the Australian Light Horse has preceded them.

The Turks and remaining German officers are fleeing! The charge at Beersheba has become such a legend that these Turks have no wish to join another and have something of a conversion on their own road to Damascus – they no longer want to fight.

•

That evening, on the southern outskirts of Damascus – to the pulsing light and throbbing roar of the Turks blowing up ammunition and fuel dumps in the near distance of the city, the ground lightly shaking 'neath their feet – Chauvel meets with Lawrence of Arabia, the latter begging him to keep his men outside the ancient city for the moment. This, as he tells the Australian, is 'because to-night would see such a carnival as the town had not held for six hundred years, and its hospitality might pervert their discipline'.[22]

(And also, as Blind Freddie and Suspicious Harry can both tell you, because Lawrence wants the honour of being the 'Liberator of Damascus' to be his alone.)

Chauvel is uncertain if this is a good idea, but such is Lawrence's stature – for he and his band of Arabs have delivered everything that they promised, and are a constant drain on Turkish resources – that he reluctantly agrees. Chauvel will, however, send his own men of the 3rd Australian Light Horse Brigade to *skirt* Damascus and cut off the road to Aleppo to the north, so that all Turks trying to flee would be captured.

So it is that on the sparkling morning of 1 October 1918, Major Arthur Olden – originally a dentist from Ballarat, whose first job in the Army had been peeling spuds – finds himself with the scouts of his own 10th Australian Light Horse Regiment, acting as Advance Guard for the 3rd Brigade, trying to skirt the city from the south-west and get on the road to Aleppo. Alas, not only is no track around the city apparent, the detritus from the previous night's battle – with dozens of corpses of Germans and Turks, together with literally hundreds of dead camels and horses spread in every direction – makes this route problematic and probably impossible.

Trying to find an easier path, Olden soon realises that, 'the only way to the Aleppo road lay through the heart of the city itself'. (Bad luck, Colonel Lawrence.) They soon head that way, only to be greeted by 'a sudden burst of Turkish rifle fire'.[23]

With things suddenly tense, Major Olden orders swords to be drawn, and leads his men on a brief charge towards the core of the ancient city.

'Across the river, two or three hundred yards away,' Henry Gullett notes 'were thousands of Turks, at the barracks. For a moment the enemy decision was in the balance. But the sight of the great Australian horses at the gallop (the Turks and natives never cease to marvel at the size of our horses), with flashing swords, and the ring of shoes upon the metal, turned the scale.'[24]

More than somewhat!

'The shooting by the Turks,' one of the officers tells Gullett, 'changed in a second to the clapping of hands by the citizens.'[25]

That clapping is soon joined by many shots ringing out, but 'the shots were now coming from native Arabs, who were expressing their feelings in the popular Arab way by blazing at the heavens'.[26]

It is mystifying to the Australians, who judge the fire to be 'ginger'[27], but there is no doubt that everything has suddenly changed.

The mood is now one of enormous celebration as the men of Damascus continue to fire into the air with sheer joy at their city being 'liberated' from the Ottoman Empire for the first time in 400 years. So much for 'skirting' . . .

Clattering across a bridge that spans the Barada River, the Australians soon come to a large square filled with a throbbing crowd assembled before the *Serail*, Hall of Government, where officials await them on the front steps.

10th Regiment . . . halt!

'Where is the Governor?' Major Olden asks, via an interpreter he has successfully called for.

They were told that he awaited them upstairs.[28]

Friendly hands reach forward to hold his horse after Olden dismounts.

Carefully now, with his .45 Webley revolver in one hand and his sword in the other, Olden and two of his equally armed officers follow the officials into the imposing building and up the grand marble stairway built two centuries earlier, and enter a magnificent room, filled on one side with yet more officials in fabulous uniforms and garb, and on the other side, sitting on a kind of throne, a small man in strangely European dress, albeit with a tarboosh, otherwise known as a fez.

This is Emir Said, grandson of Abd-El-Kader, Sultan of Algiers, and just the previous afternoon, just before fleeing the city, Djemal Pasha, Commander of the Fourth Army, had sworn him in as Governor.

The dentist from Ballarat, Major Olden, rises to the occasion. Instead of going to the Governor, he pauses in the middle of the room, and bids the Governor to come to him. That distinguished gentleman does so, bows, and says: 'In the name of the City of Damascus, I welcome the first of the British Army.' Well, they are Australians actually, but before they can get to that the Governor continues: 'What are your wishes?'

It is tempting to ask for a flying carpet, but Olden sticks to the practical path and asks for something urgent, a surrender in actions not just in words. 'The shooting in the streets must instantly cease': that is the wish of Olden.

The amused Governor explains there is nothing to fear. 'The shooting is merely an expression of excess of feelings.'[29] Joyful feelings, the British are welcomed, and so is the departure of the Turks. And now the Governor commences a flowery speech in Arabic. Olden holds up his hand and bids him stop. The British will be here soon, and it is to them you should make such speeches. They love that kind of thing. He is an Australian.

Very well then.

The Emir agrees to give them a guide – an Armenian Colonel – to get through the city, and on the road to Aleppo. In return, Olden agrees that the Governor may retain a detachment of the gendarmerie with which he is to preserve order.

Said declares himself happy to sign a document surrendering to the British Army, but Olden wants the pre-written script changed, so history will record that Damascus *actually* surrendered to the Australians of the 10th Light Horse Regiment.

'I have the greatest honour in meeting Major Arthur Olden, who was the first British officer to enter Damascus, in the bravest manner known of the Saxon race. I have written these words as Remembrance of this glorious meeting.'[30]

Returning to his men congregated outside, Major Olden – who is an ancient history buff – holds up the piece of paper and jocularly says to his Troopers: 'I'm in the line of Rameses of Egypt, Alexander the Great, and Napoleon of France!'[31]

Oh, how his men cheer.

What a lark!

Major Olden and his men take their leave, heading to Aleppo – the greatest current danger in Damascus for an Australian is being buried in rose petals.

'Pushing through the crowded streets the populace gave every indication of their great joy at the occupation of the city by British troops. The troops were sprayed from the balconies with champagne, perfumes, rose leaves and confetti on leaving the city . . .'[32]

They are memories to last a lifetime.

'Syrian girls ran beside our old horses, handing up cigars, grapes, and oranges. It was unforgettable.'[33]

The cry in Arabic of *'Ya mit Ahlan wa sahlan'*, 'A hundred welcomes!' becomes a chant along their way, even as shopkeepers rush forth to shower the Australian Troopers with everything from fresh dates to juicy fruit, sweets and cigarettes.

'Crowds hung to their stirrups and ran along with their hands on the bridle reins. They were smothered with perfumes. Every man who smoked enjoyed a gift cigar, lark-eyed women and pretty girls appeared in every window . . . Others boldly waved their hands and smiled their welcome, and threw down scents and other favours.'

After all they have been through, it is nothing less than *extraordinary*. Henry Gullett's pen told it true, as ever:

> It was a wonderful hour for our young Australian countrymen. But the long war has made them into reserved men of the world. They rode, very dusty and unshaved, their big hats battered and drooping, through the tumultuous populace of the oldest and one of the most appealing cities in the world, with the same easy, casual bearing, and the same quiet, self confidence that are their distinctive characteristics on their country tracks at home. They ate their grapes and smoked their cigars, and missed no pretty eyes at the windows. But they showed no excitement or elation. The streets of old Damascus were but a stage in the long path of the war. They have become true soldiers of fortune.
>
> Few men in any age have passed through 24 more adventurous and gratifying hours than they knew during this first day around Damascus after the greatest achievement in history. But the light horseman is not demonstrative.[34]

After they have fully left the area, it is a good two hours before the second ribbon winner, Lawrence of Arabia will arrive in – what else but – a Rolls-Royce.

He is accompanied by his colourfully attired Arab tribesmen, themselves wildly firing shots in the air. It is a couple of days later again that Lawrence's friend and princely protege Prince Feisal arrives with his Sharifian Hejaz Army and is to achieve his own reward for having roused the Arabs to rise against the Ottoman Empire. For after a military government is proclaimed, Feisal bin Hussein becomes the King of Syria.

It is a triumph for Lawrence! It would have been a better triumph if he had been first into Damascus, but Lawrence is confident that will not affect his place in history; for he intends to write the history and leave out that part. But in the present, the Australians are first and present, and Lawrence of Arabia is far from quit of this oft troublesome breed.

Ever mindful of appearance over reality, Lawrence asks Chauvel to stage a procession for Feisal. The bemused Chauvel notes the request: 'On the early morning of October 3rd Lawrence informed me that the Emir Feisal would arrive in Damascus that afternoon and that he wished to have a triumphal entry, at 3 pm, galloping in like an Arab Conqueror of old at the head of about 300 horsemen. Seeing that he, Feisal, had had very little to do with the conquest of Damascus, the suggested triumphal entry did not appeal to me very much but, having in view that the Arabs would have administration of the city I thought it would not do any harm.'[35]

What does do harm is Lawrence himself. One morning in Damascus, the Australian Adjutant of the 12th Regiment, C. L. A. Abbott, is formally, distantly (and rather haughtily) asked to help Colonel Lawrence, who he has never met. Abbott is a busy man, but out of courtesy agrees to meet Lawrence at the Town Hall. Well, he is there and Lawrence is not. Finally, Abbott sees a British officer he does know, Colonel Pierce Joyce, and starts to talk to him, when a man 'hastened up with a swirl of white silk. His headdress was bound with gold cords and there was gold embroidery on his robes. As he walked, he lifted his skirts in front exactly as a woman would.'

Lawrence of Arabia, I presume? But Lawrence does not greet Abbott or even look at him.

'He ignored me and spoke to Joyce, in a high, querulous voice.'

Lawrence tells Joyce to tell Abbott to clear the square in front of the Town Hall and keep it clear. Abbott pointedly tells Lawrence that this might be a difficult task as a number of Colonel Lawrence's Arab comrades in arms are present: 'Colonel, it is obvious there are Hejaz troops among the crowd. If they refuse to go, we'll have to charge them.'

And now the great Lawrence does finally speak to him, he positively hisses and his words about his former men are shocking.

'I don't care what you do. I've finished with them. *Hunt them out!*'

Good God! And as he speaks Abbott's eyes are drawn to Lawrence's hands, they are shaking, not with anger, but with an energy he can't control; it is hysteria, this man is about to crack, if he has not cracked already. Lawrence vanishes inside the Town Hall, departing in a swirl of silk.

Abbott is distinctly unimpressed with T. E., as he soon tells Colonel Donald Cameron of the 12th Light Horse.

'You're not the only one,' Cameron replies. 'Bourchier told me that Lawrence went tramping into the barracks hospital and began screaming at [the Commanding officer of the 4th Field Ambulance] Major Clive Single. He was working himself into a fit of hysterics, so Clive gave him a couple of slaps across the face. That quietened him and he went off.'[36]

(Lawrence will deliberately misremember the incident very differently in his *Seven Pillars of Wisdom*, with a brutish Australian Major slapping him for laughing at him; and his opinion of Australians takes a distinct dip as of this moment: 'These Australians, shouldering me in unceremonious horseplay, had put off half civilisation with their civil clothes. They were dominant tonight, too sure of themselves to be careful: and yet: – as they lazily swaggered those quick bodies, all curves with never a straight line, but with old and disillusioned eyes: and yet: – I felt them thin-tempered, hollow, instinctive; always going to do great things; with the disquieting suppleness of blades half-drawn from the scabbard. Disquieting: not dreadful.'[37])

The slap is not all that Lawrence rewrites. When it comes to the Australians having arrived in Damascus before him, he simply omits to mention that he and his men were second, only recounting their own triumphal entry.

'We drove up the long street to the government buildings on the bank of the Barada. The way was packed with people lined solid on the sidewalks, in the road, at the windows and on the balconies or house-tops. Many were crying, a few cheered faintly, some bolder ones cried our names: but mostly they looked and looked, joy shining in their eyes. A movement like a long sigh from gate to heart of the city, marked our course.'[38]

His ever lower view of Australians is confirmed.

As a breed, they are 'too sure of themselves to be careful ... thin-tempered, hollow, instinctive ... The sporting Australians saw the campaign as a point-to-point with Damascus the post.'[39]

(*Sniff.*)

Some of the British are equally unimpressed with these Johnny-come-earlies, one senior Yeomanry officer snarling, 'The Australians went through Damascus like a mob of cowboys.'[40]

And yet for his part, Major Olden takes no flak from his own superiors for having arrived first.

'General Chauvel sent for me the other day,' he will write of the event, 'and I had to tell him the whole tale, and he did not seem at all displeased.'[41]

Another small parenthesis here. When Lawrence's book comes out to give his own account of the fall of Damascus, Chauvel is *most* displeased and writes to the Director of the Australian War Memorial, to correct the record on the Englishman's claim that his men were first in: 'If any of Feisal's followers did get in during the night, they were unrecognisable as such to the enemy or ourselves ... I am personally of the opinion that the first of the Arab forces to enter Damascus were those who followed Lawrence in and, by that time an Australian Brigade [the 3rd Light Horse Brigade] and at least one regiment of Indian Cavalry had passed right through the city.'[42]

Close parenthesis.

In the there and then, Lieutenant General Sir Philip Chetwode writes to Chauvel after the fall of Damascus: 'You have made history with a vengeance, and your performance will be talked about and quoted long after many more bloody battles in France will have been almost forgotten.'[43]

And Chauvel, in turn, writes to his wife.

'I wrote you last from [Armageddon]. Since then we've marched about 120 miles and I am now writing this on Djemal Pasha's desk in his own house at Damascus. We have had a great and glorious time and the Chief, who motored from Tiberias today to see us, has just told me that our performance is the greatest cavalry feat the world has ever known ...'[44]

•

From Damascus, Allenby's forces push on to Homs, followed by Aleppo right on the Turkish border, when the Turks formally surrender, signing the 'Armistice of Mudros' aboard HMS *Agamemnon* at Port Mudros, on the island of Lemnos, on 30 October 1918.

Around the Arab world, the bells ring out, British gun-boats fire salvos of blanks just to let out the noise, even those dour men who look after the camels are observed to go 'half-crazy and commenced a corroboree at their own'.[45]

For the men of the Australian Light Horse, at this point congregated around, a double tot of rum is issued, and one Trooper takes up the Arab practice of firing his rifle into the air – shouting 'Mum and Dad and Australia! It's all over, boys. It's a bloody Armistice!'[46] – and is only mildly rebuked for his trouble.

'That night convention was relaxed as officers and Light Horse men relaxed, fraternised, and drank each other's health, in the goodly SRD rum.'[47]

The long ride is over.

Hostilities are set to cease at noon the following day, 31 October 1918, a neat year after the Last Charge at Beersheba. Not only has the war in the Middle East come to an end, but so has the Ottoman Empire after 400 years.

It means that, though three years after the event, the very purpose for which Australia had first stormed the cliffs at Gallipoli – to weaken the Ottoman Empire, and remove them as an ally of Germany – had now been fulfilled.

Less than a fortnight later Germany signs the armistice and the Great War is over.

•

And yet while it is one thing to have won the war, it is quite another to get home, and it will be many months before enough ships are assembled to get the Australian Light Horse back to Australia.

In the meantime, there will be trouble for some.

One night in December 1918, three brigades of the Anzac Mounted Division are bivouacked outside the Bedouin village of Surafend, in central Palestine.

Around midnight a Trooper in the 1st New Zealand Machine Gun Squadron is asleep in his tent right on the edge of the camp, when he wakes to the sound of someone first taking his kitbag and now running away with it. Leslie Lowry gives chase, catches the culprit in the sand dunes and brings him down with a rugby tackle. A shot rings out and Lowry slumps, dead.

In the account of Banjo Paterson, 'the New Zealanders and their blood brothers, the Highlanders, organized a revenge party. They were sick and tired of being robbed and murdered by an allegedly friendly population, and they knew that nothing would be done unless they did it themselves. A few Australians went along with them – there couldn't be any trouble on any front without an Australian being in it – and the revenge party followed the thief to his village, recovered the stolen goods, and killed every able-bodied man in the village.'[48] At least three dozen Bedouins are dead.

On hearing the news, Allenby is beyond furious. Nearly a week later the Australian and Kiwi Troopers of the Anzac Mounted Division are on their sandy parade ground, when the Bull arrives. He does not return General Chaytor's salute and cold silence falls before he speaks. Appropriately, Allenby addresses them from his high horse. He is given to understand that there has been a *slaughter* at Surafend. Revenge by blood. It is a DISGRACE. Yes, a Trooper was shot by a Bedouin, but that is no cause for what has happened. One murder does not justify three dozen murders in retribution. The General wants names of those responsible.

Silence.

As expected. The soldier's code.

In cold fury, Allenby talks to them like a headmaster at first:

'You who were not there know who were and know all about it but you are not game to come forward and say so.'[49]

Silence.

The Trooper's name was Leslie Lowry. He was murdered by a Bedouin. Shot through the chest as he chased a thief in the night, twitching in agony as he died. He was revenged.

Allenby continues, his words shooting into an army that have given all for him.

'You have committed an atrocity worse than anything the Turks ever did!'[50]

Silence.

Contemptuous silence. Silence cold as the graves of the thousands of their friends who died at the hands of the Turks, and more particularly the bloody Bedouins.

Allenby's voice grows louder to combat the silence.

'I *was* proud to command you. But now I'll have no more to do with you. You are a lot of cold-blooded murderers and cowards.'[51]

Silence no more; now the hush is broken, there is a buzzing from the men. What does it sound like? To one Trooper it is like 'millions of hives of angry bees'[52], the low hum of instant mutiny. And now one voice rings out:

'ONE.'[53]

One? Allenby gazes at them in wonder. And now a hundred voices ring out:

'TWO.'

My God, are these men actually . . .

'THREE.'

Allenby is being counted out! If the commander is still there by ten, well, numbers will be followed by actions . . .

'FOUR, FIVE, SIX, SEVEN . . .

Discretion is the better part of valour, and Allenby rides off, his face like thunder as a thunderous roar follows him . . .

'EIGHT, NINE, TEN, OUT!'

The Anzacs watch their General disappear, shrinking smaller as they grow louder and a chorus starts '*Out, you bastard, Out, you bastard, Out, you bastard.*'[54]

The ill-will for Allenby's words was manifest and felt so strongly that there are reports that the Australian authorities asked for an apology. None was forthcoming. Repercussions for the Australians at the time were minimal, beyond cancelled leave and a suspension of all gallantry awards then under consideration.

The bad blood is there; but they have spilt blood together. Despite the incident, as Banjo Paterson will chronicle, there remained enormous affection for Allenby from the Australians:

'Every Australian, down to hospital patients, turned out and wildly cheered Allenby when he made his triumphal return to Cairo after smashing up the Turks in Palestine.

'Hospital cases were carried out on stretchers and wounded men limped out on the arms of orderlies to wait by the line till his train went by. As soon as the train was sighted a roar of cheering broke out and was kept up till the train with its solitary figure on the car platform swept out of sight.'[55]

And certainly the Englishman is nothing if not generous in his remarks, as recorded in a personal letter: 'The Australian light horseman combines with a splendid physique a restless activity of mind. This mental quality renders him somewhat impatient of rigid and formal discipline but it confers upon him the gift of adaptability, and this is the secret of much of his success mounted or on foot. In this dual role, on every variety of ground – mountain, plain, desert, swamp, or jungle – the Australian light horseman has proved himself equal to the best. He has earned the gratitude of the Empire and the admiration of the world.'[56]

Something between a bouquet and an olive branch, the letter has an effect.

'There, between their great Commander-in-Chief and the Australians and New Zealanders,' the Official Historian Henry Gullett will note, 'the painful Surafend affair rested. It was characteristic of the strong temper and of the frailties of both. Both had erred in anger. The sincerity of Allenby's final words to them was never doubted by the troops. Surafend, however, should not be forgotten.'[57]

As Allenby's train pulls away, taking him to Alexandria and then home to England, Banjo Paterson records one Australian Trooper gazing after it, puffing on his pipe and pronouncing 'the Australian farewell'.

'Good-bye, Bull,' he says. 'That was a hard thing you said about us. But a man must make mistakes sometimes. I've made mistakes meself.'[58]

•

The good news for the Troopers in the early months of 1919 is . . . they are going home! The terrible news is that they are told by the Australian Army that their horses can *not* return to Australia with them, and they must be handed back to the Remount Depot.

The response is somewhere between grief and fury – and sometimes both.

Worst hit are those who have brought their own horses from Australia and have been with them through the entire campaign. They have come to these parts together on a ship, ridden together across the Sinai, charged Turks together and often bled together. The whole way through, the thought had been that they would return to Australia together, and perhaps be cheered in a parade down the main street of their home towns.

But now, after achieving victory together, the Troopers are meant to just hand their beloved horses over, to be sold to the *locals*?

It is nothing less than a complete betrayal. Of the horses. Of the Troopers. Many of them, in fact most of them, have a bond with their horse that makes them family.

'The companionship and trust of a horse are a very good thing to know,' it will be well expressed. 'The soft and welcoming whinny of a horse you have loved and cared for; a horse you have ridden often and far, it may be years ago, is something to remember always.'[59]

And now they are to break that bond, by betrayal? Leave the horse in Egypt? Why, hadn't they seen the way the locals treat horses, mistreating them, flogging them literally to death? They had to hand their horses to *them*?

No. Just no.

Many of them would rather just put a clean bullet in their horse's heads and end it, rather than have them end their days working for the Arabs.

One Trooper, Major Oliver Hogue – who will come to literary fame as 'Trooper Bluegum' – even writes a poem about it, entitled 'The Horses Stayed Behind', with a part of it reading . . .

I don't think I could stand the thought of my old fancy hack,
Just crawling round old Cairo with a Gyppo on his back . . .

No, I think I'd better shoot him and tell a little lie,
He floundered in a wombat hole and then lay down to die,
Maybe I'll get court-martialled, but I'm damned if I'm inclined
To go back to Australia and leave my horse behind.[60]

Officers, of course, are far less likely to circumvent army orders and will fret for many years to come over just what happened to their mounts. One of these is that imposing mountain of a man, Brigadier 'Bill' Granville Ryrie, who writes years later of his lost horse, sold in Cairo:

Plain Bill, you are wanted by Granville, the fellow who rode
you before
Across the bleak hills of Monaro, and over the seas to the war,
You flinched not, nor flew from gunfire, you ran at the Turk
on the plain,
And now 'tis your master is calling and wanting his waler
again . . .[61]

The bulk of the Australian Light Horse return home within six months of Armistice; 136,000 have seen service in Gallipoli and the Levant.

Trooper Maurie Evans, who had first read about the shots fired by Gavrilo Princip in Sarajevo and the immediate aftermath while having breakfast in Kyogle four years earlier, disembarks at Melbourne and writes as the last line in his diary: 'And though I have many pleasant memories of my wanderings I hope I may never wander again under the aegis of the Army. *Inshallah.*'[62]

Over to you, Banjo.

The Last Parade

Over the sea you brought us,
Over the leagues of foam:
Now we have served you fairly
Will you not take us home?

Home to the Hunter River,
To the flats where the lucerne grows;
Home where the Murrumbidgee
Runs white with the melted snows.

This is a small thing, surely!
Will not you give command
That the last of the old campaigners
Go back to their native land?

They looked at the grim commander,
But never a sign he made.
'Dismiss!' and the old campaigners
Moved off from their last parade.

EPILOGUE

Perhaps a cross, or a row of shells,
On wind-swept dusty 'rise,'
Will mark where a brave man left the race
With a willing heart and a smiling face,
His grave a Bedouin camping-place—
But memory never dies![1]

Trooper Arthur Beatty, 4th Australian Light Horse Regiment

General Harry Chauvel, GCMG, KCB, arrived home in Australia on 14 September 1919, settling in Melbourne. Within three months, he was appointed as Inspector General of the now all-volunteer Australian Military Forces, the most senior post in the Army, and made a member of the Council of Defence, becoming Chief of the General Staff in June 1923 – responsible for the overall organisation of the Army.

His rise continued throughout the 1920s, until in November 1929, under the Prime Ministership of James Scullin, in company with John Monash, he was elevated to full General, the first two Australians to be so honoured.

He retired from the Army less than six months later, taking up board positions on three companies, while also devoting himself to ex-servicemen's causes, including sitting on the committees of both the Australian and Victorian War Memorials.

'He was a great horseman, and it was a really important thing for him, to keep that horsemanship up, and . . . to feel that heritage of being a Light Horseman,' Chauvel's grandson, James Maberly, would recount. 'A particular charger was brought to him by a groom every day and he would go for a ride in South Yarra. Even on those days when he was too ill, the horse would still arrive and he would say, "I'm terribly sorry, I can't do it today," or my grandmother would go down and explain . . . but the charger always came.'[2]

For the coronation of George VI in 1937, it was General Chauvel who led the Australian contingent, a supreme honour and a measure of how highly he was regarded.

By the time of World War II, the nation was again able to harness his military experience when, in June 1940, Chauvel became the founding Inspector-in-Chief of the newly established Volunteer Defence Corps – modelled on the British Home Guard – which saw him once more in uniform and moving around the country. Alas, in 1944 he fell ill, and on 4 March 1945, he died in Melbourne aged 79.

One thing that helped keep the Chauvel name alive was the work of his nephew, Charles Edward Chauvel, an Australian filmmaker, producer and screenwriter, who made many successful films, including *Forty Thousand Horsemen*, the first film about the charge at Beersheba. Starring Chips Rafferty, the film was long on romantic sub-plots and a little short on accuracy, not to mention budget and locations. Several hundred horsemen had to make do with charging repeatedly up and down the sandhills of . . . Cronulla, instead of Egypt. Nonetheless it was a hit and captured the Australian imagination with the terrific drama of the final charge and led to Beersheba living on as a battle and much deserved legend.

Brigadier General William Grant CMG, DSO and bar, VD and Order of the Nile. After the war, Brigadier General William Grant returned to the family farm on the Darling Downs, and the following year was appointed to command the 1st Light Horse Brigade in the Citizen Military Forces. He left the Army in 1928.

Grant continued to breed sheep, cattle and horses at his property at Bowenville, until selling up in 1931 and moving to a new farm in the Dirranbandi district. He died in 1939, aged 68.

'Members of the late Brigadier General Grant's old regiment – the 11th Light Horse – formed a guard of honour . . . in Peel street today,' the *Warwick Daily News* reported, 'while his coffin was borne to the waiting gun carriage by men who served under him in the war.

'At the crematorium, to the roll of a Queensland Cameron Highlander's drum, three volleys were fired and the "Last Post" sounded.'[3]

General Edmund Allenby, 1st Viscount Allenby, GCB, GCMG, GCVO, KStJ. At the conclusion of the war, Allenby was rewarded by a grateful nation by promotion to the rank of Field Marshal, and being made a Viscount, before returning to Egypt as Great Britain's High Commissioner, a post he retained until his retirement in 1925. At this point, as noted in a report in the *Sydney Morning Herald*, he took what amounted to the first extended holiday of his adult life, with his first port of call with Lady Allenby being none other than . . . Australia.

'I am here merely as a tripper,' he told the *Sydney Morning Herald*, 'and to renew acquaintance with the men who were my good friends and followers in Palestine and France. This great country has been a revelation to me . . .'[4]

Allenby does indeed meet with many of the Australian officers and men he commanded as he and his wife tour around, but the rambunctious, ever aggressive and ever war-like man they remember is no more.

'I am sure those of you who have been through the horrors of war will agree with me,' he says in an address at the Memorial Hall of Moss Vale to a standing-room only gathering, 'that the very last thing we want is another war. We fought our fight and gained victories and saved the Empire but we lost many near and dear to us. In doing so many of our dearest friends are gone and many others are crippled for life. We fought because we had to fight but I am certain the sincere wish of all of us is that we shall never have to fight again. It is for these reasons that I am a pacifist . . .'[5]

Lord Allenby died on 14 May 1936 in London, aged 75.

General 'Hellfire' Jack Royston, CMG, DSO, survived the poison gas he had voluntarily sniffed. After the war – and still with the bullet in his leg from Romani – he returned to South Africa, where he raised sheep and cattle on his several properties in the Natal as well as, no doubt, exhausting the many horses he bred and rode. He was not forgotten by the Australians who had served under him and in 1934 was invited by the 8th Australian Light Horse Regiment Association to attend the centenary of Victoria's establishment and, more particularly, the dedication of Melbourne's Shrine of Remembrance. At all public military appearances he was cheered to the echo by his former charges and, in fact, visited three other states in his tour.

Still going strong, he was the leader of the South African contingent at the coronation of George VI, before he died in Durban on 25 April 1942, at the age of 82. His second wife would write of him that 'he loved his Australians to the last'.[6] (In an eccentric ritual that Hellfire Jack would no doubt approve of, this fine woman was known afterwards to occasionally dance naked in the moonlight in the hope of summoning his spirit.)

After General Chauvel departed for Australia in April of 1919, **Brigadier General Granville Ryrie, KCMG, CB, VD,** briefly took over as commander of the AIF in Egypt. In October of that year he was knighted, and in the same month returned to Australia three days before the Federal election, where he was again returned as the Member for North Sydney. Throwing himself once more into a career of Federal politics, he rose to the position of Assistant (Honorary) Minister of Defence in Billy Hughes' post-war government. In 1927, he retired from politics to become Australia's High Commissioner in London, a post he held for the next five years. He returned to Australia, and died in Sydney on 2 October 1937, aged 72.

Major Banjo Paterson, CBE, went back to journalism, writing for such august journals as the *Sydney Mail* and *Smith's Weekly* before becoming the editor of the *Sydney Sportsman*, a racing journal. His finest poetry was published in 1923, in a book called *Collected Verse*, and, after retiring from full-time work in 1930, he spent his remaining years writing poems, as well as the occasional story for the *Sydney Morning Herald*. He died after a brief illness, on 5 February 1941, aged 76.

As extraordinarily brave as **Colonel Alexander White** was in leading his men over the top at the Battle of the Nek, history would not judge him kindly, with Charles Bean noting, 'the gallant White, acting as a sportsman rather than a soldier, by leading forward the first line deprived his regiment of the control which should have been exercised over its operations. Its morale did not require the stimulus of personal leadership; and had his protest been added to Brazier's [Colonel Noel Brazier, commander 10th Light Horse], Antill might have discontinued the attack.'[7]

Colonel Arthur Olden, DSO, returned to Australia to resume his practice, in Perth, as a dental surgeon, filling cavities, extracting teeth and failing to mention that, as a matter of fact, he was the fellow who accepted the surrender of the city of Damascus after 400 years of Turkish rule. In 1921 he wrote *Westralian Cavalry in the War*. He died in 1949, aged 68.

After his grievous wound at Beersheba, **Lieutenant Guy Haydon** recovered in the hospital at Cairo. In the next bed was a British Cavalry Officer who had seen three years' service on the Western Front before being transferred to the Levant just in time for the Beersheba campaign.

'I have seen every action in which the British Cavalry have taken part,' he will tell the Australian, 'but the charge of the LH at Beersheba yesterday, is the finest thing that I have ever seen mounted troops do.'[8]

Haydon would always remember the accolade. He returned to the Haydon Horse Stud in early 1919, to embrace Bonnie and meet his daughter Patricia for the first time, and continue his recuperation. But his recovery from his war wound would be long, arduous, and never truly complete, though he was able to resume work as a grazier on the Liverpool Plains near Quirindi. He and Bonnie had two more children, Isabelle and John.

Though he never again found the equal of his beloved horse Midnight, he was active in the equine world, supporting the local pony club and acting as judge in many Bushmen's Carnivals. After falling ill in 1964, he died on 1 August 1965, aged 76.

The Haydon Stud remains in the family to this day and the bullet that killed Midnight and wounded Guy is a family treasure. I was privileged to be able to stay at the homestead and go through their archives for a weekend in mid-January 2023.

On a terrible day some time after November 1917, Thomas Bell of Walpeup received a strange and troubling communication.

> Dear Sir,
>
> With reference to the report of the regrettable loss of your nephew, the late No. 3650, Private H. T. Wickham, 4th Light Horse Regiment, I am now in receipt of advice which shows that he died in Beersheba, on 1 November 1917, of wounds received in action, and was buried the following day . . .[9]

Thomas Bell and his wife Margaret are deeply confused. Thomas quickly writes to the authorities, advising that, while they don't have a nephew H. T. Wickham, they do have a son, **Harry Bell**, with those initials, but he had gone droving in Queensland, and they have not heard since.

After a further exchange of letters, the dreadful truth emerges. It is indeed their second son who has been killed, fighting under an assumed name. A second blow will fall the next year, when their first-born son, Samuel, is also killed, while serving with the 57th Battalion near Villers-Bretonneux.

Trooper Thomas O'Leary was awarded the Military Medal for his derring-do at Beersheba. Returning home in February 1919, he never quite settled down, as he became something of a hermit, residing on the edge of Townsville in little more than a humpy.

In 1956, aged 72, he died and was buried in a pauper's grave in Townsville. In 2013, however, the local RSL rallied, and a memorial headstone was placed atop the grave.

In saving Captain Douglas Rutherford, **Flight Lieutenant Frank McNamara VC, CB, CBE**, received the only Victoria Cross awarded to an Australian airman in World War I. He rose to Air Vice Marshal in the Royal Australian Air Force and died in 1961.

Trooper Tibby Cotter, the Dennis Lillee of his day, is still remembered. There is a Tibby Cotter Bridge in Sydney that takes cricket fans, particularly, over busy Anzac Parade to get to the nearby SCG.

The Australian Cricketers' Association has an annual Tibby Cotter Address and the speaker in 2022 was none other than Dennis Lillee.

Tibby lies in Beersheba still, under a cypress tree in Row D, his grave adorned with a small headstone of Italian marble, bearing the inscription:

TROOPER ALBERT COTTER, 924.
12TH AUSTRALIAN LIGHT HORSE.
KILLED IN ACTION, OCTOBER 31, 1917.
AGE, 33.[10]

Trooper Ion Idriess returned to Australia and took up a sterling career – not surprisingly from how wonderfully evocative his diaries are – as a writer, going on to pen no fewer than 50 books. He averaged a book every 10 months, and would say of himself, that he could 'write like stinking hell'[11] and twice wrote and published three books in a year. (I am in awe.) He died in 1979, aged 89.

Bill the Bastard was so beloved, he was not shot, but rather placed among several packhorses sent back to Gallipoli with Charles Bean straight after the war to gather artefacts. After that trip was over he remained, finishing his days in the care of those on the staff of the War Graves Commission looking after Gallipoli's war cemeteries. Inevitably he was given a grave of his own, with the epitaph:

'BILL'
AUSTRALIAN LIGHT HORSE
1914 to 1924
A WALER AND ONE OF THE BEST[12]

Brigadier General George MacLeay Macarthur-Onslow, CMG, DSO, VD, was mentioned in dispatches and awarded the Distinguished Service Order for his service at the Battle of Romani. He was twice more mentioned in dispatches and awarded the Order of the Nile 3rd Class. Evacuated with typhoid in early 1919, he returned to Australia. In October 1919 he was appointed a Companion of the Order of St Michael and St George. He died in 1931.

Sir Ross Macpherson Smith, KBE, MC and Bar, DFC and two Bars, AFC, would go on to great fame as the winner of the Great Air Race in 1919, between England and Australia, winning £10,000 with his co-pilot and brother, Lieutenant Keith Smith, in their Vickers Vimy plane. Ross Smith returned to England in order to attempt an around the world flight in a Vickers Viking amphibian. He was killed in a test flight near London on 13 April 1922.

Lawrence of Arabia, Colonel T. E. Lawrence, CB, DSO, ended his war and began his peace still fighting for the Arabs, serving as Prince Feisal's personal representative at the Paris post-war peace conferences, given a seat at the table with Presidents and Prime Ministers to argue Prince Feisal's case at Versailles. (Lawrence also wrote a speech for Feisal to deliver at Versailles in Arabic; Lawrence then read it out in English. President Wilson informed Lawrence that the French were upset that no French version of the speech was provided, so Lawrence translated it off the cuff for their benefit!)

For years Lawrence had been promising Arab leaders, starting with Feisal, that, in return for their help in destroying the Ottoman Empire, they would be the ones who would fill the power vacuum. Alas, it does not turn out like that. Winning a war is one thing, winning the peace quite another. Why? The machine of empire was able to defeat whatever ideals Lawrence still possessed. The Sykes–Picot pact had been secretly struck, dividing up the Middle East neatly for the French and the British. As for an empowered Arab state, or states, this is not something now desired or delivered by Winston Churchill or his counterparts.

For the die is not only cast but set. Syria, for example, had been promised to Feisal as the first bastion of Arab rule, but is now in the thrall of the French. Egypt? That goes with Britain. Palestine? It falls to the British, not by war, but by accord. This is the way that the Great War began, and this is the way it shall end; with byzantine secret agreements unknown to those who fight.

Lawrence is outraged, and says so with some vigour. To whom? King George V, amongst others, and to the horror of the watching Winston Churchill, Lawrence refuses to accept his DSO from the amazed monarch and also turns down a knighthood to boot in protest against the Sykes–Picot pact.

The reality is, just as the British rule Palestine, the French rule Syria by mandate. Various 'accords' are granted to Feisal, but it is colonialism blessed by the League of Nations; not freedom or independence. But Colonel Lawrence has never been one to accept reality; he shapes it. And now he vanishes from it; resigning his rank and, in time, his identity.

Lawrence returned to an England where word of his derring-do had spread. An American journalist, Lowell Thomas, has made Lawrence into a sensation with his famous talks on the Middle East campaign, 'The Last Crusade', starring the romantic exploits and fantastic photographs of Colonel Lawrence. The talks began at Covent Garden, and were meant to last just two weeks, but were transferred to the Albert Hall when the scale of public demand was realised. Over one million people came to hear Thomas talk over the next few months about his incredible 'discovery', the man he dubbed Lawrence of Arabia. Lowell Thomas was amused to receive a telegram from Lawrence himself: 'I SAW YOUR SHOW LAST NIGHT AND THANK GOD THE LIGHTS WERE OUT!'[13]

Lawrence, unable to resist, in fact attended the talk many times unrecognised by all when entering dressed in a tweed suit. When the lights went down, all were drinking in the stories of this magical man who conquered the Turks with his will and sense of destiny; when the lights went up none realised that this elegant small man in their midst was Lawrence of Arabia, and he exited time and again into his beloved anonymity. The talks led to a book, *With Lawrence in Arabia*, and the legend was printed and has lived on ever since. Lowell Thomas himself began to doubt some of Lawrence's stories about his life before the war; when he asked Lawrence about them he received a laugh in response and this telling reply: 'History isn't made up of truth anyhow, so why worry?'[14]

Asked what the secret was to his sudden worldwide fame, Lawrence answered 'Fancy-dress'.[15] As to whether Lawrence wanted anonymity, Thomas summed it up very well in one reminiscence of his friend and subject:

'There is an old Turkish saying which admirably illustrates the character of TE and which, being interpreted, signifies: "He had a genius for backing into the limelight."'[16]

Such was Lawrence's fame and talents he could easily have remained in public life, or in high military rank, and prospered mightily. Nevertheless, despite that fame, he re-enlisted under an alias as an aircraftsman in the Royal Air Force, working in the staggeringly humble role as one of the ground crew, while living in an even more humble cottage on the edge of the aerodrome in Dorset. And yet, still he lived an extraordinary life.

Returning late from leave one day 'Aircraftman John Hume Ross', as Lawrence then called himself, apologised to his annoyed superior, and when an explanation was demanded, he offered only the excuse that he had lost track of time while dining with the Archbishop of Canterbury, George Bernard Shaw and Lady Astor. It was true.

Lawrence was lucky to get into the RAF in the first place; his admissions officer thought there was something strange about well-spoken John Ross, and asked for references. Lawrence returned the next day with beautifully written references, forged by himself. The amused admissions officer, one W. E. Johns, was an aspiring author himself, working on a book about an airman called Biggles. After ensuring that this 'John Ross' was not a criminal, he was allowed to take a medical; which noted the subject to be very nervous and also that he had evidently suffered an incredibly severe beating in the past on his legs and buttocks, for which he gave no explanation. Inevitably, the press was tipped off as to who 'John Ross' was, which led Lawrence to resign and re-enlist under another alias; a pattern that would repeat for the remainder of his life.

Back in Britain, in terms of physical excitement, Lawrence's major joy was riding his Brough Superior motorcycle too fast along the twisting and turning country lanes. Alas, on 13 May 1935, while doing precisely that, he roared up from a dip in the road to see two small boys on their bicycles just ahead. He swerved, lost control and, ultimately, his life. He was 46 years old.

'I have lost a good friend and a valued comrade,' Sir Edmund Allenby would write. 'Lawrence was under my command, but, after acquainting him with my strategical plan, I gave him a free hand. His co-operation was marked by the utmost loyalty, and I never had anything but praise for his work which, indeed, was invaluable throughout the campaign.'[17]

Lawrence's own classic account of his adventures in the Great War, *Seven Pillars of Wisdom*, helped cement his fame. It is a spellbinding account of his war-time experiences. Part reportage, part poetry, part embellishment, uniquely Lawrence; the book remains a classic of literature, if not the most reliable history book in the world. One of the many who praised it as a work of genius was George Bernard Shaw.

One of the few who knew what actually happened and was infuriated was Chauvel, who wrote despairingly to Allenby in 1929: 'My Dear Field Marshal, I am much concerned about the acceptance of so much of Lawrence's production "Revolt in the Desert". The official historian [Gullett] seems to have swallowed it whole. The proofs I have just seen are teeming with quotations from it . . . they have little or no foundation in fact . . . I am naturally most concerned about Lawrence's absurd claims re the administration of Damascus.' Unfortunately, legend trumps facts, no matter how many footnotes you might add. Chauvel included 13 points in his letter to Allenby including Point 8: 'There is the same old lie that Feisal's Arab forces had penetrated into Damascus on the night of September 30/October 1.'[18] Luckily, Chauvel did not live long enough to see David Lean's *Lawrence of Arabia*, which prevented his head from exploding.

After the war was over, the highly regarded **Colonel Ismet** went on to a hugely successful career in politics, first as one of the Prime Ministers to the first President of the Turkish republic, Mustafa Kemal Atatürk, and after Atatürk's death, the only candidate to succeed him. As President İsmet İnönü, the political achievement with which he is most credited is keeping Turkey out of World War II. He died in 1973, aged 89.

Major Richard Meinertzhagen would achieve enduring fame because of the Haversack Ruse . . . but we'll get to that. In the meantime, the intelligence officer would also claim that his ruse with dropping the opium-laden cigarettes worked and that after capture some of the Turks seemed to be notably 'befuddled', and 'barely coherent'.

After the war, he also went to the Versailles Peace Conference and became General Allenby's chief political officer, a witness and participant in the 'Palestine Mandate', which is no less than a retrospective rubber stamp to British rule handed over by the newly created League of Nations. After Meinertzhagen's first marriage fell apart, he married one Anne Constance, with whom he had three children. Alas, as a court would later solemnly maintain, just after the birth of the third child, Anne was doing target practice with her husband, when she . . . accidentally shot herself in the head.

No, seriously.

The fact that the fatal bullet entered the skull of the small woman from above seemed odd, most particularly when noting how much her husband towered over her, but nothing was proved and he was not charged. At the very least it may be maintained that Meinertzhagen did not grieve for long and began a very close live-in relationship with Tessa Clay, who he introduced as his housekeeper, his niece or his cousin, as the mood took him. She was 30 years his junior, very attractive and, remarkably, lived longer than he did. Meinertzhagen went on to have a long career in the field of intelligence, burnishing his own legend by publishing his edited and embellished diaries, one of which bore the appropriate title *Diary of a Black Sheep*, and several landmark books on ornithology, although typically enough after his death these too were exposed as including many deceptions by their mischievous and vainglorious author. (One biography of Meinertzhagen was subtitled *The Life and Legend of a Colossal Fraud*.) He died in 1967.

His principal legacy, to this day, is the Haversack Ruse – though there has been enormous controversy over just who was primarily responsible for it. The central charge by his accusers is that Meinertzhagen over-egged the whole story to make it appear like he was the sole originator and executor of the idea, and had done everything from doctor his diary to deliberately excluding from his account those who did deserve credit.

That he altered his diary is beyond dispute, though just how much of his account was full-on fabricated continues to be much debated. Whatever the fine detail, there seems no doubt that Meinertzhagen was intimately involved in the ruse, and that was certainly acknowledged in roughly contemporary accounts by everyone from Lawrence of Arabia to Winston Churchill to Lloyd George, the last of whom wrote that the ruse was suggested to Allenby 'by a brilliant young officer called Meinertzhagen, who subsequently, at the risk of his life, successfully carried it out'.[19]

At least let us say that, whatever the whys and wherefores of the actual ruse, the effect was multiplied many times over. Lawrence of Arabia himself wrote that 'after the Meinertzhagen success, deceptions, which for the ordinary general were just witty hors d'oeuvres before battle, became for Allenby a main point of strategy'.[20]

With greater objectivity, the British Official History declared accurately that the ruse was to have 'an extraordinary effect, an effect, indeed, hardly to be matched in the annals of modern war'.[21]

For, whatever else, the legend of the Haversack Ruse has been credited with spawning dozens of other schemes of subterfuge tried on the enemy. It is even said to have been the genesis of Prime Minister Winston Churchill's idea in the course of World War II to form the 'London Controlling Section', devoted to producing deception campaigns for the Allies on an industrial scale with considerable success. One such was the famed 'Operation Mincemeat', where in 1943, to aid the invasion of Sicily, a corpse, the 'man who never was', was given a false identity, that of 'Captain William Martin' and planted with false battle plans and military correspondence for the Nazis to find as he drifted ashore. The Haversack Ruse successfully enacted once more, this time with a body!

For his part, **General Friedrich Kress von Kressenstein** denied being taken in by the ruse at all.

'There is an opinion to be found in English and Turkish war literature,' he would write, 'that I was deceived by the satchel of Herr Meinertzhagen to move my only reserve (the 7th Division) behind our right wing just before the 3rd Battle of Gaza instead of sending it to Beersheba. This is false.'[22]

Fair enough. But against that, he was hardly likely to write that the ruse got me, *haken, schnur und senkblei*, 'hook, line *und* sinker', was he? And the Turkish account, *Yildirim*, by Lieutenant Colonel Hüseyin Hüsnü Emir, says the German was completely taken in, and believed in Meinertzhagen's bag ruse with high probability.[23]

Also indicating that Kress von Kressenstein was indeed taken in was his report to the Yildirim Army Group headquarters, three weeks after the charge, when, while being honest enough to say, 'I had no idea Beersheba would be captured so rapidly, and did not see the need for reinforcements,' he also insisted that, 'it was believed that the enemy's main attack was to be against Gaza, and that the attack on Beersheba was just a diversion. Besides, a possible invasion from the coast had to be watched.'[24]

Either way, Kress von Kressenstein would endeavour to make the best of the defeat, noting that the 'understrength Turkish battalion entrusted with Beersheba's defence doggedly held out with great courage and in so doing fulfilled its obligation. They held up two English cavalry divisions for six hours and had prevented them from expanding their outflanking manoeuvres around the Beersheba–Hebron Road.'[25]

In the summer of 1918, Kress von Kressenstein was transferred to a German command in the Caucasus. After the war, he returned to Germany. He retired as a Lieutenant General in 1929, and died in Munich in 1948.

Following the fall of Damascus, the Three Pashas fled into exile. **Enver Pasha** was condemned to death in his absence by the Turkish Court Martials. Enver sought refuge in Moscow, where he was granted an audience with Lenin. He returned to his home country in 1922 during the Turkish War of Independence, dying in a cavalry charge, mown down by machine-gun fire. Today, he is an infamous figure due to his involvement and attributed responsibility for the Armenian Genocide; an atrocity that has become increasingly recognised as one of the great horrors of the twentieth century.

Djemal Pasha went into exile in Switzerland; like Enver Pasha he was sentenced to death *in absentia*. Djemal then trained another army, the Royal Army of Afghanistan. While attempting to negotiate an accord with the Bolsheviks, he was assassinated on the 21st of July 1922, by the Armenian Revolution Federation. Djemal had been singled out as a perpetrator of the Armenian Genocide; one of eight men killed as part of 'Operation Nemesis', named after the Greek goddess of divine retribution.

In mid-November 1917, the parents of **Flight Lieutenant Alaric Pinder Boor,** received the cable they had been dreading for three years.

> Deeply regret to inform you that Lieutenant A. P. Boor,
> General List and R. F. C. died of wounds October 31st.
>
> Army Council expresses sympathy. [26]

Though devastated at his loss, they were at least honoured on his behalf to receive another cable shortly afterwards.

> Dear Sir, — The King and Queen deeply regret to hear of
> the loss you and the Army have sustained by the death of
> your son in the service of his Country, and I am commanded
> to convey to you the expression of their Majesties' true
> sympathy with you in your sorrow, —
>
> Yours very
> faithfully,
> F. M. PONSONBY
> Keeper of the Privy Purse[27]

Boor's Commanding Officer, Major Horace Haycock, in turn, also wrote to Alaric's parents.

'Knowing from him the affection you had for him, for often he spoke of his mother and father and of the happy times he had at home and of the fact that my own Mother and Dad have lost a son I can feel and sympathise with you – his everlasting topics were home, his people, and his fiancée. In the few months I knew him I came to know you deeply [and] how almost yearningly he longed to get back to see you all. Oh it is cruel! and my deepest sympathy goes out to you who are left to mourn his loss.'

Haycock signed off his letter:

'With the very deepest sympathy for you who had so grand a man for a son. Believe me.'[28]

Alaric's beloved fiancée, Ida Rawlings, mourned him for the rest of her days. She eventually married a shoe salesman and they had one son.

•

There has long been a claim that there is a direct line between the Last Charge at Beersheba, the Balfour Declaration, and the establishment of the State of Israel in 1948.

On the occasion of the centenary of the charge, in a ceremony held at the Commonwealth War Graves Cemetery in Beersheba where the likes of Tibby Cotter, Harry Wickham, Ben Meredith, Alaric Boor and all the rest are buried, the Israeli Prime Minister Benjamin Netanyahu did not hold back:

'Nearly 4000 years ago Abraham came to Beersheba, the city of seven wells.

'Exactly 100 years ago brave ANZAC soldiers liberated Beersheba for the sons and daughters of Abraham and opened the gateway for the Jewish people to re-enter the stage of history.'

The Australian Prime Minister Malcolm Turnbull broadly agreed saying: 'Had the Ottoman rule in Palestine and Syria not been overthrown by the Australians and the New Zealanders, the Balfour Declaration would have been empty words.'[29]

The caveat, of course, is that beyond completely ignoring the efforts and sacrifice of the British 20th Corps in taking Beersheba, the remarks are uttered by politicians for purposes political rather than historians only interested in what actually happened. In a lecture on 30 October 2017, delivered at the Australian National University, the esteemed Australian military historian Dr Jean Bou noted of Turnbull's and Netanyahu's speeches, 'I think it's pretty fair to observe this is an idea that is being pushed by politics and vested interests. Clearly the Australian Government, for various reasons, is trying to build closer ties with Israel and vice versa, and Beersheba is becoming the vehicle by and large, by which this is done to a large extent . . . I think you have to draw a pretty long bow to say that Australia somehow has had a role in the creation of the State of Israel.'[30]

Against that, for the Balfour Declaration of 1917 – which promised a state for Jews to be established in Palestine – to be fulfilled, Britain first had to capture Palestine. And to do so Britain was heavily dependent on the Australian Light Horse, so although Bou's long bow is indeed long – and it winds around far more battles than just Beersheba – it is there.

Either way no-one disputes, then or now, the wonder of that charge and the accomplishments of the mighty Australian Light Horse overall. It remains so revered in the Australian Armed Forces that, to this day, even in an entirely mechanised age, the 'Light Horse' live on in six units. And even though now mounted on Armoured Personnel Carriers, the traditions of the Light Horse are maintained and the accomplishments of the original units hailed as stars to steer by. One of the cavalry units of APCs, the 4/19th Prince of Wales Light Horse, maintains the shoulder patch of the 4th Light Horse, and carries Beersheba as one of the battle honours on the regiment's flag. Serving members of that regiment commemorate the charge each year on the day the anniversary falls.

Whatever the whys and wherefores of the geopolitical impact of that charge, nothing changes the allure of the story. For, well over a century after they charged towards the setting sun in the ultimate death-or-glory ride, the story of what was accomplished in that thundering twilight still has the capacity to 'stiffen the sinews and summon up the blood' among their fellow Australians.

In late April 2023 I journeyed to Beersheba to see up close the place where it all happened. The once tiny settlement is now a bustling town of 250,000 people. In Beersheba I gazed upon the ancient surrounds that indeed reminded me – through the shimmering heat, the rolling sands and clinging bushes – of the Australian outback. That Anzac Day, in a corner of a foreign field that is forever a war grave cemetery, I went to pay my respects to those who never saw their home again, and was able to lay yellow roses on the graves of the likes of Tibby Cotter, Alaric Pinder Boor and the forever young Harry Bell.

As an Australian writer, I do my best to make our history come alive. I feel both a duty to get it right, and endlessly privileged that I have the opportunity to bring such extraordinary stories to a wider audience. The sad part is that more often than not I am writing about people long gone, which means there is no chance of personally shaking the hands of these heroes who are mostly long forgotten, men whom I have come to know.

And here was a case in point. For here they were, in this quiet grave-yard of white headstones while, around them the once-tiny hamlet of Beersheba has grown, their deeds no more than a footnote, if that, in the collective consciousness.

But allow me to say, at least here: Bravo, gentlemen, to you and yours.

What a story. What a ride!

After leaving the cemetery, as the sun started to fade just as it did on that remarkable day, I stood atop Tel el Saba itself, gazing east. There, the ground they charged over is remarkably unchanged, more easily allowing the indulgence of squinting my eyes and cocking my ear to imagine just what it would have been like to see and hear them charging forth.

Echoes of the final lines of Banjo's most famous poem came to me, and I feel sure that Banjo – of all people – would excuse me if I adapt those lines a little, and finish thus:

> The Last Charge at Beersheba is a household yarn today,
> And Australians tell the story of that ride . . .

THE END

NOTES

Epigraph

1 Idriess, *The Desert Column*, ETT Imprint, Sydney, 2017, e-book, p. 8.

Dramatis personae

1 Paterson, *Happy Dispatches*, Angus & Roberston, Sydney, 1935, chapter 15.
2 Gullett, *The Australian Imperial Force in Sinai and Palestine, 1914–1918*, Angus & Robertson, Sydney, 1923, p. 380.

Introduction and acknowledgements

1 *Minyip Guardian and Sheep Hills Advocate*, 25 February 1918, p. 3.

Prologue   The Charge of the Light Brigade

1 UK National Army Museum, 'The order that launched the charge of the Light Brigade, 1854', Accession Number NAM. 1962-11-4-3.

Chapter one   The guns of August

1 Bean, *Official History of Australia in the War of 1914–1918, Vol. I*, Angus & Robertson, Sydney, 1941, p. 93.
2 Maurice Evans, war diaries, August 1914 – December 1918, Mitchell Library, MLMSS 1576/Item 1.
3 Great Britain, Parliament, The Governor-General to the Secretary of State, Telegram No. 13, 3 August 1914 (Received 6:30 p.m.), *Correspondence Regarding the Overseas Assistance Afforded to His Majesty's Government by His Majesty's Overseas Dominions*, T. Fisher Unwin, London, 1914, p. 4.
4 Bean, *Official History of Australia in the War of 1914–1918, Vol. II*, Angus & Robertson, Sydney, 1941, p. 31.
5 Kannengiesser, *The Campaign in Gallipoli*, Hutchinson & Co., London, 1928, p. 25.

6 Kannengiesser, *The Campaign in Gallipoli*, p. 25.

7 Kannengiesser, *The Campaign in Gallipoli*, p. 26.

8 Kannengiesser, *The Campaign in Gallipoli*, p. 26.

9 Jones, *A Thousand Miles of Battles*, Time-Life Books, Australia, 1987, p. 8.

10 Jones, *A Thousand Miles of Battles*, p. 8.

11 Hill, 'Grant, William (1870–1939)', *Australian Dictionary of Biography*, National Centre of Biography, Australian National University, 1983.

12 Author's note: Technically it was still the 6th Light Horse Regiment, but things are already in train to re-badge it as the 8th Light Horse Regiment, as it will stay for the rest of the war.

13 *The Argus*, 3 May 1914, p. 14.

14 *The Queanbeyan Observer*, 4 December 1914, p. 3.

15 *South Western Times*, 6 November 1917, p. 3.

16 Paterson, 'Queensland Mounted Infantry', poem, 1900.

17 Idriess, *The Desert Column*, p. 98.

18 *Sunday Times*, 6 December 1914, p. 14.

19 *Sunday Times*, 6 December 1914, p. 14.

20 *The Sydney Morning Herald*, 1 January 1915, p. 3.

21 *The London Gazette*, 5 November 1914, Issue No. 28963, p. 8997.

22 Djemal Pasha, *Memories of a Turkish Statesman*, Hutchinson & Co., London, 1922, p. 137.

23 Pasha, *Memories of a Turkish Statesman*, p. 138 [reported speech].

24 Pasha, *Memories of a Turkish Statesman*, p. 138 [reported speech].

25 Drane, *Complete Anzac Gallipoli War Diary*, 15 December 1914.

26 *The Sydney Morning Herald*, 12 January 1915, p. 9.

27 Archibald Barwick, diary, undated, in FitzSimons, *Gallipoli*, p. 113; diary ML MSS1493/1/Box1/Item 1, Mitchell Library, SLNSW.

28 Frederick Forrest, war diary, 9 December 1914, p. 10.

29 Bean, *Official History of Australia in the War of 1914–1918, Vol. I*, pp. 125–6.

30 Department of Veterans' Affairs, *Training Australian army recruits during World War I*, DVA Anzac Portal, 2001.

31 McMullen, *Pompey Elliott*, Scribe, Melbourne, 2008, p. 100.

32 Robertson, *Anzac and Empire: the Tragedy and Glory of Gallipoli*, Hamlyn Australia, Richmond, 1990, pp. 43–44.

Chapter two   Death in the sun

1 Idriess, *The Desert Column*, p. 93.

2 *Sydney Mail*, 14 October 1908, p. 1028.

3 Montefiore, *Jerusalem: The Biography*, Hachette, UK, 2011, p. 501.

4 Montefiore, *Jerusalem*, p. 501.

5   Pasha, *Memories of a Turkish Statesman*, p. 154.

6   Haydon, *Midnight Warhorse*, 2017, p. 21.

7   Pasha, *Memories of a Turkish Statesman*, p. 156.

8   Pasha, *Memories of a Turkish Statesman*, pp. 156–157.

9   Pasha, *Memories of a Turkish Statesman*, p. 157.

10 Jones, *A Thousand Miles of Battles*, p. 39.

11 Hogue, *Trooper Bluegum at the Dardanelles*, 2nd ed., Andrew Melrose, London, 1916, p. 51.

12 Knightley, *Australia*, Jonathan Cape, London, 2000, p. 64.

13 Bean, war diary, 2 April 1915, p. 29, AWM38, 3DRL606/3/1 – March – April 1915 [reported speech].

14 Eric Harford Ward, diary, Mitchell Library, MLDOC 1300.

15 'War Letters of Sir John Monash', *Courier Mail*, 13 November 1934, p. 13.

16 Hogue, *Trooper Bluegum at the Dardanelles*, p. 81.

17 *South Gippsland Shire Echo*, 18 June 1915, p. 3.

18 Berrie, *Under Furred Hats*, Naval & Military Press, London, 2009, pp. 20–22.

19 Mitchell, *The Light Horse: The Story of Australia's Mounted Troops*, Macmillan, Sydney, 1978, p. 35.

20 Mitchell, *The Light Horse*, p. 35.

21 Idriess, *The Desert Column*, p. 15.

22 Hogue, *Trooper Bluegum at the Dardanelles*, p. 95 [reported speech].

23 Hogue, *Trooper Bluegum at the Dardanelles*, p. 95.

24 Bean, *Official History of Australia in the War of 1914–1918*, Vol. II, Angus & Robertson, 1941, p. 91.

25 Jones, *A Thousand Miles of Battles*, p. 25.

26 Jones, *A Thousand Miles of Battles*, p. 27.

27 Horner, *The Commanders: Australian Military Leadership in the Twentieth Century*, Routledge, London, 2021, p. 107.

28 *The Sydney Morning Herald*, 20 July 1915, p. 8.

29 Burness, *The Nek: The Tragic Charge of the Light Horse at Gallipoli*, Kangaroo Press, Kenthurst, 1996, p. 75.

30 John Hamilton, *Goodbye Cobber, God Bless You*, Pan Macmillan, Sydney, 2004, p. 243.

31 *The Herald*, 8 August 1919, p. 7.

32 Hamilton, *Goodbye Cobber, God Bless You*, p. 285.

33 Schuler, *Australia in Arms*, T. Fisher Unwin, London, 1916, p. 241.

34 Comments by Lieutenant Colonel N. M. Brazier, Official History 1914–1918 War Records of Charles E. W. Bean, Correspondence 1926–31, AWM, 3DRL 7953/27, Part 3, Ch. XVIII, [no page numbers].

35 Simpson, *Maygar's Boys: A Biographical History of the 8th Light Horse Regiment A.I.F. 1914–19*, Just Soldiers, Military Research & Publications, Moorooduc, 1998, p. 279.

36 *The West Australian*, 28 September 1915, p. 5.
37 Bean, *Official History of Australia in the War of 1914–1918, Vol. II*, p. 614.
38 Bean, *Official History of Australia in the War of 1914–1918, Vol. II*, p. 614.
39 Comments by Lieutenant Colonel N. M. Brazier, Official History 1914–1918 War Records of Charles E. W. Bean, Ch. XVIII, [no page numbers].
40 *The Canberra Times*, Friday, 25 April 1986, p. 8.
41 Comments by Lieutenant Colonel N. M. Brazier, Official History 1914–1918 War Records of Charles E. W. Bean, Ch. XVIII, [no page numbers].
42 Örnek and Toker, *Gallipoli: Companion to the Feature Length Documentary*, Ekip Film Ltd, 2005, p. 94.
43 Jones, *A Thousand Miles of Battles*, p. 34.
44 King, *Palestine Diaries*, Scribe Publications, Australia, 2017, e-book, p. 66.
45 Bean, *Official History of Australia in the War of 1914–1918, Vol. II*, p. 618.
46 Bean, *Official History of Australia in the War of 1914–1918, Vol. II*, p. 633.
47 awm.gov.au/collection/E8470. Author's note: The Australian troops were essentially sent on a suicide mission at the Nek that morning. The troops came to place the blame on Godley, and renamed the Nek, 'Godley's Abattoir'. The Turks, on the other hand, subsequently called the area Cesarettepe, meaning 'Bravery' or 'Courage' Hill.
48 *The Daily Telegraph*, 20 October 1915, p. 11.
49 Haydon, *Midnight Warhorse*, 2017.
50 Perry, *The Australian Light Horse: The Magnificent Australian Force and its Decisive Victories in Arabia in World War I*, Hachette, Australia, 2009, p. 114.
51 Faulkner, *Lawrence of Arabia's War*, Yale University Press, New Haven, 2016, p. 194.
52 *The W.A. Record*, 17 November 1915, p. 17.
53 *The W.A. Record*, 17 November 1915, p. 17.
54 Middlebrook, *The Kaiser's Battle*, Penguin, Harmondsworth, 2000, p. 56.
55 *The W.A. Record*, 27 November 1915, p. 17.
56 *The W.A. Record*, 27 November 1915, p. 17.
57 Hill, *Chauvel of the Light Horse: A Biography of Sir Harry Chauvel*, Melbourne University Press, Melbourne, 1978, p. 61.
58 Pasha, *Memories of a Turkish Statesman*, pp. 163 and 167.
59 Pasha, *Memories of a Turkish Statesman*, p. 163.
60 Pasha, *Memories of a Turkish Statesman*, p. 163.
61 Hogue, *Trooper Bluegum at the Dardanelles*, p. 269.
62 Haydon, *Midnight Warhorse*, 2017.
63 *Crookwell Gazette*, 8 March 1934, p. 3.
64 Vincent, *My Darling Mick: The Life of Granville Ryrie, 1865–1937*, National Library of Australia, 1997, p. 98.
65 Vincent, *My Darling Mick*, p. 98.
66 Letter, Guy Haydon, 24/12/15, Haydon Family Archive.

67 Letter, Granville Ryrie to Mrs Granville Ryrie, 23 December 1915, AWM PR84/193, pp. 202–203.

68 Hogue, *Trooper Bluegum at the Dardanelles*, p. 256.

69 Further reading: Bean, *Official History of Australia in the War of 1914–1918*, Vol. II, p. 883.

70 Wiltshire, war diary, 20 December 1915, p. 19, 12 December 1915–16 March 1916, MLMSS 3058/Box 1/Item 4.,

71 Hogue, *Trooper Bluegum at the Dardanelles*, p. 278.

72 Hogue, *Trooper Bluegum at the Dardanelles*, p. 278.

73 Hogue, *Trooper Bluegum at the Dardanelles*, p. 278.

74 Hogue, *Trooper Bluegum at the Dardanelles*, p. 278.

75 Wiltshire, war diary, 20 December 1915, p. 19.

Chapter three   The sins of the Sinai

1 Thomas O'Leary, Court Martial Proceedings, National Archives of Australia: A471, 6646, Item ID: 6826919.

2 Letters, Private Stanley Broome, 12th Australian Light Horse Regiment, AWM PR91/053.

3 Records of H. S. Gullett 60/300, AWM40.

4 Idriess, *The Desert Column*, p. 82.

5 Campbell, *Banjo Paterson: A Life in Pictures and Words from the Banjo Paterson Family Archive*, Macmillan Publishers Australia, e-book, 2022, p. 198.

6 Paterson, *Happy Dispatches*, Lansdowne Press, p. 195.

7 John Ernest (Chook) Fowler, AWM MS 888, p. 13.

8 Jones, 'Royston, John Robinson (1860–1942)', *Australian Dictionary of Biography*, National Centre of Biography, Australian National University, Vol. 11, 1988.

9 Jones, *A Thousand Miles of Battles*, p. 14.

10 Private Papers of General Sir Archibald Murray, Imperial War Museum, collected letters, 79/48/2, p. 54.

11 Private Papers of General Sir Archibald Murray, p. 64.

12 Idriess, *The Desert Column*, p. 83.

13 Idriess, *The Desert Column*, p. 84.

14 Idriess, *The Desert Column*, p. 85.

15 Idriess, *The Desert Column*, p. 84.

16 Idriess, *The Desert Column*, p. 88.

17 Records of H. S. Gullett, AWM40 68, p. 4.

18 Grainger, *The Battle for Palestine 1917*, Boydell Press, 2006, p. 101.

19 Bean, *Official History of Australia in the War of 1914–1918*, Vol. I, p. 138.

20 Idriess, *The Desert Column*, p. 87.

21 Idriess, *The Desert Column*, p. 85.

22 Idriess, *The Desert Column*, p. 98.

23 Private Papers of General Sir Archibald Murray, p. 87.

24 Maurice Evans, war diaries, Mitchell Library.

25 Maurice Evans, war diaries, Mitchell Library.

26 Maurice Evans, war diaries, Mitchell Library.

27 *The Bulletin*, 26 April 1890.

28 Paterson, *Happy Dispatches*, Lansdowne Press, p. 41.

29 Paterson, *Happy Dispatches*, Lansdowne Press, p. 124.

30 Paterson, *Happy Dispatches*, Lansdowne Press, p. 125.

31 Paterson, *Happy Dispatches*, Lansdowne Press, p. 125.

32 Paterson, *Happy Dispatches*, Lansdowne Press, p. 125.

33 Paterson, *Happy Dispatches*, Lansdowne Press, p. 124.

34 Paterson, *Happy Dispatches*, Lansdowne Press, p. 126.

35 *Western Mail* (Perth), 3 January 1935, p. 3.

36 Idriess, *The Desert Column*, p. 88.

37 Idriess, *The Desert Column*, p. 89.

38 Idriess, *The Desert Column*, p. 89.

39 Idriess, *The Desert Column*, p. 89.

40 Idriess, *The Desert Column*, p. 96.

41 Jones, *A Thousand Miles of Battles*, p. 42.

42 Gullett, *The Australian Imperial Force in Sinai and Palestine*, Angus & Robertson, p. 191.

43 Anglesey, *A History of the British Cavalry: Vol. 5: 1914–1919 Egypt, Palestine and Syria*, Pen & Sword Books Limited, 1994, e-book, p. 55.

44 John Collie Stephen, diary and letters, AWM 3DRL/3584.

45 Thomas O'Leary, Court Martial Proceedings, NAA.

46 Thomas O'Leary, Court Martial Proceedings, NAA.

47 Elizabeth Riddell (ed.), *With Fond Regards: Private Lives Through Letters*, National Library of Australia, Canberra, 1995, p. 34.

48 Idriess, *The Desert Column*, p. 84.

Chapter four   Horsemen for the Apocalypse

1 Jones, *A Thousand Miles of Battles*, p. xii.

2 *Shepparton Advertiser*, 12 October 1934, p. 1.

3 Jones, *A Thousand Miles of Battles*, p. 44.

4 Hill, *Chauvel of the Light Horse*, p. 73.

5 Author's note: While actual Taubes were mostly used as reconnaissance aircraft, distinctive for their swept-back wings in the manner of a dove – which the German word 'taube' translates to – there were actually very few if any of those kind of planes active in the desert theatre from early 1916 onwards, as

their delicate form simply did not suit the robust conditions. But even when they were withdrawn, the argot of calling all kinds of German monoplanes 'Taubes' remained.

6 Maurice Evans, war diaries, Mitchell Library.

7 Maurice Evans, war diaries, Mitchell Library.

8 Idriess, *The Desert Column*, p. 141.

9 Idriess, *The Desert Column*, p. 142.

10 John Collie Stephen, diary and letters, AWM 3DRL/3584.

11 Bradley, *Australian Light Horse: The Campaign in the Middle East 1916–1918*, Allen & Unwin, Crows Nest, 2016, p. 20.

12 Sergeant Leslie S. Horder, diary, AWM 3DRL/6595.

13 Jones, *A Thousand Miles of Battles*, p. 46.

14 Jones, *A Thousand Miles of Battles*, p. 46.

15 Idriess, *The Desert Column*, p. 150.

16 Bradley, *Australian Light Horse*, p. 20.

17 Idriess, *The Desert Column*, p. 153.

18 John Dudley Hobbs, diary, AWM PR85 289.

19 Idriess, *The Desert Column*, p. 147.

20 'In memory of Bill of the Sixth Light Horse Regiment', The Chauvel Foundation, [reported speech].

21 Idriess, *The Desert Column*, p. 153.

22 Letter, Trooper Oliver Clarke, 7th Light Horse, AWM RCDIG0000374, p. 4.

23 Letter, Trooper Oliver Clarke, AWM, p. 4.

24 Letter, Trooper Oliver Clarke, AWM, p. 4.

25 John Dudley Hobbs, diary, AWM PR85 289.

26 Jones, *A Thousand Miles of Battles*, p. 5.

27 Bradley, *Australian Light Horse*, p. 13.

28 Idriess, *The Desert Column*, p. 154.

29 Bradley, *Australian Light Horse*, p. 25.

30 Maurice Evans, war diaries, Mitchell Library.

31 Bradley, *Australian Light Horse*, p. 26.

32 Bradley, *Australian Light Horse*, p. 23.

33 Fred Tomlins, war diaries, 21 August 1914 – 28 April 1917, Mitchell Library, MLMSS 5975 (CY 3348, frames 1–479).

34 Paterson, *Happy Dispatches*, Lansdowne Press, p. 122.

35 Paterson, *Happy Dispatches*, Lansdowne Press, p. 122.

36 Paterson, *Happy Dispatches*, Lansdowne Press, p. 123.

37 Jones, *A Thousand Miles of Battles*, p. 49.

38 Verner Gladders Knuckey, diary, AWM PR 03193, Book 3, p. 5.

39 Maurice Evans, war diaries, Mitchell Library.

40 Kinloch, *Devils on Horses*, Exisle, Auckland, 2007, p. 92.

41 Chauvel to Gullett, Records of H. S. Gullett, AWM 40, 53/40.

42 Anglesey, *A History of British Cavalry*, Cooper, London, 1995, p. 56.

43 Letter, Trooper Oliver Clarke, AWM, p. 5 [reported speech].

44 Letter, Trooper Oliver Clarke, AWM, p. 5 [reported speech].

45 Letter, Trooper Oliver Clarke, AWM, p. 5.

46 Jones, *A Thousand Miles of Battles*, p. 49.

47 Bradley, *Australian Light Horse*, p. 25.

48 Captain Arthur Rhodes, diary entry dated 4 August 1916, quoted in Kinloch, *Devils on Horses*, p. 92.

49 Bradley, *Australian Light Horse*, p. 33.

50 Bradley, *Australian Light Horse*, p. 33.

51 Verner Gladders Knuckey, diary, Book 3, p. 8.

52 Letters of Ross Smith, A World Away, South Australia's War 1914–18 website.

53 Anglesey, *A History of the British Cavalry*, Pen & Sword Books, p. 72.

54 Letter, Heinrich Romer Andrea, AWM PR 89/179.

55 Maurice Evans, war diaries, Mitchell Library.

56 Letter, Trooper Oliver Clarke, AWM, p. 1.

57 Verner Gladders Knuckey, diary, Book 3, p. 6.

58 Maurice Evans, war diaries, Mitchell Library.

59 Idriess, *The Desert Column*, p. 155.

60 Idriess, *The Desert Column*, p. 155.

61 Idriess, *The Desert Column*, p. 156.

62 Idriess, *The Desert Column*, p. 156.

63 Ion Idriess, diary, AWM RCDIG0000448.

64 Idriess, *The Desert Column*, p. 159.

65 Idriess, *The Desert Column*, p. 160.

66 Idriess, *The Desert Column*, p. 162.

67 Maurice Evelyn Pearce, diary, Mitchell Library, MSS 2940.

68 Idriess, *The Desert Column*, p. 166.

69 Idriess, *The Desert Column*, p. 167.

70 Hill, *Chauvel of the Light Horse*, p. 80.

71 Ion Idriess, diary, AWM RCDIG0000448.

72 Records of H. S. Gullett, AWM 40 68, p. 5.

73 Hill, *Chauvel of the Light Horse*, p. 75.

74 Mitchell, *The Light Horse*, pp. 48–49.

75 Ion Idriess, diary, AWM RCDIG0000448.

76 Private Papers of General Sir Archibald Murray, p. 92.

77 Leo Hanly, diary, AWM PR05366.

78 Maurice Evans, war diaries, Mitchell Library.

79 Ion Idriess, diary, AWM RCDIG0000448.

Chapter five   Pomp and circumstances

1 Gullett, *The Australian Imperial Force in Sinai and Palestine*, p. 29.
2 Jones, *A Thousand Miles of Battles*, p. 1.
3 Letter, Guy Haydon, 1 August 1916, Haydon Family Archive.
4 Haydon, *Midnight Warhorse*, 2017, p. 41.
5 Cutlack, *Official Histories: First World War*, Vol. VIII, *The Australian Flying Corps in the Western and Eastern Theatres of War, 1914–1918*, Angus & Robertson, Sydney, Australia, 1941, p. 421.
6 Lloyd George, *The Great Crusade: Extracts from Speeches Delivered During the War*, George H. Doran Company, New York, 1918, p. 212.
7 *Southern Times*, 25 November 1916, p. 3 [reported speech].
8 *Southern Times*, 25 November 1916, p. 3 [reported speech].
9 Lawrence, *Seven Pillars of Wisdom – A Triumph*, Oxford University Press, 1940, p. 104.
10 Perry, *The Australian Light Horse: The Magnificent Australian Force and its Decisive Victories in Arabia in World War I*, Hachette, Australia, 2009, p. 183.
11 Pasha, *Memories of a Turkish Statesman*, p. 139.
12 Letters, General Granville Ryrie, AWM PR84/193.
13 Faulkner, *Lawrence of Arabia's War*, p. 241.
14 Records of H. S. Gullett, AWM40 65, p. 3.
15 King, *Palestine Diaries*, p. 105.
16 *The Telegraph*, 25 August 1916, p. 4.
17 Robbins, *British Generalship on the Western Front*, p. 205.
18 Bradley, *Australian Light Horse*, p. 44.
19 King, *Palestine Diaries*, p. 108.
20 Perry, *The Australian Light Horse*, p. 197.
21 Gullett, *The Australian Imperial Force in Sinai and Palestine*, p. 207.
22 Jones, *A Thousand Miles of Battles*, p. 2.
23 Sibyl Chauvel, diary, 16 April 1917, Chauvel Papers, AWM.
24 Letters, General Granville Ryrie, AWM PR84/193.
25 Bradley, *Australian Light Horse*, p. 45.
26 Jones, *A Thousand Miles of Battles*, p. 66.
27 Bradley, *Australian Light Horse*, p. 45.
28 Jones, *A Thousand Miles of Battles*, p. 66.
29 Australian Imperial Force Unit Diaries, AWM4, Item 10/1/29.
30 Gullett, *The Australian Imperial Force in Sinai and Palestine*, p. 221.
31 Author's note: Though the Official Historian Henry Gullett refers to this man as Lieutenant F. W. Cox, it was in fact Brigadier General Charles Frederick Cox, known as 'Fighting Charlie'.
32 Gullett, *The Australian Imperial Force in Sinai and Palestine*, p. 221.
33 King, *Palestine Diaries*, p. 126.

34 Gullett, *The Australian Imperial Force in Sinai and Palestine*, pp. 223–224.

35 Idriess, *The Desert Column*, pp. 242–243.

36 *The Sydney Morning Herald*, 12 January 1915, p. 9.

37 Bradley, *Australian Light Horse*, p. 54.

38 King, *Palestine Diaries*, p. xx.

39 Hill, *Chauvel of the Light Horse*, p. 101.

40 Idriess, *The Desert Column*, p. 243.

41 Maurice Evans, war diaries, Mitchell Library.

42 Idriess, *The Desert Column*, p. 261.

43 Idriess, *The Desert Column*, p. 261.

44 Hill, *Chauvel of the Light Horse*, p. 102.

45 John Ernest (Chook) Fowler, AWM MS 888.

46 Mitchell, *The Light Horse*, p. 53.

47 Letters, Private Stanley Broome, AWM PR91/053.

48 Idriess, *The Desert Column*, p. 256.

49 Grainger, *The Battle for Palestine 1917*, p. 3.

50 Smith, *Fiery Ted: Anzac Commander*, Nationwide Books, Christchurch, 2008, p. 163.

51 Bradley, *Australian Light Horse*, p. 53.

52 Private Papers of General Sir Archibald Murray, p. 202.

53 Idriess, *The Desert Column*, p. 287.

54 Idriess, *The Desert Column*, p. 254 [reported speech].

55 Falls and MacMunn, *Military Operations: Egypt and Palestine*, Vol. I, His Majesty's Stationery Office, London, 1928, p. 78.

56 Idriess, *The Desert Column*, p. 83.

57 John Ernest (Chook) Fowler, AWM MS 888, p. 15.

58 John Ernest (Chook) Fowler, AWM MS 888, p. 15.

59 Dearberg, *Desert Anzacs: The Under-Told Story of the Sinai Palestine Campaign 1916–1918*, Interactive Publications, 2017, p. 128.

60 Pasha, *Memories of a Turkish Statesman*, p. 171.

61 Pasha, *Memories of a Turkish Statesman*, p. 179.

62 Pasha, *Memories of a Turkish Statesman*, p. 172.

63 Lawrence, *Seven Pillars of Wisdom*, p. 309.

64 Lawrence, *Seven Pillars of Wisdom*, p. 312.

Chapter six Defeat in victory

1 Idriess, *The Desert Column*, p. 5.

2 Jones, *A Thousand Miles of Battles*, p. 66.

3 Letters, Private Stanley Broome, AWM PR91/053.

4 Murray, *Sir Archibald Murray's Despatches (June 1916 – June 1917)*, J. M. Dent, New York, E. P. Dutton, London, 1920, p. 139.

5 Idriess, *The Desert Column*, p. 262.
6 Ross Smith, diary, PRG 18/19, South Australia Library.
7 Papers of Joseph Bull, AWM PRO1547.
8 *The Register*, 26 May 1917, p. 7.
9 *The Register*, 26 May 1917, p. 7.
10 *The Register*, 26 May 1917, p. 7.
11 *The Register*, 26 May 1917, p. 7.
12 *The Register*, 26 May 1917, p. 7.
13 *The Register*, 26 May 1917, p. 7.
14 *The Register*, 26 May 1917, p. 7.
15 Bradley, *Australian Light Horse*, p. 60.
16 *The Gundagai Times and Tumut, Adelong and Murrumbidgee District Advertiser*, 5 June 1917, p. 2.
17 Author's note: Henry Gullett's official history of *The Australian Imperial Force in Sinai and Palestine, 1914–1918* provides a nominal title of 'Tala Bey' for the commander of the Gaza garrison during the First Battle of Gaza. Gullett appears to have taken this name from the Desert Column War Diary recording a message received detailing the testimony of a captured Turkish soldier naming the commander of the Gaza garrison as such. However, after researching other sources, including primary documents, I believe this is a German officer, Major Ernst Tiller, who commanded 'Group Tiller' consisting of seven battalions comprising the Ottoman 79th and 125th Regiments, and 2nd Battalion, 81st Regiment.
18 Gullett, *The Australian Imperial Force in Sinai and Palestine*, p. 267.
19 Housman, *A Shropshire Lad*, Branden Books, Wellesley, 1896, p. 39.
20 Idriess, *The Desert Column*, p. 274.
21 Idriess, *The Desert Column*, p. 275.
22 Idriess, *The Desert Column*, p. 276.
23 Idriess, *The Desert Column*, p. 277.
24 Idriess, *The Desert Column*, p. 274.
25 Idriess, *The Desert Column*, p. 276.
26 Idriess, *The Desert Column*, p. 276.
27 Idriess, *The Desert Column*, p. 276.
28 Gullett, *The Australian Imperial Force in Sinai and Palestine*, p. 268.
29 *Wagga Wagga Express*, 7 June 1917, p. 1.
30 Leacock, *Nonsense Novels*, Bodley Head, London, 1911, p. 63.
31 *Wagga Wagga Express*, 7 June 1917, p. 1.
32 Idriess, *The Desert Column*, p. 277.
33 Idriess, *The Desert Column*, p. 277.
34 Idriess, *The Desert Column*, p. 278.
35 Idriess, *The Desert Column*, p. 278.
36 Vincent, *My Darling Mick*, pp. 130–134.

37 Idriess, *The Desert Column*, p. 279.
38 Idriess, *The Desert Column*, p. 279.
39 Idriess, *The Desert Column*, p. 279.
40 Ion Llewellyn Idriess, diary, 1917, AWM, 1DRL/0373.
41 Falls, *Military Operations: Egypt And Palestine*, His Majesty's Stationery Office, 1930, London, p. 321.
42 Gullett, *The Australian Imperial Force in Sinai and Palestine*, p. 273.
43 Gullett, *The Australian Imperial Force in Sinai and Palestine*, p. 273.
44 Gullett, *The Australian Imperial Force in Sinai and Palestine*, p. 274.
45 Idriess, *The Desert Column*, pp. 280–281.
46 Bradley, *Australian Light Horse*, p. 64.
47 Idriess, *The Desert Column*, p. 281.
48 Gullett, *The Australian Imperial Force in Sinai and Palestine*, p. 278.
49 Bradley, *Australian Light Horse*, p. 65.
50 Idriess, *The Desert Column*, pp. 283–284.
51 Idriess, *The Desert Column*, p. 284.
52 Idriess, *The Desert Column*, p. 284.
53 Vincent, *My Darling Mick*, pp. 130–134.
54 Idriess, *The Desert Column*, p. 294.
55 Idriess, *The Desert Column*, p. 284.
56 Ross Smith, diary, PRG 18/19, State Library of South Australia.
57 Gullett, *The Australian Imperial Force in Sinai and Palestine*, p. 279.
58 Idriess, *The Desert Column*, p. 288.
59 Falls and MacMunn, *Military Operations: Egypt And Palestine*, p. 310.
60 Gullett, *The Australian Imperial Force in Sinai and Palestine*, p. 294.
61 Gullett, *The Australian Imperial Force in Sinai and Palestine*, p. 294.
62 Prowles, *The New Zealanders in Sinai and Palestine*, Whitcombe and Tombs Limited, Auckland, 1922.
63 Australian Imperial Force Diaries, General Staff HQ, Anzac Mounted Division, March 1917, AWM4 1/60/13.
64 Australian Imperial Force Diaries, March 1917, AWM4 1/60/13.
65 Gullett, *Official History of Australia in the War of 1914–1918, Vol. VII – The Australian Imperial Force in Sinai and Palestine, 1914–1918*, Chapter XXIII, Battle of Beersheba, Angus & Robertson, 1941, p. 282.
66 Idriess, *The Desert Column*, p. 288.
67 Idriess, *The Desert Column*, p. 288.
68 Idriess, *The Desert Column*, p. 288.
69 Idriess, *The Desert Column*, p. 288.
70 Idriess, *The Desert Column*, p. 289.
71 Idriess, *The Desert Column*, p. 292.
72 Gullett, *Official History of Australia in the War of 1914–1918, Vol. VII*, Chapter XVII, First Gaza Engagement, p. 286.

73 Gullett, *The Australian Imperial Force in Sinai and Palestine*, p. 284.
74 King, *Palestine Diaries*, p. 183.
75 Gullett, *The Australian Imperial Force in Sinai and Palestine*, p. 285.
76 Gullett, *The Australian Imperial Force in Sinai and Palestine*, p. 294.
77 Stanley Parkes, diary, AWM PR01077.
78 Idriess, *The Desert Column*, p. 86.
79 Gullett, *The Australian Imperial Force in Sinai and Palestine*, p. 289.
80 Gullett, *The Australian Imperial Force in Sinai and Palestine*, p. 289.
81 Falls and MacMunn, *Military Operations: Egypt And Palestine*, p. 310.
82 Mitchell, *The Light Horse*, p. xx.
83 Bradley, *Australian Light Horse*, p. 68.
84 Gullett, *The Australian Imperial Force in Sinai and Palestine*, p. 293.
85 Gullett, *The Australian Imperial Force in Sinai and Palestine*, pp. 293–94.
86 Bradley, *Australian Light Horse*, p. 69.
87 Gullett, *The Australian Imperial Force in Sinai and Palestine*, p. 291.
88 Gullett, *The Australian Imperial Force in Sinai and Palestine*, p. 296.
89 Bradley, *Australian Light Horse*, p. 69.
90 Robert Valentine Fell, war diaries, Mitchell Library, Microfilm: CY 4893, frames 145–516.
91 Idriess, *The Desert Column*, p. 297.
92 Hughes, *General Allenby and the campaign of the Egyptian Expeditionary Force, June 1917 – November 1919*, Thesis, King's College London, 1995.
93 Murray, *Sir Archibald Murray's Despatches*, p. 133.
94 Gullett, *Official History of Australia in the War of 1914–1918*, Vol. VII, p. 300.
95 Gullett, *Official History of Australia in the War of 1914–1918*, Vol. VII, p. 300.
96 Papers of Joseph Bull, AWM PRO1547.
97 Bradley, *Australian Light Horse*, p. 72.
98 Jones, *A Thousand Miles of Battles*, p. 73.
99 Jones, *A Thousand Miles of Battles*, p. 73.

Chapter seven   The Second Battle of Gaza

1 Gullett, *The Australian Imperial Force in Sinai and Palestine*, p. 63.
2 Hopkins, *Alaric Pinder Boor: A Life Reimagined*, MoshPit Publishing, NSW, 2020, p. 270.
3 Murray, *Sir Archibald Murray's Despatches*, p. 155.
4 Murray, *Sir Archibald Murray's Despatches*, p. 133.
5 Fred Tomlins, war diaries, Mitchell Library.
6 Letter, Trooper Oliver Clarke, AWM, pp. 1–2.
7 Idriess, *The Desert Column*, p. 298.

8 Hughes, *General Allenby and the Campaign of the Egyptian Expeditionary Force, June 1917 – November 1919*, King's College London.

9 Hughes, *General Allenby and the Campaign of the Egyptian Expeditionary Force, June 1917 – November 1919*, King's College London.

10 Gullett, *The Australian Imperial Force in Sinai and Palestine*, p. 303.

11 Mitchell, *The Light Horse*, p. 64.

12 Idriess, *The Desert Column*, p. 309.

13 Harris, The 4th Brigade Trek from the Canal to Khan Yunis and the 2nd Gaza Battle, handwritten ms, p. 8.

14 Haydon, *Midnight Warhorse*, p. 31.

15 John Ernest (Chook) Fowler, AWM MS 888.

16 John Ernest (Chook) Fowler, AWM MS 888.

17 John Ernest (Chook) Fowler, AWM MS 888.

18 Bostock, *The Great Ride: The Diary of a Light Horse Brigade Scout, World War I*, Artlook Books, Perth, 1982, p. 71.

19 John Ernest (Chook) Fowler, AWM MS 888.

20 Haydon, *Midnight Warhorse*, p. 31.

21 Smithers, *A New Excalibur*, Butler and Tanner, London, p. 186.

22 Smithers, *A New Excalibur*, p. 104.

23 Idriess, *The Desert Column*, p. 311.

24 Idriess, *The Desert Column*, p. 311.

25 Bradley, *Australian Light Horse*, p. 76.

26 Idriess, *The Desert Column*, p. 311.

27 Bradley, *Australian Light Horse*, p. 76.

28 Bradley, *Australian Light Horse*, p. 76.

29 Bradley, *Australian Light Horse*, p. 76.

30 Haydon, *Midnight Warhorse*, p. 31.

31 Idriess, *The Desert Column*, pp. 302–303.

32 Gullett, *Official History of Australia in the War of 1914–1918, Vol. VII*, p. 327.

33 Gullett, *Official History of Australia in the War of 1914–1918, Vol. VII*, p. 327.

34 Gullett, *Official History of Australia in the War of 1914–1918, Vol. VII*, p. 401.

35 Idriess, *The Desert Column*, p. 304.

36 Letter, John Collie Stephen, AWM 3DRL/3584.

37 Haydon, *Midnight Warhorse*, p. 31.

38 Idriess, *The Desert Column*, p. 314.

39 Idriess, *The Desert Column*, p. 313.

40 Idriess, *The Desert Column*, p. 314.

41 Murray, *Sir Archibald Murray's Despatches*, p. 164.

42 Idriess, *The Desert Column*, p. 315.

43 Idriess, *The Desert Column*, p. 333.
44 Idriess, *The Desert Column*, p. 333.
45 Paterson, *Happy Dispatches*, Lansdowne Press, p. 79.
46 Murray, *Sir Archibald Murray's Despatches*, p. 134.
47 Murray, *Sir Archibald Murray's Despatches*, p. 134.
48 Gullett, *The Australian Imperial Force in Sinai and Palestine*, p. 338.
49 Wavell, *Allenby: A Study in Greatness*, OUP, New York, 1941, p. 171.
50 Wavell, *Allenby: A Study in Greatness*, p. 171.
51 Wavell, *Allenby: A Study in Greatness*, p. 185.
52 James, *Imperial Warrior: The Life and Times of Field Marshal Viscount Allenby*, Weidenfeld & Nicolson, London, 1993, p. 105.
53 Hughes, *General Allenby and the Campaign of the Egyptian Expeditionary Force, June 1917 – November 1919*, King's College London.
54 Wavell, *Allenby: A Study in Greatness*, p. 186.
55 Weintraub, *The Recovery of Palestine, 1917: Jerusalem for Christmas*, Cambridge Scholars Publishing, Newcastle upon Tyne, 2017, p. 52.
56 Maurice Evans, war diaries, Mitchell Library.
57 Maurice Evans, war diaries, Mitchell Library.

Chapter eight   Enter Allenby

1 Paterson, *Happy Dispatches*, Lansdowne Press, p. 81.
2 Wavell, *Allenby: A Study in Greatness*, p. 188.
3 Wavell, *Allenby: A Study in Greatness*, p. 188 [reported speech].
4 Wavell, *Allenby: A Study in Greatness*, p. 188 [reported speech].
5 Letter, Oliver Cromwell, 3 August 1650, http://www.olivercromwell.org/Letters_and_speeches/letters/Letter_129
6 Falls, *Military Operations: Egypt And Palestine*, p. 9.
7 Fox, *Learning to Fight: Military Innovation and Change in the British Army*, Cambridge University Press, Cambridge, 2018, p. 221.
8 Paterson, *Happy Dispatches*, Lansdowne Press, p. 83.
9 Paterson, *Happy Dispatches*, Lansdowne Press, p. 83.
10 Paterson, *Happy Dispatches*, Lansdowne Press, p. 83.
11 James, *Imperial Warrior*, p. 115.
12 Gardner, *Allenby of Arabia, Lawrence's General*, Coward-McCann, New York, 1966, p. xviii.
13 Paterson, *Happy Dispatches*, Lansdowne Press, p. 83.
14 Carver, *The Warlords*, Weidenfeld & Nicolson, London, 1976, p. 149.
15 De Marco and Radway, *Twentieth Century World*, Stanley Thornes, Cheltenham, 1995, vii.
16 Meinertzhagen, *Kenya Diary 1902–1906*, Eland Books, London, 1984, p. v.
17 Wavell, *Allenby: A Study in Greatness*, p. 198.

18 Gullett, *The Australian Imperial Force in Sinai and Palestine*, p. 357.
19 Allenby Papers, Liddle Hart Centre for Military Archives, King's College London, 2/1/1-76; 1/8/6-39. Author's note: Allenby used the word 'Nebi'. In modern Arabic, it is 'Nabiun'.
20 Smith, *The Historical Geography of the Holy Land*, George H. Doran Company, New York, 1920, p. 284.
21 Wavell, *Allenby: A Study in Greatness*, p. 192.
22 Wavell, *Allenby: A Study in Greatness*, p. 192.
23 Roy James Dunk, manuscript, AWM PR00469, p. 3.
24 Allenby Papers, 2/1/1-76.
25 Lawrence, *Seven Pillars of Wisdom*, p. 326.
26 Lawrence, *Seven Pillars of Wisdom*, p. 328.
27 Lawrence, *Seven Pillars of Wisdom*, p. 328.
28 Lawrence, *Seven Pillars of Wisdom*, p. 330.
29 Lawrence, *Seven Pillars of Wisdom*, p. 330.
30 Idriess, *The Desert Column*, p. 83.
31 Gullett, *The Australian Imperial Force in Sinai and Palestine*, p. 364.
32 James, *Imperial Warrior*, p. 126.
33 Allenby Papers, 1/8/6-39.
34 Paterson, *Happy Dispatches*, Lansdowne Press, p. 122.
35 Paterson, *Happy Dispatches*, Lansdowne Press, p. 123.
36 Paterson, *Happy Dispatches*, Lansdowne Press, p. 123 [reported speech].
37 Sergeant D. W. Harris, AWM 40 45, Official History, 1914–1918 War: Records of Henry S. Gullett, p. 2.
38 Sergeant D. W. Harris, AWM 40 45, p. 2.
39 Jones, *A Thousand Miles of Battles*, p. 85.
40 Preston, *The Desert Mounted Corps*, Houghton Mifflin Company, Boston and New York, 1921, p. 6.
41 Hill, *Chauvel of the Light Horse*, p. 118.
42 Allenby Papers, 1/8/6-39.
43 *Daily News* (Perth), 19 January 1933, p. 7.
44 Grainger, *The Battle for Palestine 1917*, p. 89.
45 Paterson, *Happy Dispatches*, Lansdowne Press, p. 127.
46 Allenby Papers, 2/5 Miscellaneous Correspondence.
47 Preston, *The Desert Mounted Corps*, p. 20.
48 War Diary GSO GHQ EEF, September 1917, WO 95/4368, p. 3.
49 Jones, *A Thousand Miles of Battles*, p. 86.

Chapter nine Positions, everyone

1 Gullett, *The Australian Imperial Force in Sinai and Palestine*, p. 379.
2 Lawrence, *Seven Pillars of Wisdom*, p. 352.

3 Lawrence, *Seven Pillars of Wisdom*, p. 352 [reported speech].

4 Lawrence, *Seven Pillars of Wisdom*, p. 352 [reported speech].

5 Lawrence, *Seven Pillars of Wisdom*, p. 27.

6 Lawrence, *Seven Pillars of Wisdom*, p. 376.

7 Lawrence, *Seven Pillars of Wisdom*, p. 352

8 Lawrence, *Seven Pillars of Wisdom*, p. 639.

9 Idriess, *The Desert Column*, p. 92.

10 Actual map and notes provided by the family of Peter Haydon at Bloomfield.

11 Fox, *Learning to Fight*, p. 221.

12 Preston, *The Desert Mounted Corps*, p. 14.

13 Grainger, *The Battle for Palestine 1917*, p. 94.

14 Roy James Dunk, manuscript, AWM PR00469, p. 2.

15 Roy James Dunk, manuscript, AWM PR00469, p. 1.

16 Grainger, *The Battle for Palestine 1917*, p. 86.

17 Anglesey, *A History of British Cavalry*, Cooper, pp. 56–57.

18 Allenby Papers, 1/8/6-39.

19 Author's note: Brian Garfield, author of *The Meinertzhagen Mystery* – a very strong critic of Meinertzhagen's claims – states that the J. D. Belgrave working with Meinertzhagen was one James Dacres Belgrave. In fact, thanks to my researcher, Barbara Kelly – subsequently confirmed by Lieutenant Colonel Renfrey Pearson (retired) of the British Army digging into the archives of the National Army Museum, and doubly confirmed by Dr Peter Williams – I respectfully submit that this Belgrave is not the man who worked as General Staff Officer Grade One for the EEF during 1917. The Belgrave in question was in fact Lieutenant Colonel John Dalrymple Belgrave. He was with the EEF Intelligence unit from 2 August 1917 to 17 September 1917, after which he was transferred to Cyprus, liaising with the British colonial administration on the island and its High Commissioner, Sir John Clauson. James Dacres Belgrave was a Captain with the Royal Flying Corps, and the recipient of two Military Crosses. He was killed after being shot down east of Albert, France, on 13 June 1918. John Dalrymple Belgrave served out the Great War and retired from the army in 1932.

20 Lawrence, *Seven Pillars of Wisdom*, p. 393.

21 Memorandum from Lt Col. J. D. Belgrave to Commanding General EEF, TNA WO 95/4368.

22 Memorandum from Lt Col. J. D. Belgrave to Commanding General EEF, TNA WO 95/4368, p. 6.

23 Memorandum from Lt Col. J. D. Belgrave to Commanding General EEF, TNA WO 95/4368, p. 6.

24 Paterson, *Happy Dispatches*, Lansdowne Press, p. 76.

25 Paterson, *Happy Dispatches*, Lansdowne Press, p. 77.

26 Daley, *Beersheba: A Journey through Australia's Forgotten War*, Melbourne University Press, Melbourne, 2009, p. 91.

27 Paterson, *Happy Dispatches*, Lansdowne Press, p. 81.

28 Paterson, *Happy Dispatches*, Lansdowne Press, p. 82.

29 Paterson, *Happy Dispatches*, Lansdowne Press, p. 82.

30 Allenby Papers, 1/8/6-39.

31 Çiçek, *War and State Formation in Syria: Cemal Pasha's Governorate During World War I, 1914–1917*, Routledge, New York, 2014, p. 261.

32 Mustafa Kemal to Enver Pasha, 20 September 1917, in F. J. Moberly, *The Campaign in Mesopotamia 1914–1918*, Vol. IV, His Majesty's Stationery Office, London, 1927, p. 351.

33 *The Western Mail* (Perth), 1 November 1934, p. 4.

34 Rubenstein and Whaley, *The Art and Science of Military Deception*, Artech House, UK, 2013, pp. 57–58.

35 Rubenstein and Whaley, *The Art and Science of Military Deception*, p. 58.

36 Tuohy, *The Secret Corps: A Tale of 'Intelligence' on all Fronts*, John Murray, London, 1920, p. 284.

37 Tuohy, *The Secret Corps*, p. 284.

38 Tuohy, *The Secret Corps*, p. 285.

39 Raugh, 'The Haversack Ruse In Gaza Impressed Even Lawrence Of Arabia', Warfare History Network.

40 Maurice Evans, war diaries, Mitchell Library.

41 Author's note: This is a saga in dispute, with so many claims and counter-claims it is hard to keep track. The best I can work out, however, Major Richard Meinertzhagen was indeed serving as a General Staff Officer Grade Two with the Intelligence Unit of the EEF during 1917. He was certainly heavily involved in organising material to be included in what later became known as the 'Haversack Ruse'. Another credible claimant is Captain Arthur Neate who was also involved and first made a drop of documents on 12 September 1917. Richard Meinertzhagen undertook a further drop on 10 October the same year. It appears that Meinertzhagen identified himself among the documents later picked up by a Turkish patrol, his name often being referenced in subsequent Turkish narratives of the event. Whether there was a ruse on the ruse is possible, and it seems indisputable that, beyond subterfuge, self-promotion was one of Meinertzhagen's key skills and credit for the ruse goes a lot wider than just him. And yet contemporary witnesses who credit him include David Lloyd George, T. E. Lawrence and Cyril Falls, compiler of the British Official History.

42 Emir, *Yildirim*, Genelkurmay Basim Evi, Ankara, 2002, p. 100.

43 Emir, *Yildirim*, p. 100. Author's note: True, Kress von Kressenstein will later insist that he did not believe the documents were real: 'The English knew they could not begin a large campaign after the beginning of the rainy season

... there could be no doubt that the attack on Beersheba and Gaza was to begin very soon. Therefore I was sure the information of the satchel must be dismissed as fake.' (Brian Garfield, *The Meinertzhagen Mystery*, Potomac Books, Washington, 2007.) But, under the circumstances, my view is that Colonel Hüsnü is a more reliable witness, and it is unlikely that Kress von Kressenstein would ever acknowledge the success of the ruse.

44 Emir, *Yildirim*, p. 100.
45 *The World's News*, 24 April 1920, p. 4.
46 *The World's News*, 24 April 1920, p. 4.
47 U. S. Army Intelligence Center & School, *Military Intelligence*, Volumes 10–12, Ed. Frederick J. Britton, US Government Printing Office, Arizona, 1984, p. 12.

Chapter ten   Well met by moonlight

1 Lawrence, *Seven Pillars of Wisdom*, p. 199.
2 Gammage, *The Broken Years: Australian Soldiers and the Great War*, ANU Press, Canberra, 1974, p. 146.
3 Jones, *The Australian Light Horse*, Australians at War, Time-Life Books, Australia, 1987, p. 96.
4 Emir, *Yildirim*, p. 110.
5 Campbell, *Banjo Paterson*, p. 205.
6 Campbell, *Banjo Paterson*, p. 205.
7 Paterson, 'A Bushman's Song', *The Man From Snowy River and Other Verses*, Angus & Robertson, Sydney, 1896, p. 125.
8 Paterson, *Happy Dispatches*, Lansdowne Press, p. 86.
9 Paterson, *Happy Dispatches*, Lansdowne Press, p. 86.
10 Idriess, *The Desert Column*, p. 352.
11 Idriess, *The Desert Column*, p. 243.
12 Idriess, *The Desert Column*, p. 243.
13 Idriess, *The Desert Column*, p. 356.
14 Teichman, *The Diary of a Yeomanry M.O., Egypt, Gallipoli, Palestine and Italy*, T. Fisher Unwin, London, 1921, p. 172.
15 Australian Imperial Force unit war diaries, 1914–18 War, Australian Remount Depot, AWM4, Item No. 28/1/1 Part 2.
16 Paterson, *Happy Dispatches*, Lansdowne Press, p. 86.
17 Richard Meinertzhagen, *Army Diary 1899–1926*, Oliver and Boyd, Edinburgh, 1960, p. 220.
18 Australian Imperial Force unit war diaries, 1914–18 War, Australian Mounted Division, AWM 4, Item No. 1/58/4 Part 3.
19 Australian Imperial Force unit war diaries 1914–18 War, Australian Mounted Division, AWM 4, Item No. 1/58/4 Part 3.

20 Australian Imperial Force unit war diaries 1914–18 War, Australian Mounted Division, AWM 4, Item No. 1/58/4 Part 3.

21 Falls, *Military Operations: Egypt And Palestine*, p. 65.

22 *Camden News*, 5 December 1918, p. 1.

23 *The Albury Banner and Wodonga Express*, 7 June 1918, p. 13.

24 Allenby Papers, 1/8/6-39.

25 Campbell, *Banjo Paterson*, p. 205.

26 Emir, *Yildirim*, p. 111.

27 Preston, *The Desert Mounted Corps*, pp. 5–6.

28 *The Albury Banner and Wodonga Express*, 7 June 1918, p. 13.

29 Jones, *The War in the Air*, Vol. V, Clarendon Press, 1935, p. 236.

30 Hill, *Chauvel of the Light Horse*, p. 122.

31 Campbell, *Banjo Paterson*, p. 205.

32 Campbell, *Banjo Paterson*, p. 205.

33 Maurice Evans, war diaries, Mitchell Library.

34 Sergeant Arthur Pickford, diary, 'Days in Conflict 1917: Battle of Beersheba', ABC website.

35 'The Battle of Beersheba', 4th Light Horse Regiment, AIF Unit History Account.

36 Australian Imperial Force unit war diaries, 1914–18 War, 12th Light Horse Regiment, AWM4, Item No. 10/17/9.

37 Hammond, *History of the 11th Light Horse Regiment, Fourth Light Horse Brigade, Australian Imperial Forces, war 1914–1919*, Wide Bay Antique Militaria, Singapore, 1984, pp. 78–84.

38 Hammond, *History of the 11th Light Horse Regiment*, pp. 78–84.

39 Smith, *Men of Beersheba: a History of the 4th Light Horse Regiment, 1914–1919*, Mostly Unsung Military History Research and Publications, Melbourne, 1993, pp. 111–132.

40 *Western Mail* (Perth), 1 November 1934, p. 6 [reported speech].

41 *Smith's Weekly*, 14 February 1931, p. 18.

42 *Referee*, 31 October 1917, p. 12.

43 *Smith's Weekly*, 14 February 1931, p. 4.

44 Roy James Dunk, manuscript, AWM PR00469, p. 4.

Chapter eleven   Beersheba besieged

1 *The Herald* (Melbourne), 16 February 1918, p. 4.

2 Gullett, *The Australian Imperial Force in Sinai and Palestine*, p. 397.

3 Idriess, *The Desert Column*, p. 358.

4 Smith, *Men of Beersheba*, pp. 111–132.

5 Ion Llewellyn Idriess, diary, 1917–1918, AWM, 1DRL/0373.

6 *Western Mail* (Perth), 1 November 1934, p. 6.

7 *Bunbury Herald*, 12 June 1918, p. 4.

8 Gullett, *Australia in Palestine*, Angus & Robertson, Sydney, 1919, p. 95.

9 Preston, *The Desert Mounted Corps*, p. 26.

10 *The W.A. Record*, 27 November 1915, p. 17.

11 Kempe, *Participation*, Hawthorn Press, Melbourne, 1973, p. 87.

12 Kempe, *Participation*, p. 87.

13 Perry, *The Australian Light Horse*, p. 314.

14 *Barrier Miner*, 17 February 1918, p. 2.

15 Australian Imperial Force unit war diaries, 1914–18 War, General Staff, Headquarters Anzac Mounted Division, AWM 4, Item No. 1/60/20 Part 2.

16 Idriess, *The Desert Column*, p. 359.

17 Idriess, *The Desert Column*, p. 360.

18 Ion Llewellyn Idriess, diary, 1917–1918, AWM, 1DRL/0373.

19 Idriess, *The Desert Column*, p. 361.

20 *The London Evening News*, *500 of the Best Cockney War Stories*, Associated Newspapers Ltd., London, 1921, p. 133.

21 Idriess, *The Desert Column*, p. 362.

22 Idriess, *The Desert Column*, p. 362.

23 Hopkins, *Alaric Pinder Boor*, pp. 275–276.

24 Hopkins, *Alaric Pinder Boor*, pp. 275–276.

25 Woodward, *Hell in the Holy Land: World War I in the Middle East*, University Press of Kentucky, 2014, p. 107.

26 Preston, *The Desert Mounted Corps*, p. 25.

27 Idriess, *The Desert Column*, p. 363.

28 War Diary GSO GHQ EEF, September 1917, WO 95/4368, p. 2.

29 *Western Mail*, 1 November 1934, p. 6.

30 *Western Mail*, 1 November 1934, p. 6. Author's note: These marvellous words and images are from *The Wells of Beersheba* by Frank Dalby Davison. Ironically, Davison was not present at the charge or even in this theatre, but his fascination with the charge and his assembly of accounts and 'patient inquiry of those who were in it' (*The Age*, 17 February 1951, p. 4) produced the best account of the entire charge, one that was acclaimed, endorsed and quoted by the men who actually did it!

31 *Western Mail*, 1 November 1934, p. 6.

32 *The London Evening News*, *500 of the Best Cockney War Stories*, p. 95.

33 *Western Mail*, 1 November 1934, p. 6.

34 *Western Mail*, 1 November 1934, p. 6.

35 Smith, *Men of Beersheba*, p. 117.

36 Steve Butler, 'The taking of Tel el Saba, or the role the New Zealanders played in the taking of Beersheba', The Australian Light Horse Association website.

37 Nicol, *The Story of Two Campaigns: Official War History of the Auckland Mounted Rifles, Regiment, 1914–1919*, Wilson and Horton, Auckland, 1921, p. 157.

38 Butler, 'The taking of Tel el Saba'.

39 Emir, *Yildirim*, p. 117.

40 Emir, *Yildirim*, p. 125.

41 Emir, *Yildirim*, p. 117.

42 Emir, *Yildirim*, p. 125.

43 *Camden News*, 5 December 1918, p. 1.

44 Haydon, *Midnight Warhorse*, letter from Cairo Hospital, p. 35.

45 Australian War Memorial, 'The charge of the 4th Light Horse Brigade at Beersheba', 30 October 2007.

46 Gullett, *The Australian Imperial Force in Sinai and Palestine*, p. 392.

47 Gullett, *The Australian Imperial Force in Sinai and Palestine*, pp. 393–94.

48 Gullett, *Official History of Australia in the War of 1914–1918*, Volume VII, p. 404.

49 *Western Mail*, 1 November 1934, p. 6 [reported speech].

50 Gullett, *Official History of Australia in the War of 1914–1918*, Volume VII, p. 393.

51 Australian Light Horse Studies Centre, (online), Desert Column, The Battle of Beersheba, Palestine, 31 October 1917 'Put Grant straight at it'.

52 Gullett, *The Australian Imperial Force in Sinai and Palestine*, p. 393.

53 King, *Palestine Diaries*, p. 256.

54 Gullett, *The Australian Imperial Force in Sinai and Palestine*, p. 394.

55 Perry, *The Australian Light Horse*, p. 5.

56 Haydon, *Midnight Warhorse*, letter from Cairo Hospital, p. 35.

57 *Spur* (Official Australian Light Horse Association Magazine), April 1999, 4th Regiment History, p. 25.

58 John Ernest (Chook) Fowler, AWM MS 888.

59 Letter, Edward Cornelius Dengate, AWM 3DRL 7678.

60 Haydon, *Midnight Warhorse*, letter from Cairo Hospital, p. 35.

Chapter twelve   Straight at 'em

1 Bean, *Anzac to Amiens*, Australian War Memorial, 1983, p. 386.

2 *Bealiba Times*, 11 January 1918, p. 3.

3 John Ernest (Chook) Fowler, AWM MS 888.

4 *The Albury Banner and Wodonga Express*, 7 June 1918, p. 13.

5 Colin Bull, AWM2017.1.304 [reported speech], https://www.awm.gov.au/articles/blog/remembering-colin-bull-and-the-battle-of-beersheba

6 Ernest Craggs, Australian War Memorial, https://www.awm.gov.au/collection/C103702

7 *Sydney Morning Herald*, 18 October 2017.

8 Shakespeare, *Richard III*, Act V, Sc. 3.

9 Author's note: Although Henry Gullett, in his Official History, names the Essex Battery as the force which silenced the machine guns on Hill 1180, I believe he was mistaken. The Notts Battery were attached to the Australian Mounted Division at this juncture, and had been brought up to the point of deployment for the Charge. Brigadier General Grant ordered the O. C. of the Notts Battery to open fire on Hill 1180. This is also recorded in the Notts Battery War Diary.

10 *Foster Mirror and South Gippsland Shire Advocate*, 28 February 1918, p. 3.

11 Australian War Memorial, 'The Charge of the 4th Light Horse Brigade at Beersheba', 30 October 2007.

12 *The Albury Banner and Wodonga Express*, 7 June 1918, p. 13.

13 Idriess, *The Desert Column*, p. 359.

14 Edward Cornelius Dengate, AWM 3DRL 7678.

15 King, *Palestine Diaries*, p. 256.

16 John Ernest (Chook) Fowler, AWM MS 888.

17 Perry, *The Australian Light Horse*, p. 8.

18 *The Albury Banner and Wodonga Express*, 7 June 1918, p. 13.

19 *Camden News*, 5 December 1918, p. 1.

20 Preston, *The Desert Mounted Corps*, p. 29.

21 Idriess, *The Desert Column*, p. 365.

22 *Camden News*, 5 December 1918, p. 1.

23 Colin Bull, AWM2017.1.304 [reported speech].

24 Edward Cornelius Dengate, AWM 3DRL 7678.

25 Idriess, *The Desert Column*, p. 365.

26 Ernest Craggs, AWM C103702.

27 Haydon, *Midnight Warhorse*, letter from Cairo Hospital, p. 35.

28 Idriess, *The Desert Column*, p. 364.

29 Jones, *A Thousand Miles of Battles*, p. 44.

30 *Albury Banner & Wodonga Express*, 7 June 1918, p. 13.

31 Preston, *The Desert Mounted Corps*, p. 29.

32 Idriess, *The Desert Column*, p. 365.

33 *Foster Mirror and South Gippsland Shire Advocate*, 28 February 1918, p. 3.

34 Smith, *Men of Beersheba*, p. 124.

35 Idriess, *The Desert Column*, p. 365.

36 Australian War Memorial, 'The charge of the 4th Light Horse Brigade at Beersheba', 30 October 2007.

37 Trooper Sloan Bolton D.C.M., diary, A Dream of the Past, 4th Light Horse Regiment 1914–1918, privately published.

38 Haydon, *Midnight Warhorse*, letter from Cairo Hospital, p. 35.

39 John Ernest (Chook) Fowler, AWM MS 888.

40 John Ernest (Chook) Fowler, AWM MS 888.

41 John Ernest (Chook) Fowler, AWM MS 888.

42 John Ernest (Chook) Fowler, AWM MS 888.

43 John Ernest (Chook) Fowler, AWM MS 888.

44 Gullett, *The Australian Imperial Force in Sinai and Palestine*, p. 397.

45 Edward Cornelius Dengate, AWM 3DRL 7678.

46 John Ernest (Chook) Fowler, AWM MS 888.

47 John Ernest (Chook) Fowler, AWM MS 888.

48 Davies, 'An Account of the Charge at Beersheba', The Australian Light Horse Association website.

49 Preston, *The Desert Mounted Corps*, p. 30.

50 Sergeant D. W. Harris, AWM 40 45, p. 10.

51 Trooper Sloan Bolton D.C.M., diary, Dream of the Past, 4th Light Horse Regiment 1914–1918.

52 Trooper Sloan Bolton D.C.M., diary, Dream of the Past, 4th Light Horse Regiment 1914–1918.

53 Davies, 'An Account of the Charge at Beersheba', The Australian Light Horse Association website.

54 *Smith's Weekly*, 14 February 1931, p. 4.

55 *Western Mail* (Perth), 1 November 1934, p. 6 [reported speech].

56 Haydon, *Midnight Warhorse*, p. 36.

57 Haydon, *Midnight Warhorse*, p. 36.

58 Haydon, *Midnight Warhorse*, p. 40.

59 Haydon, *Midnight Warhorse*, p. 36.

60 *Camden News*, 5 December 1918, p. 1.

61 *Foster Mirror and South Gippsland Shire Advocate*, 28 February 1918, p. 3.

62 *The Sun* (Sydney), 23 February 1918, p. 3.

63 Sergeant D. W. Harris, AWM 40 45, p. 14.

64 Preston, *The Desert Mounted Corps*, p. 33.

65 Military History and Heritage Victoria Inc., *Busting Beersheba*, 18 November 2018.

66 *Kerang New Times*, 25 December 1917, p. 3.

67 Patrick M. Hamilton, diary, AWM 3DRL7521.

68 Patrick M. Hamilton, diary, AWM 3DRL7521.

69 Patrick M. Hamilton, diary, AWM 3DRL7521.

70 Patrick M. Hamilton, diary, AWM 3DRL7521.

71 Haydon, *Midnight Warhorse*, p. 36.

72 Patrick M. Hamilton, diary, AWM 3DRL7521.

73 Patrick M. Hamilton, diary, AWM 3DRL7521.

74 Patrick M. Hamilton, diary, AWM 3DRL7521, p. 5.

75 Campbell, *Banjo Paterson*, p. 206.

76 Campbell, *Banjo Paterson*, p. 206.

77 Preston, *The Desert Mounted Corps*, p. 33.

78 Campbell, *Banjo Paterson*, p. 206.

79 Grainger, *The Battle for Palestine 1917*, p. 89.

80 The Australian Light Horse Association, 'Albert Whitmore – 9th Light Horse Regiment'.

81 List No. 315, Appointments, Commissions, Rewards, 1 November 1917.

82 *Minyip Guardian and Sheep Hills Advocate*, 25 February 1918, p. 3 [reported speech].

83 Haydon, *Midnight Warhorse*, p. 42.

84 Woodward, *Hell in the Holy Land*, p. 108.

85 *Crookwell Gazette*, 8 March 1934, p. 3.

86 *Daily Pictorial*, 23 December 1930, p. 6.

87 *The Albury Banner and Wodonga Express*, 7 June 1918, p. 13.

88 *Tweed Daily*, 4 April 1918, p. 4.

89 Papers of Lt Col. Murray Bourchier, AWM 2DRL0444.

The aftermath

1 Preston, *The Desert Mounted Corps*, p. 31.

2 The Australian Light Horse Association, 'Albert Whitmore – 9th Light Horse Regiment'.

3 *The Guardian*, 9 November 2009.

4 Preston, *The Desert Mounted Corps*, p. 98.

5 *The Herald*, 16 February 1918, p. 4.

6 Major Vivian Gilbert, *The Romance of the Last Crusade: With Allenby to Jerusalem*, Appleton & Co., New York, 1923, p. 170.

7 *Camden News*, 5 December 1918, p. 1.

8 Preston, *The Desert Mounted Corps*, p. 31.

9 Gullett, *The Australian Imperial Force in Sinai and Palestine*, p. 404.

10 *The Argus*, 24 October 1942, p. 1.

11 *The Argus*, 24 October 1942, p. 1.

12 *The Argus*, 24 October 1942, p. 1.

13 Wavell, *Allenby: A Study in Greatness*, p. 289.

14 Jones, *A Thousand Miles of Battles*, p. 179.

15 Jones, *A Thousand Miles of Battles*, p. 179.

16 Dale and Bowers, *Armageddon: Two Men on an Anzac Trail*, Melbourne University Press, Melbourne, 2011, p. 199.

17 Gullett, *The Australian Imperial Force in Sinai and Palestine*, p. 727.

18 *The Grenfell Record and Lachlan District Advertiser*, 8 November 1937, p. 4.

19 Jones, *The Australian Light Horse*, p. 168.

20 Jones, *The Australian Light Horse*, p. 165.

21 Jones, *The Australian Light Horse*, pp. 155–157.

22 Lawrence, *Seven Pillars of Wisdom*, p. 668.

23 *The Register*, 23 December 1918, p. 8.

24 *The Register*, 23 December 1918, p. 8.
25 *The Register*, 23 December 1918, p. 8.
26 *The Register*, 23 December 1918, p. 8.
27 *Ballarat Star*, 10 January 1920, p. 5.
28 *The Register*, 23 December 1918, p. 8.
29 *The Register*, 23 December 1918, p. 8.
30 Jones, 'Olden, Arthur Charles (1881–1949)', *Australian Dictionary of Biography*, National Centre of Biography, Australian National University, 1988.
31 *The Waler, Australia's Greatest War Horse*, Mago Films, Screen Producers Australia, 2015.
32 Australian Imperial Force unit war diaries, 1914–18 War, 10th Light Horse Regiment War Diary, AWM4 10/15/40, 1 October 1918.
33 *The Argus*, 24 October 1942, p. 1.
34 *The Register*, 23 December 1918, p. 8.
35 Letter, Chauvel to Allenby, 22 October 1929: Allenby Papers, 2/5 Miscellaneous Correspondence.
36 'Who Slapped Lawrence of Arabia?', unattributed newspaper clipping, 1970. Author's note: There will be another claimant as to who the Australian was, who slapped Lawrence of Arabia in Damascus. Corporal Leslie Lang Tip, who had covered himself in glory for the charge at Kaukab the evening before, now passes by an oddly attired British officer shouting at sick Turkish soldiers. Lang Tip told him to stop. The English officer not only refuses, but starts shouting at Lang Tip. What is a man to do? Lang Tip belts him one. It has been a long war, and he is very tired.
37 Lawrence, *Seven Pillars of Wisdom*, p. 663.
38 Lawrence, *Seven Pillars of Wisdom*, p. 666.
39 Lawrence, *Seven Pillars of Wisdom*, p. 664.
40 *Western Mail*, 5 December 1935, p. 2.
41 *Great Southern Leader*, 20 December 1918, p. 5.
42 Knightley, *The Secret Lives Of Lawrence Of Arabia*, Thomas Nelson and Sons Ltd, London, 1969, p. 88.
43 Bradley, *Australian Light Horse*, p. 16.
44 Mitchell, *The Light Horse*, p. 102.
45 *The Argus*, 24 October 1942, p. 1.
46 *The Argus*, 24 October 1942, p. 1.
47 *The Argus*, 24 October 1942, p. 1.
48 Paterson, *Happy Dispatches*, Lansdowne Press, p. 88.
49 Daley, *Beersheba: Travels Through a Forgotten Australian Victory*, p. 263.
50 Perry, *The Australian Light Horse*, p. 494.
51 Daley, *Beersheba: Travels Through a Forgotten Australian Victory*, p. 263.
52 Daley, *Beersheba: Travels Through a Forgotten Australian Victory*, p. 264.

53 *The Times*, 24 November 1964.

54 Daley, *Beersheba: Travels Through a Forgotten Australian Victory*, p. 264 [reported speech].

55 Paterson, *Happy Dispatches*, Lansdowne Press, chapter XVII.

56 Gullett, *The Australian Imperial Force in Sinai and Palestine*, p. 791.

57 Gullett, *The Australian Imperial Force in Sinai and Palestine*, p. 791.

58 Paterson, *Happy Dispatches*, Lansdowne Press, p. 89.

59 *Advocate* (Burnie), 2 July 1942, p. 6.

60 Bou, 'They shot the horses – didn't they?', *Wartime* magazine, Issue 44, Australian War Memorial, September 2008, pp. 54–57.

61 Vincent, *My Darling Mick*, p. 213.

62 M. C. Evans, war diary, 11 September – 24 December 1918, MLMSS 1576/ Item 8, Mitchell Library, State Library of NSW.

Epilogue

1 *The Australasian*, 21 September 1918, p. 53.

2 Hunter, 'He never forgot he was a lighthorseman', AWM Memorial Article, 31 October 2018.

3 *Warwick Daily News*, 27 May 1939.

4 *Sydney Morning Herald*, 18 January 1926, p. 14.

5 *Sydney Morning Herald*, 18 January 1926, p. 14.

6 Ian Jones, 'Royston, John Robinson (1860–1942)', *Australian Dictionary of Biography*.

7 Bean, *Official History of Australia in the War of 1914–1918, Vol. II*, pp. 631–632.

8 Haydon, *Midnight Warhorse*, p. 35.

9 National Archives of Australia, NAA: B2455, Wickham, Harold Thomas, p. 22.

10 *Newcastle Sun*, 24 December 1940, p. 8.

11 Croft, 'Idriess, Ion Llewellyn (1889–1979)', *Australian Dictionary of Biography*, National Centre of Biography, Australian National University, 1983.

12 *Examiner*, 3 December 1924, p. 5.

13 Lawrence, *T. E. Lawrence By His Friends*, Jonathan Cape, London, 1937, p. 209.

14 Lawrence, *T. E. Lawrence By His Friends*, p. 214.

15 Lawrence, *T. E. Lawrence By His Friends*, p. 234.

16 Lawrence, *T. E. Lawrence By His Friends*, p. 215.

17 PBS, Lawrence of Arabia, Allenby radio interview, *The Listener*, 22 May 1935.

18 Letter, Chauvel to Allenby, 22 October 1929, Allenby Papers, 2/5 Miscellaneous Correspondence.

19 *The Courier-Mail*, 3 October 1936, p. 22.

20 Lawrence, *Seven Pillars of Wisdom*, pp. 553–554.

21 Cyril Falls, *Military Operations: Egypt and Palestine*, p. 312.

22 Garfield, *The Meinertzhagen Mystery: The Life and Legend of a Colossal Fraud*, Potomac Books Inc., Washington D.C., 2007, p. 29.

23 Emir, *Yildirim*.

24 Australian War Memorial, 'The View From the Other Side', School Resources.

25 Kress von Kressenstein, *Mit den Türken zum Suezkanal*, Otto Schlegel, 1938, p. 279.

26 *South Western Times*, 6 November 1917, p. 3.

27 *Bunbury Herald*, 12 June 1918, p. 4.

28 Hopkins, *Alaric Pinder Boor*, pp. 275–276.

29 France 24, 'Israeli, Australian, New Zealand leaders mark landmark WWI battle', 31 October 2017.

30 Bou, *The Battle of Beersheba – Myths and History, 100 Years On*, Coral Bell School of Asia Pacific Affairs, ANU College of Asia & the Pacific.

BIBLIOGRAPHY

Books

Anglesey, George Charles Henry Victor Paget, Marquis of, *A History of the British Cavalry: Vol. 5: 1914–1919 Egypt, Palestine and Syria*, Pen & Sword Books Limited, 1994, e-book

Bean, C. E. W., *Anzac to Amiens*, Australian War Memorial, 1983, Monograph https://www.awm.gov.au/collection/LIB32452

Bean, C. E. W., *Official History of Australia in the War of 1914–1918*, Vol. I, Angus & Robertson, Sydney, 1941

Bean, C. E. W., *Official History of Australia in the War of 1914–1918*, Vol. II, Angus & Robertson, Sydney, 1941

Berrie, G. L., *Under Furred Hats (6th Australian Light Horse Regiment)*, Naval & Military Press, London, 2009

Bostock, Henry P., *The Great Ride: The Diary of a Light Horse Brigade Scout*, World War I, Artlook Books, Perth, 1982

Bradley, Phillip, *Australian Light Horse: The Campaign in the Middle East 1916–1918*, Allen & Unwin, Crows Nest, 2016

Burness, Peter, *The Nek: The Tragic Charge of the Light Horse at Gallipoli*, Kangaroo Press, Kenthurst, 1996

Campbell, Alistair, *Banjo Paterson: A Life in Pictures and Words from the Banjo Paterson Family Archive*, Pan Macmillan Australia, e-book, 2022

Carver, Michael, *The Warlords*, Weidenfeld & Nicolson, London, 1976

Çiçek, M. Talha, *War and State Formation in Syria: Cemal Pasha's Governorate during World War I, 1914–1917*, Routledge, New York, 2014

Cutlack, F. M., *Official Histories: First World War Vol. VIII, The Australian Flying Corps in the Western and Eastern Theatres of War, 1914–1918*, Angus & Robertson, Sydney, 1941

Daley, Paul and Bowers, Michael, *Armageddon: Two Men on an Anzac Trail*, Melbourne University Press, Melbourne, 2011

Davison, Frank Dalby, *The Wells of Beersheba*, Angus & Robertson, North Ryde, 1985

De Marco, Neil and Radway, Richard, *Twentieth Century World*, Stanley Thornes, Cheltenham, 1995

Dearberg, Neil, *Desert Anzacs: The Under-Told Story of the Sinai Palestine Campaign 1916–1918*, Interactive Publications, Carindale, 2017

Emir, Lieutenant Colonel Hüseyin Hüsnü, *Yildirim*, Genelkurmay Basim Evi, Ankara, 2002

Falls, Cyril, *Military Operations: Egypt And Palestine*, His Majesty's Stationery Office, London, 1930

Falls, Cyril and MacMunn, George, *Military Operations: Egypt And Palestine*, His Majesty's Stationery Office, London, 1928

Faulkner, Neil, *Lawrence of Arabia's War*, Yale University Press, New Haven, 2016

Fox, Aimee, *Learning to Fight: Military Innovation and Change in the British Army*, Cambridge University Press, Cambridge, 2018

Gammage, Bill, *The Broken Years: Australian Soldiers and the Great War*, ANU Press, Canberra, 1974

Gardner, Brian, *Allenby of Arabia, Lawrence's General*, Coward-McCann, New York, 1966

Garfield, Brian, *The Meinertzhagen Mystery: The Life and Legend of a Colossal Fraud*, Potomac Books Inc., Washington D.C., 2007

Grainger, John D., *The Battle for Palestine 1917*, Boydell Press, 2006

Great Britain, Parliament, *Correspondence Regarding the Overseas Assistance Afforded to His Majesty's Government by His Majesty's Overseas Dominions*, T. Fisher Unwin, London, 1914

Gullett, Henry Somer, *Australia in Palestine*, Angus & Robertson, Sydney, 1919

Gullett, Henry Somer, *The Australian Imperial Force in Sinai and Palestine, 1914–1918*, Angus & Robertson, Sydney, 1923

Gullett Henry Somer, *Official History of Australia in the War of 1914–1918, Vol. VII – The Australian Imperial Force in Sinai and Palestine, 1914–1918*, Angus & Robertson, Sydney, 1941

Hamilton, John, *Goodbye Cobber, God Bless You*, Pan Macmillan, Sydney, 2004

Hammond, E. W., *History of the 11th Light Horse Regiment, Fourth Light Horse Brigade, Australian Imperial Forces, War 1914–1919*, Wide Bay Antique Militaria, Singapore, 1984

Hill, Alec, *Chauvel of the Light Horse: A Biography of Sir Harry Chauvel*, Melbourne University Press, Melbourne, 1978

Hogue, Oliver, *Trooper Bluegum at the Dardanelles*, 2nd ed., Andrew Melrose, London, 1916

Hopkins, Jeff, *Alaric Pinder Boor: A Life Reimagined*, MoshPit Publishing, NSW, 2020

Horner, David, *The Commanders: Australian Military Leadership in the Twentieth Century*, Routledge, London, 2021

Housman, A. E., *A Shropshire Lad*, Branden Books, Wellesley (MA), 1896

Idriess, Ion, *The Desert Column*, ETT Imprint, Sydney, 2017, e-book

James, Lawrence, *Imperial Warrior: The Life and Times of Field Marshal Viscount Allenby*, Weidenfeld & Nicolson, London, 1993

Jones, H. A., *The War in the Air, Vol. V*, Clarendon Press, Oxford, 1935

Jones, Ian, *A Thousand Miles of Battles*, Time-Life Books, Australia, 1987

Jones, Ian, *The Australian Light Horse*, Australians at War, Time-Life Books, Australia, 1987

Leacock, Stephen, *Nonsense Novels*, Bodley Head, London, 1911

Lloyd George, David, *The Great Crusade: Extracts from Speeches Delivered During the War*, George H. Doran Company, New York, 1918

Kannengiesser, Hans, *The Campaign in Gallipoli*, Hutchinson & Co., London, 1928

Kempe, Humphrey, *Participation*, Hawthorn Press, Melbourne, 1973

King, Jonathan, *Palestine Diaries*, Scribe Publications, Australia, 2017, e-book

Kinloch, Terry, *Devils on Horses*, Exisle, Auckland, 2007

Knightley, Phillip, *Australia*, Jonathan Cape, London, 2000

Knightley, Phillip, *The Secret Lives of Lawrence of Arabia*, Thomas Nelson and Sons Ltd, London, 1969

Kress von Kressenstein, Friedrich Freiherr, *Mit den Teurken zum Suezkanal*, Otto Schlegel, Berlin, 1938

Lawrence, A. E., *T. E. Lawrence By His Friends*, Jonathan Cape, London, 1937

Lawrence, T. E., *Seven Pillars of Wisdom – A Triumph*, Oxford University Press, 1940

The London Evening News, 500 of the Best Cockney War Stories, Associated Newspapers Ltd., London, 1921

McMullen, Ross, *Pompey Elliott*, Scribe, Melbourne, 2008

Meinertzhagen, Richard, *Army Diary 1899–1926*, Oliver and Boyd, Edinburgh, 1960

Meinertzhagen, Richard, *Kenya Diary 1902–1906*, Eland Books, London, 1984

Middlebrook, Martin, *The Kaiser's Battle*, Penguin, Harmondsworth, 2000

Mitchell, Elyne, *The Light Horse: The Story of Australia's Mounted Troops*, Macmillan, Sydney, 1978

Moberly, F. J., *The Campaign in Mesopotamia 1914–1918, Vol. IV*, His Majesty's Stationery Office, London, 1927

Montefiore, Simon Sebag, *Jerusalem: The Biography*, Hachette, UK, 2011

Murray, Sir Archibald, *Sir Archibald Murray's Despatches (June 1916 – June 1917)*, E.P. Dutton, London, 1920

Nicol, Sergeant Charles Gordon, *The Story Of Two Campaigns: Official War History of the Auckland Mounted Rifles, Regiment, 1914–1919*, Wilson and Horton, Auckland, 1921

Örnek, Tolga and Toker, Feza, *Gallipoli: Companion to the Feature Length Documentary*, Ekip Film Ltd, Istanbul, 2005

Pasha, Djemal, *Memories of a Turkish Statesman*, Hutchinson & Co., London, 1922

Paterson, A. B. (Banjo), *Happy Dispatches*, Angus & Roberston, Sydney, 1935

Paterson, A. B. (Banjo), *Happy Dispatches*, Lansdowne Press, Sydney, 1980

Paterson, A. B. (Banjo), *The Man From Snowy River and Other Verses*, Angus & Robertson, Sydney, 1896

Perry, Roland, *The Australian Light Horse: The Magnificent Australian Force and its Decisive Victories in Arabia in World War I*, Hachette, Australia, 2009

Preston, Richard, *The Desert Mounted Corps*, Houghton Mifflin Company, Boston and New York, 1921

Prowles, Lieutenant Colonel C. Guy, *The New Zealanders in Sinai and Palestine*, Whitcombe and Tombs Limited, Auckland, 1922

Riddell, Elizabeth, *With Fond Regards: Private Lives Through Letters*, National Library of Australia, Canberra, 1995

Robbins, Simon, *British Generalship on the Western Front*, Routledge, London, 1995,

Robertson, John, *Anzac and Empire: the Tragedy and Glory of Gallipoli*, Hamlyn Australia, Richmond, 1990

Rubenstein, Hy and Whaley, Barton, *The Art and Science of Military Deception*, Artech House, UK, 2013

Schuler, Phillip, *Australia in Arms*, T. Fisher Unwin, London, 1916

Simpson, Cameron Victor, *Maygar's Boys: A Biographical History of the 8th Light Horse Regiment A.I.F. 1914–19*, Just Soldiers, Military Research & Publications, Moorooduc, 1998

Smith, George Adam, *The Historical Geography of the Holy Land*, George H. Doran Company, New York, 1920

Smith, Michael, *Fiery Ted: Anzac Commander*, Nationwide Books, Christchurch, 2008

Smith, Lieutenant-Colonel N. C., *Men of Beersheba: A History of the 4th Light Horse Regiment, 1914–1919*, Mostly Unsung Military History Research and Publications, Melbourne, 1993

Smithers, A. J., *A New Excalibur*, Butler and Tanner, London, 1986

Teichman, Oskar, *The Diary of a Yeomanry M. O.*, Egypt, Gallipoli, Palestine and Italy, T. Fisher Unwin, London, 1921

Tuohy, Ferdinand, *The Secret Corps: A Tale of 'Intelligence' on all Fronts*, John Murray, London, 1920

US Army Intelligence Center & School, *Military Intelligence, Volumes 10–12*, ed. Frederick J. Britton, US Government Printing Office, Arizona, 1984

Vincent, Phoebe, *My Darling Mick: The Life of Granville Ryrie, 1865–1937*, National Library of Australia, 1997

Wavell, Sir Archibald, *Allenby: A Study in Greatness*, Oxford University Press, New York, 1941

Weintraub, Stanley, *The Recovery of Palestine, 1917: Jerusalem for Christmas*, Cambridge Scholars Publishing, 2017

Woodward, David R., *Hell in the Holy Land: World War I in the Middle East*, University Press of Kentucky, 2014

Journals and magazines

Military Heritage magazine, April issue, Sovereign Media, Reston, Virginia, 2001

Spur (Official Australian Light Horse Association Magazine)

Bou, Jean 'They shot the horses – didn't they?', *Wartime* magazine, Issue 44, Australian War Memorial, September 2008, https://www.awm.gov.au/wartime/44/page54_bou

Newspapers

The Advocate (Burnie)
Albury Banner and Wodonga Express
The Argus
The Australasian
Ballarat Star
Barrier Miner
Bealiba Times
The Bulletin
Bunbury Herald
Camden News
Canberra Times
Courier-Mail
Crookwell Gazette
Daily News (Perth)
Daily Pictorial
Daily Telegraph
Examiner
Foster Mirror and South Gippsland Shire Advocate
Great Southern Leader
Grenfell Record and Lachlan District Advertiser
The Guardian
Gundagai Times and Tumut, Adelong and Murrumbidgee District Advertiser
The Herald (Melbourne)
Kerang New Times

London Evening News
London Gazette
Minyip Guardian and Sheep Hills Advocate
Newcastle Sun
Queanbeyan Observer
Referee
The Register
Shepparton Advertiser
Smith's Weekly
South Gippsland Shire Echo
South Western Times
Southern Times
The Sun (Sydney)
Sunday Times
Sydney Mail
The Sydney Morning Herald
The Telegraph
The Times
Tweed Daily
Wagga Wagga Express
W.A. Record
Warwick Daily News
West Australian
Western Mail (Perth)
The World's News

Archives/State Collections

Diaries

Barwick, Archibald, diary, undated, 22 August 1914–September 1915, MLMSS 1493/1 Box 1/Item 1, Mitchell Library, State Library of NSW

Bean, C. E. W., war diary, 2 April 1915, AWM38, 3DRL606/3/1 – March – April 1915

Chauvel, Sibyl, diary, 16 April 1917, Chauvel Papers, AWM

Evans, Maurice C., war diaries, August 1914 – December 1918, MLMSS 1576, Mitchell Library, State Library of NSW

Fell, Robert Valentine, war diaries, Mitchell Library, Microfilm: CY 4893, frames 145–516

Forrest, Frederick E., war diary, 19 October 1914 – 8 September 1917, https://web. archive.org/web/20180309230102/http://amosa.org.au/schools/mhp/diaries/ War%20diary%20-Frederick%20Forrest.pdf

Hamilton, Patrick M., diary, AWM 3DRL7521

Hanly, Leo, diary, AWM PR05366, https://www.awm.gov.au/collection/C1303792

Harris, David, The 4th Brigade Trek from the Canal to Khan Yunis and the 2nd Gaza Battle, handwritten manuscript, Australian Light Horse Studies Centre https://alh-research.tripod.com/ the_4th_brigade_trek_from_the_canal_to_khan_yunis_and_the_2nd_gaza_battle/

Hobbs, John Dudley, diary, AWM PR85 289, https://www.awm.gov.au/collection/ C88655

Horder, Sergeant Leslie S., diary, AWM 3DRL/6595https://www.awm.gov.au/ collection/C90146

Idriess, Ion, diary, AWM RCDIG0000448, https://www.awm.gov.au/collection/ C1357925

Idriess, Ion Llewellyn, diary, 1917, AWM 1DRL/0373

Knuckey, Verner Gladders, diary, 8th Light Horse Regiment, AWM PR 03193, Book 3, https://www.awm.gov.au/collection/C1358010

Parkes, Stanley, diary, AWM PR01077https://www.awm.gov.au/collection/C373811

Pearce, Maurice Evelyn, diary, Mitchell Library, MSS 2940

Pickford, Sergeant Arthur, diary, A Squadron, 4th Australian Light Horse Regiment, 'Days in Conflict 1917: Battle of Beersheba', ABC website. https://www.abc.net. au/ww1-Anzac/beersheba/analysis-diaries-and-footage/

Smith, Ross, diary, PRG 18/19, South Australia Library, No. 1 Squadron, A.F.C. 24/10/1916 – 15/2/1918

Tomlins, Fred, war diaries, 21 August 1914 – 28 April 1917, Mitchell Library, MLMSS 5975 (CY 3348, frames 1–479)

War Diary GSO GHQ EEF, September 1917, WO 95/4368, National Archives, UK

Ward, Eric Harford, diary, State Library of New South Wales, MLDOC 1300, https://www.sl.nsw.gov.au/collection-items/diary-eric-harford-ward

Wiltshire, A. R., war diary, 20 December 1915, 12 December 1915–16 March 1916, MLMSS 3058/Box 1/Item 4, https://acms.sl.nsw.gov.au/_transcript/2011/ D12301/a3357.htm

Letters

Andrea, Heinrich Romer, AWM PR 89/179, https://www.awm.gov.au/collection/ C92313

Broome, Private Stanley, 12th Australian Light Horse Regiment, AWM PR91/053

Clarke, Trooper Oliver Joseph Burke, 7th Light Horse, AWM RCDIG0000374

Dengate, Edward Cornelius, AWM 3DRL 7678

Haydon, Guy, 24/12/15, Haydon Family Archive

Haydon, Guy, 1 August 1916, Haydon Family Archive

Ryrie, Granville to Mrs Granville Ryrie, 23 December 1915, AWM PR84/193, https://www.awm.gov.au/collection/C91774

Stephen, John Collie, AWM 3DRL/3584

Other items

Allenby Papers, Liddle Hart Centre for Military Archives, King's College London

Australian Imperial Force unit war diaries, 1914–18 War, Australian Mounted Division, AWM 4, Item No. 1/58/4 Part 3, https://www.awm.gov.au/collection/C1351117

Australian Imperial Force unit war diaries, 1914–18 War, Australian Remount Depot, AWM4, Item number 28/1/1 Part 2. https://s3-ap-southeast-2.amazonaws.com/awm-media/collection/RCDIG1002954/bundled/RCDIG1002954.pdf

Australian Imperial Force unit war diaries, 1914–18 War, General Staff HQ, Anzac Mounted Division, March 1917, AWM4 1/60/13, https://www.awm.gov.au/collection/C1351756

Australian Imperial Force unit war diaries, 1914–18 War, General Staff, Headquarters Anzac Mounted Division, Item No. 1/60/20 Part 2, https://www.awm.gov.au/collection/C1351050

Australian Imperial Force unit war diaries, 1914–18 War, Light Horse, 1st Light Horse Brigade, AWM4, Item 10/1/29, https://s3-ap-southeast-2.amazonaws.com/awm-media/collection/RCDIG1013009/bundled/RCDIG1013009.pdf

Australian Imperial Force unit war diaries, 1914–18 War, 10th Light Horse Regiment War Diary, AWM4 10/15/40, 1 October 1918, https://www.awm.gov.au/collection/C1352129

Australian Imperial Force unit war diaries, 1914–18 War, 12th Light Horse Regiment, AWM4, Item No. 10/17/9, https://www.awm.gov.au/collection/C1351638

Bean, C. E. W., Official History 1914–1918, War Records of Charles E. W. Bean, Correspondence 1926–31, AWM, 3DRL 7953/27, https://www.awm.gov.au/collection/C1377970

Bolton, Trooper Sloan 'Scotty' DCM, diary, A Dream of the Past, 4th Light Horse Regiment 1914–1918, privately published

Bolton, Trooper Sloan 'Scotty' DCM, https://anzacday.org.au/trooper-sloan-scotty-bolton-dcm

Bourchier, Lt Col. Murray, papers, AWM 2DRL0444

Bull, Colin, AWM2017.1.304, https://www.awm.gov.au/collection/C2278617

Bull, Joseph, papers, AWM PRO1547

Dunk, Roy James, manuscript, AWMPR00469

Fowler, John Ernest (Chook), AWM MS 888

Gullett, H. S., Records, 60/300, AWM40

Harris, Sergeant D. W., AWM40 45, Official History, 1914–1918 War: Records of Henry S. Gullett

Murray, General Sir Archibald, Private Papers, Imperial War Museum, collected
    letters, 79/48/2
O'Leary, Thomas, Court Martial Proceedings, NAA: A471, 6646, Item ID: 6826919
UK National Army Museum, 'The order that launched the charge of the Light
    Brigade, 1854', Accession Number NAM, 1962-11-4-3, https://collection.nam.
    ac.uk/detail.php?acc=1962-11-4-3
Wickham, Harold Thomas, service record, National Archives of Australia, NAA:
    B2455

Online Sources

Australian Light Horse Association, 'Albert Whitmore – 9th Light Horse Regiment',
    https://www.lighthorse.org.au/albert-whitmore/
Australian Light Horse Studies Centre, Desert Column, The Battle of Beersheba,
    Palestine, 31 October 1917, 'Put Grant straight at it.', https://alh-research.
    tripod.com/Light_Horse/index.blog/1847762/put-grant-straight-at-it/
Australian War Memorial, Bull, Trooper Colin, https://www.awm.gov.au/articles/
    blog/remembering-colin-bull-and-the-battle-of-beersheba
Australian War Memorial, 'The charge of the 4th Light Horse Brigade at
    Beersheba', 30 October 2007, https://www.awm.gov.au/articles/blog/
    the-charge-of-the-4th-light-horse-brigade-at-beersheba
Australian War Memorial, Craggs, Trooper Ernest James, https://www.awm.gov.au/
    collection/C1037028
Australian War Memorial, 'The View From the Other Side', School Resources,
    https://www.awm.gov.au/learn/schools/resources/back-to-the-source/beersheba/6
Butler, Steve, 'The taking of Tel el Saba, or the role the New Zealanders played
    in the taking of Beersheba', The Australian Light Horse Association website,
    https://www.lighthorse.org.au/the-taking-of-tel-el-saba-or-the-role-the-new-
    zealanders-played-in-the-taking-of-beersheba-by-steve-butler/
Chauvel Foundation, 'In memory of Bill of the Sixth Light Horse Regiment',
    https://chauvelfoundation.org/home/anthology/contents/the-horses/
    in-memory-of-bill-of-the-6th
Croft, Julian, 'Idriess, Ion Llewellyn (1889–1979)', Australian Dictionary of
    Biography, National Centre of Biography, Australian National University,
    https://adb.anu.edu.au/biography/idriess-ion-llewellyn-6786/text11739,
    published first in hardcopy 1983
Davies, Colonel Jack, 'An Account of the Charge at Beersheba', The Australian
    Light Horse Association website, https://www.lighthorse.org.au/
    an-account-of-the-charge-at-beersheba/
Department of Veterans' Affairs, Training Australian army recruits during
    World War I, DVA Anzac Portal, 2001, https://Anzacportal.dva.gov.au/
    wars-and-missions/ww1/military-organisation/training

Drane, T. E., *Complete Anzac Gallipoli War Diary*, http://bushroots.com/wp/2009/04/Anzac-gallipoli-war-diary-by-tedrane/

France 24, 'Israeli, Australian, New Zealand leaders mark landmark WWI battle', 31 October 2017, https://www.france24.com/en/20171031-israeli-australian-new-zealand-leaders-mark-landmark-wwi-battle-0.

Haydon, Peter, *Midnight Warhorse*, 2017, http://www.haydonhorsestud.com.au/wp-content/uploads/2015/03/Midnight-Warhorse2.pdf

Hill, A.J., 'Grant, William (1870–1939)', *Australian Dictionary of Biography*, National Centre of Biography, Australian National University, https://adb.anu.edu.au/biography/grant-william-6457/text11055, published first in hardcopy 1983

Hunter, Claire, 'He never forgot he was a lighthorseman', AWM Memorial Article, 31 October 2018 https://www.awm.gov.au/articles/blog/sir-harry-chauvel.

Jones, Ian, 'Olden, Arthur Charles (1881–1949)', *Australian Dictionary of Biography*, National Centre of Biography, Australian National University, https://adb.anu.edu.au/biography/olden-arthur-charles-7899/text13735, published first in hardcopy 1988

Jones, Ian, 'Royston, John Robinson (1860–1942)', *Australian Dictionary of Biography*, National Centre of Biography, Australian National University, https://adb.anu.edu.au/biography/royston-john-robinson-8290/text14529, published first in hardcopy 1988

Military History and Heritage Victoria Inc., *Busting Beersheba*, 18 November 2018. http://www.mhhv.org.au/wp-content/uploads/Sir-Harry-His-Horses-And-The-Quiet-Lady-Chauvel.pdf.

Paterson, A. B. (Banjo), 'Queensland Mounted Infantry', 1900, https://monumentaustralia.org.au/themes/conflict/boer/display/92773-queensland-mounted-infantry/photo/2; https://allpoetry.com/Queensland-Mounted-Infantry

PBS, Lawrence of Arabia, Allenby radio interview, *The Listener*, 22 May 1935. https://www.pbs.org/lawrenceofarabia/players/allenby2.html

Raugh, Harold, 'The Haversack Ruse In Gaza Impressed Even Lawrence Of Arabia', Warfare History Network, https://warfarehistorynetwork.com/the-haversack-ruse-in-gaza-impressed-even-lawrence-of-arabia/

South Australia's War 1914–18 website, Letters of Ross Smith, A World Away, https://southaustraliaswar.history.sa.gov.au/blog-posts/smith-ross-august-1916/

Thesis

Hughes, Matthew Dominic, General Allenby and the campaign of the Egyptian Expeditionary Force, June 1917 – November 1919, King's College London, https://kclpure.kcl.ac.uk/portal/en/studentTheses/general-allenby-and-the-campaign-of-the-egyptian-expeditionary-fo

TV, Film and Video

Bou, Jean, *The Battle of Beersheba – Myths and History, 100 Years On*, video, Coral Bell School of Asia Pacific Affairs, ANU College of Asia & the Pacific. https://sdsc.bellschool.anu.edu.au/news-events/podcasts/video/5761/battle-beersheba-myths-and-history100-years

The Waler, Australia's Greatest War Horse, Mago Films, Screen Producers Australia, 2015

INDEX